ALSO BY NICHOLAS HASLAM

Sheer Opulence

REDEEMING FEATURES

REDEEMING FEATURES

· A MEMOIR ·

NICHOLAS HASLAM

ALFRED A. KNOPF NEW YORK 2009

THIS IS A BORZOI BOOK
PUBLISHED BY ALFRED A. KNOPF

www.aaknopf.com

Knopf, Borzoi Books, and the colophon are registered trademarks
of Random House, Inc.

Library of Congress Cataloging-in-Publication Data

Haslam, Nicholas.
Redeeming features : a memoir / by Nicholas Haslam. — 1st ed.
p. cm.
ISBN 978-0-307-27167-9
1. Haslam, Nicholas.   2. Interior decorators—Great Britain—Biography.
I. Title.
NK2047.6.H37A2 2009   747.092—dc22   [B]   2009027440

Manufactured in the United States of America
First Edition

FOR MY GODCHILDREN

Carina Haslam
Jessica Heathcote Amory
Louisa Fox
Otis Ferry
Eleanor Pilkington
Rex von Hofmannsthal
And, in memoriam, Jacob Zimmer

Acknowledgments

First and foremost, my thanks are due to Flora Connell, my beloved and irreplaceable right hand, without whom this book would not exist, and to Shelley Wanger, my enchanting editor at Knopf. Equally, to Dan Franklin, my brilliant editor at Jonathan Cape, who had faith from the start.

I owe many thanks to Graydon Carter and Chris Garrett at *Vanity Fair* for their excellent advice and enthusiasm. And a debt of gratitude to my agent Gillon Aitken who has made all the right decisions. Hugh Cecil originally cast a writing fly over the pools of my memory. David Jenkins and Catherine Snow generously read and tailored my manuscript. Adam Tyler Moore researched and corrected dates and details. Andrew Wilson sent me examples of how to really write. Mark Lucas, Matthew Sturgis, Alan Sampson, and Celia Hayley all played early, crucial roles in shaping the book. I owe a special debt of gratitude to Evelyn de Rothschild and Victoria de Rothschild; likewise to Charles Saatchi and Stuart Sapcote.

Those who have constantly encouraged, sustained, and advised me over the years must be paramount in my thanks. Such love and friendship, new and old, I treasure, particularly that of Dominick Dunne, Natasha Kagalovsky, Carol Galley, and Hannah Rothschild. I hope Susan Crewe, Alexandra Shulman, Rupert Thomas, Lynn Barber, and Mark Amory are aware of how grateful I am for their support.

Min Hogg and other beloved friends of a lifetime, Romana McEwen, Christopher Gibbs, James Fox, John Richardson, Jane von Westenholz, James Davison, Candida Lycett-Green, Danny Moynihan, and Michael Haslam graciously responded to my frequent calls on their memory and fished out long-forgotten photographs. James Moores gave me permission to reproduce the John Deakin portrait on the dust jacket. Richard and Susan Young allowed me to raid their astonishingly extensive archive, and Robin Muir of British *Vogue* delved into back issues. Condé Nast publications also provided "W" archive photographs by Tim Jenkins, and Norma Stevens at The Avedon Foundation generously let us use Avedon's *Harper's Bazaar* cover. Jerry Schatzberg and David

Bailey generously allowed me to use their work, and the estate of Diane
Arbus kindly granted permission to reproduce the portrait of Mae West
that Diane gave me.

Gilly King of Whitelands College showed me round Parkstead House.
Her enthusiam for my ancestors' past in that exquisite building by Sir
William Chambers brilliantly illuminated my theretofore scant knowledge.

Carol and Reinhard Winkler in Klosters and the Alpes-Maritimes,
Janet de Botton in Provence, Carole and Anthony Bamford on boats and
in Barbados, and Paddy and Lizzie Rountree in Mauritius all provided
havens of calm and beauty in which to write. I am grateful beyond words
for such times of sybaritic luxury. For more than twenty years John and
Jean Major have made my own retreat in Hampshire, the Hunting Lodge,
a joy to return to.

My heartfelt thanks go to Kate Howard in my office and Ken Schneider
at Knopf for cheerfully re-re-typing my manuscript, which was then in-
structively copyedited by Susan Llewellyn.

My steadfast, beautiful, and handsome colleagues at NH Design, especially Colette van den Thillart, Jena Quinn, and Freddy van Zevenbergen,
delight and inspire me every day, as does each member of my staff past
and present. I could never have finished this book without their care, diligence, responsibility, and understanding. My driver, Nash Chowdery, has
unlimited skill and patience.

To all those mentioned above, and to the myriad others who have so
memorably touched my life, I can only crave indulgence for any errors in
Redeeming Features. They are no one's fault but my own.

NH
Hampshire, 2009

REDEEMING
FEATURES

Then did I dwell within a world of light,
Distinct and separate from all men's sight,
Where I did feel strange thoughts, and such things see
That were, or seemed, only revealed to me,
There I saw all the world enjoyed by one;
There I was in the world myself alone;
No business serious seemed but one; no work
But one was found, and that in me did lurk.
D'you ask me what? It was with clearer eyes
To see all creatures full of deities.

No ear,
But eyes themselves were all the hearers there,
And every stone and every star a tongue,
And every gale of wind a curious song.

—THOMAS TRAHERNE

· ONE ·

I
T IS EARLY MORNING. Beyond the open window of my attic room is
a sky so blue it seems to throb. I feel irresistibly drawn by its radi-
ance. Somehow I must try and reach it, touch it, must try to get there
from my bed with its mattress made rigid by boards. I push away the
metal-ribbed dome that prevents the covers from weighing on my legs.
With hesitant steps I cross the room toward the shining square. I reach
the window's embrasure, grasp the sill, and look out into the blue, blue
heady as ether. And then, below the blue, in an orchard set in cobweb-
spangled grass, apple trees stand layered with deep drifts of blossom, fat
clusters of snow white petals smudged with crimson, bouquets like clouds
gathering before sailing up into that vivid sky, leaving their black shadows to fragment on the silvery ground. I am transfixed by this sight, this
new vision of remembered mornings, this vibrant spring.

I hear the door open, and Teresa's voice behind me. "Back to bed
now?"

Three years earlier, at the age of seven, I had caught polio. It was
Teresa who, for the thousand days the disease paralyzed my body, had
tended to my every need. With her patience and help I was just learning
to walk again.

"In a minute," I answer.

Outside the orchard's walls the drive, along which, so long ago it
seemed a London ambulance had brought me, curved gently up over a
ridge, through chalky flat fields furrowed by the sharp spears of green
wheat, to meet the walls enclosing the garden below. Beyond, on one
side, was a barrier of tall dark trees; on the other, the rusty pink bricks
of outbuildings, stables, storerooms, granaries, and garages were dwarfed
by the creosote-blackened boards of tall barns. Above them, roofs of
lichen-speckled tiles lay like an undulating patchwork, gently tucking
their eaves around the hay-filled darkness. Farther away, in the hazy
morning distance, the fields were fringed by ragged hawthorn hedges
fuzzy with garlands of old-man's beard. Irregular massive elms, coral-
like against the sun, studded with the jagged islands of rooks' nests,

would soon cast pools of shade splashed with the noisy pink of dog roses. All around the ridge fell gently away, folding into canopies of green woodlands, lime green beeches, yellow-green oaks, the blue-green steeples of yew. Devil's Den, Willow Copse, and Herbert's Hole, these woods were called—names as ancient as the valleys and hills in this primeval Chiltern landscape.

Across the chalk-and-flint-strewn fields, a coppice of gnarled, mistletoe-swathed branches stood stark against the glassy sky. They marked the ley of a lane to a sandy heath. I had always known that Gypsy families drew their painted wagons into circles around fires ringed with stones, and brown-limbed, long-haired children raced whooping through the labyrinth of dark tunnels they'd formed beneath the high bracken. One heat-heavy evening three summers before, near naked myself, I had run the mile across the shardlike stubble, peered through the saplings to watch them. After a while, though I was unable to understand their strange speech, they signaled me to join them, explore their tunnels, and join the stone circle, where, feeling a kind of thrilling sensuality, I watched sinewy arms reach for soot-blackened kettles that hissed on dying embers. Smoky shadows rose and deepened. Then for a moment the setting sun infused the facade of Hundridge, distant across the fields, with a fiery gleam beckoning me back to my own world. As I ran I looked over my shoulder, wanting to return but stumbling on, my heart thumping. I was feeling a strange new emotion, different from any I'd yet experienced: I realized I was somehow enviously attracted to those figures and faces I'd just seen. The strength of this sensation made me suddenly scared. Was it a sin to feel this way? Could I be punished for it? Breathless, I stopped, looked back—just one last glance. Now the line of elm trees stood dark against the sky, like a barrier, guardians of the secret beyond.

Other emotions crowded in, jangling, pell-mell. I felt for the first time that I was in some way two people in one, that there was a second being within me who would always look longingly at beauty, at an attractive figure, at a different life. I turned away from this disconcertingly thrilling unknown and walked toward the consolingly familiar.

GREAT HUNDRIDGE MANOR, built in 1696, was a perfect example of William and Mary provincial architecture, its absolutely symmetrical facade composed of dark pink brick. Many of these had been glazed and glittered in the sunshine, glowed at sunset. When my father found the house in the 1920s, before he married, it had languished for more than a hundred years as a ramshackle farm on the estate of the Lowndes family, the local landowners in nearby Chesham. Deeds revealed it had been, in James I's reign, the property of a family called Chase until they upped and went to America, eventually to found the Chase Manhattan Bank. Chase descendants still live in a white clapboard homestead called Little Hundridge in Deerfield, Massachusetts.

From time to time the family would write to my father, offering, to my intense terror mingled with disbelief, to buy Hundridge and ship it, brick by pink brick, to America. Twenty years later in South Carolina I saw an entire plantation house being floated down the Charleston River on pontoons to some new destination, and I realized my fears had not been factually unfounded.

The *délabré* state of the house in no way deterred my father. Clearing the detritus of several centuries of grime, farm ordure, and broken implements revealed an untouched architectural jewel. Mercifully escaping any kind of modernization over the centuries, its finely carved pine staircases, doorways, and architraves were intact, and all the original fire surrounds remained, except the one in the room my father had chosen as his study, which was shaped like an elaborate scallop shell and had been added in the Regency. Several of the rooms still retained the original elaborately painted paneling and were considered to be among the most interesting seventeenth-century provincial interiors in England.

He assembled a brilliant team to transform Hundridge into the ideal retreat. Additions were commissioned from the renowned Welsh architect Clough Williams-Ellis, and the creation of gardens and grounds from the landscape designer Cecil Pinsent, while the interior's decoration was entrusted to his distant cousin and close friend the author and aesthete Geoffrey Scott, with whom he traveled, shared houses, interests, and a circle of friends. For several years in the 1920s Scott lived in an elegant and simply decorated mews behind my father's London house in Hanover Terrace. Some of the furniture he chose for both these rooms, and those at Hundridge, is around me as I write.

My father's early albums contain many photographs of Scott. His tall gangling figure is always impeccably dressed in the tweed or gray flannel suits, narrow jacketed and floppy trousered, of the period, and frequently sporting the newfangled neckwear, a colored bow tie. Scott had a slightly simian face and wore his thick, dark hair brushed back. A scholar of exceptional erudition and visual acumen, he had a passion for Italian and English art, and his first book, *The Architecture of Humanism,* was a critically acclaimed sensation. He had hoped to follow it with an expanded history of taste, a project ideally suited to his interests and abilities, but at the time of his death a decade later, the manuscript had not progressed beyond the unpromising opening statement, "It is very difficult. . . ." Perhaps he would have had empathy with the present queen, who, asked what she thought of taste, replied, "Well, I don't think it *helps.*"

Geoffrey became secretary and librarian to the distinguished collector and dealer Bernard Berenson, for whom he was extending and decorating I Tatti, the Berensons' villa above Florence. He was almost simultaneously having an affair with BB's wife, Mary, and Vita Sackville-West. Cecil Pinsent had laid out the gardens there, as he was to do at Hundridge a decade later. Hundridge was thus to become an extension of the intellectual and artistic coterie from the period my father had spent in Italy. When I was fourteen, on our first journey to Italy together, my father took me to I Tatti to have tea with Berenson's amanuensis, Nicky Mariano, in one of those lofty *salones* in which the old maestro had authenticated so many dud old masters for so much gullible new money.

Geoffrey Scott took the simple yet ideal proportions of Hundridge into account when furnishing its interior. Having not been modernized since the time it was built, the house retained its late-seventeenth-century details, its beautiful wrought-iron window latches, engraved brass door plates and handles, and architecturally influenced carving of cornices and door surrounds. Bold forms and overscaling were Scott's watchwords in furniture, mixed with the purest of baroque art and objects picked up in London for a song on frequent trawls of Roman and Florentine antique dealers, or London's Caledonian Market beyond King's Cross.

In the main sitting room, always called the Long Room after Clough Williams-Ellis doubled its size, Geoffrey's never-changed scheme was of plain white walls, curtains of red glazed cotton printed with a stylized lily, and enormous sofas covered in rough white linen. A towering Dutch baroque cupboard was balanced by a huge Italian oil painting depicting shelves of vellum-covered books with exquisite calligraphy on their spines, which hung above a large mahogany *retour d'Egypte* sarcophagus, annoyingly unsittable-on during parties due to its sloping pyramid-shaped lid.

My mother's store-cupboard was off this room—forbidden territory, and smelling of candles and cloves. Here she kept her records, mainly Chopin and Bach, though those of American musicals, or "La Vie en Rose," "Lili Marlene," and the "Harry Lime Theme" from *The Third Man,* were almost permanently on the radiogram's turntable, ready for a quick fox-trot.

The stone-floored, pine-paneled staircase hall had a rectangular oak table, its wood faded to pewter gray, which stood on bulbous melon legs under the semicircle of a viridian silk-velvet Elizabethan cloak bordered in dull silver metallic thread. Opposite stood a pine bench concealing a radiator, considered a brilliant modern trick of Scott's, especially as the hinged seat could be lifted to dry damp picnic rugs. On the staircase hung another large painting, a European version of an Oriental landscape in a marbleized frame, and an eighteenth-century portrait of a Venetian noblewoman wearing an astonishing pair of dangling diamond earrings, feeding biscuits to a tiny dog.

A little sitting room, or parlor, on the left of the hall was done up in stuff of tobacco brown and pale gold-gray satins, and near-black fringes. It had walls that had been ingeniously decorated by some itinerant artisan-artist, the 1690s counterpart of a specialist painter. The panels of sham burr-walnut wood graining, separated by stiles and rails of black lacquer scattered with stylized Chinoiserie scenes and figures, were contained in moldings, cornices, and skirtings painted to resemble violet-streaked yellow marble.

Opposite, looking out on a low wall topped by simple iron railings that separated the garden from the fields beyond, was my father's study. Its irregular paneling and shutters were painted white, and the furniture covered in plain pale brown rep. This serenity was countered by the strong smell of tobacco—my father had a little serrated acorn-shaped metal tool that made a very satisfactory noise as I scraped out the bowls of his pipes—and the searing scaly stink coming from a pot of thick fish glue, sent yearly and boiled up from the detritus of the Hull fish-filleting factory he had bought on a whim. I remember titles of books on the shelves: *The Ragged Trousered Philanthropists; Cry, the Beloved Country; The World of Don Camillo; The Sea Around Us*—this last, for some reason, being the cause of a violent row between him and my mother.

Upstairs my parents slept in their respective four-post beds. My father's was a very elaborate affair that Geoffrey had had made, inspired by Saint Ursula's in Carpaccio's mystical painting of her vision which hangs in the Accademia in Venice. This bed was among the few things my father left me when he died. As I have always liked to live in the intimacy of small rooms, while hoping others will have vast ones needing much furniture and materials, I sold this stately and somewhat unwieldy memento to the Victoria and Albert Museum, which displays it in their English furniture department to this day. The room itself had astonishing paneling swirled with paint in the strange *grottesque* style, so called because of its almost surreal, rocklike forms. The panel over the fireplace alone devolved into a barely discernible landscape, a rock-teetering, tow-ered castle. This fanciful conceit had been carried out in imitation *scag-liola,* in itself a faux finish made by pulverizing and coloring stone fixed in gesso.

When Hundridge was photographed for *Country Life* in 1942, a revered architectural historian wrote: "This painted imitation of a syn-thetic substance counterfeiting paint is a *tour de force.* Representation cubed, pastiche to the third degree." The glowing dark red in this triple *fauxness* was obtained from dried bulls' blood, which, mixed with pow-dered chalk from the Roman quarry in the woods below the house, made the almost transparent brownish pigment that the painter had used to give these walls their startling chiaroscuro. For my mother's bedroom, which was painted the pale blue-gray of her eyes, Geoffrey had arranged a simpler bed—slim dark posts surmounted by a barreled white canopy outlined in gray baroque gadrooning. High and narrow, as was then the fashion, the bed was quite an effort to climb up into in the morning, to snuggle up to Mum as she lay listening to the latest songs on the wireless—Nat Gonella singing "The Isle of Capri" is the first tune I re-member. The bed seemed hardly wide enough for both of us, but it never occurred to me that there was certainly no room for my father. Perhaps people didn't sleep all night together in those days, or maybe double beds were new and considered common.

Above a Queen Anne chest of drawers, and another in whitened oak, hung Gaudier-Brzeska drawings and a charming oil-sketch head by the fashionable portrait painter of the time, Robin Guthrie, of the ballerina Moira Shearer, whom my mother greatly admired. Over the dressing table was a painting of roses by a family friend, which my mother regu-larly refreshed with her latest lipstick. A door led to a balcony, built over the Long Room. On summer evenings we gathered there at sundown as my mother, looking so lovely with her arms folded behind her blond head, warmed by the last rays of heat from the tiles of the roof that sloped up behind the parapet on which she lay.

Opposite these rooms, in the south and east corners of the square that formed the footprint of the house, were guest bedrooms. The first, some-what arbitrarily, as it was painted blue, was always called the Pink Room. It contained a pretty little Regency faux-bamboo tester bed of even more astonishing narrowness. So it seems most odd that this was the one cho-sen by the royal gynecologist, E. Lane-Roberts—who had played a key role in the birth of both the queen and Princess Margaret—for my own birth, at eight in the evening, in September 1939. It was about the second week of the "phony war." It's always rather irked me that I can't claim to having been born prewar. Nevertheless, in labor, my mother heard a pain-piercing ringing of alarmlike bells in the room below.

"Do go and find out what on earth's that ghastly racket," she said to Nurse Blackie, the midwife. The din continued. Blackie bustled back.

"It's just Mr. Haslam, mum, ringing for another helping of Queen's pudding." There could have been no question of my father witnessing the birth of any of his sons: Not only was it not the custom of the time, but he was distinctly squeamish. Being so, he wasn't much help when, a few weeks later, I nearly bled to death at the circumcision he insisted on, an operation that has subconsciously made me extremely wary of anyone touching that part of my anatomy.

The room that completed this floor, with gilt-edged, brown-black lacquer panels and umber faux marble wainscot, was called, with the same arbitrariness, the Blue Room, and it was there that I was to spend the years of polio. It was connected to the Pink Room by a tiny cabinet with a marble washbasin, just as my parents' bedrooms were joined by a secret dressing room. I loved these cubbyholes, warm and dark, so different from the long cold corridor to the nursery wing. I truly dreaded that passage, which was hung with black-framed engravings of my mother's more illustrious forebears carrying out their country's duty— Lord Cornwallis "receiving" the pathetic, cringing, turbaned children of Tippoo Sahib at Seringapatam, for instance, or Lord Raglan charging with the Light Brigade—terrified that, while gingerly navigating its icy length, I should be set upon by, of all unlikely things, packs of howling wolves.

Putting off bedtime till the last possible moment, I would hang about the kitchen or the servants' hall next door while our beloved cook, Sersee, would sing along to hymns on the wireless, or shush me if I interrupted Sandy MacPherson at his Theatre Organ. A great joy was to be taken into her larder to look at the eggs suspended in water glass that she "put down" each week, preserving Biddy and the other hens' output in a strange glutinous liquid, or to help rummage in a sack filled with straw for potatoes with the fewest eyes and to turn the ripening tomatoes on the windowsill. Then there would be a thick chunk of toast spread with beef dripping before "Now off with you," and the dreaded corridor.

The nursery end of the corridor, past the wolves, had been built into one part of a huge barn. Soon after I was born, the upstairs rooms— where my two older brothers had slept—were given over to my father's secretary and her family, safely removed from air raids in London. But the ground floor was still, for my earliest years, Nanny Baker's domain. On the right a playroom, with a curved window of special glass that magnified the sun's heat, had been built for my brother John, who had been born with seriously turned-backward feet. As a child he'd had to wear corrective leg braces, and in early childhood could play only, while supervised, either here or in the sandpit outside.

The playroom seemed rather forlorn in my later childhood, with cupboards full of Michael and John's outgrown toys: headless lead soldiers, bent feathers from forgotten Red Indian headdresses, their prep school cricket gear with strange hard white triangles sprouting straps they referred to, unhelpfully, as boxes, and mangled tracks for Hornby 00 model electric trains.

Behind this was a gloomy "day" nursery, as cold as the playroom was hot, and by now containing only a Ping-Pong table that, each December, would be heaped with holly boughs. My father would dragoon everybody into stripping off the leaves, which, with an outsize needle, he threaded onto wires, making the prickly dark green chains he considered the only acceptable form of Christmas decoration.

Beside this room were the "night" nursery and two bedrooms, mine a peculiar pointed shape, sandwiched into an odd corner between the old barn and the stairs. One of my earliest memories is of Nanny Baker nightly tucking yards of thick black cloth over my nursery window. Because of the blackout I had a luminous Scottie dog lamp, its strange lemony glow lasting only a few minutes—enough to keep the wolves at bay—after which it would be dark until morning; when Nanny came to remove the carefully placed material. Then I could see Butter—the fat little cob that had gently borne John around in a sort of basketwork howdah, and eventually would become my pony—maneuvering his white-maned neck over his stall door opposite, while Nanny made endless cuppas in which to dunk rationed Rich Tea biscuits, and jeered at the ranting voice of Lord Haw-Haw, the Nazis' pet English propagandist, coming through from Berlin on her shortwave wireless. I slept in this room until Nanny retired, when I moved over to the attic floor above my parents' bedrooms; Teresa was in the room next door, with her sewing room at the top of the stairs and, opposite, a bedroom reserved for Nanny's visits. In the middle of the landing, under a central skylight stood a pale wood chest of drawers with a Greuze engraving above it, both relics of my grandfather's house in the North of England, as indeed were the contents of some cupboards; his tall hats, frock coats, and trousers pressed with perfect creases from seam to seam in the late Victorian style.

Behind the 1696 main house stood a medieval chapel, with a fine Perpendicular east window, dated 1199 and dedicated to Edward II, the "king and martyr." It had been converted successively into a vast-ovened kitchen, and then into a brewhouse, with the furnace and copper vat still intact. Early Georgian owners added a cider press. I made a den, one of many, in the round receptacle for fruit at the press's top, and filled it with fossils and arrowheads found in the Roman flint quarry in the woods. Tacked on to the west end was a lath-and-plaster cottage, with the curious words "Seldom Sene" crudely inscribed in the lintel of its low doorway, its windows originally looking into a walled nut orchard, in which my father installed one of the earliest outdoor swimming pools in England. Its amusing primitive lavatory, with two adult seats side by side and a smaller child's version with a step next to them, became the changing room. Less funny was the day my brother Michael said, "Come on, jump in the pool, I'll catch you." I did, he didn't. I sank like a brick and saw green bubbles streaming out of my mouth as I sank. Suddenly there was a *whoooosh*ing push from below. My mother, realizing what had happened, dived to my rescue fully clothed. As I was backslapped into coughing, I saw her tobacco brown suede loafers, filled with water, at the pool's edge.

Nearer the main building had stood a wooden wellhouse, the brick-lined shaft of the well descending hundreds of feet through the Chiltern flint to a just-visible glitter of dark water. My father decided to incorporate this well into a new south wing, and our Christmas tradition was to unbolt the stout wooden cover and drop lighted paper flares weighted with stones, counting the many seconds till a distant plop and dim fizz. Opposite lay an irregular complex of stables and farm buildings, tall brick barns, tractor sheds, and apple storage rooms.

Cecil Pinsent had kept his garden design for Hundridge appropriately simple. Around the house there were those apple trees standing in square beds, some big lawns, and long herbaceous borders against the old brick walls, into which, at one corner, a pretty white trellised summerhouse had been built by some carefree Georgian. There were the usual attempts at a cutting garden, and rows of vegetables near some not very spruce greenhouses. These beds were edged in thick wood beams. Naturally I used to walk on them, rather than the path. One day my father saw me and became suddenly and inexplicably angry: the "If I ever catch you doing that again" routine. It was the only time he ever threatened to hit me.

My father had a strange love-hate relationship with woods in general.

Though the house was surrounded by them, they were kept severely at bay. The woodsman, aptly named Mr. Wood, was constantly cutting down and sawing up enormous trees into logs to be dragged up to the house by his huge gray horse. And when my father, in very old age, came to visit my house, the Hunting Lodge in Hampshire, he ran from it within half an hour, pleading arboreal claustrophobia.

IN 1946 I WAS SEVEN YEARS OLD. For all but one those had been war years, and Hundridge, a mere forty miles outside London, was on the flight path back to base for the Luftwaffe bombers. Having dropped some of their deadly load on the capital, they would lighten their return journey by dumping the metallic leftovers on our chalky Chiltern valleys and hills as they lumbered to Peenemünde to stock up for the next raid. Thus not a chink of light could glow from our windows after dark. I can picture helping Mary, the housekeeper, at her evening routine of "shutting up" the main house, where the recessed shutters in their paneled embrasures still folded out to fit across the panes with seventeenth-century precision, and heavy curtains were pulled across with that satisfying rasp of metal runners on their tracks as we tugged on the bronze acorns dangling on the beeswax-rubbed white cords, leaving my hands smelling faintly of honey.

I rather loved the inky seclusion of the blackout, and maybe it contributed to my lasting lack of fear of the dark. In the brightness of daylight it was a routine to find out from Mr. Wood whether a bomb had actually landed anywhere nearby. Occasionally there were thumps and bangs in the night, and a few bombs did fall in the woods, but there was never a near-hit. I remember standing at the edge of quite big craters, the freshly thrown-up earth looking like huge molehills, and the exposed jigsaw of tree roots. I can see my father asking for the operator on the big Bakelite telephone in an alcove in the kitchen corridor, and telling the Home Guard of suspected unexploded shells, or being called to go and help with a defusion nearby. Sometimes the less destructive incendiary bombs fell in the woods, and my parents would rush out with their dinner guests to see how pretty the trees looked all lit up, especially with the long strands of silvery metal—was it called flak?—that the air force would drop to baffle German radar, dripping like tinsel from the branches. My mother would curse like a fiend when brambles snagged her precious nylons, which all too rarely—stockings being a government-forbidden luxury—were smuggled in by the fairly constant flow of American big brass, both army and navy, who frequently came to stay at Hundridge.

Looking back, it seems extraordinary how little these nocturnal activities of the Germans disrupted the daily regularity of our lives. Perhaps by now the writing was on the bunker wall, and Hitler's mad plans were being redirected eastward; or perhaps because I'd known nothing else, those wartime years seemed positively rosy. The postman delivered like clockwork, often twice a day. My father went by train to his office in London, where he was a company director. People came to stay almost every weekend. It was a great treat to be allowed to meet them when they changed trains at Chalfont station, riding there and back on the branch line to Chesham in the open engine cab of the driver, Mr. Popplesthwaite, whose whistling bright pink lips gleamed in his goggled, coal-dust-encrusted face.

My parents, somewhat surprisingly, given—or perhaps because of—their Victorian upbringings, encouraged their children to interact with their friends. "Children should be obscene but not absurd," my father would say. My eldest brother, Michael, my tousle-headed, daring older god, remembers playing a game of Grandmother's Footsteps with H. G. Wells as he sat hidden by the high back of a chair in the parlor. When braveheart eventually dared to tag him, Wells shot from his seat onto all fours and barked like a rabid dog, sending Michael howling for Nanny. HG would usually bring one of the loves of his life, the enormous Russian countess Moura Budberg, who towered over him. Moura was often said to be a spy, a theory given a certain credence by her diplomat husband having been shot by Bolshevik assassins before her eyes at their Estonian estate, though this didn't impede her long affair with Maxim Gorky, both in and out of Russia. Wells would spend hours begging my mother to persuade Moura to marry him, but to no avail. She preferred to retain her amatory freedom for lovers like Bruce Lockhart, author of *Comes the Reckoning,* and, by the time I remember her, her role as fixer to the film mogul Alexander Korda. She and my father played endless games of tennis, very badly, bundled up whatever the weather in vast prickly Fair Isle sweaters, so stiff they could hardly put their arms to their sides (not unlike Randolph Hearst, who at San Simeon would have a racquet tied to each outstretched arm and two men to push him, twirling, toward the ball). I remember playing one summer wearing a rare and proudly displayed present, a Hawaiian shirt. "Aren't you hot?" my father sneeringly inquired from his woolly carapace.

The portrait painter Simon Elwes would come with his wife Golly, sis-

ter of my godfather Francis Rennell, and their sons, the most enchanting
of whom was the youngest, Dominic. He was sent for safety to America
during the war (a strategy my mother thought a bit common) and came
back to live for a few months at Hundridge, a gum-chewing, chino-
wearing, crew-cut, pink-skinned, softly accented vision. I knew he was
the most beautiful thing I'd ever seen, and I was smitten by male beauty,
not for the first time. It was a love that increased as I grew up with admiration for Dominic's hilarious wit, uncanny mimicry, and his physical
and sartorial perfection. All too tragically to end with his suicide. My
mother was regrettably never painted by Simon Elwes in his just-not-too-
sugary chocolate-box style, though later she did sit for her portrait, wearing an elaborate Aage Thaarup hat, by his less famous rival, Robin
Guthrie. The picture was shown that year at the Royal Academy.

A good friend of my mother's was Mel Russell-Cooke, to me morbidly
fascinating, as her father had been captain of the *Titanic*. Other guests
were Golly's brother Peter Rodd, married at the time to Nancy Mitford,
from whom my mother got the feeling that Buckinghamshire was on a
par, county-wise, with stockbroker Surrey. The willowy young Randlord
Alfred Beit, who was married to Nancy's cousin Clementine, and the
composer A. P. Herbert and his wife, Gwen, to whose house in Ham-
mersmith Terrace we would make an annual journey for their party to
watch the Oxford and Cambridge Boat Race, were more particularly
friends of my father's, as was Maynard Keynes, who came with various
boyfriends, among them Duncan Grant. My father's diplomatic-world
contemporary, Gladwyn Jebb (later, as Lord Gladwyn, to be ambassador in Paris), brought his tiny, charmingly overdressed wife, Cynthia,
who was the great-granddaughter of Isambard Kingdom Brunel. My father had quite a "yen," as the word was, for Bin, the nickname we all
called her. Into his old age he would send her scatologically obscene
rhymes and tidbits, which must at least have relieved the tedium of Gladwyn's company.

IN SOME WAYS, as the youngest by many years, I felt almost like an only
child. Anne, my mother's daughter by her first marriage, seemed impossibly remote since she lived with her father in New York; my brother
Michael was ten years older than me, and the middle son, John, six. I remember their being away far more that I remember them being at home.
There had been a third, who died in infancy, but I never heard my parents refer to his life or death. Being older, my brothers were away at

school: Michael at Kirkby Lonsdale in distant Cumberland, John much nearer at Lockers Park in Berkhamsted. Even during the holidays I saw very little of them: They would be in another part of the house while I would stay upstairs with Teresa. Of the two, Michael was the more conventionally beautiful, tall and dark with thick brown hair on a beautifully shaped head, while John, due to the misfortune of his turned-back feet, was shorter and with a muscular torso because his legs never grew to their full length. He, too, had a beautiful face, almost angelic with bright blue eyes, white-blond hair, and perfect lips, and of the two the sunnier disposition. Michael was rather poetically withdrawn. Neither, unsurprisingly, was particularly interested in me.

The strictures of war made overt spoiling of any of us fairly impossible. I had known only a world of rationing in which everyone was issued with little buff-colored paper books of blotchily printed coupons; milk was a luxury, cream unheard of, and butter had been replaced by a repulsive whale-fat slime called Snoek. We dined on Pom, powdered potatoes and dried eggs, which fleshed out the supply from the hens that strutted and scratched in their run below the kitchen door. Sugar was scarce, there were no sweets (sweet rationing was still in force when I went to Eton several years later), and imported fruit was a treat. I remember, as do many people born around the same time as I was, my first banana, and someone coming from London cradling two avocado pears as if they were the Holy Grail. Each week my mother would collect two tiny screw-top blue glass medicine bottles of what was called orange juice—though I believe now it was in fact dyed turnip or swede—from, of all unlikely places, the post office in Chesham. There appeared to be no shortage of spirits for grown-ups to add to this concoction. There was mainly gin—vodka being unheard of, while whiskey and brandy had medicinal overtones—and, less frequently, sherry, which stood for months souring in an opened bottle and was drunk disgustingly but fashionably warm. Wine was rare; some venerable bottles moldered in the cellar, to be produced at grander weekends. Michael drank cider, and for special occasions he and John made a very basic wine cup. Not greedy, and certainly not gourmets, my parents ate perfectly well off the land during the war. Neither of them shot, so game, rabbit, and even squirrel—pronounced delicious—were bagged by Rumens, a sort of keeper-cum-chauffeur, who lived in a hideous cottage, designed by Clough Williams-Ellis, which loomed among beech and oak trees beside the drive. By the time I became conscious of food as different things for different meals, meat was obtainable, though I imagine scrupulously rationed. Fresh fish was a rarity, since there were few nearby rivers in those chalky hills so distant from any coast. But gold-glinting fat kippers were sent down from the fish-filleting business in Hull in rough pine crates, packed between layers of thick yellow waxy paper; and I can still recall the wet flat wooden boxes filled with bladderwrack-buried oysters, my mother's favorite food, that periodically arrived from an admirer living near Colchester.

I saw little of my father during the week, as he came back from his London office after my bedtime, though he sometimes climbed up to my room to say goodnight. His arrival was announced by a farting noise he could make with his palms, which I hated. My mother hardly ever came to my attic floor, but I could hear her running her bath and changing after her day doing diverse local war work; at one point she drove a horse-and-cart milk round, though sadly I was too young to witness this hilariously incongruous sight. I did frequently go with her to Chesham in a tiny tinny Ford—her imported American Buick had long since been put up on blocks in a barn—to wheedle a forbidden half gallon of gas (as she called it, having learned to drive in New York) out of Mrs. Ratcliffe, who manned the pumps, or cajole some lard from Mr. Kingham, the butcher.

Knowing how well the color suited her, my mother almost always wore her red square-shouldered wool coat to facilitate the wheedling. In Kingham's we sometimes met our glamorous and deflatingly funny neighbor Lady Ranfurly. "Di, darling!" Hermione once said. "That coat! Too heavenly! You *must* lend it to me next time I'm pregnant."

From as early as I can remember until I was ten and able to go away to school, my world was the staff. They were my only friends. Teresa, Sersee (a contraction in my baby talk of Miss Hersee), who ruled the kitchen and the roosters in her hen yard, and Mary Walkling, the housekeeper, all became, for all of my youth, my closest, most beloved companions. My mother's loving nature, trusting and flirtatious, enabled her to engage staff who, by turning a deaf ear to the not infrequent tension between her and my father, remained at Hundridge for decades. They had for the most part been the staff at 8 Hanover Terrace, my parents' London home in Regent's Park, where they had lived in the early 1930s before war seemed inevitable. Mary had started there as a parlor maid—her title in that faraway parlance—but came to Hundridge as housekeeper. Her uniform, with its nunlike headdress of pleated starched linen nodding above the stiff white apron elaborately buttoned to the front of her long blue overall, made her look like a less outré version of Marie, the whey-faced, kohl-eyed dowager queen of Romania, famous for her self-designed "medieval" uniforms. Our equally regal but hardly flamboyant Mary took holidays in a tiny yellow cement terrace house at Broadstairs in Kent, shared with her brother. It was my greatest treat to be allowed to spend a few days with them, the seaside spellbinding after landlocked Buckinghamshire. Sersee hardly ever left Hundridge for more than a day; her idea of a holiday was an hour with the hairdresser in Chesham. Instead her near-identical sister Bertha, sweet-spoken and hymn humming, would come to stay. Only after many years did my mother learn they were the daughters of an aristocratic girl who had eloped with a groom and consequently been ejected from her family.

The Hundridge gardens were looked after—"tended" is too strong a word—by a rotund whiskery codger called Reginald Gibbs. He wobbled over each morning from a nearby hamlet—where he shared an Arts and Craftsy pebble-dashed council cottage with his spinster sister—on a high, old fashioned bicycle, wearing a brown bowler hat, a collarless shirt with a front stud, weskit, trousers tied with string at the knees, and enormous boots. He would gnaw on a huge ham bone in his shed, swig from a stoneware bottle, do a bit of digging or tying up, and then wobble away down the drive, shouting somewhat bibulously, "Goo'day, Nick-o-las!" Sometimes, at weekends we would see him in the post-office-cum-general-shop in Hyde Heath, manned by Miss Murrell, an old lady of astonishing age and sprightly sharpness at totting up one's bill on a little blackboard kept by the money draw. Reg would be dressed in his best—a blue suit, rigid enough to stand alone—and there would be more "Goo'day Nick-o-las's," though less slurred. One imagines the spinster sister ruled with a steel rod.

So indeed did the mother of Len, the so-called butler. A weedy young man, too "delicate" to have been in the forces, Len shared Rowan Cottage, about a mile up the road, with this termagant, who certainly wouldn't have condoned her son's sitting listlessly around at home chain-smoking, and cross-legged to boot, the way he did in his pantry at Hundridge. My mother, always charmingly indulgent toward staff, could never find it in her to give him a ticking off. I used to enjoy helping him wash up—we "stacked," wickedly, it being deemed dreadfully wasteful of soap and water to dirty both sides of plates—and was thrilled by the faintly sensual ammonia smell of silver polish. He also used to tune his wireless, sotto voce, to the Forces Favourites program, which seemed distinctly racy compared to Sersee's Theatre Organ listening.

Of all the household it was Teresa who was most important to me. A sturdy, strong-willed, and proud country girl from Steirmark, the Aus-

trian province between Vienna and the Italian border, she had come to my
mother as a lady's maid in the early thirties. At the rumblings of war she
was sent to the Isle of Man, as an enemy alien, but my parents pulled
strings to prevent a long internment, or—a worse fate, for Teresa was
part Jewish—deportation. Teresa was a passionate filmgoer, and on her
day off would come back from the cinema in Chesham having walked the
four miles through woods, alone, in the dark. The next day she would tell
me the stories, sing the songs, describe the stars. I can still see her acting
out Bob Hope crooning "Buttons and Bows," the song from *The Pale-
face,* but for some reason at that point I absolutely hated films. Perhaps
it was my father's terrifying habit of dressing up as an old lady at parties.
I'd been carried screaming from my first film, Walt Disney's *Sleeping
Beauty;* buried my face in my hands at *My Friend Flicka,* howled through
National Velvet. It was Teresa who gradually weaned me of film fear, and
even now I can remember the feeling of triumph at finally enjoying one,
even if it was Mario Lanza in the deeply corny but at least more adult
Toast of New Orleans. It was pleasure that would last only if I was accompanied by Teresa to reassure me. When I went to private school, my
terror returned even with such innocuous, educational films as *Nanook
of the North* or *Tarka the Otter.* True joy in the world of celluloid was
not to be mine until I saw Irving Berlin's *Call Me Madam.* I became word-
perfect in every lyric, and grew obsessed with Ethel Merman. Not long
after this revelation, some local children whom I hardly knew invited
me to a fancy-dress party. I was determined to go as Ethel—surprisingly
encouraged by my mother. But fatherly feet were firmly put down, and
Teresa was told to drag the Red Indian costume out of the dressing-
up box.

Teresa was, for the first fourteen years of my life, the person I trusted
and loved above anyone, and vice versa. She slept beside my bed all the
nights I was critically—and potentially contagiously—ill; nursed me tire-
lessly though immobility to convalescence, taught me how my legs could
walk. That I, by a single careless remark, would demolish such devotion,
was an early and lasting lesson in humiliating sorrow. I had had no contact with her for ten years, until one day there was a ring on the doorbell
of a Manhattan apartment I had rented from Marcel Duchamp and his
wife, Teeny. I opened it to see Teresa, smiling. Why was she in New York?
I forget. Why? To forgive? Perhaps, but nothing can ever absolve that
one shouted, shaming, outburst: "You're only a servant!" Teresa had
packed that night and was gone by morning.

The one other figure I saw daily was my grandmother Evelyn Ponsonby, an erect but frail and gentle lady who stayed mainly in her room, dressed invariably in a sweet-pea-colored lace peignoir. She treated me with the gracious but unfamiliar manner of her time and class. I would sit by her dressing table, lulled by the scent of violets in her silver-topped, cut-glass toilette, or thrilled by the ammonia reek of her smelling salts, as she would gently brush her long hair until it crackled with electricity and was ready to be put up over "rats" in preparation for the attachment of the rather perky turn-of-the-century-style hats she invariably wore to leave her bedroom. Such excursions were hardly ever more exotic than coming downstairs to have tea with the mother of my father's secretary, Miss Findon, who lived in at Hundridge for the duration of the war. On fine afternoons she would walk gently in the garden, parasol in gloved hand, her pointed, buckled shoe leaving only the faintest imprint on new-mown grass.

Evelyn Sillery, as she was before marrying my Ponsonby grandfather, had French blood; her forebears possessed vineyards in Champagne. (Meeting M. Krug of the eponymous champagne house, I asked if he had ever heard of a de Sillery vineyard. He replied that he not only knew it but that it was one of the earliest and finest *marques,* and that he had recently bought the land.) Evelyn died at Hundridge while I was still quite young, the only one of my grandparents I ever knew, and I the only one of her grandsons to be given her patrician married name.

· TWO ·

OUR BRANCH OF THE HASLAMS—one of the oldest names in Britain, as I discovered from a BBC program a decade or so ago, pre-Norse and meaning "land of hazels"—was a Lancashire family who made its fortune on the boom in cotton spinning. By the time my father was born in 1886, they had become tycoons in, and eventually grandees of, Bolton. My grandfather had been made mayor of the town, living in some style at Whitebank, a large and rather dour villa fitted out entirely by the furniture manufacturers Messrs. Gillows. A vast sign reading HASLAM dominated Manchester's Piccadilly skyline, frequently painted by L. S. Lowry, who was an almost exact contemporary of my father. He admired and collected the artist's work from the start, and over the years Lowry became a close friend.

While pillars of industrial northern society, they were not provincially minded. My grandfather, great-grandfather, and great-great-grandfather variously had traveled extensively in the United States, Russia, Egypt, and the Holy Land, while a cousin, Fanny, had decided to visit the Argentine, where she married and became the grandmother of that country's greatest writer, Jorge Luis Borges. My father and his brothers owned the first motorcar in Bolton, in fact one of the first in England. It ran on electricity, and a man walked in front of it waving a red flag to warn of its approach; not a bad idea, given my father's consequent driving ability or indeed his understanding of internal-combustion engines. He once sent back a new Austin "because it thumps"—he had been driving over the recently installed cat's-eyes.

There are still a Haslam Hospital and a Haslam Park in Bolton—though no longer any Haslams of our branch, as by family consent they sold the business to Amalgamated Cotton Spinners. My staunchly northern grandmother moved, most surprisingly, to London, and moreover to a house on "Millionaires' Row"—Kensington Palace Gardens, albeit at the somewhat less sumptuous Bayswater end—and with her daughters, Mildred and Winifred, safely married to suitable northern businessmen, her three sons set out on their various careers.

Oliver, my father's middle brother, delicate in health, had been advised to spend a few years in the dryness of the high Arizona deserts. There he lived among the Hopi Indians in Oraibi and was at the opening of the first hotel to be built at the Grand Canyon, sending back vivid letters to his mother via Pony Express. My father inherited those letters, and with his misguided lifelong belief that the subject is more valuable than the object—*he* himself wrote in the names of the many famous guests in the Hundridge visitor's book—copied them and destroyed the originals, envelopes, stamps, and all. When, years later, I lived on a ranch in Arizona, museum directors made me acutely aware of the fantastic value of such Wild West memorabilia.

Oliver subsequently returned to England, working for a while in the cotton industry and upon his marriage, settled permanently at Cairngill in Scotland with his wife, Agnes, their daughter, Di-dee, and his inventions.

My uncle Robert, the eldest, was sent (as its first experimental boy pupil) to all-female Bedales, Yorkshire-based until it moved to Hampshire. Such petticoat education only stimulated his sex drive, spendthriftiness, and dandyism. He was given, in his salad days, to tooling around Europe in a selection of ever larger Rolls-Royces, and wearing ever larger checked suits, his hand on the hooter and girls in the rumble seat.

For a time Robert was apprenticed to the Arts and Crafts architect C. F. A. Voysey, before setting up his own somewhat lackadaisical practice. He designed a handful of houses in a faintly Voyseyesque style near Bognor before the sybaritic sybil beckoned once more, in the form of a Kabuki-faced, orange-haired Irish artist named Dolores. She became his second or third wife, and with her he inhabited vernacular residences in London, Wastwater, Brighton, and Capri, though they mainly lived beside a vast millpond at Wonersh in Surrey, building at its very edge a pitch-dark house filled with twisting oak staircases, precious Chinese porcelains, and Pekingeses—all of which were something of a hazard to his three nephews' ebullient youthfulness.

My father was his mother's favorite son. Christened William Heywood (her family name), he was always called Mike in his youth, and Bill in later life. Her innate intellectualism and as-yet undenominated feminism mapped out a solid education for him. His early education was at the local dame school in Bolton, after which he was dispatched to, and survived, the disconcertingly rugged Yorkshire public school Sedbergh. Roaming the hills surrounding the slate gray school buildings—bare, rounded, rain-ridged hills that look like the backs of gigantic elephants clustered around some invisible water hole—he acquired a lasting love of remote landscapes.

He went to France to learn the language—to Tours, at the time considered to have the purest spoken French. This seems to have been something of a failure; later in life he spoke Italian and Spanish fairly fluently, but he never mastered French. However, sharing digs with a Siamese prince named Mom Chow Skon—one of the many sons of the exotic king of *The King and I,* who had been a pupil of Anna Leonowens—he picked up a few words of Welsh-accented Siamese. He completed his education at King's, Cambridge, where among his contemporaries were E. M. Forster, Lytton Strachey, Harold Nicolson, and the poets James Elroy Flecker and Rupert Brooke. (The latter introduced him into the Marlowe Society where, as his obituary in the King's College Annual Report quaintly put it, "he flourished as a player of female parts.") I imagine I might have seen some of these illustrious old cronies when my mother and I went with him in the late forties to the great service for the rededication of King's College Chapel, which had been damaged during the war. I vividly remember thinking the ceremony was for the king himself, who with the queen and Princesses Elizabeth and Margaret Rose passed within inches of my nose as they crossed the lawn from the chapel to the banquet. My father brought home a champagne cork in a little wire crinoline that he promised was from the royal table, and it joined my treasure hoard, becoming a much-swanked exhibit.

Of all the friends he made at this time, it was Maynard Keynes, who would be the most important and whom he introduced into the City in the early twenties. Meanwhile, after a brief and entirely landlocked spell in the navy, it was decided that his immediate future should be in the diplomatic corps. This decision led to a first posting, in 1909, as a very junior secretary to Sir Rennell Rodd, the British ambassador to Rome. Escaping the somewhat stuffy atmosphere that Sir Rennell and Lady Rodd's embassy induced, he fell in with a livelier circle of young would-be diplomats, among them Gerald Tyrwhitt-Drake, later Lord Berners; Gerry Wellesley, eventual inheritor of the Wellington dukedom; and Harold Nicolson, yet to be married to Vita Sackville-West.

But of this group, the most intimate was Geoffrey Scott, with whom he had for some time shared a flat on the Trinità dei Monti, sky-high above the Spanish Steps, forever romantically known as the one where John Keats had lived during his Italian years. My father had met Edith Wharton in Paris and the Eternal City of his time was the very one described by Wharton in her short story "Roman Fever." Much of Rome was still to be excavated, and gardens and pastures lapped the sculpted stones of the monumental ruins; at dusk shepherds could be heard calling their flocks into the safety of the grassy Colosseum. The aristocracy, both Black and White, with their diverse but rigid allegiance to either the papal Vatican or the royal Quirinale, still used swaying painted-leather carriages with caparisoned horses and liveried footmen, and dark-eyed, brown-bodied urchins dived among the time-smoothed stone dolphins and deities of Bernini's fountain in the Piazza Navona.

With Geoffrey as guide, at each weekend the group would clamber into an open Isotto-Franchini and hurtle along dusty country roads in search of the classical and baroque churches, villas, and palaces Geoffrey would teach my father to admire. Evenings were spent at some vinetrellised *taverna* in Trastevere, drinking young Frascati wine, and smoking Franz Josefs, the long wonky cigars with a straw threaded through, favored by the already old emperor of Austria. Geoffrey would doodle architectural theories, Wellesley drew caricatures of eminent contemporaries—somewhere I have one of Lytton Strachey doing unspeakably indelicate things to Queen Victoria—while Berners would write obscene limericks about the dullness of the Rodds. Many had to be shielded from the brilliant blue eyes of the Rennells' handsome but somewhat humorless son, Francis, who was to become another of my father's close friends and eventually, as Lord Rennell, my godfather.

When Geoffrey was engaged by Bernard and Mary Berenson to make the additions and alterations to I Tatti, this self-entertaining company would entrain to Florence, to wander in the gaslit Uffizi and Pitti galleries, to visit Sir William Acton at La Pietra, Sir George Sitwell at Montegufoni, or to explore remote hilltop villages. When my father took me to Italy in the late 1950s we went to a restaurant in one such village. "I dined here with Caruso," he said. It was in Florence that my father met Cecil Pinsent, the garden designer of I Tatti and many other Tuscan villas, and it was there that Geoffrey became enamored of Lady Sybil Cuffe, at that time the wife of Bostonian millionaire William Bayard Cutting. The Cuttings were living at the Villa Medici in Fiesole with their daughter, the future writer Iris Origo. Bayard Cutting died, it appears of depression, aged thirty-one. Sybil, equally depressive, and Geoffrey were married soon after. For my father, the youthful idyll of Rome, of the Trinità dei Monti, of a country still in many aspects trapped in the eighteenth or nineteenth century, came to an end; he decided to leave Italy, but not before securing the pledge of another godparent for his intended family in Iris, by now Geoffrey Scott's step-daughter.

JUDGING BY EARLY PHOTOGRAPHS, my father was clearly a very beautiful young man. Slight, with pale, perfect features inherited from his mother, and humorous eyes, he looks innocent yet self-assured even wearing the flounced dresses little boys wore at the time; the high stiff collars and fashionably slightly ill-fitting suits of the pre–World War I years, and then later the neat close-cut uniforms of his short stint in the navy. His looks suggest meekness, though he had, in fact, a covert dual personality: docile in some relationships, inflexible in others. He certainly must have been a magnet for lustful glances, and perhaps the advances, of the largely homosexual circle of his youth, but there is no proof, not even a hint, that he had affairs with any of them. He had affection for them all, always, and especially Ralph Hamlyn, whom he met in 1921, and who was to exert a strong, strange, almost loverlike lifelong thrall over him.

Their friendship was forged during early business deals. Ralph was the prototype of the entrepreneur, dabbling in many areas, and his business acumen was widely admired; he eventually became the founder of the accountancy firm of Binder Hamlyn. As a person he was a nightmare. He presented himself as a typical British colonel, though he was in fact from New Zealand, and despite the horribly manly image—he sported a bristling mustache and a peremptory manner—was a homosexual, something I discovered only years later, when I saw him entertaining a group of boys in a low club. He expected everyone to do his bidding. This included my father, who showed his meek side by constantly kowtowing to Ralph's panjandrum-like decrees and fits of fury.

Perhaps his mild reaction to this was due to the complete lack of jealousy in my father's makeup, or to his undeveloped but certainly existent feminine side. What seems certain is that my father was very different from his Lancashire forebears, those "vintage Puritan families," as one history of them puts it, from Bolton—the Calvinist stronghold known as the "Geneva of the North." He was lighthearted compared to his grandfather, my great-grandfather Robert Heywood, who was born in 1786, a few years before Europe was thrown into the turmoil of the French Revolution. The family had been weavers of fustians—and later the fabric "jean" (the name arose from the shade of blue peculiar to Genoese dyes)—since 1600. Robert's grandfather was among the first to acquire spinning mules, which could be worked by hand once installed in laborers' cottages. Not that these newfangled mules brought in much money; Robert's father had to earn a further penny a week by reading the newspaper to local villagers.

The Heywood business gradually expanded into cotton mills, foundries, and bleach works. Robert wed for the first time at the ripe age of sixty-two; his bride, Elisabeth Shawcross, was a forebear of the writer

William Shawcross. Their daughter, Mary Heywood, who married the Manchester cotton magnate John Haslam, was my father's mother.

It seems to have been this John Haslam who introduced the artistic strain that ran in the blood of their three sons. While my father may not have been as practical as his brothers, Robert the architect manqué and Oliver the sometime inventor, he had more appreciation, nurtured by influential minds such as Scott's, of Continental and, indeed, world culture, and his discerning eye was manifested in Hanover Terrace and Hundridge, the houses he later bought and had decorated. My mother's upbringing could not have been more different from my father's. She was the daughter of the Honorable Arthur Ponsonby, a younger brother of the eighth Earl of Bessborough (their father had been one of the fourteen children of the seventh earl), but her childhood had been anything but secure. The Bessborough fortunes had been steadily diminished by my mother's great-great-grandmother (born Lady Harriet Spencer, and thus an ancestor of Diana, Princess of Wales), who had traveled extensively on the Continent, meeting Queen Marie Antoinette—"sadly altered, her belly quite big, and no hair at all"—as well as such luminaries as Talleyrand and Mme Récamier, at Versailles. In a single decade the family fortune was reduced even more drastically by Harriet's sister, Georgiana, Duchess of Devonshire, at the gaming tables so essential to Whig society; and in an even more scandalous way by the willful excesses of my mother's great-great-aunt, Lady Caroline Lamb, the most infamous of these being her passion for the "mad, bad, and dangerous to know" Lord Byron. Another, John Ponsonby, Lord Imokilly, famous for being the handsomest man in England, seems to have been a role model for the Scarlet Pimpernel; like his Bessborough cousins, the daredevil was irresistibly drawn to Revolutionary Paris, but his good looks saved him from being hanged by the mob. And twenty years later, a William Ponsonby "went about, with Lord Hartington, as two tall young ladies, dressed in the last fashion, with diamonds, spotted muslin, and silver turbans and feathers."

MY GRANDPARENTS, poor but happy, lived in a newly built terrace on Putney Hill, land formerly belonging to the family's country house at Roehampton. In the century before, this estate had covered several hundred acres, bounded by Richmond Park and the road up to Wimbledon, but by their time the estate had shrunk and the house itself, designed by the young architect William Chambers in the classical taste set by De-

vonshire cousins at Chiswick, had been let, as successive earls had decided to live more or less permanently at Bessborough, their original Irish
seat in County Kilkenny. In spite of my grandparents' lack of funds—
indeed, in a move perhaps calculated to improve them—and encouraged
by the fact that one cousin, Sir Frederick Ponsonby, was Private Secretary,
and another Keeper of the Privy Purse, to Queen Victoria—they asked the
monarch to be godmother to my mother, who had been born on the very
day of the Diamond Jubilee of the queen-empress and named Diamond
in her honor (a name she would soon transmute into Diana, to prevent
people from instantly knowing her age). She faintly remembered the
queen smiling through seed-pearly teeth and being very sweet and play-
ful with children, and in Victoria's will she was left a large purple plush
pincushion, garishly bedecked with a picture of Windsor Castle in bead-
work. It lay, royally venerated but aesthetically mocked, on a table in one
of the painted rooms at Hundridge.

Of his five children Diamond Louise Constance was the one her father found the most beguiling. She was not the prettiest—her slightly
younger sister, my aunt Judith, was that—but from her birth, Diamond's
huge gray-blue eyes, engaging, slightly asymmetric smile, and forthright
manner made her his favorite. It was she who would be tipped off as to
where presents were hidden—revealed by following a shaft of light darting from my grandfather's shaving mirror—the first to get a gold sover-
eign from his pocket roll. Cupboard love or not, she adored him in
return. One can see why. Photographs of him in bowler hat and black
coat with tweed britches and matching buttoned gaiters, mounted on the
glossy docked-tail hunters he habitually rode, show him to have been
well built and tall, with lustrous dark eyes and full curved lips below the
requisite luxuriant mustache, a figure much admired by ladies, particularly the actress Gertrude Kingston.

Arthur's love of the chase took him all round Wales and the West
Country, and thence to Bessborough, Ballynatray, Kilcooley Abbey, and
other Ponsonby family houses in Ireland. My mother would often ac-
company him for happy summer weeks spent with her Duncannon,
Drogheda, Oranmore and Browne relations until the threat of the Trou-
bles put an end to such visits and, within a decade, the whole Protestant
Ascendancy way of life. During the night of 22 February 1923, Bessborough was burned to the ground by forty men from the Irish Republican
Army.

Meanwhile financial difficulties had begun to plague Arthur and Evelyn Ponsonby, and their Putney house had to be sold. Furthermore

Arthur's handsome looks and roving eye won him no end of lady friends, especially on visits to Barbados, where he had sugar interests and stayed with the plantation owner Sir Graham Briggs at Farley Hill. Since ruined, and now a Barbadian national monument, this was a vast "great house," from which his visits to the seedier side of downtown Bridgetown ensured that my mother acquired some Bajan siblings. To alleviate the fiscal constraints he was plunging into, my grandfather moved into "bachelor" rooms on London's Ebury Street, while Evelyn took the family, now expanded to three girls and two boys, across the Channel to Le Touquet, where living was considerably cheaper.

While this period of her youth instilled in my mother a lifelong if somewhat romanticized love of France, and an equally romantic belief she could speak the language, it was overshadowed by the antics of her eldest sister, Iris. While finishing her education in Germany, Iris had, like some turn-of-the-century precursor of Unity Mitford, met and become obsessed with Houston Stewart Chamberlain, the English-hating son of a British admiral who had married Wagner's daughter. Foreshadowing Hitler, Chamberlain loudly espoused the purity of the Aryan, and particularly German, race. Having become his vociferous devotee, Iris was brought back to England under a cloud, and dismissed by her family to Brighton, where she compounded her sins by marrying a Communist beach photographer. While I remember my mother going somewhat secretively to see her, we were never allowed to meet Aunt Iris.

Perhaps because of this slight blot on the Ponsonby escutcheon, but more certainly due to her parents' continuing incompatibility, my mother was made a ward of court, her guardian being a bachelor diplomat family friend named Sir William Goode. At the end of World War I, he was to be nominated the senior British member of the Allied Reparations Committee in Austria. He asked Diana—who had been, like many girls of her station, a Volunteer Aid Detachment (VAD) nurse at Guy's Hospital in London, tending horrifically wounded soldiers—to go with him to Vienna and run his household. They broke the journey to Austria by stopping in Paris, where Goode was attending the Congress of Versailles, which resulted in the treaty that sealed the Allies' victory over Germany. In her new, if still loosely defined role Diana was present at the signing. By chance a junior appointee to this same reparations committee was my father.

It is one of my lasting regrets that I never asked my mother about this very emotionally important period in her life. It seems extraordinary to think that when she arrived in Austria it was still an empire. Indeed, Emperor Franz Josef, aged widower of the beautiful Elisabeth, known as Sisi, had died a mere three years before. The tragedy at Mayerling, when Crown Prince Rudolf had shot his mistress, Marie Vetsera, and then himself, was still as deeply etched on the national psyche as the nightly operettas at the Volksoper, or Dr. Freud's revelatory analysis. The young Hapsburg couple, Karl and Zita, were novices on the imperial throne (though the empress would live until the 1980s—with a sense of romance, I attended her memorial service at the Holy Redeemer in Chelsea). No one in Vienna at the beginning of this new reign could possibly foresee that the centuries-old Austro-Hungarian Empire would be swept away with Karl's premature death in 1922.

SINCE THEY WERE PART OF SUCH a small circle in such a small city as Vienna, it was inevitable that my parents would meet. When they did, my mother fell in love almost instantly, attracted by his dazzling looks combined with his subtly flirtatious manner. My father, though interested and flattered, was not so hasty hearted. He was in no hurry to get married, happily entrenched with his set of young male friends, both English and Austrian. Through the latter my father came to know the actress Katharina Schratt, who for many years had been if not the mistress certainly the confidante of old Franz Josef.

Many of his set were a sort of sequel to my father's admirers in his Cambridge years, and clearly fancied him. One of them, Chester Purvis, when my mother begged him to talk my father into marrying her, declined on the grounds that it would be cutting off his nose to spite his face. After several further humiliating brush-offs, the gilt began to pall on the Viennese gingerbread, and my mother, realizing the situation seemed hopeless, took the brave but surely heartrending decision to put a lot of space between them. Flying in the face of William Goode's guardianship and advice, she left Austria. I don't think she had any inkling, as the Stambul Express carried her home toward England, exactly how wide that space was soon to be. The family situation had worsened; her parents were living apart. There was no family money, and she was hardly skilled in any occupation that would produce any.

Her brothers had gone to America—Cecil, her favorite, to New York, where he was then the athletics tutor to the children of the astonishingly rich Otto Kahn, creator of a new Florida resort, Palm Beach, and benefactor of the Metropolitan Opera House, who lived in splendor in a richly appointed uptown mansion and a vast estate on Long Island. Janet

Rhinelander Stewart, whose pale beauty reminded Cecil Beaton of "the first primrose," told me of the first time she went, as a sassy young girl, to stay at the Kahns' estate on Long Island. "The luxury was unbelievable. If you thought of a martini, one came out of the wall at you. At dinner Mr. Kahn asked if there was anything lacking in my bedroom. Cheekily, I replied there was no pornography. When I went to bed, the room was stacked with porn of every sort, books, pictures, objects, fans, watches, jewels, you name it. And all museum quality."

It must have been Uncle Cecil's example that gave my mother the idea, even the courage, to follow him to the United States. What better way could there have been of easing the memory of unrequited love than going abroad, especially to a country where having a comparatively menial job did not cast the aspersions on a young woman of her class that it would have at home? She somehow secured the position of what we now think of as an au pair with a family called Loomis, in Boston, and sailed there from Liverpool just as the wartime decade eased into the Roaring Twenties.

The Loomises seem to have been proper Bostonian intellectuals and, if not precisely Brahmins in the city where Lowells speak only to Cabots and Cabots speak only to God, pretty straitlaced. Massachusetts' finest soon became too tame for Diana's newfound sense of adventure, and with Bill all but forgotten, her eyes turned toward New York, where Cecil introduced her into his fast-growing circle of friends.

From one of these friends, she learned that the great comedienne and *Ziegfeld Follies* star Fanny Brice, whose life became the subject of the film *Funny Girl,* was looking for a social secretary. Then as now an English accent could melt American hearts, and though Diana's shorthand skills were minimal, Fanny's endearingly schmaltzy nature dissolved at her beauty, unrequited-love story, and enthusiasm. Many nights my mother would stand in the wings of the Music Box Theater as Fanny sang her great hit, "My Man." During the final "walkdown" she would get a broad wink from Fanny, the signal for her to alert the driver. After the curtain calls, the dressers, aided by the newly invented zippers, would have Miss Brice out of the plumes and stays and sequins in a trice, and she and Diana would hurry to the purring Oldsmobile, bowling upstate through the night. The destination would be Sing Sing, the state prison known to its inmates as the "Walled-off Astoria," where Fanny's then husband, the handsome gambler Nicky Arnstein, was doing time for racketeering. Though the boxes of food from Sardi's on the front seat were meant for Nicky and his con friends, Fanny would often say, "Gee,

I'm hungry, kid—stop the car," and tuck in to a hearty second supper, adding, "Those crooks'll just have to make do with the meatballs."

Once there was a power cut during rehearsal of an act involving Fanny, as her famous character Baby Snooks, and a troupe of midgets. My mother called out, "Miss Brice, are you okay?" From the dark came the lisping voice: "No. I'm up to my ath in dwarvthes."

Fanny and Diana became great friends, my mother visiting her whenever she went to New York. She took my father, after their marriage, to see Fanny in a *Follies* show. Fanny spied them from the stage, saw Diana was wearing a white dress, saw my dad in black tie. The show had a black-and-white finale, and Fanny sent a stagehand to get them to join her for the walkdown of that seemingly endless staircase—a pretty girl *is* like a melody.

New York on the cusp of the 1920s must have been a spectacular place to be, especially for a young English girl. But Diana was neither hedonistic nor opportunistic. While she had an amusing job, which naturally provided admirers and gaiety and parties, Diana's inborn reserve held her back from overstepping any bounds. There appears to have been one affair with a married man, a friend of the Pulitzer Prize–winning Herbert Bayard Swope, which ruffled the feathers of Manhattan and Southampton matrons, but it was not long before she fell properly in love. A Jewish doctor born in Albany, Henry Marks was the complete opposite of Bill: older but uncomplicated, rugged yet tender, and extremely handsome in the Spencer Tracy mold. His wife had recently died, and he was keen to become a father. They married almost immediately and, in the golden dawn of a carefree United States in the early twenties, led a happy life in a small apartment on Beekman Place. They would drive for long vacations up to the almost undiscovered Martha's Vineyard, where they bought one of the three original fishermen's cottages overlooking the harbor at Menemsha. After a couple of summers there, my mother felt that the Vineyard was becoming overcrowded, and insisted they also get a cabin in Montauk, at the far end of Long Island, then a veritable wilderness. During this time they had the child Henry so badly wanted, a daughter they named Diana, but known always in the family as Anne.

It seemed an idyllic existence, but a fly was about to buzz into the ointment. My father, encouraged by Ralph Hamlyn, whose Machiavellian mind had determined that his beloved Bill should now father some children, began to send letters to Diana implying that, after deep consideration, she was the wife of his dreams and the only possible mother of his children. Flattered, but thinking little of such a plan, she replied in desultory, noncommittal terms, stressing that she loved Henry, adored Anne, and delighted in their life together.

Unfazed, my father sent Hamlyn to New York to plead his suit. Still no dice. Ralph Hamlyn returned without the prize, and the letters from my father ceased. Henry breathed again; the summer at Montauk was hotter and lazier than the last.

One April day in 1928 at about eleven thirty in the morning, the bell rang at the apartment on Beekman Place. My mother opened the door. My father stood there, young and vulnerable.

There was a lot to arrange. Henry was completely understanding and gracious. Even so, divorce was not easy, even then, even in America, except in a few far-flung states. Then there was Anne. Henry insisted she should remain with him, and to try and ease the natural sense of guilt my mother had in what was to all intents and purposes abandoning her, it was agreed that Anne, now aged seven, should have sessions with a Jungian psychiatrist colleague of her father. Psychiatry itself was in its infancy at the time, and Anne was an early guinea pig for this particular treatment.

Needless to say it never worked properly, and though my mother and Anne were on the surface fond and loving, deep in their souls was a nagging shame in one, and sense of irreparable loss in the other.

My mother went to Reno, Nevada, for her divorce. Nominally a "quickie," it nevertheless required several weeks' residency, so she rented a small ranch house. The house came with a cowboy who, she long after—not unproudly—confessed, would take her riding in the cool of the evening. Under those diamond-bright desert stars, they made love. I suspect my mother thought she had better get some good sex under her belt before reversing her path and returning to my father, to a marriage, to Hanover Terrace, and to Hundridge. And to Ralph Hamlyn.

· THREE ·

THE END OF THE WAR coincided with the onset of all the usual tiresome things that plague a seven-year-old child. The fact that the doctors and dentists were in London was the bright side of having to undergo the terrifying extraction of teeth, with the attendant claustrophobic rubber mask and tube of vile-smelling gas, entailing twenty-four hours of "ice cream only." The first time we went to London, we emerged from the still blacked-out Marylebone Station into a sunlit windy day, with smuts and ashes swirling into one's eyes and mouth, and barrage balloons among the clouds above, rocking at their invisible moorings.

Willow herb was already rampant on bomb sites: Windows and doors, and even furniture could be seen swinging recklessly high above our heads from buildings shorn in two by doodlebugs.

Walking down Park Lane, I was astonished by the grime that covered every surface. Sitting in Gunter's, in the big window that looked out over Curzon Street, we were served some form of ice cream sundaes, which also had a light film of soot over the whipped cream, by waitresses in beige-gray uniforms with pleated lace aprons and headbands. After a suitable digestive pause—"Go run round the block," my mother used to say—she took me to swim at the International Sportsman's Club, a fine old establishment, mosaicked and marbled, long since torn down. There we saw a very beautiful couple wearing matching white sharkskin bathing costumes that glistened in the water, sometimes doing lengths, now swimming entwined like sleek dolphins. They emerged, she pulling the white rubber cap from her luscious hair and pushing back his dark locks with her red-nailed fingers. My mother whispered to me that they were Tyrone Power and Linda Christian. Though I had not yet seen them on the screen, I was agog at clocking up my first celebrities, genuine film stars.

The incredibly severe winter of 1947 put paid to journeys to London for many weeks. Relentless frost followed snowfall after snowfall, the last shoveled piles of it remaining till May. Trains were frequently canceled, and roads were sometimes impassable for several days at a time, so my father stayed in town with Ralph Hamlyn. The bitter weather played into my mother's hands, as her daughter, Anne, was coming over from New York for her first postwar visit to England. The last thing Diana wanted was Ralph coming to Hundridge and bossing everyone about.

Being at the time barely aware of my mother's first marriage, I had no conception of this sister beyond the expectation that she would, as a much older person of sixteen, have little time for me.

After many changes of plan due to the snow, the morning of Anne's arrival came. I dressed—appropriately, I must have thought—in a cowboy costume and waited with a tiny sled on the hill at the top of the drive. I could hear the car approaching, the clank of its chains echoing through the snow-laden woods, long before it came in sight; and then in no time Anne disembarked, advancing to greet this curious welcoming committee of one astride its sled.

Her milk-and-honey-fed skin, the thickly lashed eyes under distinctive dark brows, the breath from her pale lips and the warmth of her fur jacket melted the frosty air. She came over, not saying a word, and sat down behind me on the sled. With a *whoosh* we shot down the ice-hard gravel and, shrieking, careened into the banked-up snow. I was, naturally, her slave for the rest of her stay at Hundridge, reveling in the attractiveness of her accent and expressions and clothes, which had so fascinated me when Dominic Elwes had come to stay a few months earlier. But the thought that one might be able to visit the Valhalla these immortals came from never crossed my mind.

OFTEN WE SET OFF in the just-fallen dusk, my mother laughing as she weaved the little Ford between the smooth gray trunks of beech trees that loomed suddenly scarily close in the headlights' feeble beams, for the lake below Shardeloes, a lovely Adam house between Old Amersham and Little Missenden, to join friends skating on the thickly frozen surface, holding candle ends in jam jars. Pat Harrison—a Bloomsburyesque figure with her Virginia Woolf–ish nose, complete with drip, which I expectantly watched and waited to fall when she came each week to teach me to play the piano (Bartók, so daringly modern)—squeezed waltzes and polkas out of a little white leather accordion as the skaters circled the ice.

At Christmas we all piled into cars—a Hillman had joined the Ford—and drove for what seemed forever, though it was a mere twenty miles, to the Farm, an agricultural venture near Wing that my father shared with Ralph Hamlyn. While the food at these festivities was traditionally delicious and abundant, I dreaded the moment when Ralph, in prickly pepper-and-salt tweed suits, would pull me to him for a rough embrace. It was almost as bad as the dry, rice-powdery ones from Ralph's two be-whiskered spinster sisters, Dora and Rachel. These ordeals were sweet-ened by the knowledge that their Christmas presents would always be an envelope containing a new pound note, while Ralph's was, thrillingly, one of those huge old fivers, its fine black script scrolling all over the white tissue-thin paper.

After a vast lunch we were made to bundle up and inspected the work-ings of the farm, the size of silage heaps, the fatness of heifers. As evening darkness fell we took lanterns and in the flickering yellow light watched the cowman Bernard Winter and his sons shoo the herd into the byre. They milked each beast by hand, snuggling stools and buckets deftly against the haunches of their beloved pet-named animals, whose soft low-ing and hot breath curled up to the barn's rafters, enticing one to be given a creamy-smelling, rasp-tongued lick. The charm of this bucolic scene would be shattered by Ralph having one of his frequent furious tantrums, probably because I had failed to douse a light or shut a gate, and once, famously, when he noticed that Amy Binder, the wife of his partner at Binder Hamlyn, was wearing too-townish peep-toe shoes, deemed inap-propriate for such agriculturally instructive excursions.

Sometimes we would go back to the Farm for the lambing. The flock was housed, incongruously, in a jagged crescent of old railway carriages my father had bought in a Yorkshire scrapyard. Each brood had chosen its own berth, the mother ewes stretched out luxuriously on the thread-bare plush. The tups looked incredibly comical, wandering aimlessly along the corridors like little lost travelers, and they seemed to lighten Ralph's mood. He once jovially bet me half a crown I couldn't catch one. He was right. Lambs are very sturdy and wriggle like snakes.

After long white frosty winters, the Hundridge garden transformed it-self suddenly and brilliantly into scintillating spring. The fruit trees, hav-ing secretly thrived under their frozen blankets, exchanged them for those snowy drifts of pink-smudged blossom, followed by dense clusters of fruit. In the flower beds, plants that had been tangled sodden clumps shot into spears of perfumed color, roses ran riot over warm brick. I used to pull bedding down from my attic room and sleep in the little trellised gazebo in the crook of the garden's walls. The big bronze tap began its daylong task of filling the swimming pool, a process I had to monitor every few minutes, disappointed at its slowness. With my snuffly old mongrel, Annie, and Pablo (whom I'd named, somewhat precociously, after Picasso), a bounding poodle puppy, I'd scour the Roman quarry in Devil's Den for flints for my haphazard collection housed high in the chapel's tower, or fruitlessly watch the badger sets on an earthy bank in the farthest part of the wood, where rampant laurels made it almost impenetrable, dark and thrillingly frightening.

When summer came we would go to Scotland, to my uncle Oliver's house in Dumfriesshire, on the shores of the Solway Firth. His wife, Agnes, whom I had never known, had been "delicate" in the unspecified fashion of her Edwardian era, and for her health's sake Uncle Oliver had built a villa with suitably delicate white porches, shutters, and balconies, set in a fashionably bamboo-groved and Japanese-pooled garden overlooking the sea. Below lay a crescent swath of beach from which the sea rushed away, seemingly to the horizon, after every tide, leaving glittering wave-patterned mudflats, crisscrossed with shining freshwater rivulets fed by the burn that gurgled down past Oliver's gingerbread summerhouse. Farther out toward the point that cradled the bay like a rocky arm, there were quicksands to be very aware of, and on the point itself an excitingly spooky cave in which, Oliver warned me so sternly my hair stood on end, one would drown if trapped by a fast-turning tide.

Each August we traveled up to Cairngill on the night train from King's Cross, taking supper in hampers and our own cutlery and bed linen, and usually waking in the depth of night as the engine noisily shunted the carriages into and out of Crewe. We would lift a corner of the leather blind to watch the linemen, who carried lanterns swinging from poles over their shoulders, shouting incomprehensible orders so the carriages would creak over manually switched points. At first dawn, as the train rattled toward—magic words—"the border," we lurched along the corridor to the dining car, where stewards brought bowls of salty porridge. Faces pressed to the steamy windows, we beheld a thrillingly different landscape. Beyond the railway embankments, dark fells and feathery waterfalls merged into the distant hills, heathery mauve below a pale green sky, sprinkled silver with a few lazy stars. Leaving Carlisle, the line dipped down to meet the Solway Firth, shimmering in the brightening light, and then, steaming through Gretna with its romantic connotations, we knew we had entered Scotland. This was the gateway to a two-month-long summer world, one of sandals and Aertex shirts, fishing in rock pools, riding Shetland ponies bareback, and hearing remembered sounds: burn water the color of bark cascading down over moss-dappled rocks, making a white foam that gathered, fizzing, at the edge of dark pools; the metallic clang as Duncan, the blacksmith, forged heavy shoes for the brawny horses, their flanks twitching with impatience, that would harrow the stony pastures up on the hills; the sharp, hard call of curlews; and sunset hymns rising from the nearby village hall.

At Dumfries we had to disembark and change to the meandering branch line to the little town of Dalbeattie, where Uncle Oliver, his hair gleaming on his parchment white head, would be waiting by a small procession of vehicles to transport us bag and baggage to Cairngill.

Oliver Haslam, in middle age, had become "an inventor." Among other much-needed gadgets, he had devised an H-shaped chimney pot that didn't smoke out the rooms below, particularly popular on this winter-windy coast, and an early version of automatic gates. They wobbled open as you positioned, precariously, and with much reversing and cursing, the driver's-side wheels on to a narrow metal ramp. Another eccentricity of construction was his private golf course, laid out on a forty-five-degree mountainside, where a bosh shot sent one's ball sailing away into the Solway Firth below. The caddies for a round on this literally breathtaking course were Shetland ponies, wearing a kind of willow pergola strapped to their backs for carrying golf bags.

Oliver was continually working on some esoteric project in his cluttered Cairngill workshop, a whitewashed bothy beside the burn to which I was sent before meals to fill a glass jug with the peaty water. Sometimes he would hear me and call me into his workshop. Inside, in the sudden dark, there were the nose-wrinkling dry smells of rabbit's-foot size, glue, and turps that hit the back of one's throat, the ear-splitting whine of an electric lathe showering the dusty air with a brilliance of stars as Oliver milled metal, or the sudden flare of blue green flame from his welding torch. But it was the miniature theater he had built that I found completely captivating. Oliver's passion was to experiment with the mix of narrative and music through the manipulation of light, and this fascinating toy was his ultimate realization. Seemingly nothing more complicated than a large box on spindly legs, with a rectangular mouth for a stage, it operated entirely mechanically. Oliver merely set its machinery in motion, stood away, and for half an hour the story of, say, *Faust,* was acted out, with music, lights, and scenery magically creating the illusion of characters.

It was too expensive an experiment to manufacture copies for the many people who asked Oliver for a theater of their own. Far ahead of its time, it was in many ways the precursor of what is now achieved with lasers, and to watch it was an experience that must have fired my later enthusiasm for stage and costume design. I don't imagine Oliver made, or indeed needed to make, any money from his inventions, but of all his immediate family he alone displayed some of the practical imagination, or imaginative practicality, that had devised the machines that were the basis of the Haslam family business.

In my memory's eye Uncle Oliver remains a silver-haired, eternally young adult, the exact opposite of Uncle Ralph. Loving and forgiving, he instructed me in his imaginative ability and instilled in me a desire to create visually beautiful things.

TERESA WAS WITH ME AS USUAL that sunlit evening on the long crescent beach below Cairngill; the distant rocky points lulled a running tide. Riding a little skewbald pony along the breaking surf, I suddenly felt a surge of intense pain, a violent electric current coursing through me. There was no time to scream or even call out. In a split second the current seemed to concentrate itself down the right side of my body, and then—nothing. The pain had gone, but something more sinister had taken its place: I was paralyzed.

Somehow Teresa got me off the pony, carrying me along the beach, through the dense shade of navy green trees fringing it, and up past the peat brown burn to the house. Unable to lug my limp six-year-old body farther up to our rooms in the wing, she laid me in the one that had long ago been Aunt Agnes's. Cool and white, its striped blinds holding back the sunlight from lilac-bough-printed curtains and summer slipcovered furniture, it had been kept by Oliver as she had arranged it. Now it became an instant sickroom. Oliver was called from his workshop, Dr. Alexander hastily summoned from Dalbeattie, and my parents, who were on a rare holiday together in the Shetland Islands, alerted. They hired a plane to fly back to Cairngill. Even in my inert state, I registered the drama of so extravagant a decision, and that their evident concern must mean I was seriously ill.

The absence, now, of any pain was oddly disconcerting. Up till that moment, whenever I had felt ill, something had ached or itched or hurt, making the illness at least understandable. There was nothing I could do but surrender myself to the strange sense of helplessness my body had acquired, and bleakly watch the process developing around me.

News of my collapse spread around the area like wildfire. Polio, or infantile paralysis as it was called in those pre–Salk vaccine days, scared like the Black Death. Cairngill became a no-go area, its inhabitants pariahs.

Tradesman refused to trade, the postman refused to post, the fishmonger refused to monger. My illness had come at the apogee of this, the last great polio panic. Most people believed, like Henry's parents in *Ruthless Rhymes for Heartless Homes,* that there was no cure for this disease.

Dr. Alexander, having cheeringly announced that he thought if I lived, I'd never walk again, consulted London specialists by the only telephone in the house, brass and wood and hanging on the wall of the silver-cleaning room beside the knife-polishing drum. I could hear him shouting that I should be sent away to the terrifying-sounding Dumfries Infirmary. A few days later I was hauled into a rickety local ambulance with Teresa holding me, and the doors clanged shut on my last view of the summer green hills and rough stone walls above Cairngill.

Eventually I slept and awoke later in the almost workhouselike infirmary's long narrow public ward. It was dark and high, with a few yellowing lamps on long iron rods gleaming feebly above some of the other beds, on which lay inert bundles whose cries and moans echoed off the grimy stone walls. There was no sign of my parents or, worse, of Teresa. I was utterly alone in a totally alien place for the first time in my life.

Not for long: A little old man came hobbling along the aisle between the metal beds. He stopped at mine, peered, squinting, and drew closer. Who can he have been? How did he come to be there? He was holding some kind of wooden box with a handle. Looking intently at me he turned the handle; tinny music came tinkling from the box. Then suddenly there was a flash of movement, and a tiny monkey, dressed in red velveteen britches and waistcoat with a little tinsel-tasseled hat, leaped onto my bed, dancing to the music, and shaking a miniature tambourine, minute teeth gleaming like seed pearls in its smiling lips. From that moment all I ever wanted was a monkey. It climbed onto my chest, the coal black button eyes staring intently into mine, as if willing me to recover. A woman came and shooed the organ grinder away, the monkey looking back at me from his shoulder. The next day the doctors told my parents I'd be dead within a week.

The monkey knew better. Maybe in some way he did will me to live. Anyway, I didn't die. I lay for the next days and nights watching the doorway beyond the rows of battered metal beds. When a week had passed Teresa appeared, but not to take me back to Cairngill. Instead I was to be transferred to Lauriston Hall, a gloomy liver-colored sanatorium outside Dumfries. Segregated now in a huge featureless room, with an ink-dark cedar of Lebanon outside its rainswept plate-glass windows, I had to be injected with penicillin about once an hour, day and night, with enormous thick needles that painfully punctured the unparalyzed parts of my body. Those penicillin shots were made endurable, just, by the beautiful young Scottish nurse who administered them.

She, too, was called Nicky, which established an instant bond between us. "Nicky will look after Nicky," she used to say as she prepared the needles. And as I became more drowsy, she'd sing "The Skye Boat Song" in the sweetest, softest voice. Along with the injections, I was also put into a rigid cast made from plaster of Paris, a sort of coffinlike trough resembling the lower half of an Egyptian mummy's sarcophagus. As I lay in this, bandages were wrapped tightly under it and over my torso, so that the only limbs I could move were my arms, below the elbow.

Thus, after a month, when the decision was made to move me to London, it seemed only natural that Nurse Nicky should come with me. For the second and last time in their lives my parents hired a private plane, but there was precious little glamour attached to my first flight. It was by far the most terrifying I've ever known. We lurched and tossed and dived in lightning storms all the way, my castbound body on its stretcher literally bouncing up to the aircraft's metal-ribbed ceiling, my parents and Nicky struggling to stay upright as they tried to anchor me. Nicky agreed to remain in London for the few months I had to be in the nursing home at 27 Welbeck Street, and when it became clear my polio would get no worse, if no better, came for a few weeks to help Teresa settle me in at home, at Hundridge.

THE HUNDRIDGE I RETURNED TO with polio had been reorganized to accommodate my disability. My Ponsonby grandmother was by now dead, and the room she had always occupied, the Blue Room, was designated my sickroom. Where other children my age were expanding their horizons with school and new friends, my boundaries had contracted to four seventeenth-century walls. I was to spend three years of my childhood lying immobile, coming to know every twist and turn of the painted marble cornice, each flower gathered in the bouquets of the black-background early-Victorian needlework carpet. This room was the vortex of my youth, and I its motionless center, bound by bandages into my plaster shell amid the pulleys, posts, and paraphernalia of my Heath Robinson–like sickbed. From that contraption, with its planks and portable potties, lying prone and almost immobile in my cast, I could see only the roof of the nursery barn, the topmost branches of elm and beech trees stretching away to the woods beyond.

During the first months, in Scotland and London, the sensation of not having sensations had been curiously pervasive, and my brain felt as numb as my body. Once back at Hundridge, the familiar rhythms of the machinery of the house, filtering through to me in this half-familiar room, began to awaken me. Trapped as I was by my paralysis, with no certain prognosis of recovery, my thoughts veered between dumb acceptance and an understandable panic. Would I be lying here forever? Though I could glimpse it from my window, the safe world of Hundridge itself—let alone the sensual, dazzling world that belonged to the Gypsies beyond—seemed as though it would be always unattainable. The people who entered my life now were doctors—London specialists and local GPs. My most frequent visitor was the looming presence of Dr. Rolt. As he leaned over my inert body, murmuring encouragement, I could see the anxious furrows on his high, pale-domed brow.

Incarcerated I may have been, but everyone in the household made supreme efforts to rally my spirits, and treated me as solicitously as the princess and her pea. The everyday life of the house didn't totally revolve around me, but it certainly flowed through my room. The door was always open. The servants would gather to gossip by my bed; visitors would constantly drop in to see me; my mother would entertain her friends there in the evening, often bringing the cocktail shaker, the 78s, and the gramophone, rolling up the carpet and dancing to the tunes of the latest American musicals, *Oklahoma!, Porgy and Bess,* or *Annie Get Your Gun,* the last with the mesmerizingly powerful voice of Ethel Merman. I would watch and listen and sing along, though unable to take part in any of such sophisticated action.

For a short while before I caught polio, I had attended the pre-prep division of a local school, the Beacon—now very sought-after by upwardly mobile parents—on the hill between Chesham and Amersham, where my father dropped me off on his way to get the train to his City office. Winterbourne, a postwar version of the Dame School in Bolton my father had been to in his infancy, was housed in a Mr. McGregor-y wooden shed in a kitchen garden at the far end of the Beacon's playing fields. With several other tots in ragbag uniforms, I would crocodile along the cinder paths to the ramshackle schoolroom, impressed by how neatly the rows of onions and mounds of lettuce were kept compared to Gibbs's haphazard hoeing. Inside, the classroom was almost too dark to actually see or do anything. Here we were taught, or exposed to, rather, the three Rs. The other tots and I would fitfully listen to a cheerful-looking round ball with an unruly bun on her head until it was time to unwrap the somewhat bland rock cakes Sersee had packed for my lunch.

When I became bedbound, this basic education continued in the same vein. I am sure my parents must have arranged for some kind of lessons, but embarrassingly, almost the only thing I can remember is someone reading me *Hiawatha*. Far more engaging was Teresa's radio, with daily doses of *Dick Barton, Special Agent* or *ITMA (It's That Man Again)*— Tommy Handley was near God to my father—and *Paul Temple,* starring Kim Peacock, a handsome actor who lived near Hundridge, but whose house I was later strictly forbidden from visiting, due to some scandal.

There had been no attempt in our household at any conventional religion. My mother sometimes took me with her when she arranged the altar flowers in the church in Chesham, but such community work didn't entail attending regular Sunday service. For major religious holidays they went to Great Missenden, to the church where I had been christened. (The home movie of that seminal event was thought more inspirational than anything divine, and shown so often I could have been forgiven for believing mine had been an infantile Second Coming. My mother's astonishing but fashionable "halo" hat did give her a spurious saintliness, but I think the film's fascination lay in its phony-war devil-may-carelessness.)

My parents flirted for a time with the teaching of the Russian mystic philosophers Gurdjieff and Ouspensky, but any like-minded groupies needed to share the "RARE THING YOU HAD DONE" were hard to find in petrol-rationed rurality. There was a brief fling with the Oxford Movement, a curious nod toward Rome, but in the end it was the arcane theories of Mary Baker Eddy that they went for. At Ralph Hamlyn's unavoidable insistence the whole family had their copies of *Science and Health*. By the time I was old enough to partake (once I had been disabused of my certainty that a purple-faced neighbor with a vast stomach called Mrs. Eddy had written these precious tracts), "daily readings" became the norm, with a bumper session on Sundays. No one dared admit they hadn't understood a word, and the arguments that ensued were even more heated than raked-over bridge coals. A measure of the efficacy of *Key to the Scriptures* was claimed by my father after "a reader," Miss Hochsteter, was put on my polio case, but eventually family interest dwindled, and even he and Ralph had to admit that physicians won out over "heal thyself."

Eventually trusting in the doctors began to pay off. After several months the specialist appeared by my bedside, but not, this time, for his regular checkup. Lying rigid in the cast had made moving my arms impossible, but now it was decreed that the constricting bandages around my upper body could be unwound, and I could start to move them. I can remember the extraordinary whiteness of my arms as Teresa unraveled my mummylike bindings. There was a sensation of lightness. A burden had been removed—and not just literally. With that, the long-interrupted momentum of my childhood kicked into life again.

This advance coincided with the arrival of an enormous dollhouse perfect in every detail and mercifully sans little inhabitants. I can't imagine how it came. Maybe I asked for it, though I expect the answer would have been a dusty no, and I certainly don't remember anyone suggesting it. Possibly its maker, A. P. Herbert's daughter Lavender, just saw that it would be a good idea. Anyway, the house could be pulled right up over the bed. With its facade lifted away, I could endlessly change its rooms, rearrange the furniture, make pictures for the walls, even glue up curtains. I don't know if this toy can be held responsible for what I was ultimately, nearly forty years later, to make my career, but it was certainly the most memorable plaything, somewhat akin to Uncle Oliver's automatic theater, with which to pass those last, dragging months I had to remain in bed.

I remember this period as being the most enervating of the entire time I was ill. Liberation was predicted but not certain. First it had to be established whether I could walk again, whether the muscles had atrophied. A physical therapist was sent for: Miss Field strode into the room looking like a nun in her long cardigan and gray skirt. After several visits she coaxed me to the edge of the bed and swung my legs over its seemingly precipitous height. My feet, touching the ground for the first time in nearly three years, felt like jelly. Terrifyingly, I had forgotten how to walk. Though I could see you had to put one foot in front of the other, I didn't know how to do it: That part of my brain had shut down. Miss Field would hold my hands or my waist as though she were teaching me to dance. "Don't look down, follow me, look into my eyes," she would say as I would stumble falteringly after her. When I first made it across the room unaided, Teresa hugged me, and I noticed tears in her eyes.

For me, overjoyed as I was at regaining this longed-for rebirth, the sense of exhilaration was tinged perhaps with nervousness. After being so long confined to one place, there seemed an almost visible barrier across the threshold of my room. I had to screw up my courage to make this step into a wider sphere. Hours, days, weeks were to be spent rediscovering the Hundridge I remembered. Being able to run as far as the ha-ha at the end of the lawn, and eventually cross it into those longed-for green remembered woods, tasted like unimaginable freedom.

The first time I really knew that I was alive again came when Teresa started arranging normal childish activities. I remember, one afternoon, playing hunt-the-thimble in the attics. As I hid it in what I thought was an ingenious spot inside a metal lamp, I touched the filament and reeled back with the shock, knocked unconscious. Perhaps it would have been better if I had remained safely strapped into my plaster shell.

While I was bedbound, Hermione Ranfurly—her husband, Dan, had succeeded the Duke of Windsor as governor of the Bahamas—came almost daily to amuse me, with her parrot, Coco, on her shoulder, and her frankly risqué stories.

When I was eventually able to leave the confines of the house, I would walk through the woods and fields to Pednor, Hermione's sprawling 1900s milk-chocolate-colored brick house built somewhat strangely straddling a narrow country road. The walk entailed passing the weatherbeaten wood-and-canvas caravan of a very ancient, bent woman with shawl, stick, cat, and all. Far from being witchlike, she was the dearest thing, and cooed with pleasure at the Victoria sponge cake Sersee had given me to take to her. She would insist on sharing it, both of us sitting on the steep narrow steps of the caravan and drinking ink-black tea from floral cups.

Hermione herself was the first grown-up outside the Hundridge circle to treat me as an adult, having that most endearing trait, incurable curiosity. She planned different treats each visit, once giving me a longed-for Parker 51 fountain pen, or taking me to tea with a neighbor called Beryl Allom, whose aunt had recently been murdered by Haig in his notorious "acid bath." Hermione found ghoulishness in every moment of the dainty tea party, indicating with a stage wink that we should avoid the fairy cakes, which were iced in a lurid shade of poison green.

A Hermione highlight was being invited to Pednor for one of the visits of Queen Mary, to whom Dan's aunt, Lady Constance "Puss" Milnes-Gaskell, was a lady-in-waiting. "Come early," Hermione said, "and help me put things away." We stashed silver and gold objects, little jeweled frames, in various hiding places, substituting, in pole position as a test of the queen's famously acquisitive habit, a small and rather hideous pink jade Fabergé pig. The royal eye glinted at this treasure, the royal toque nodded, the royal umbrella stabbed toward it, and none-too-discreet royal harrumphs were directed at Aunt Puss. But Hermione was no sucker for royal favor, and the jade pig remained firmly where we had placed it, known forever after between Hermione and me as "you *lucky* Pig." Another joy was visiting Dan's decidedly fast mother, Hilda Lezzard, who had had five husbands, now married to Lizzie, the notorious ladykiller, who had had fives wives, at their house high above Great Missenden. Both drank like fish and laughed like drains, but that didn't stop them tearing around the country lanes in sparkling, long-bodied sports cars, Hilda's hands—in exquisitely sewn driving gloves—clutching a martini as she double-declutched into a corner.

When my parents decided to move from Hundridge, Hermione and her family were the people I missed most. I saw her too infrequently in London, and occasionally visited her in Pednor. She went on to write two books: *The Ugly One,* which described her highly irregular Welsh upbringing, and *To War with Whitaker,* which showed how extremely close to high command in wartime Cairo she was, and how she was privy to many secrets of the Italian campaign. John Egremont once observed that "two people ran the war in the Mediterranean, General 'Jumbo' Wilson and Lady Ranfurly." Both books confirm her humor and self-effacing tenderness. Later she was to found the Ranfurly Library, supplying books to needy countries the world over. Dan and Hermione, to their intense disappointment, had no son, only an adored daughter, Caroline Knox, which may partly explain her kindness to my youthful self.

But what effect had the years in bed had on me? I dismissed the memory of that somehow pointless time as best I could, but I do know that though I was still merely nine, I gravitated much more to the company of adults, their conversation, and their humor. And I was anxious to taste life. Even though formal education was only now looming, I was already looking beyond it.

· FOUR ·

ONCE UP AND VERY MUCH ABOUT—"underfoot," as Sersee put it—I was old enough, though barely bright enough, to go back to school at the Beacon for a few terms. The doctors believed I should not yet be away from home for any length of time. Once again my father would drive me on his way to London, making me count the telegraph poles beside the road into Chesham in Italian. He was always livid at my inevitable stumble at the numerical switch between sixteen and seventeen. I remember little of the Beacon except its higgledy-piggledy staircases, and my terror at the headmaster, Mr. Fieldhouse, dressing up as Charley's Aunt on a parents' day and doing elaborately unfunny routines with his reticule and umbrella. He would scamper among pupils and parents, leering horribly under his feathered bonnet, and revealing lurid striped stockings beneath his frowsy skirts. I was petrified, and for many years howled in horror at the sight of anyone in fancy dress. I made no friends except a boy called Dendy, who lived at Chartridge, a couple of valleys over from Hundridge, and liked cats, and a smarmy blond boy named Reeves, whom I realize now I found attractive.

I much preferred accompanying my mother on outings to play bridge with friends, when I was left to explore their rooms and attics for the afternoon. I remember looking at the vast collection of paintings and drawings amassed by the tiny, stiff-collared, and morning-suited Sir Bruce Ingram, proprietor of *Illustrated London News* magazine and Colnaghi's Gallery in Bond Street, and his huge powdered cromlech of a wife, unsuitably named Lily. He had quite a crush on Diana, sometimes giving her pretty things by minor masters.

The Ingrams had a large toothy daughter called Avril, who had married a Colonel Blimpish Parisian, something to do with SHAEF. My mother and I went to stay with them in their hideous flat in a block in Neuilly. I had, very exotically for the time, already been to Paris soon after the war, in the year of the New Look. My mother had felt that it was time for me to see the city she loved—"to get his eye in," she told my father, who hadn't been a bit pleased with her plan. I don't remember much except going to Jacques Fath, where she bought a black dress with big buttons diagonally down the skirt, and "1948" written in gilt nails all around the belt. We bought some sweets that looked like real chestnuts, and I must have scoffed the lot. I was violently sick on the plane home, embarrassing her no end, even more when the huge face of a leathery old lesbian appeared around the seat and said, "Would he like a Kwell?" My mother nearly hit her. Like her forebears she had no truck with minor illness. She thought the cure-all was to push aside the furniture and dance, preferably to Greta Keller singing "I Get Along Without You Very Well." My brother John once merely *felt* sick when yachting with her: "Oh, for God's sake, boy, go below and have a doughnut."

On this second visit the Blimp's fluttering batman, Dennis, was detailed to show me the more important monuments of the city. Our short evening tour ended at the barracks in the Champ de Mars. I sat watching corps de garde buff their lacquered and feathered helmets while Dennis disappeared into the arms of *Le Grande Armée*. It seems extraordinary that my parents were perfectly happy to let me associate with, let alone be entrusted to, someone like him. They were certainly not morally lax. Though they had homosexual friends, even admirers, of both sexes, they indulged only, I am certain, in heterosexual relationships; perhaps for this reason they assumed that I would follow suit. A neighbor, Di Baerlein, daughter of Richard Baerlein (the much-read and -respected racing correspondent "The Scout"), was neat as a pin in gray flannel trousers and men's check shirts, and obviously deeply in love with my mother. She came frequently to Hundridge, her moist, dark blue, slightly pop eyes following my mother's every move over the rim of a constantly refilled tumbler of whiskey. Diana was clearly flattered, but I never witnessed a suggestive or sexually motivated word. Equally, though I now know that Ralph Hamlyn was in fact homosexual, his feelings for my father were never made obvious. In hindsight I see that Hamlyn's bullying nature and hectoring tone were in effect playing the sadist to my father's gentle demeanor and perhaps slight, indeed latent, trait of masochism. This relationship steadily made my mother unhappy and jealous, but my father, being a complete stranger to jealousy, did not mind my mother's admirers, female or male. It can't be that he simply didn't notice, as my mother certainly didn't hide them. In the years following the war, Dick Ellis, a young naval officer, had practically lived at Hundridge. My brother now tells me he suspects that Dick was Mother's lover, but at the time I thought he was just another of those young adults, members of the forces, who often visited Hundridge. Through Dick she developed a love of sailing, and they both spent much time on the yacht she bought. One summer she took a house for herself, Teresa, and me at Burnham-on-Crouch, while Dick stayed on the boat. The gramophone needle wore deep grooves in Dietrich's rendition of "La Vie en Rose."

My mother adored dancing, a pastime only infrequently shared with my father. To satisfy her need for rhythm, live as well as recorded, she would bundle guests and family alike into her Standard and drive us to the Millstream, a low-beamed coaching inn on the road to Aylesbury at Old Amersham, transformed into a roadhouse, as they were then called. The Millstream was a magnet for the showbiz world, whose members, including a young Dirk Bogarde, lived in garishly white or heavily half-timbered houses in nearby villages, handy for the Denham and Elstree studios. This place seemed to me, as I watched the others regularly punish the parquet, or sat with them in the chatter-filled restaurant, the height of sophistication.

And thrillingly, these rooms straddled a real millstream; by opening a hatch one could stare down at water roiling over a stone dam, the noise instantly drowning out the one-two-one-two beat of the band and the restaurant's clatter. When my head got woozy from cigarette smoke and sleepiness, I could get a refreshing blast from this roaring river, invigorating me enough to join my mother and her friends on the dance floor, and gingerly try out the fox-trots and quicksteps her sister Judith had been teaching me in the Long Room at home.

To fuel my mother's stock of dance tunes we would go to the electrical shop in Chesham, where, among the glowing-coal fires and primeval Teasmades, there was a tiny stock of records. One snowy winter evening, as a mouselike assistant let us play Frankie Laine singing "Good Night Irene," I saw, by the light of the shop spilling onto the pavement, a group of Teddy Boys lounging and laughing outside. Their long jackets and narrow trousers, thin ties and thick-soled shoes, pale faces and shiny quiffs of hair gave me the same sensation as the Gypsy children so long ago. Part of me instantly wanted to join them, be part of their insolent glamour.

IN THE SPRING OF 1950 my sister, Anne, arrived from New York with the news she was engaged, and my parents decided to give a ball at Hundridge in her honor. A giant, or so it seemed, marquee was attached to the back of the house, and for days a brown-yellow light filtered into the rooms, often accompanied by the doggy smell of wet canvas. My father always insisted on peeing outside if possible, and to this purpose took some friends out on the lawns beyond the tent in the dark, where they tripped over the guy ropes. Ralph Hamlyn, to my mother's ill-concealed joy, ripped the leg of his prickly tweed trousers.

The tent was in the last throes of being decorated, my ten-year-old eyes agog as the garlands and lights were being hauled into place, when Anne's fiancé and his brothers walked unannounced into it. My jaw dropped at the sight. Who were these godlike beings, with their buffed tans and *en brosse* hair? Their snow white teeth, T-shirts, crew-neck sweaters tied around slim hips, tip-tilted little bottoms encased in spotless chinos, white-socked feet shod in pale buckskins made quite an impression. I stared, remembering every detail: how they moved, how they spoke, smiled, and laughed. My longing to visit America, to be among these paragons of male loveliness, intensified at that moment.

Sending me to school at the Beacon had been planned as a springboard to a proper prep school, as a proper boarder, at the age of ten. Forres was chosen, as it had originally been sited at Penn, a village nearby. At the outbreak of war, however, it had decamped from a mellow old rambling mansion in deep Buckinghamshire primrose woods, to Swanage, in Dorset. Unluckily for me it decided to stay on in a dark, pebble-dashed gray building, high on a wind-lashed ridge above that yellow-stone-built town, perched beside a flint-cold sea. Its owners, Mr. and Mrs. Chadwick, enamored of this rarely sunny south, had added to the already gloomy building the even gloomier necessities of a boys' school. There was a gym with greasy climbing ropes dangling from a disconcertingly distant ceiling, a stage for nerve-rending school celebrations, a poky chapel, rows of Izalled outdoor lavatories with slate-hard Izal paper, zinc-lined plunges containing five inches of near-frozen water, corridors not to be run in, and a dining hall with its attendant stale smells of sweat and soup that one longed to flee from.

Getting there was half the hell. Rain drizzled on the platform at war-scarred Waterloo as mothers in half hats ("both practical *and* smart," as copywriters put it) with fox head-gripping-tail fur tippets, clasped other howling brats to their knobbly bodies before coaxing them into the grimy school train, which all too soon lurched into life. Grinding and hooting our way past walls bearing myriad magenta-and-white advertisements for Virol—"*Anaemic girls need it,*" "*Expectant mothers need it,*" "*Growing boys need it*" (I'll say)—past waving clumps of weeds clinging to blackened bomb sites, out through soiled suburbs into sodden countryside. Snotty noses of the first-timers, who had to go to this fresh hell a day earlier, snuffled against rain-stained windows or stared warily up at the sepia photographs of British "beauty spots," consciously avoiding, for fear of blubbing, any mutual contact.

Eventually glimpses of a sullen sea appeared on the right-hand side of the train, visible only fitfully as we trundled around the outskirts of Bournemouth, skirted Poole Harbor, and trundled into Wareham. What seemed hours later we lugged unwieldy tuck boxes up the granite hill into allotted dormitories that were named somewhat belligerently after wartime leaders: Tedder, Montgomery, Wavell.

I studied my dorm mates. I hadn't ever lived in the same house, let alone room, with children of my own age. What were these scuggy little mites who picked their noses, farted, and talked an unknown language about "corners," "scrums," "silly-mid-ons," or "nets"? I tried to make what I assumed was adult small talk to the more approachable masters, particularly the Chadwicks' good-looking son Peter, who really wasn't very interested in whether Carol Bruce's recording of *Pal Joey* was more pleasurable than Dolores Gray's version of Annie in *Annie Get Your Gun*. I dreaded Matron's morning inspection of our "business," which lay nakedly in peculiarly flat-panned lavatories. "A little less paper, please, Haslam" was her sneering response to my attempt at covering my shame.

There were the obligatory games, the obligatory tentative sexual experiments, the obligatory parental visits with stilted lunches and teas in the better hotels of the area, where one sat on hard serge sofas that irritated the backs of one's legs and pretended, for their sake, to be happy. I secretly longed for them to go, panicked that I might display even more of my ignorance and ineptness, and feeling that, whatever there was to be learned, it was not here, on this sullen seashore, amid these dull, stereotypical children. It was somewhere else, among Gypsies or Teddy Boys or dazzling-smiled Americans.

A major difficulty, I found, was trying to make sense of many of the subjects I was being taught. The method seemed labored and impersonal compared with the fragments of history, the snatches of foreign languages, the schadenfreude and wit and humor that had flown around my bed at Hundridge. But sports were worse. One of the few famous old boys Forres had ever produced was Christopher Chataway, an early four-minute miler, but I imitated his prowess in sport even less than I did that of another alumnus, Paul Foot, in academe.

I dreaded the rickety bus rides to play matches against local schools, bar one, which took us near Corfe Castle ruins. In summer we could climb those slippery chalk ramparts and lie in the grass that smelled of

salty thyme, staring up at the soaring stone walls. It was all the more romantic to me because the chapel at Hundridge had been dedicated to the
castle's builder, Edward II, the martyr king. Another occasional bright
spot was the musical entertainment the music master, Mr. Farjeon, wrote
for the end of each term. They were hardly the brilliant Broadway productions of my imagination, but at least had some catchy songs, one or
two of which I can still hum in my head. One song contained the first ref-
erence to Chanel that I recall hearing.

After an obligatory visit to the Festival of Britain, at which I was most
impressed by the Shot Tower, seemingly sky-high with its silhouetted lion,
I begged my mother to take me to see Marlene Dietrich in cabaret at the
Café de Paris. She was up for it, but her entreaties were firmly nixed by
my father on the grounds that Dietrich, though old enough to *be* my
mother and with that overblown come-on, was too sexy for me to be exposed to. My parents were weird about things like that. My mother had
recently warned me against roughhousing with Ruth, the pretty preteen
daughter of their chauffeur, because "she might get sexy." You can't win.

Apart from being informed, in hushed tones during an algebra lesson,
that the king had died, I don't remember anything I was meant to learn
at Forres. I was given increasingly dreadful reports, which made the
longed-for holidays agony, and my parents engaged a tutor to coach
me. He was the son of my mother's cousin, Frieda Somerset. Handsome,
with long dark hair, tall, erudite, aesthetic, and amusing, Richard Hughes-
Hallet was also—*how could they not see?*—gay. After a couple of
lessons—my mother's studio sitting room had been turned into a makeshift schoolroom—he very gently started kissing me and holding me in
his arms. I loved every minute, but his attentions never went any further.
My parents never knew of our relationship, though I think Teresa had
twigged its existence, and it continued for several years, long beyond
the time of tutoring. I would sometimes spend the night with Richard
at his mother's pretty house in Philimore Terrace, where he lived with his
equally handsome though straight twin brother, John, a successful portrait painter. Both of them took immense care in opening my eyes to art
and classical architecture, each having a horror of the Victorian period
that was just creeping back into fashion. My pleasure in their company
lasted many years, until Richard committed suicide in a bed-sit in Hove,
following soon after his twin who had done the same.

Their kind of education, sexual and otherwise, did not do much to improve my concentration at, and reports from, Forres. After a particularly
rotten one, my father, realizing that this conventional schooling had been

a dismal flop, and that there were slim hopes of my getting into Eton unless they changed tack, cast around for a crammer.

Hawkhurst Court had been recommended by a Hundridge neighbor with an equally dim son. Housed in a carelessly nondescript Regency country mansion, it had been, I later read, a seat of the earls Dysart, forebears of Iris Origo's. It still lay deep in the summery Sussex countryside of gold-green meadows and dense chestnut woods. In the trees below the school, almost hidden, was a ramshackle studio hut, as thrillingly crammed with the accoutrements of painting and sculpture and just fiddling about as Uncle Oliver's Cairngill workshop. It was home to a charming, hermitlike gentleman, the artist son of Alfred Gilbert, who had created the statue of Eros in Piccadilly Circus.

I loved it from the start. Attend lessons, listen, do your prep, and apart from that, no rules, no sports. It was fun to share my passion for American music with a budding homosexual friend, or tune in to the radio programs *Grand Hotel* and *Palm Court* while lounging on bottomless sofas, admiring the handsome Oliver Smedley, the knitwear heir, until an unproscribed bedtime. The "equally dim" neighbor, Jonathan Lawrence—now a major hedge fund manager—had a fabulously glamorous mother, a ringer for Veronica Lake. On our frequent days out Mrs. Lawrence would let me drive her scarlet-upholstered cream Cadillac through dark green cathedral-like lanes to picnics consisting almost solely of alcohol and cigarettes.

The intense method of teaching, one-to-one and uninterrupted with cousinly embraces, by interesting teachers, was a speeded-up, vivid version of what had seemed so dull at Forres. The cramming was in a way hypnotic, and since I am delightfully susceptible to hypnotism, it somehow managed to instill in me enough knowledge to attempt the Common Entrance examination to Eton.

To Hundridge, after an anxious August, came the results. I'd passed, and with a distinction: that of being bottom of Eton's entire college of seventeen hundred boys.

IN A PHOTOGRAPH OF ME aged thirteen, I am standing in the garden at Hundridge dressed proudly in the new tailcoat and striped trousers I would soon be wearing daily at Eton. I remember even then being pleased that I was too tall to wear the uniform imposed on shorter boys—the stiff, wide, eponymous collar and a cropped jacket known as a bumfreezer. I hold my top hat, my hair is shining blond, my skin flawless, and even though I was actually somewhat dreading the actual scholastic in-carceration, I have the broadest smile on my face. This may have been due to the fact that, a couple of nights before, my father had come up to my attic bedroom, making the farting noise with his hands that I had al-ways found repellent, to give me a sex razz, as my future Etonian con-temporaries called parental talks about the birds and the bees. Though my mother had always lightly referred to sex, and in a layby near Oxford had gingerly questioned me about my inclinations, I had never discussed such matters in any form with my father. After a bit of embarrassed pre-amble he came to the point, in his own somewhat arcane way: "When you get to Eton, there will be lots of temptations of the flesh. There will be older boys who will want to play with your tail," he finished. Yikes! My tail? I felt surreptitiously for this unseen growth on my spine. His well-intentioned lecture had fallen on already fully flowering ground.

What I wanted to say was, "If you mean men will make love to me in the way I have already experienced, I can't think of anything nicer," but it wasn't until many years later that I told them about Richard Hughes-Hallet or any other encounter.

WITH THE MEMORIES AND PRIVATIONS of the war years fading, my mother had been taking various flats in London. The first was in Chiltern Court, an airless and sooty 1930s block built bang on top of Baker Street station but nevertheless convenient for coming up from and going back by train to Hundridge. I can remember the pleasure of sitting on the floor in those stiflingly hot little rooms surrounded by shellac 78 rpm records, and screwing the steel needles that came in small but pleasantly heavy boxes into the wind-up gramophone my mother could barely travel without.

Far now from finding films frightening, I was turning into a veritable cineaste. The Marble Arch Odeon was a constant lure and an easy walk during which my mother felt I could come to no harm. After a rollicking evening in the two-and-ninepennies watching David Tomlinson, a con-ventionally good-looking if somewhat fleshy Ealing comedy star, dearly beloved by Sersee, in some equally conventional froth, I followed a hand-some iron-gray-haired man along Baker Street and down the stone steps of a green-painted trellis-metal public lavatory. A dim light glowing above the grubby tiles with a naughty allure was swiftly counteracted by the unflushed stench.

After momentary physical contact he lost his nerve at my transparent inexperience, but he certainly made me laugh. He was the actor Hugh Paddick, Kenneth Williams's costar in the outrageous radio program *Round the Horne,* and I would consequently go to Hugh's dressing room at the Criterion Theatre where he was appearing in a very risqué revue.

I HAD NEVER SEEN Eton before my first day there. My brothers, Michael and John, had left several years before, but even though Hundridge was a mere hour's drive away there had never been any suggestion of taking me to look at the place, to at least familiarize me with its age, its aura, its scale. Perhaps my father, with his memories of seriously tough Sedbergh, believed Eton was a soft option in comparison, while my mother sniffed slightly at the Etonian ethos, Harrow being the choice of Whig families like the Ponsonbys.

I was, of course, awed by the first sight of my new surroundings. The buildings seemed so huge, so old, so overpowering, forbidding, and authoritative. As in other schools I'd attended, new pupils arrived a day ahead of the rest of the boys. I can still recall the forced smiles of anxious parents and preoccupied housemasters, as well as the little tweed jackets and trembling pink lips of my fellow new entrants. Some of them were so small, goggle-eyed, young and—as it seemed to me—furry, they made me think of Beatrix Potter illustrations. I felt, for the first time in my life, a recognizable flush of pride at being older and thus taller, closer to the sophisticated adult sphere I longed to inhabit. If I had my own pangs of apprehension, they were less concerned with potential homesickness than with the prospect of being cut off from the grown-up world.

Many of my contemporaries found that Eton immediately took the place of home. But for many, school—and particularly this huge, uncharted institution, even with the promise of one's own room rather than shared dorms—seemed in those first weeks a decidedly alien environment.

A mere handful of boys at the places where I had been educated up till then had gone on to Eton, most of them older, and none in my year, and I was almost a whole year older than any of the other boys who arrived that summer "half" (as Eton terms are so mystifyingly called) of 1953. And, despite what should have been an intellectual advantage of age, my position as bottom of the entire school was one I was to hold on to in certain subjects—notably math and chemistry—for several future halves. New arrivals, years my junior, would sail up past me. We didn't have complexes in those days, or I should most certainly have developed one about my stupidity and general academic incompetence. After hearing this last word directed at me repeatedly during my first term, I finally asked my father what it meant. He looked somewhat alarmed.

"M'tutor," or housemaster, was Mr. How, referred to by "his" boys as Fred, his Christian name, but to the rest of the school he was "Oily How," a singularly inappropriate nickname for he was a bone-dry, wiry, semireclusive individual, with a passion for skiing. His "tutor's"—Eton jargon for the places boys lived—were in Godolphin House, a large, late Georgian building that lay across the road from the great Tudor quadrangle of the original school with its superb soaring College Chapel, and hard by the pompous Edwardian School Hall, and thus at the very center of Eton life. Built to house schoolboys, it featured a broad central staircase with creaking, worn treads, off which were the boys' bed-sit rooms. The paneled walls and stairs were densely carved with former pupils' names—a practice, by my time, forbidden.

The facade of the house was dominated by a large elegant porch and front door, but these were used only by Mr. How and our dame, Miss Byron, and other visiting grown-ups. The Boys' Entrance was on the left, leading into a poky lobby, almost entirely taken up by a zinc-topped table surmounted by tiers of pigeonholes for muddy football boots and scuffed shoes. In charge of cleaning these rows of footwear, caked with that sacred-playing-fields-of-Eton soil, was the ruddy, bewarted houseman, Horace Brown. A truly Dickensian figure, Horace was busy all day, in all seasons, at the zinc table, wearing a canvas apron and stiff thick serge trousers held up by a wide leather belt, his huge bottom turned to a tiny smoldering fire, guarding the boys' door like an ogre. You had to face his tirades if a return after lockup was anticipated. It was a frightening ordeal, though eventually I learned to melt his stern facade, and he would hide the key behind a loose brick outside. From this gloomy hall a door led into the boys' dining room, painted a dingy green, while steep stairs rose to our sleeping quarters. Up this staircase, on my first day, I lugged my boxes in a tearful blur.

The room I had been allotted was chilly and narrow, no more than a large box, though with a surprisingly big window giving on to the porch. And at least it was my own. There was just enough space to house the four elements common, I was to discover, to all Eton boys' rooms: a fold-down bed, a "burry" (Eton's slang contraction of "bureau"), its attendant desk chair, and a washstand, for which the boys' maid brought a metal jug of hottish water early each morning. I unpacked my little pile of prescribed clothes: the tailcoat, stiff collars, and paper ties. The day before they had seemed so exotic; from tomorrow they would be workaday. Someone helped me hang my gray-green geometrically patterned curtains at the window (they were too short) and around the bed. Boys were expected to bring their own, and to a man their parents chose cretonnes printed with flying pheasants, so mine seemed outrageous. On the skimpy shelves I placed a few pathetic reminders of home: a photograph of Annie, my mongrel; the jar of precious sweets—still, and for a year or so to come, on rationing—that Sersee had given me a few hours earlier; and a Bible. I tucked new pajamas into the drawers of the hand-me-down, battered burry and kissed my parents good-bye. And though in that action I knew I was cutting bonds that could never be retied in the same way, I felt, as at Forres, that I quite wanted them to go. I needed to ingratiate myself with the new, and many, adults who now surrounded me. Of these, I was to discover that there were three—Mr. How, my Classics master, Julian "Legge" Lambart (a sweet old thing who still spoke the "waynee, weedee, winkee" form of Latin and had been my brother Michael's housemaster), and m'dame, Nora Byron—who were the most important.

But for the rest of that first day, we "scugs" wandered around, stand-offishness gradually giving way to shyness and then hesitant conversation, probing for possible friendships. Many of them already knew each other, having been to the accepted pre-Eton preparatory schools, which Forres most definitely was not. Though I was quite nice looking, the fear that I had no sporting or academic achievements to swank about made me initially nervous of any in-depth friendships. Once again adults had to be my target, and the palpable sophistication that Eton exuded, and the fact that all "beaks"—masters greeted one in the street in response to one's "capping" them, gave me a new confidence.

Mr. How, scarcely a "hands-on" housemaster, left the day-to-day running of the house to an elected body of senior boys. They ruled from the "library," a communal room through whose rarely open door I would sometimes glimpse these terrifying grand creatures slumped in exaggerated poses of relaxation. I soon came to realize that How's was, in comparison to others, a fairly "slack" house. Luckily for me, it had only a moderate reputation for sporting achievements or academic prowess.

In the daytime all activity centered around the house notice boards and Miss Byron's sitting room. Both these busy social hubs were just outside my tiny room. While her taste in decoration veered toward the dainty with chintzes and china ornaments, Nora Byron was a caricature matron, squat and round and astonishingly plain. Yet despite her unpromising physical characteristics, she was proud of the fact that, had she been born a boy, she would have been Lord Byron, being descended directly from the romantically handsome poet.

Deprived by this caprice of genetics of her inheritance and a seat in the Lords, she became instead dame to many a young lordling, a role she had filled with gruff diligence for a number of years. When my brother Michael had been at the same house under her dameship, he had been, due to their shared love of literature, something of a pet. She would tell me about this brother I hardly knew, and his antics with her other favorite, Mark Birley, son of the fashionable New Zealand–born portrait painter Sir Oswald Birley, and himself a dabbler at painting. "I have an early Birley," she would boom. She failed to tell me, however, that it was Mark, bursting into Michael's room, who saved him from the vigorous but unwanted advances of another member of their house, the young Jeremy Thorpe, future Liberal Party leader whose career was ruined by a homosexual scandal.

Miss Byron gradually transferred some of that residual affection onto me. I was pleased at the distinction. Squat and plain she may have been, but she was very wise, if brusque, and very musical—she had an unreciprocated crush on the head of Music, Dr. Sydney Watson, a man most unlikely to tickle her ivories—and instilled in me my first operatic leanings. She was appalled to hear I had been taken to see the lowbrow *Carmen* during the visit to Paris. She was also very, very frugal. My mother, visiting Michael some years before, once witnessed a tragic accident in Eton High Street. White as a sheet, she sought Nora Byron, who asked if she would like some brandy. My mother brightened. Miss Byron shuffled away, returning with a glass smaller than a thimble. "I *have* watered it down," she bellowed.

Being already an incurable snoop, I was very pleased that my room was so near the center of things. I was glad, too, that it was at the front of the house. From my window I could watch the *va et vient* of school life, leaning over the sill and craning my neck to watch such passing beauties as Charlie Shelburne, Robie Uniacke, and Toby Tennant. I developed an early passion for one Anthony Forbes who boarded at Wyke's, the tutor's next door. I considered his long, smarmed-back flaxen hair and his parents' square-lined Rover sedan the pinnacle of sophistication.

We had fagging at Eton all the years I was there, along with Early School and its pre-breakfast classes—up at six to write the précis put off from the evening before, then running, tails flying like rooks and stiff collars askew, into Div, as forms were called, by seven-thirty. Fags were summoned by a Boy Call at any moment of the day or early evening, the usual noises of the house would be drowned out by the drawn-out shout of "Boyyyyyyyy-up!" from a member of the library. Anyone still in Lower School had to race helter-skelter to the caller's door: the last to skid along the passage being given some minor errand to run, or a message, known as a Fag Note and written on paper folded in a prescribed form, to take to another house.

Frequently I was the last but, on account of my curiosity about people and settings, rather enjoyed the tasks. It was fascinating to be sent to masters' private rooms, sometimes meeting their wives "doing the flowers" in the hall, or to admire elder boys' houses and to see, however fleetingly, their rooms, their clothes, their libraries. One might catch a glimpse of real grandees like Jacob Rothschild, legendary for having presented a television to his house library. "A television!" It was hard to believe.

I enjoyed the opportunity to get into buildings otherwise forbidden to lower boys, especially College, the oldest and most romantic part of the school, with its low, pitch-dark rooms literally smothered with incised names of many famous scholars or passages of Greek and Latin. Some chores were less fun than others, especially if one had to wait for a reply. An airhead member of another library could forget one was there, and as one was not allowed to sit or even speak, one could stand outside a closed door for what seemed hours.

Each member of one's own house library was assigned two fags who had to look after his room and cook his teatime "mess"—which involved charring sausages and burning toast on the flickering gas rings in a cupboard on each floor, and being soundly abused for doing so. Never having shot, I was early on humiliated by Simon Boscawen, the first hulk I was assigned to, for not knowing that "two brace" of eggs meant four. In retribution I would regularly piss all over his football shorts and Corps fatigues before hanging them, another fag task, in the drying cupboard.

Though I wasn't very good at fagging, obsequiousness even then not being one of my strong suits, I managed to avoid being beaten, or "swiped," too often by my library for cheek, or worse, showing off ("side"—a cardinal Eton sin). While I was once swiped for bad work, the beak assigned to administer the punishment was Legge Lambart, a man of such gentleness he was practically crying as he inflicted the few not very painful strokes. I never experienced the seriously dreaded "pop-tanning," when—it was bruited—one was wedged, bum in, head out, under a sash window at the end of a long corridor, for each beefy member of that elite group to charge and thwack their vicious, notched-bamboo pop canes on one's naked quivering behind.

I rather regret now that I managed to have only one serious pass made at me. It was an hour or so of sheer terror with a recently deceased historian of Oriental art that took place in his room, which shared a wall with m'tutor's study. I could hear the tutor's every word and move as Oliver and I fumbled about, until I crept guiltily but gratefully back to my own room, carefully avoiding the interest of Miss Capel, the "night watchman," an extraordinary woman in a long white gown topped by a wimple above a huge moon white face, gliding silently on vast white blanco'ed rubber-soled shoes. Nervous new boys had been known to faint with fright on encountering this ghostlike sight, who Miss Byron said was "very well born, you know, but rather come down in the world."

The Eton College Corps and most sports passed me by, figuratively and literally. I couldn't kick, catch, bowl, or head a ball. During my brief time at my horribly hearty prep school, I had endured all the clichés of athletic incompetence—running in the wrong direction; getting out of the way, rather than into the path, of speeding balls; failing to understand either instructions or rules. I still have no idea what "offside" is. At Eton, though, it all seemed to matter rather less. I was vaguely aware when Mr. How's boys beat another team, but I hardly envied the players: all that cold and mud in winter, the sweaty heat of summer. I did admire them though, in their fabulously long, multistriped house- or sports-colored scarves, which, worn in a particularly complicated way, gave them an enviable swagger.

I was, even if becoming a rather spotty teenager, sophisticated and precocious. At least I wanted to be. I was enthralled by glamour and abroad, particularly America and its new, vital, postwar culture. My contemporaries were necessarily still insular. There were almost no foreigners at Eton in the early 1950s, let alone Asians or Africans.

The presence of Philip Harari, who was partly, exotically, Egyptian, provoked untold excitement. "You know he's *Egyptian*!" we would whisper as we reverently stepped aside to allow the unimpeded progress of this dark-eyed, glossy-black-haired pharaonic creature. Hardly anyone traveled, you could only take fifty quid abroad. The fact that I had been to Paris was considered very dashing. Skiing was a rarity, summers in the Mediterranean unthought of. People, if they went anywhere, went to Scotland.

Glamour was in short supply, but it could be discovered in magazines that were hardly the standard reading matter for schoolboys. I would get *Picture Post* and thrill at pictures of, say, the ravishing Empress Soraya buying her clothes at the Paris collections. I chased glamour as far as the dim lights of Slough; one of my first Etonian misdemeanors, luckily undetected, was to sneak there, running along ditches and behind hedges, until I could safely board a forbidden bus, irresistibly lured by Ethel Merman (and a sensational young blond, called Marilyn Monroe) in *There's No Business Like Show Business*. I tried taking the *New York Herald Tribune* as my paper but this was considered outlandish and abruptly stopped. I would buy a cheap cologne called 4711 from the chemist's in town, believing that its scent was redolent of Paris models and the world of fashion. "How can you be interested in all that rubbish?" my friend Grey Ruthven, now Lord Gowrie, would say. I was fascinated by the arcane royal warrants emblazoned on the windows of the Eton High Street tailors and hosiers—*By appointment to HRH Princess Christian of Hanover* in New & Lingwood's, or *Makers of shooting costumes to HRH The Duchess of Connaught* in Welsh & Jefferies—which conjured up a world of courts and Ruritania. There was a music shop in an alley off Eton High Street run by a very pretty girl who would let me listen to records in one of a line of small blue-painted booths. I would spend hours there soaking up American show tunes. Though I didn't have a record player in my room at school, I'd buy the newly invented LPs and study the covers intently, reveling in the casts' names: Mary Martin, Alfred Drake, Vera-Ellen, Lilo. I remember distinctly reproducing the Tom Keogh pastiche-Lautrec sleeve of Cole Porter's *Can-Can* during a geometry lesson.

My best friends in my tutor's were Bill Montgomery and Greville Howard. For many years we messed together—the school slang for boys sharing tea in one of their rooms. We would make basic fry-ups and toast, which we wolfed down in order not to need the notoriously unappealing house dinner we had to attend later. (There was a much-repeated story of David Harlech, father of my friends Jane and Julian Ormsby-Gore, being questioned by his tutor about a boy who had tragically committed suicide. "S-s-s-sir, c-c-c-could it b-b-be the f-f-f-food?" ventured David.) As lower boys Greville and I had to cook our fag masters' "mess" before our own. Greville was even worse at this than I, constantly being yelled at for burning everything in the frying pan. He would think up disgustingly foul but to us incredibly funny retributions; it's astonishing the whole library wasn't constantly heaving with dire poisoning.

Both Bill and Greville took Etonian life very casually. Bill was already concentrating on becoming a "deb's delight" in the future and final presentation year of 1958. Almost everything made Greville laugh, which gave no hint of his future career as a political force and self-made multimillionaire peer. Despite a tragic childhood, throughout which he barely knew his parents, he had the kindest, most trusting nature, and this sometimes led to his being exploited by bullying boys.

There was a terrible triumvirate of thugs—rather looked down upon, I fear, for being from state schools—named Wrangham, Owston, and Beech-Peal. These three forced the most pliant boys of the house to carry out extremely humiliating tasks in public, and thus were feared as much as disliked. The last I heard of Beech-Peal, the cruelest of the perpetrators, was that he was living in the Kenyan bush as a Masai wife—that's *as*, not *with*.

And occasionally the elegant approached Eton. One chilly winter afternoon I was standing under the damp halo of a hissing gas lamp in New Schools Yard with a recently made friend, "Little" Winston Churchill, grandson of the prime minister. The traffic on the main Bath road that bisected Eton in those days was at a snail's pace in the acrid yellow fog. A small Rolls-Royce turned off by School Hall, its gauntleted chauffeur a silhouette. The car stopped and a light lit the interior, framing a golden-tanned, Titian-red head above a cloud of fur, against the oval back window. A suede-gloved arm reached for the door; crocodile shoes momentarily touched the running board, the shimmer of exquisite nylon-stockinged legs followed. This was my first never-to-be-forgotten sight of Winston's mother, the infamously seductive Pamela Churchill, lover of Elie and Aly and Gianni, and very soon to marry Leland Hayward, the Broadway producer of, among other shows, *My Fair Lady*. When Pamela flew Winston to New York for the opening, I was openmouthed at the sheer glamour of such intercontinental excursions, my earliest inkling of the newly emerging jet set.

Living in New York a decade later, I saw Leland and Pam quite frequently, and witnessed her extraordinary knack of being able to make not only her husbands and lovers but every man on whom she trained her beam, sexual or otherwise, believe he was the only person in the world who mattered to her. She told me that as a very young child she had been out driving with her mother when the car broke down. Her mother hopeless, the two of them helpless, Pamela just stamped her foot and said, "Man will come. Man will help." Man did: This was, Pamela said, laughing, to be the pattern of her life.

My affectations were tolerated by the beaks and even some of the older boys, though they wouldn't have tolerated the fact that, even with my everyday classmates, I would dissemble. My many failings were overlooked on account of my one area of ability: I could draw. From the outset, in the very subtle way that Eton worked, I was encouraged in this direction. The art school, a 1930s building at the far end of the tar-macked parade ground, became my salvation. With three half-holidays a week, and almost invariably able to avoid any sports, I had plenty of free time. Although I passed some of it browsing in the many old book and antique shops that then abounded in Eton and Windsor, I spent far more drawing. The head of the art schools was Wilfred Blunt. He was the most benign of men, big, bow-tied, his proud head as classically baroque as the sculpture and architecture about which he wrote many inspirational books. His handwriting was perfect italic, and he insisted that I learn it too, along with the basic skills of painting, anatomy, and perspective. His somewhat drier, even more erudite brother, Anthony—then the revered Keeper of the Queen's Pictures but later despised as the "traitor spy"—admired some of my efforts. And it was in art that I received the only glowing report I ever had. Toward the end of my time at school Blunt wrote, "Haslam is undoubtedly the genius of his generation."

A "genius" I was not. But I truly enjoyed drawing and painting. I started doing portraits of my schoolmates. It proved a ready way to acceptance and popularity. Early on I painted a picture that was bought by a pink-and-white old gentleman called Sir Rex Benson. He entered my painting in an exhibition of amateur artists—among them Princess Marina, Duchess of Kent, no less—at the Trafford Gallery in Mount Street, run by the social mountaineer Charles Harding. My housemaster, after the enlightened Eton fashion, let me go up to London for the opening evening party. To my delight my painting and I were photographed and appeared in the press next day.

It was a first taste of fame. The canker had got into the rose. The following summer half, which could have seemed endless, was in fact made delightfully spasmodic by the coronation. Naturally Eton was *en fête* for its royal neighbor's big day, and there were many diversions throughout the summer. Heads of state, arriving in steady succession to pay their official compliments to the ravishing young queen, usually visited Eton as well. I particularly remember standing on "the wall" for the visit of a tiny, wiry nut-brown figure in a dusty black, elaborately gold-braided uniform. It was Haile Selassie, the emperor of Ethiopia. He passed by close enough for me to get a faint but distinctly pungent whiff of his exotic empire.

"Long-leave," the half-term holiday, was made a day longer, with a separate break for the coronation itself. My father and I waded through torrential rains at dawn to St. James's, to his favorite club, Brooks's, to see the great procession in the damp flesh and watch the ceremony on minute televisions that relayed events from Westminster Abbey in an eerie greenish hue. I saw for the first time those treasures of English art, the great set of portraits (many of them my mother's ancestors) of the Dilettanti Society, while we ate a breakfast of bridge rolls with ersatz coffee. Perhaps in honor of the now monarch, women were allowed to enter those hallowed male precincts for the day, and among my father's guests was my godmother, Iris Origo, by now herself a distinguished writer. I was disappointed—as an ignorant fourteen-year-old—that someone with the wonderfully romantic name of her noble Tuscan husband should have such an apparently gloomy and dour personality, though perhaps it was merely a reaction to the sheets of water cascading from the flapping awning that soaked our balcony seats as we watched the two crowd-pleasing queens, Elizabeth of England and Salote of Tonga, trundle by in their gilded and lacquered carriages. It was only several years later, as the evening sun faded against the stone of the Teatro Marcello, her Roman home, when she awed me with the precision and depth of her knowledge, that I came to realize why my father so admired Iris.

· FIVE ·

IN AN ATTEMPT TO MAKE ME get some favorable reports, or at least to try my best that initial year at Eton, my mother had promised to take me to New York for the first time, to stay with my sister, by now married and the mother of two children. Somehow I scraped up enough "passes," and we flew from Heathrow—still merely a few Nissen huts in a field—on a great lumbering Stratocruiser. It had proper curtained-off, pull-down beds, and needed to stop for refueling. Goose Bay? Gander? Anyway, somewhere quite cold and windswept in Canada, a great contrast to the furnace blast of Idlewild's tarmac, and an hour later, the fuggy heat of a Manhattan August.

Anne and her husband, John Loeb, whose family owned Brillo, the scouring-pad manufacturers, lived on Sixty-sixth and Madison Avenue. Their apartment (third floor, slightly disappointing—I'd imagined my head in the clouds) was done in the Jewish-*moderne* style popularized by the decorator William Pahlmann, corner sofas in rough checked material, and some rather good paintings. A large Léger hung over the— recessed, of course—fireplace. Distance had lent an enchantment to my relationship with Anne, and I was longing to see more of her, but, since it was summer, she was at their house in Connecticut with Virginia, my niece, while their son, David, was in camp, so my mother and I had the run of the sultry city and the refreshing coolness of the apartment.

We went to the Metropolitan Museum, where Diana particularly admired El Greco. We went to the Modern for *Les Demoiselles d'Avignon*. We went to her old haunts: Beekman Place, Bonwit Teller, Hattie Carnegie, Bergdorf's. She took me, controversially, to a matinee of Tennessee Williams's *Cat on a Hot Tin Roof* with Barbara Bel Geddes as Maggie to Burl Ives's Big Daddy. We went around Manhattan on a boat, and around the park in a carriage. We went way west to see a Brillo commercial being aired live (joy of joys, the burned piecrust stuck resolutely to the pan), and north to Harlem by subway—risky then, but my mother was fearless on that level. We went of course up the Empire State Building, and drove via Greenwich Village to Wall Street. In an alley off Broadway we found the Music Box Theater and asked to see Miss Brice's dressing room, where Diana—Diamond—became momentarily emotional. On Broadway we saw *The Pajama Game,* and I witnessed my first standing ovation, lauding Carol Haney for her rendition of "Steam Heat." Afterward, we dined—and the adults drank highballs—in the Rainbow Room with Charles Collingwood, CBS's then legendarily handsome newscaster, and his wife, the minor movie star Louise Albritton. Voluptuous magnolia shoulders, strapless black satin Mainbocher, and a tiny Lilly Daché feathered, veiled pillbox. Heaven! The only blot on the horizon came when we heard that Fanny Brice had died. She had moved to California since my mother's last meeting with her and become a somewhat idiosyncratic decorator. Her daughter Fran had married the film producer Ray Stark, and bought Humphrey Bogart's old house, later inherited by their daughter Wendy, complete with Fanny's decor.

After a couple of weeks even Diana had run out of inventive steam, and agreed I could now get around on my own. After a movie on Forty-second Street—Deborah Kerr in *From Here to Eternity,* I was about to get on the shuttle train between Penn Station and Grand Central when I noticed a young man—and noticed him noticing me. His name was Raymond Foster, and he was in acting school. As it happened, Ray lived not far from Anne's East Sixty-sixth Street building, but exciting worlds apart in a small flat he shared over on Fifty-ninth Street, in the shadow of the Third Avenue El, which clattered and clanged with spark-showering frequency.

I went there quite often that week. Ray was funny, obsessed by Hollywood and its stars, particularly Guy Madison, and tender. He smelled of sun and sand and, I suppose, sex. I told my mother, intentionally sketchily, and she seemed pleased I'd found a crony. On Thursday, Ray asked if I'd like to go with him to a friend's in the country for the weekend. There *were* rules, so I asked permission.

"W-e-ll . . . who is the friend?" said my mother.

Later that afternoon: a darkened room, slanted sun through shutters. Somewhere nearby a television blared out a soap.

"Ray, who is this friend?"

"She's called Tallulah Bankhead." He grinned. "Miz Tallooolah Bayankhayed."

Thank God, a girl. The name rang a bell, but not an alarm. Till later.

"She's called Tallulah Bankhead, Mummy."

"Tallulah *Bankhead*! *Tallulah Bank*head!"

Her eyes were wild.

"Do *you* mean to tell *me* that *you* want to go to *Tallulah Bankhead's*? Of all the things, of all the people—"

She stopped, turned away.

That same evening, late, she said: "Of course you must go. Goodnight. Oh, and give her my love. She won't remember, but give it to her."

Ray and I went to Windows, Miss Bankhead's house upstate, in his old Fairlane. It had a white plastic steering wheel and a banquette front seat. I lay with my head on Ray's blue-jeaned thighs, the smell of newly washed denim over his golden skin intoxicating. By now I had been filled in about our hostess by my mother, who had met her in Fanny Brice's circle. She had concentrated mainly on her beauty and talent rather than her wayward if picturesque past. As he drove, Ray was now telling me of her distinctly racy present, her varied sexual appetite, her feuds, her remarks, and her particular, unique speaking voice. No exaggeration on either of their parts could have prepared me for the whirlwind I was about to reap.

They were by the pool: Miss Bankhead and her girlfriend, the great character actress Estelle Winwood, leading man Franchot Tone, only recently divorced from Joan Crawford, and Sally Cooper, twentyish daughter of Dame Gladys. Ray and I walked out of the long, narrow stone building and down the sloping lawn toward them. Tallulah took off her dark glasses; the green eyes narrowed.

"Daaahling!"

It was the first, and it will always be the best.

"And what have you got there, dahling? . . . At Eton? Fifteen? Really, dahling, even for *us* that's a bit"—to me now—"*I* was thrown out of Eton, you know, dahling. No, dahling, *physically,* me and Tony Wilson, on that June day you celebrate. That was in the twenties, dahling. I expect it's all much more, er"—she shrugged—"*modern* these days. Now come, you know all these people, don't you, dahling? Have a julep, sit here. And this is my dog." She thrust a minute apricot mutt into my arms, along with the frosty silver mug. "Name? Name?" She looked at it, puzzled. "I don't think it's got a name, dahling." Tallulah would one day tell me she had a chronic inability to remember *any* name, though *"Miss! Bette!! Davis!!!"* whiplashed off her tongue with scornful frequency, along with, that first day, some highly graphic stories about crooner Johnny "Crybaby" Ray's sex life. They included rubber pants and sheets and Dorothy Kilgallen—New York's leading celebrity gossip columnist, later to be involved with Joan Crawford.

As well as the dog, Tallulah had another toy: the earliest Polaroid camera. It was huge and cumbersome, and produced fairly instant, very grainy black-and-white photographs, about four times the size of later models. We were entranced, mugging for the taker and laughing at the results. She gave me all of them. Sadly, I didn't know they needed "fixing," and within no time they had become ghost pale. I also idiotically lost another, more touching, more intrinsically valuable record of those extraordinary hours. As we were leaving, Tallulah said, "I want to give you something." She took a picture from the wall of her living room. It was a signed Walt Disney cartoon, composed of layers of colored acetate, of the beautiful but wicked stepmother in Disney's *Snow White,* her image based on Tallulah's face and voice. On the back, in handwriting, was "Love from Walt," to which Tallulah added, "and Tallulah, to Nicky."

I was so obsessed by Ray that, on the day we were about to leave New York, I decided that enough was enough with Diana. I left a note on the kitchen table in Anne's flat to say I was leaving to start a new life, crept down the service stairs, and hurried over to Ray's apartment. A woman opened the door. And shut it again. Thus rejected, I could only return to my sister's. She had come back from Connecticut and had my note in her hands. Perhaps because of her own problems with our mother, she winked as she tore it up.

My mother and I went back to England by boat. Before we sailed, Ray sent flowers and the best seller of the season, Patrick Dennis's *Auntie Mame,* to the dock, and to my cabin a cable. *"Tu me manqueras,"* he'd written. I blubbed over that, but Diana said, "Oh, do pull yourself together. He's only a boy." I did, and at least my boy's book let laughter mingle with tears during the crossing.

Back at school, of course, I wrote to Ray. Innocent young-crush first-love letters, but indiscreet. He didn't reply. I felt, for the first time, and with a kind of panic, the faintest tremors of a heartbreak. One evening after Boy's Dinner my tutor came to my room. "I want to see you in my study tomorrow after morning school. This is very serious. Your parents will be there."

They were. Silent, clouded with fury, but, I could sense, oddly uncensorious. There too, on Mr. How's desk, were my letters to Ray. The woman at the door, his mother, watching the soaps I'd heard through the wall, had opened every one.

I was not sacked from Eton. My heart stayed in my mouth for several days, but I had not committed the sin during term time. Everyone, including, I think, Fred How, gave a sigh of relief. The incident was never referred to by anyone again.

Ten years or so on, I finally did give Tallulah my mother's love. "Remember her? Dahling, of course I do. With Fanny Brice, dahling. Diamond something. Beautiful English girl with the deep voice." Well, well, well.

ABOUT A YEAR after I went to Eton, my parents decided to sell Hundridge. At continual, and frequently vituperative, loggerheads over the influence of Ralph Hamlyn, they had arrived at the conclusion the best way to try to save their marriage might be by living permanently in London, where both would have more freedom. But in fact the move was just a prelude to separation. Hundridge had been a lifetime's pleasure to my father, and Diana, never fully at heart a country person, only belatedly realized that her security rug—the tie that ultimately bound her to Bill—had been sold from under her feet.

Looking back, it seems extraordinary that I only heard of the sale of Hundridge and my parents' separation in a letter my brother John wrote to me saying, "Don't let it upset you . . ." But with the callowness of lily-white youth, I didn't really mind either of these drastic decisions. I was excited when told they had bought a huge house in the grandest of Regent's Park terraces, Cumberland, where Wallis Simpson had lived for part of her kingly courtship, and frankly relieved when, not long after, my father moved out.

He went to live with Uncle Ralph, in his tall dark house in Seymour Street, its manly gloom relieved by some silvery waterscapes by Lowry. I had always dreaded the nights, when, as a child, I would be taken to stay there, with its uncomfortable hard chairs, its narrow beds from which slippery counterpanes always slid, its stale-dining-room smell, and the grinning yellow teeth of Kental, Uncle Ralph's butler. With my father gone, my mother let me decorate a downstairs sitting room at Cumberland Terrace. I am ashamed to say I elected to paper one wall only with a strident modern design. My brother Michael was so distressed by this scheme that he could hardly be induced to come across from his own flat at the back of the house, and quite soon after his marriage to the enchanting Judy Browne, they left Regent's Park for a flat of their own in racily cheap Earl's Court.

During one spring holiday I was asked to a dance to be given by some friends in the country. They lived near Hundridge, so it seemed fun to go and see former neighbors. There, among the guests, was James Hogg, a couple of years senior to me at Eton, and—as a result—scarily unapproachable. He, however, greeted me with nerve-settling nonschool informality, and introduced me to the girl he was with. She had long dark hair, rather naughty eyes, and, like him, the tiniest gap in her front teeth. It gave her smile a special attractiveness. She was wearing a strapless red dress, almost matching her shoulders and face, which were violently flushed. Her first words to me were "I've just had a *frightfully* hot bath." She was James's sister, Min, and she became then and there, and has remained, the closest, most beloved person in my life.

In the course of that evening Min and I discovered that we lived very near each other in Regent's Park. Together with James we went back to London in the cronky little car that Min would—over the coming couple of years—so frequently drive down to Eton. Her parents lived in doctorland, at 2 Upper Harley Street, as her father, Sir Cecil Hogg, was the country's leading ear, nose, and throat doctor, with all the royal family among his patients. He would bring back from his calls to the palaces paper handkerchiefs smudged with the queen's or Princess Margaret's lipstick, which we treasured. The Hoggs' house very soon became my home from home. Min's mother, Polly, had humor, taste, and understated elegance. She was to prove a great influence on both Min's and my aesthetic development. My mother, like almost everyone else, also adored Min on sight, though there was a certain wariness between Diana and Lady Hogg, which Min and I thought was just as well. We didn't want them interfering with our newfound friendship.

My mother decided that the following summer was the right time for her projected visit to Paris, and suggested that Min—who was with her parents in Germany, where her brother, James, by now in the army, was stationed with his regiment near Kiel—meet us there. There was to be another traveler with us, in the shape of the youngest so far of my mother's many admirers, and the only one who could justly be called by the (then unknown) epithet "toy boy."

Archie Norman must have been all of twenty-six, shy, slender, with long lashes around the big dark eyes that followed my mother's every movement. He had tufty black hair that he tried to smarm down, and curly lips that trembled at any tiny slight from my mother. And there were plenty: "Archie, you look exactly like a squashed bluebottle!" Tremble. "Oh, *do* stop mooning around. Did you get the ice?" Tremble. "Change the record. Like all boys your age, you have absolutely no sense of rhythm!" One could almost feel the tears about to trickle down his pale cheeks. The slavish attention he paid her, however, made her mood ever mellower as we neared the city that she held in such touchingly louche regard. Archie was also very sweet with me, never hinting that I was in the way. Perhaps I wasn't. I never quite knew how far my mother took these "affairs." She only ever confessed a short fling with J. B. Priestley to me.

In Paris we were met by Chester Purvis. Reed-thin, polished, and iron gray in a haze of blue cigarette smoke, he was among the oldest and most open-minded of my parents' mutual friends. He had become the in-demand translator for the top brass at UNESCO. My mother never held against him the rebuff he had given her in Vienna, when she asked him to "put her case" to Bill. She was always totally lacking in resentment. Or perhaps she had so much for Ralph Hamlyn that she didn't harbor it for anyone else. The friendship she and Chester had subsequently forged was deep yet lighthearted.

Chester had found us rooms in the Rue du Colisée, near his flat off the Champs-Élysées. The hotel had an almost Mediterranean atmosphere ("The south of France," as Nancy Mitford noted, "begins in Paris"), with balconied rooms looking onto a plane-tree-filled courtyard inside tall stone gates. A few tables and chairs were placed on the street itself.

Sitting there on our first evening, Min and I were fascinated to discover that quite nearby was the famous old nightclub Le Boeuf sur Le Toît, which even we knew of as the erstwhile haunt of Jean Cocteau, Christian Bérard and *les Surréalistes*. But opposite was a more garish, more modern establishment, its name, Le Carrousel, proclaimed in garishly flashing lights. On the hoarding above was a huge poster of the star, Coccinelle, and a smaller one of "notre vedette nouvelle, Bambi," both beautiful, busty blondes. There was something a bit odd about them—"exaggerated," perhaps. We watched bug eyed as these showgirls arrived, some tottering on their heels, the stars being dropped off by sleek dark young men in sleek dark cars.

Within a couple of years I would go frequently to Le Carrousel, reveling in its tawdry allure, its cheap plush banquettes circling a gaudily curtained stage, and eagerly expecting the tinny scratch of the song associated with each performer, all of whom had, by Prefecture law, to whip off their wigs at the end of their act. Even the sublime Coccinelle, the most glamorous of women, was perforce reduced to revealing his stubbly male pate. We were intrigued by a newcomer to the troupe, the slightly gauche Toni April, who sang a parody of "Get Me to the Church on Time." Toni would eventually transform himself, with the help of Moroccan surgeons, into April Ashley, now as beautiful, sophisticated, and elegant-voiced as any duchess. April briefly married the eldest son of Lord Rowallan, the chief Boy Scout: "I have a great sense of history," April once told me, "And I think by being the first male peeress I have made it."

I would later know Bambi. One night I offered to take him out to dinner. Thrillingly, Bambi accepted and, feeling like an Edwardian boulevardier, I suggested some famously grand restaurant, probably Le Grand Véfour. "Comme c'est lugubre ici" was Bambi's pouty comment as the white foxes slid from his flawless shoulders. However, that first Paris evening, Min and I were more interested in hair color. She thought it would be a good idea if I were to go blond too, and, with the aid of some very basic bleach, she turned me what can only be described as a not-too-subtle shade of brass.

The next morning my mother was livid. "I'm cross, Chester's cross, and what's more," her voice rising, "*Archie's* cross."

This fury lasted all of an hour. By noon Archie just shrugged conspiratorially as we settled into Chester's open tourer. With Min and me in the dickey seat, we drove out of Paris and into a new world: a previously undiscovered panoply of French country houses. The visions of Tanlay, Anet, Vaux-le-Vicomte, and many lesser, even prettier ones, seen in the golden light of those August afternoons are stamped on my brain, picture-postcard clear.

And on those summer nights, as soon as possible after dinner, Min and I would get the Métro to St.-Germain-des-Prés, spending all hours and every sou we had in the Café de Flore or Les Deux Magots. When we couldn't persuade a taxi to take us home for free, we walked through the dawn, through fountains, through dewy grass, shoes in hand.

Toward the end of our stay my mother decreed we would all go to a proper grown-up nightclub. I imagine she envisaged the can-can and ostrich plumes, Follies Bergère-style, or something in the manner of Josephine Baker. She chose one called Les Naturistes, as it was handy. Taking her prediction of only modest near-nudity with a pinch of salt, we went. On a small stage six feet from our noses, acts of such gripping filth took place that all five of us got strident giggles and soon were unceremoniously shown *la porte*. Later my mother said, "Of all the things! And in front of Archie, too."

BACK IN LONDON, Archie's adoration was gathering pace. I suppose my mother had never had this kind of calf-love before. The affair got serious enough for us to spend a Saturday night at the Normans' vast family estate near Maidstone in Kent, in order for Archie to show her off to his parents. It didn't go well. My mother deemed the house dreary in the extreme ("No gramophone, did you notice?") and hated their prized Dutch seascapes. Lady Norman was a dull old stick, and from the frosty reception she gave us—no question of "Now, how about a drink?"—my mother deduced it was hardly worth unpacking. Not long after, the Normans, *père et mère,* decided enough was already too much and shipped

Archie off to work in Peru or somewhere, far from my mother's dangerous allure.

It would be wrong to suppose that my mother was "fast." I am quite sure she really loved only my father all her life. But she was a flirt of the nicest sort, outgoing, generous, and spontaneous by nature and, while not guileless, extremely honest. She was not vain and never required false flattery, but she relished attention and was drawn to anyone who would extend her somewhat limited bounds of intellect. She admired cerebral courage rather than physical prowess. She herself had innate gumption, an almost reckless bravery, exemplified by her decision to throw in the towel at my father's noncommittal attitude when they had first met in Vienna, and, poor and alone, set off for alien America. There was a sentimental side to her nature but no sign of nostalgia. She found it extremely difficult to tell a lie, a trait she passed on to her children in varying degrees. She believed, as was then quite common, that she had psychic visions. She firmly maintained that twice, when romantically taken by a handsome young Canadian poet, George Whalley, who was writing the definitive marginalia of Samuel Taylor Coleridge, they had both seen and spoken to Coleridge in the parlor at Hundridge.

Earthly treasures did not interest her. Her jewels were minimal. My father never would have pressed Cartier *parures* on her, though he did have some earrings copied from the eighteenth-century Italian portrait that had hung on the staircase at Hundridge. She had hardly any inherited pieces (rather gray, diamondy bits) and a few somewhat brighter bought things. She liked the new "costume" jewelry, which often, to my chagrin—I loved those gilt seahorses on green plastic clips—she would take off and give spontaneously to friends. She said she preferred furs, but except for a worn raccoon trench coat, a short swingback leopard, and a rather too-ginger mink, had nothing very distinguished. Her clothes were good or hideous after the fashion of the moment, and in either she could look stunning. She liked people to choose them for her, and to please by wearing them. Unlike the mothers of other boys, she never embarrassed me when visiting school. Her method was simple, and much to be recommended. She would arrive at the appointed place, open the car door, almost without stopping, yell, "Get in!" and then drive away at top speed.

My father, on the other hand, in Hundridge days often came to my house in what we called his "hedging" clothes—I was lucky if he remembered to put down his billhook. These visits were sometimes embarrassing. Once a contemporary, Gerald Clarkson, was reading in my room when my father walked in, together with his great friend, L. S. Lowry, wearing a dirty mackintosh. Gerald didn't stir until my awkward stammer, "Erm . . . Gerry . . . er . . . my dad . . ." budged him. At boys' supper that evening Gerald said, "I'm so sorry. I thought it was the plumbers."

ONE SPRING HOLIDAY FROM ETON when I was about sixteen, a couple of years after we had moved from Hundridge to Cumberland Terrace in Regent's Park, I'd planned a visit to the National Gallery. I caught a bus down Albany Street, but when I proffered the only money I had—a five-pound note—to the clippie for my tuppenny ticket, she started shouting, "How d'you think I've got change for all that? You rich people!!! Get off." So, not yet having mastered the tube, I set off for Trafalgar Square on foot, with no sure knowledge of that part of London.

I didn't reach my objective that day. As I walked up Duncannon Street, named after my mother's family, the most beguiling apparition came toward me: a toweringly tall figure in thigh-high leather boots, loud checked trousers, and a navy pea jacket. His nonchalant, sweet-expressioned features—wide-open eyes, and snub nose—bobbed and swayed above the people around him, many of whom were turning to stare as they passed. I was one of them, and found myself looking straight up into his smiling face as he also turned.

"I'm Simon," he said.

I told him my name. He said he had just had lunch with another Nicky, that two Nickys in one day could only be fortuitous, that our meeting was meant to happen, that we must celebrate immediately. Simon's boundless enthusiasm for life swept over and embraced me from that first moment. His torrent of talk entranced:

"I'm working at the *Observer* film exhibition, just over there. It's a spectacular show on the history of films. Cram full of the most wonderful things—portraits, film clips, props, costumes, posters—everyone from Mae Murray to Marlon Brando. You'd love it. A friend of mine has organized the whole thing, and he's arranged for me to run the movie memorabilia stall. You should see it. What are you doing right now? Let's go this minute. Come on. You can help me on the stall. . ."

Still talking, Simon led me through the square—"I want to put you on a pedestal, like Nelson"; around the fountains—"Let's throw in some coins for luck"; to the corner of the war-damaged gallery, where the Sainsbury wing now stands. "My darling friend Dicky Buckle has created the whole exhibition on this old bomb site. Isn't it magical? And if he hadn't, I wouldn't have met you."

Later that afternoon, after we had seen the magic, and as I was reluctantly saying good-bye, Simon said, "Come for a drink at my house tomorrow—22 Bury Walk. Everyone calls it the Gothic Box."

Bury Walk, a short, hidden, narrow street, lies between the Fulham and King's Roads, bordered on one side by higgledy-piggledy mews houses that face an old converted factory. The prettiest of these, possibly at one time a dairy, juts out toward the road farther than its immediate neighbors and is built to resemble a toy Gothic castle. A tiny square Regency box, it has pointed windows and castellated roofline that can be seen if you flatten yourself against the wall opposite the tall wood palings that enclose its minute garden. On its facade is a memorial plaque to SOPHIE FEDOROVITCH, COSTUME DESIGNER, a Russian émigrée who designed the sets and costumes for many operas and ballets at Covent Garden after the war. This romantically dotty little folly was the location for one of the most extraordinary periods of my youth, and its owner, the equally romantic Simon Fleet, became as beloved a friend, mentor, and guide as anyone could hope to encounter.

Simon's real—or, rather, his original—name, I was to discover, was Harry Carnes. As a very young man he had been incredibly handsome. It appears that before some *bal costumé* in Palermo, his then-lover Fulco Verdura had inadvertently remarked that Simon's looks could be bettered only by having—"Don't you agree, Cecil? *What do you think*, Willie?"— a mere millimeter or so shaved off his nose. Always willing try anything new, Simon persuaded some shark surgeon to carry out this small improvement. But given his curiosity and enthusiasm, Simon probably asked for a few extra facial flourishes. The operation went awry, and he emerged drastically altered, his nose a pronounced snub, his eyes with that curiously always-open look. However he was still dazzlingly attractive, perhaps even more so, as a string of famous admirers—the author and matinée idol Ivor Novello and Parisian couturier Jacques Fath among them—and a multitude of friends attested. Simon faced his new appearance with typical aplomb. All right, he thought. I've got a different face, I'll be a different person. I'll choose a new name. I like "Simon," and I love sailors: Harry Carnes was reborn as Simon Fleet.

As Harry Carnes he had been on the stage, worked as an extra in films, written sketches for reviews, drawn, and painted. Simon Fleet, though still steeped in the world of theater, dance, and art, emerged with a new passion: antiques. Not the grand and the gilded but the unfashionable, the forgotten, the overlooked, the stylish and witty—and above all, the cheap. As well as his temporary movie memorabilia stall at the Film Exhibition, he had one selling "tat" in Portobello Road each Saturday morning, and a weekly collectors' column in the *Observer* headed "Consultant Antiquary." In fact this tongue-in-cheek title was the one his friends inscribed under his name on the now-vanished plaque on the front of the Gothic Box. But in truth, if he was to have any title, it should have been "Giver of Bounties." More than anyone I have ever met, he had the gift of spreading happiness, of making things, days, and nights full of interest and excitement, and with that perhaps most important quality, instantaneousness.

The Gothic Box was his perfect setting. The gate in the palings was ajar when I arrived. Simon's friendship had already made me fearless, and I stepped inside. In the little courtyard a jasmine and lemon geranium jungle billowed everywhere, smothering the walls and scenting the evening air, all reflected by a mildewed mirror, a herm of Apollo on a plinth against it. As I looked up at the toy-town cottage, my heart leaped at seeing for the first time the baby battlements, the diamond-paned, lancet-pointed windows, the primrose facade fading paler in the dusk.

The front door was also open, but first I paused for a moment to look in through the wide window that gave onto this green, perfumed garden. No curtains veiled the view, and inside the lamps were lit, affording a long, tantalizing glimpse of many shapes and colors as if looking through a kaleidoscope, all crazily fragmented by the lattice, of the room beyond. I peered though the doorway. A hodgepodge of books, pictures, more books, more pictures, glass domes, lights, candles, books teetering in piles on books, busts, hats on busts, beaded cushions, frames and fringes, toile de Jouy and uniform jackets, open books, cuttings, cartoons, postcards, programs, books on chairs, on sofas, on the floor, on chairs, on stairs. And on the floor, written in green ink, on paper with a little oval drawing of the Gothic Box, "N. Back in a mo. Si."

Within seconds Simon appeared from the garden, open champagne bottle in hand. But before we drank he showed me more of this magic domain. He had added an upper floor to the original studio. An open stair led up to a room that was mostly a bed hung with a green felt baldachin. The walls were purply brown and smothered with ballet and opera costume sketches. There was a faded emerald damask sofa under the windows, with a tall Empire *semainier,* its drawers spilling stiff collars, gloves, dotted cotton kerchiefs, and yellow socks nearby. Opposite, a bathroom—with a huge metal tub, bottles of Guerlain's Mitsouko, and cupboards bursting with Simon's distinctive suits—lay behind looped felt curtains.

It was certainly the most romantic place I had seen, new and strange, and yet welcoming. During the next few weeks I was to experience how entirely Simon would gather me into his heart and life. Just as he had amassed the diverse elements in the Box with such insouciant skill, he brought people together with the same flair. There was hardly an evening at his house that people did not casually drop by, or when Simon did not give a party. The first large gathering he asked me to was my introduction to such diverse figures as Cecil Beaton, who looked like an eighteenth-century drawing; the scruffy avant-garde writer Colin Wilson, whose book *The Outsider* had just been sensationally published; the young and supremely elegant Hubert de Givenchy; Michael Duff, whose endearing stutter made his wicked conversation all the funnier; a rotund and red-faced M.P. and diarist, Chips Channon—he was to die within a few months—with his companion, Peter Coats, an editor of *House & Garden* at the time; Oliver Messel; the Austrian actress-dancer Tilly Losch ("We always call her Silly Tosh," the comedienne Hermione Baddeley would say); Francis Poulenc, composer of *Les Biches,* a ballet Simon loved; the playwright Terence Rattigan; and the now unjustly forgotten decorator Felix Harbord. While I knew by then a few of Simon's friends and could see that each one was something extraordinary in their own right, I was naive enough not to know that these were stars of great magnitude. They were simply Simon's friends.

The most central figure in that party at the Gothic Box, the person everyone revolved around, was soon pointed out to me as Diana Cooper, one of the most famous women of her time. She was wearing, she was to tell me, a dress of red silk bought from the cardinals' robemakers in the Vatican. Diana turned her huge butterfly-wing blue eyes on me and said, in her oddly mournful voice, "But you haven't got a drink."

"Simon's run out of clean glasses," I answered.

The blue eyes opened wide. "Clean? Who cares about clean? Here, have mine." Then a gleam of conspiratorial smile crossed her face. "Look!" A woman standing with her back to us was wearing a fur stole with bobbles fringing it. "Just the job," said Diana, winking stealthily. She took a fur bobble and wiped the lipstick and the dregs of her drink from her glass. "There," she said, "whistle-clean. Now, who do you want to meet?"

This initial encounter with Diana was a compressed lesson in her enchantress's realm of unexpectedness, her love of devilry, her disregard of convention in thought and behavior (she would happily eat anything that fell on the floor) and her lifelong love of the unexpected in people, things, ideas—provided they informed, or made her laugh.

Her luminous beauty was already legendary, her performance as the Madonna in Max Reinhardt's *The Miracle* remembered with awe. Her recent enlivenment of the Paris Embassy with her beloved husband, Duff, was spoken of with admiration by most and by some with envy. Her wit, erudition, and spontaneity had been written of by the most brilliant minds of her century. I came to know that she herself believed none of this. She never believed in her own beauty, except as a facade or a useful lever. She wished she had been tall and dark (like her niece, Lady Elizabeth Paget, whose looks she admired above any—though she would always say, "Such a pity. Knows she's a beauty"). She thought she was badly educated as she never went to school; she had been taught whatever she knew by her unconventional mother, Violet, Duchess of Rutland, who dressed her in black satin as a child, and, as she admitted, encouraged Diana's tendency to claim center stage. But as she always said, "Why do people say, 'Don't try to be funny?' It seems the least one can do."

She had an odd, ungainly ducklike walk, as though her legs were too far apart. She had little dress sense, preferring the "frankly frumpish"— as she too harshly put it—to the classic or chic. By day she always wore a large felt hat (or admiral's caps from the time that Duff was First Sea Lord) with a gold-and-enamel unicorn brooch on it and some false curls underneath as "time under a dryer is time wasted." On a visit to the private zoo and casino owner John Aspinall's one day, his gorillas tenderly pulled off both hat and curls and lovingly licked Diana's lockless forehead.

She knew her power over men, and women, for that matter, and felt embarrassed by it, as well as using it for all it was worth. A "lover," Paul-Louis Weiler, gave her a mink—she called it "the coat of shame." Another gave her a front door. She affixed a plaque—THE GIFT OF PAUL GETTY—so as to counteract his reputation for meanness. "Don't worry, I'll get my friend Nose to do it," meant the ever-willing Violet Wyndham would be sent on a lonesome chore. She, on the other hand, gave what she could, and more. The information she imparted came from a fathomless well, such as her description of one of the parties of the Marchesa Casati in Venice in 1911, where the decor consisted of black apes in gilded cages holding sheaves of tuberoses. She gave friendship, her own and others'—including that of her granddaughter, Artemis, whom in those days we would take to Christmas pantomimes when she was five. And above all she gave that blue gaze, blank to the novice, but which said to the initiated, What's next?

All this was in the future that night at Simon's. At the door Diana said casually: "Come to Chantilly when you're in Paris." A few months later I took up the invitation. I went down on the train with her friend Figi Ralli, a chic Greek woman who worked for Dior. "You know, Christian has found the most brilliant young man to work in the atelier. His name is Yves Saint Laurent. Do let me know if you have time to see the new collection," Figi said en route.

At the château Diana was running down the slope to the lake, little Artemis's kite in her hand. No chance of stopping, she was knee-deep in water when she turned her blank blue gaze on us: "There's a jug of house poison on the grog tray," she shouted.

DURING THE NEXT FEW HALVES at Eton, Simon would send me "essential reading." Short stories by Somerset Maugham, a former lover; Alice Duer Miller's *The White Cliffs;* the early memoirs of Lord Berners, the composer peer and friend of my father's, but now more famously remembered for dyeing white doves at Farringdon the most garish of colors (he was, I suspect, another of Simon's lovers); Colette's *Chéri;* Edith Sitwell's poems; Paul Poiret's autobiography; Serge Lifar's *Ma Vie;* some of Beverley Nichols; all of Cecil Beaton; and an enchanting story that always made him laugh: *His Monkey Wife,* by John Collier. He would also send interesting snippets from the papers, articles he thought I would enjoy, postcards almost daily. If he was on holiday in Rome or Sicily, the postcards would be of classical sculpture or paintings with "Not NEARLY as beautiful as you" scribbled on them. He sent movie mementos when the *Observer* film exhibition closed, bottles of toilet water from an old-fashioned scent shop, G. N. Taylor in Mortimer Street, and swatches of material for the suits he was having made for me. I wore the first of these, sponge-bag-checked with pink linings, for a lunch Simon arranged at the Box to introduce me to the rich and rouged dress designer Bunny Roger, famously flamboyant and party giver supreme.

The other guests that day were Tom Parr and Tony Armstrong-Jones, at the time lovers. Tom's stepfather was Ralph Hamlyn's partner, and as a friend of my brother Michael's, Tom used to come to Hundridge when I could not help but admire his lanky elegance, clothes, and very worldly charm. Tony, not yet known as a photographer, was small and neat, with pretty, slightly simian features. He was somewhat reserved and faintly mocking, and I felt he was sizing me up.

Bunny I loved unreservedly on sight, and a lifelong friendship started then and there. Initially, during holidays, I would visit him at Fortnum &

Mason, where he had a couture dressmaking salon under his proper name, Neil Roger. He dismissed his work as "boring things for knights' wives. Like my mother," he'd hastily add. In fact the clothes he showed on the catwalk were far more stylish than that, Hollywood-inspired, in the mold of Travis Banton and Gilbert Adrian, with references drawn from the exotic costumes of the heyday of his screen idols, especially Gloria Swanson, Pola Negri, and Marlene Dietrich, whose glittering sheaths and cock feathers he loved to re-create, wearing them himself at his spectacular parties.

Sometimes I took friends from school with the express purpose of showing Bunny off; they would gasp at his square-shouldered suits, the corsetlike waistcoats over exaggeratedly skirted jackets and narrowest drainpipe trousers, cut to accentuate his lifelong twenty-six-inch waist. Crusty old military men often leered at Bunny, whispering, "Do you lace?" Up at Oxford he used to go to parties dressed as any of those film-star pinups, seducing the notoriously straight Shimi Lovat in the process, though drag was not a sexual turn-on for Bunny. He preferred male costume, and admitted to me that the Edwardian look he had perfected was what he fancied on other people. "Such a mistake," he'd sigh. "One never gets *anyone.*"

Bunny's style of entertaining was less haphazard than Simon's but could hardly be called formal, even though guests were expected to dress to the nines for the dinners he and his straight brother, Sandy, gave in their house in Walton Street. Its drawing-room walls were hung with early paintings by a friend, Edward Burra, and offered a contrast to the scotch gothic set off by Roger tartan, conveniently mauve and pale yellow, of the dining room. These dinners continued in their next, much bigger house in Addison Road, which was, Bunny admitted, inspired more by the films of Lana Turner than the frills of John Fowler, another friend. And of course, in the days when no one would have dreamed of going abroad, or even of leaving London over the Christmas period, there were the famous Roger New Year's Eve balls.

Though I was at all the precious-stone-themed balls Bunny later gave for his sixtieth, seventieth, and eightieth birthdays, I went to only the final New Year's Eve party—the one that made them infamous. The theme was fetishes, and several unwisely dressed celebrities ended up, all too recognizable in rubber corsets and fishnets, in the *News of the World,* but previous themes had been less contentious, and invitations were worded in a sort of code. "The Enchanted will meet in another part of the Forest," read one, at which Margot Fonteyn and Freddie Ashton swapped their roles from *Cinderella,* Fonteyn as an Ugly Sister, Freddie as Cinders. For another, "Miss Norma Desmond. At Home. 2024 Sunset Boulevard," the house was transformed into the film's set, with huge silver-framed photographs by Angus McBean of Bunny as Gloria Swanson, the host dressed as his favorite star. All the guests knew they had to make an enormous effort with their costumes. No one who witnessed Felix Harbord at Bunny's "Royal" party got up to a tee as Queen Victoria, including a mobile plinth to reduce Felix's enormous bulk to appropriately dwarflike Guelph proportions, will ever forget the sight.

Bunny liked nursery food (and had perfected a menu somehow consisting of suet and cream in every course), good looks, conversational ping-pong, and paper games. His guests—whether they were film stars such as Laurence Harvey or Stewart Granger (with whom Bunny had had a short—"he's got the biggest bum I've ever seen"—fling), beauties like the fashion models Barbara Goalen and Bronwen Pugh, dancers and painters, John French (at that time *the* fashion photographer) and his wife, Vere—were always at their brightest and best in Bunny's house.

His legendary parties, his houses, his dandified approach and outré taste were but a soufflé. They masked an encyclopedic mind, a sense of history, nerves of steel, passionate loyalty, deep patriotism, and the most patrician of values.

Bunny himself was made of burnished metal. Physically very fit—I saw him *run* up mountains in Scotland, at the summit adjusting his makeup from a compact kept in his sporran—he was also fearless. He'd be the first to pick up a poker and go outside if there was a strange noise. As a captain in the Italian campaign, even if his tent was lined in mauve with gilt chairs, and his army overcoats altered to look like Garbo's redingotes, he was revered by his men for the number of Germans he shot— "some right up the arse"—and after the war refused ever to set foot in Germany. He saw the funny side of it too. After Anzio, while surveying a bombed-out village, he ran into a friend who greeted him: "Bun! What're *you* doing here?" Bunny looked at the destruction around them. "Shopping," he replied. Although appalled and incensed by what he had witnessed during the war, he had the good taste to make light of it. "Now that I've shot so many Nazis," he observed, "Daddy will *have* to buy me a sable coat."

He had a sweet, self-deprecating side. He used to tell how his mother had taken her sons to Hollywood in the thirties. They were having lunch in the MGM commissary with some studio bigwigs when one said, "Lady Roger, has your youngest son ever thought of going into the movies?"

Bunny thought, At last! This is it. I'm going to be the male Dietrich, as his mother responded, "No, why?" The bigwig said, "Because we think he looks exactly like George Arliss." Arliss was an old, plain character actor who had just played Disraeli.

His parents, both children of stationmasters in neighboring villages on the main railway line from Perth to Inverness in the 1880s, became rich. Through his interests in Colombian tin mines, Brazilian railways, trams in Portugal, and telegraph services worldwide, his father, Alexander Roger, swiftly rose to tycoon status and accepted with alacrity the inevitably proffered knighthood, though he remained deeply conscious and proud of his roots. Lady Roger complemented her husband's position with an innately perfect dress sense; she decorated and ran a series of ever-larger country houses, the last of which, Binfield, near Henley, had a beautiful drawing room with tall white-curtained Gothic windows and vast sofas of rose- and carnation-printed chintz, always taken up by Bunny's three enormous bulldogs. In the hall hung Orpen's portrait of Sir Alexander, stately in robes and orders. "Who's the guy in drag?" asked film star Diana Dors.

While she adored her three sons, who from birth quickly assimilated the manners, knowledge, and style of their adopted class, Lady Roger must have been a mite disappointed that somewhat against the law of averages not one of them was the marrying kind. Sandy, the middle brother, did flirt mildly with ladies, but his fondness for hard liquor, which actually only and uniquely made him funnier and more lovable, did not encourage the requisite hardness in other areas. The eldest, Alan, was a Sinophile, having been a spy in China, as was the rumor for some years. He lived an almost totally Oriental lifestyle, speaking Mandarin, wearing Chinese clothes, and eating Chinese food prepared by his Chinese staff. It was left to Bunny, by far the most capable of the three, to look after his mother. He adored her as much as she did him, though he could be very funny about her. Later in life Lady Roger had to have both legs removed. "So lucky," Bunny said. "She'd never have fitted into the new lift with them on."

Bunny and his brothers had bought a vast, beautiful estate in wildest Wester Ross. From Garve, a hamlet west of Inverness, forty miles of single-track road led through mountains and across desolate moorland, eventually bringing one to Dundonnell, a square, stone, eighteenth-century manse in a wide wooded valley, its river running down to a sea loch, a Pictish fort silhouetted on the brae above, and thence to the sea itself. In the garden Bunny built a whitewashed, antler-chandelier-lit ballroom exactly the size to contain two sets of eightsome reels. Each Saturday night Bunny, wearing a suit of that most ravishing tartan, the Jacobite, would play 78s of the lesser-known reels, patiently guiding his two-left-footed guests through intricate sets of the "Duchess of Hamilton" or the "Duke of Perth."

In the house itself a blue-and-white-chintz-walled, -curtained, and -upholstered sitting room was my first lesson in furnishing a room with just one material. Opposite was a coffee brown silk-hung dining room with gilded Gothic chairs from Windsor Castle. A gray-and-mauve Chinese drawing room, from which a vast white, though incontinent, Persian cat would shoot like a comet the moment one opened the door—"There goes Pussy, arse streaming," said Bunny—as it ran the full length of the silk-carpeted floors. More Edward Burra paintings, cards for an extremely complicated form of patience, Georgian silver-gilt boxes for Turkish cigarettes, pencils and paper for after-dinner games, dark brown eggs, violet creams, lobsters, port (always drunk through a layer of cream), scrapbooks, and records delighted the senses, until cold linen pillows and stone-water-bottle-warmed sheets, topped by mountainous feather eiderdowns, the smell of the bracken, and the rushing rill below lulled one into the deepest sleep.

Though deep snow at Christmas was always certain, the Gulf Stream blew its warm winds over Dundonnell's hills and valleys. A walled garden, heady with lilies and old-fashioned roses, could support fig, apricot, and peach trees, under which scampered blue-gray puffball chickens with sturdy white-feathered legs like Suffolk Punches. These were nurtured by an ancient, long-retired keeper, Hector McDonald, who lived in a tiny bothy by the river. He spoke mostly Gaelic and had never been away from the parish, even to Inverness. We would visit him most mornings. Bunny once happened to mention Mary, Queen of Scots, and Hector's old eyes sparkled. "They say she's the loveliest woman in the land," he said.

When I remarked on this to Bunny, he said time-capsule memory was quite common in the area. On buying the house, he'd asked a local lady, "What is it like, living in Scotland these days?" She replied, "It would be quite all right if he hadn't turned back at Derby." Bunny had meant the availability of servants. Lady Fortescue meant Bonnie Prince Charlie.

SIX

A MONG SIMON'S CLOSE COTERIE of friends was Cecil Beaton. When, one snowy winter afternoon, we walked the few hundred yards from the Gothic Box to 8 Pelham Place, Cecil was at the height of his fame and talent. As well as regular royal portraits, and his photographs of virtually every famous literary figure in his newly published book *Persona Grata*, with text by Kenneth Tynan, Beaton had recently designed the costumes for the staggeringly successful Broadway musical *My Fair Lady*.

Cecil, long-legged and silver-haired, with a nursery pink-and-white complexion as soft as that of his sisters, Baba and Nancy, was dressed in a slightly dandified suit in one of the paler pastel shades. A flowing scarf took the place of a tie, and his feet, which one felt never touched the ground, were shod in exquisite pumps, as narrow and supple as those made for the ultra-elegant Edwardian New Yorker Rita Lydig, whose shoe trees, I had read in Cecil's book *The Glass of Fashion*, were made from the wood of Stradivarius violins. The drawing room around him, walled in crimson velvet, gilt-mirrored and candle-sconced, contained an armada of *capitonné* crimson-damask-covered furniture skittering from Aubusson rugs onto polished floors, palm trees in Chinese vases, bronzes and bibelots on myriad surfaces. He rose from a tasseled, cushioned sofa, and advanced, a lilac figure in a rose red bower.

"I'm really t-e-a-r-ably, t-e-a-r-ably sorry about the house," he said inclining a pale pink cheek. "I'm afraid it looks t-e-a-r-ably shabby and bare. No flowers, you see." The room looked chockablock to me, but in his cultured drawl, Cecil went on to explain he was now "fed up with this Queen Alexandra decor." When he left for New York the next morning to discuss the film version of *My Fair Lady*, the house was to be stripped and completely redecorated by Felix Harbord. "It's going to have a thrillingly modern look. You must come and see me when it's finished." I felt I had been invited to nirvana, and indeed I came to know Harbord's radically different decoration—the black walls and pink, orange, and turquoise furniture—very well, partly from visiting Cecil for many years until he sold the house, and later myself renting it from the new owner, with this astonishing decor complete, for a year in the 1980s. As Simon and I shuffled home through the snow, he remarked that we were probably the last people to see Cecil's ersatz Edwardian splendor.

Cecil's renown had, at this point, totally eclipsed that of his bitter rival, the saturnine designer Oliver Messel, also a friend of Simon's, who lived with his large Danish lover Vagn Rees Hansen ("There is *nothing* like a Dane," people sang) in a flower-bower of a house almost opposite Cecil in Pelham Place. There was soon to be a momentary reversal in these fortunes when Oliver's nephew, Tony Armstrong-Jones, already treading Beaton's path as a fashionable photographer, announced his engagement to Princess Margaret. This engagement engendered a lifelong jealousy in Cecil of Oliver, Tony, and his mother, Anne, Lady Rosse. Known as "Tugboat Annie" (from pushing from peer to peer), Lady Rosse was undeniably a beauty, and a brilliant decorator and hostess. Cecil delighted in spreading subtly malicious stories about her, especially the supposed closeness between her and "my *darling* daughter-in-law," as she liked to refer to Princess Margaret. One relentlessly rainy weekend at Birr, the Rosse castle in Ireland, with the guests bored witless, the butler announced, "Lord Snowdon on the line, m'lady." Tugboat disappeared, coming back wreathed in smiles. "It's all right. It's raining at Windsor too."

Another of Simon's greatest friends, whom I met for the first time at the Gothic Box, was Frederick Ashton. One of the world's two leading choreographers—the other being his friendly rival George Balanchine—Fred was slightly out of fashion workwise at that time. A few years later he was to leap back on top, orchestrating the great partnership of Rudolf Nureyev and Margot Fonteyn. He was a brilliant mimic, especially of the royal family. While his party piece had formerly been Queen Alexandra, he'd now updated it to a brilliant imitation of Queen Elizabeth, the Queen Mother, having to sit through a Wagner opera and wanting to go to the lav. All this stemmed from firsthand experience, as he was a great friend of Marina, Duchess of Kent, and her sister Olga, Princess Paul of Yugoslavia (whose husband, the regent of that country, was an erstwhile lover of Chips Channon). Fred often took these poor but beautiful royal sisters to matinees, where he would be irritated by their insistence on having a large, rustling box of chocolates. He imitated their slightly horselike jaws swiveling as they chomped away on marzipans and caramels on either side of him.

Fred had been born in Peru, one of a large family of boys. He used to say, "The reason I'm queer is because I was buggered by my brothers from the age of six onwards," which gives a whole new meaning to South American playboys. He came to Europe, determined to be a dancer, and was soon partnering every great ballerina, becoming, with Ninette de Valois, the founder of English ballet as it exists today. In the late 1940s, when my parents took me to the Royal Opera House for my first ballet, Fred and Robert Helpmann were dancing the Ugly Sisters in *Cinderella.*

With his high forehead and aquiline features, Fred was anything but ugly. The fourth finger of one hand refused to uncurl, giving his constant smoking a fascinating twist. Extremely attractive to women, Fred was deeply loved by, among others, Alice Astor, whose father had drowned on the *Titanic,* leaving her an enormous fortune. Becoming pregnant with what may have been Fred's child, Alice very much wanted to marry him. But as Fred once said to me, "I can't ever believe women don't have cocks," so perhaps it was more appropriate that Alice married his great friend Philip Harding, and that Fred was godfather to the Hardings' daughter, Emily, whose son, Jacob, was, in turn, my godson.

Fred had two idols. One was Lady Cunard, and his vivid memories of her parties, her conversation, and her sometimes almost surreal wit made me wish, not for the first time, that I'd known the dazzling Emerald. The other was the prima ballerina assoluta Anna Pavlova. He would demonstrate how she moved, and could imitate her "dying swan" so lithely people believed they were watching the diva herself dance. Pavlova apart, he loathed talking shop and would rarely discuss ballet. He used to come to New York each year for the Royal Ballet's season, a highlight of spring throughout the early 1960s.

One memorable evening, some years earlier, I had met the legendary Russian ballerina Tamara Karsavina, Nijinsky's most famous partner. I had been asked by Juliet Duff and Simon Fleet to the Theatre Royal, Drury Lane for a charity ballet performance in which Rudolf Nureyev would appear for the first time in England, having just defected at the end of the Kirov's season in Paris. The piece was Alexander Scriabin's *Poème Tragique,* which Fred had choreographed specially for Rudi to dance that night. To my amazement, Karsavina was also in our box. I can still picture her leaning forward, applauding the grace and beauty of Nureyev, the footlights illuminating her face, down which tears streamed, as she said, "Oh, to be young again and to dance with *him.*" When I told Fred all this, he merely said somewhat acidly he hoped Karsavina wouldn't give Rudi a hernia, as she had to Fred when he had lifted her in his youth. Later I heard a sweeter remark of Fred's. Sitting in the audience at the ballet with Bobby Helpmann, they both looked up in admiration at the Queen Mother, resplendently entering the royal box. After the national anthem was played and Her Majesty, smiling and waving, took her seat, Bobby whispered to Fred, "*What* a performance." Fred turned. "But what a *role*," he answered.

VIOLET WYNDHAM ALSO CAME into my life through Simon Fleet and Diana Cooper. The author of historical biographies, Violet was the daughter of a writer, Ada Leverson, and the mother of another, Francis Wyndham. Ada I knew only by repute. She was a socking great hit novelist, 1880-ish. Her style was mockable—"he smiled a smile as blank as a ceiling"—for its overtones of camp, and indeed one does occasionally feel Ronald Firbank is peeping over the pages. But her books were not her only memorial. Being the adored best friend of Oscar Wilde gave her fin-de-siècle immortality. It was to Ada he turned when his world crumbled; it was she who met him at the gaol's gate. He called her "Sphinx." When Wilde confided to Ada that in Paris he had been followed around by a young male apache dancer "with a knife in one hand," Ada shot back, "Yes, Oscar, and I'm quite sure with a fork in the other."

Violet, Ada's daughter, lived in the prettiest little house at the top end of Trevor Square, one of the two that look down toward Harrods, where, in a tiny dining room she entertained with aplomb. The first time I met the famously hard-to-please "best-dressed woman in the world," Daisy Fellowes, was at a lunch Violet gave for the photographer of the moment, Roloff Benny. After she had blanked her hostess, changed the seating plan, and left every morsel uneaten, Mrs. Fellowes was a comparatively easy guest.

Also known as Auntie Nose, Violet was extremely canny in seeing the writing on the Knightsbridge wall. She cashed in and hightailed it to the then deeply unfashionable Notting Hill, finding an even smaller and even prettier cottage in Lonsdale Road, and began her new book, a life of the Duke of Monmouth. Violet shared this new abode with Francis, who was at the time literary editor of *The Sunday Times*.

Almost instantly this tiny house became a salon, the last true salon in the eighteenth-century mold. Violet entertained most days from lunchtime till six, and Francis continued till late after dinner. There *were* intervals when Francis *had* to lie down, and moments when Violet needed to powder her—well—nose, but otherwise it was a nonstop turnover of David Hockney, Mark Boxer (creator of the first-ever color supplement),

Lucian Freud, Antonia Fraser. Violet was the Mme de Stael of the sixties and seventies and, like her, loved to dabble in statecraft. Many years later she was to introduce Roddy Llewellyn, with whom I had been living for a year or so, to Princess Margaret. They fell in love at almost first sight. To Violet's intense delight, Roddy took his trophy to lunch in Lonsdale Road. Later Violet rang me. "They do seem terribly happy, don't they?" I said I was delighted. Violet then asked, "Darling, do you think that, in our own small way, we may have changed the course of history?"

Simon also had a long-standing, complicated relationship with an extraordinary woman called Lady Juliet Duff. By the time I met her she was about seventy, immensely tall, angular and *racé*-looking, with a long pale face and hazel-blue eyes with a quizzical, somewhat owl-like expression. She was a granddaughter of the boxing-belt-famous "Yellow" Earl of Lonsdale and had hence been born in Lowther Castle. Her mother, the Countess of Lonsdale, then Lady de Grey, and finally Lady Ripon, one of the few women in Edwardian society to be interested in the performing arts, had been essential in bringing the Diaghilev Ballet to England before World War I, and had raised her daughter to share her passion. Janet Flanner, *The New Yorker*'s sharp-eyed Paris correspondent for several decades, wrote in the 1930s that "besides being six foot tall, Juliet dresses smartly and is excellent company. Her intimates include Diana Cooper, the Lunts, Noël Coward, Ivor Novello (she is extremely stage-struck), Hilaire Belloc, Maurice Baring, Anthony Powell and Harold Nicolson. Winston Churchill plays piquet with her each Thursday evening. I found all the men who were part of Juliet's entourage amusing even when they were being serious." Though a few of that entourage had died, this description held exactly true when I knew Juliet some twenty-five years later.

Juliet and Simon didn't exactly live together, but neither did they live apart. Juliet's flat in Sydney Street could be reached via the back door of the Gothic Box. And at Bulbridge, the dower house on the Wilton estate near Salisbury which was Lady Juliet's country house, Simon, having first been allotted an abandoned Nissen hut on the grounds, had progressed to a tumbledown pink cottage adjoining the mellow Regency main building.

I'm not sure anyone believed Juliet and Simon had ever been physical lovers, but Simon genuinely loved Juliet, and one felt Juliet was more than a little in love with Simon. There were jokes that because of her height Juliet was really a guardsman in drag, or that once Simon had felt he should try, only for Juliet to squeak in horror, "Goodness, Si, I'd really rather read my book." Intelligent, with a prodigious memory, she was a great gardener, though considered by some a bit of a goose, and renowned for foot-in-mouth remarks. During the war she was driving up to London, the car loaded with plants and produce for the week ahead, when a uniformed soldier tried to thumb a lift. Juliet sailed past, but after a few hundred yards she had a terrible pang of remorse and, reversing to the delighted soldier, wound down the window and explained, "Sorry! No room. Too many flowers!"

Cecil Beaton, a neighbor in the country, both adored and was irritated by Juliet, and during frequent patches of nonspeaks could be quite vitriolic about her. Juliet responded in kind, remarking acidly, "One can tell Cecil's common. Loves his mother."

There was more than bitchy flippancy underlying this dig. Juliet had never had a happy relationship with her only son, Michael. Even taller and more languidly elegant than his mother, Michael was dazzlingly handsome, funny in that special way unintellectual people can be and, like Fred Ashton, a devastating mimic—principally of Queen Mary, of whose successor, Queen Elizabeth, he was an intimate. Michael had married twice, most recently to the beautiful Lady Caroline Paget, Diana Cooper's lesbian niece. For the obvious reasons, despite an adopted son, the marriage was not a huge success. Michael searched elsewhere for the affection that his mother had never been able to bestow, and the fact that he became such a friend and playmate of Simon's—they had collaborated on several theatrical ventures—only complicated matters, exacerbating Juliet's coldness to him.

Michael's visits to Bulbridge, and Juliet's to Vaynol, the immense Duff estates in Snowdonia, were infrequent, uneasy, and tense. Juliet, though, was not jealous of Simon's other friendships. She accepted me implicitly. Like Simon, she loved youth and spirit and curiosity. She enjoyed sharing a lifetime's history, knowledge, and romance with those who might appreciate it. On my first visit to Bulbridge, she took a little Léon Bakst drawing over to the light to show me. It was of Nijinsky in *Le Spectre de la rose*. On this memento of ballet's most legendary dancer was written *Juliet! Du Spectre, à la Rose*.

She encouraged us to lug her mother Lady Ripon's huge red albums onto the white fur rug in front of her sitting-room fire, and pore over those records of grand Edwardian life: the vast houses, the vast house parties, the vast shoots, yachts, hydrangeas, tiaras and aigrettes, the letters to "Beloved Gladys" from—and about—Queen Alexandra. ("She does *not* enamel," Lady Ripon scolds one critical correspondent who had suggested that the queen used makeup.) One could unfold letters from the czar, the kaiser, from kings and prime ministers and presidents. There were telegrams from Tchaikovsky and Stravinsky, cards from actresses as many poles apart as Mrs. Patrick Campbell and Mary Pickford.

Juliet's house was a cornucopia of comfort, volupté and luxe, with its atmospheric nature-morte paintings, its *White Swan* by Oudry, its furniture by Jacob, its huge chintz armchairs with baggy covers, and—in line with Juliet's decorating mantra, "something pink, and something ugly, in every room"—riots of roses and hideous tooled leather covers for the *Radio Times*. But Juliet could also be very frugal. That afternoon Simon suggested to Juliet that I should stay the night. "I'll just have to ask Andrews"—her roost-ruling butler. A little later she returned. "Yes, Andrews says there's enough pie." At dinner, Juliet said, "Isn't it extraordinary that during the war we all ate the crust of pies."

Like many of the lighter intellectuals of the period, Juliet, as Janet Flanner had noted, was obsessed with Alfred Lunt and Lynn Fontanne, at the time the ultra-famous and respected American husband-and-wife acting team. They played elegant happily married or happily divorcing couples in frothy stage plays—*Idiot's Delight* by Robert Sherwood, and Noël Coward's *Quadrille* among them—nearly as convincingly as they did in real life. Alfred, a tall, man with a strong, handsome head and a keen eye for the boys, was in fact meek as a mouse, and Lynn, a near-beauty, hid a steely spirit beneath her exceptionally well-dressed theatrical facade. Whether in a play or not, they would come most summers to London.

This would engender a lot of "Alfred says" or "Darling Lynnie thinks" from Juliet before, during, and after their stay, which was often with her at Bulbridge, or, dangerous rivalry, with Cecil at Broadchalke. Parties were given for the Lunts by the cream of the theater and film world, by Terence Rattigan in Eaton Square, or Binkie Beaumont, the West End impresario, in Lord North Street, where they were treated like the royalty their profession—and they themselves—considered them to be. The Lunts invariably acted together, the seminal opening nights being the acme of lime- and footlit performances.

One season, however, the Lunts bucked their usual trend and appeared in *The Visit,* by Friedrich Dürrenmatt. Simon took me to the first night, at the old Stoll Theatre in Kingsway, of this very gloomy offering. Their usual lightheartedness was deadened by an avalanche of heavy Germanic expressionism, with both of them in ripped, grubby clothes and unflattering lighting. It was far from the dramatic triumph of the season the Lunts were accustomed to.

One Saturday soon after this debacle, Diana Cooper and I drove down to lunch at Enid Bagnold's pretty pre-Raphaelite house, North End, in

Rottingdean. The Lunts were also guests. Lynn, partly I think to preempt Alfred, whose eyes had widened appreciatively when he saw me, from doing so first, turned on her immense charm full throttle and made a great fuss of me, saying I reminded her of Donald Maclean, the extremely good-looking and socially adored Cambridge spy, who had, only weeks before, defected to Russia with Guy Burgess.

Then Alfred said that if I went to America, I must come and stay with them one weekend at their farm, in Genesee Depot, which sounded wonderfully rural. When I eventually did go to New York, I inquired about trains to the Lunts' farm, only to find it took a couple of days, as the rurality of Genesee Depot was in deepest Wisconsin.

However, in New York a few years later, there was a coda to my meetings with this legendary couple. Jean Shrimpton was coming over to do a modeling assignment, and I went that evening to meet her at Idlewild airport wearing my then uniform of dirty torn blue jeans and leather. Jean came through immigration with her hair a mess, no makeup, in a disheveled and extremely skimpy miniskirt, just then becoming fashion's rage. Driving back to Manhattan, I told her that Jean Howard, the glamorous wife of Hollywood's leading agent, Charles Feldman, had invited us to a small party she was giving for Jack Kennedy. Shrimp said, "Well, I'm not coming if I have to change; I'm too tired." So we drove straight to Jean's apartment on Seventy-eighth Street. In we walked, two grubby, bedraggled nervous brats. There was instant, utter silence, as several of the most famous faces on the planet swiveled toward the door. The silence was palpable. Then, very, very clearly, Noël Coward said, "My God. It's the Lunts."

WITH SUCH DISTRACTIONS and such new friends, school became even more of a slog. Simon often drove down to Eton in the bubble car Diana Cooper had given him when she bought herself a Mini, which she frequently drove into people's basements, and would park anywhere with various notes on the lines of "Warden. So sorry. Taking cross child to pictures. Please forgive." Simon himself could hardly fit into the bubble, so I would be bent triple in the tail end, but, after they'd arranged to meet me in some safely hidden spot, we would go off on expeditions to nearby houses, Cliveden, or Hampshire, Simon explaining the romantic history of these places rather than their architectural importance. If Simon could borrow Juliet's car, Min, too, came with us. That she and Simon had become such firm friends was for me an enormous pleasure.

I spent too much time and money on the telephone to Min from Welsh &

Jefferies, the school tailors in Eton High Street. The bill one term came to thirty-two pounds, a huge amount—my father was livid but eventually paid it. I was determined to make my Eton life as sophisticated as the one I longed for in London. I decorated my new room, happily larger than my first cupboardlike cell, in a style transparently inspired by Simon's eclectic Gothic Box and enlisted his help. He took me to Dazian's, a wonderful theatrical material shop, where I fell for fake ocelot skin for curtains, and consequently made cut-paper ostrich-plume pelmets to go above them. The carpet was bright green artificial grass, which we cadged off a flower seller in Belgrave Square. We rescued a huge photograph of James Dean and "Buzz" in *Rebel Without a Cause* from the film exhibition, which hung above my burry, lit by carriage lamps. The whole effect was kind of "barococo-surreal," and even the most blasé of my schoolmates were astonished. M'dame and my housemaster didn't mind a scrap—Eton ethics again—in fact Fred How used to bring his guests to see it after dinner, as though it were a sort of cabaret.

I designed the scenery for the school play, one of those interminable "Henry XIX Part 23" jobs, performed as always in the echoing Edwardian vastness of School Hall, but somehow I managed to make it look like an extension of my room, with Agincourt being planned from masses of dear little striped pink tents topped with curling plumes. And by now I had a small but tight-knit group of friends with whom I could laugh and drink shandy at Tap, a sort of bar for older boys in the High Street, and smoke under Arches, a long viaduct taking the railway across the Thames, a misdemeanor that warranted instant sacking. Nevertheless I found myself always longing for the holidays and long-leaves, for the chance to be back at the Gothic Box, back to the world that Simon brought into being, and where I perceived new vistas opening up.

I was right. Weekends during the holidays at Simon's cottage at Bulbridge always entailed visits to neighboring houses. Some grand, some less so: all interesting. On rare occasions—perhaps, for a Sunday lunch party—we'd make the short walk along the river Nadder, over the famous Palladian bridge and across the vast cedar-shaded lawns to "the big house," Wilton itself. The Pembrokes had led a very royal life. Mary, the Countess of Pembroke, had, however, inherited few of the diplomatic manners of her father, the Marquess of Linlithgow, a former viceroy of India. She could be quite blunt, and often unintentionally cutting. Simon always cherished one of her vehemently snobbish put-downs: He was driving her to London on the old A30, at Aldershot, when he pointed out the gorse and rhododendrons, saying, "It looks just like Sandringham." Mary shot back. "Don't be so silly, Simon. How could you possibly know?"

Sidney Pembroke had long since turned to his own sex, but any such proclivity was kept firmly for town. If the atmosphere at Wilton had a certain tenseness, it was relieved by the presence of the Pembrokes' children. Henry Herbert was my contemporary at Eton, and if he was surprised to see me in such a different *galère* from our respective tutor's, he never showed it. His sister, Diana, radiated film star beauty, and the Pembrokes, true to form, had marked her as a potential bride for the young Duke of Kent.

Sidney Pembroke's younger brother, David Herbert, another of Simon's greatest friends, was living at the time on the grounds in a shell-encrusted grottolike folly designed by Inigo Jones, known as the Park School. He left this dream house not long afterward, settling more or less permanently in more liberally minded Tangier. Simon was sad at so decisive a move, as David was a fund of stories of aristocratic foibles, and his ever more infrequent returns to England always signaled a special party at the Box. The Park School was subsequently taken by Lord John Hope and his wife, Liza, the only outcome of the unlikely union of Somerset Maugham and his wife, the paint-everything-white decorator Syrie.

More often we would visit farther afield, driving over to see huge-footed, corduroy-suited Siegfried Sassoon and his boyfriend at Heytesbury, both sitting gloomily in the dark hall, in anguish at the bypass being forcibly rammed through their park, or to the by now embarrassingly roué Augustus John at Friern Court on the edge of the New Forest. Dorelia would be in the kitchen, which was filled with wildflowers in jam jars, still dressed in exactly the hazy blue peasant clothes that John so often had painted her wearing. Their children and grandchildren were often in evidence, among them Poppet Pol, whose daughter, Talitha, I would later watch, over the course of several summers in Saint-Tropez, growing from nymph-child to raving beauty. Talitha married Paul Getty, Jr., but died too soon afterward of an overdose, her exquisite young body unable to tolerate the newly fashionable heroin she and many of her friends were pumping into themselves.

At Long Crichel we would call on the three literary lions, Eddie Sackville-West, Eardley Knollys, and Raymond Mortimer, all sharing a house, a library, and a record collection but not the gin or the jam. Supplies were carefully marked and closely guarded—at least by them. ("Oh dear, Simon, you've helped yourself from Raymond's," the other two would say, smirking.) At Longleat, lanky Henry Bath, still extremely handsome despite a deep attachment to the bottle, had recently handed over the running of the estate, with its newly imported lions, to his heir, the almost more handsome but even then somewhat wacky Alexander Weymouth, much to the annoyance of his two slightly more circumspect younger brothers. Long since divorced from their mother, the wild and witty Daphne—whose brother, Lord Vivian, had been shot by his lover Mavis de Vere (she went to prison, but after she got out he took her back, and they lived together happily ever after)—Henry Bath, once equally wild, was now leading a quietish life in a pretty house on the estate called Job's Mill, with his second wife, the beautiful Virginia. Her first husband, David Tennant, had been the owner of the Gargoyle Club in Soho, decorated with murals by Matisse, all now, of course, demolished.

Diana Cooper and I once drove the "safari route" through Longleat's park. The car was beset by apes. One reached in and snatched Diana's lit cigarette. Sitting on the bonnet, it tried stuffing the butt up its privates. "Oh, *not* in your placey, darling," Diana's blinking blue gaze pleaded.

Raine Pitman, a niece of John Singer Sargent, lived at Odstock near Salisbury. For her Christmas party one year—snow lay in shoulder-deep drifts each side of ice-rink roads—Raine had lit the whole house entirely with tall ecclesiastical candles, a heretofore unencountered extravagance, and the contrast of the flickering golden light inside to the still, white snowscape outside was magically memorable.

Down at Wilsford, in the Wylie Valley, resided the extraordinary topaz-beringed and shawl-bedecked, package-blond-dyed and panstick-bronzed poet and painter, a self-enchanted *fantaisiste,* the reclusive ("They call me the Garbo of Wiltshire") Stephen Tennant. He was renowned for great beauty in his youth, his love affair with his now un-spoken-to neighbor the poet Siegfried Sassoon, and more recently his habit of tipping astonished porters at Salisbury station with a single calla lily. Even I, on first meeting him, though forewarned, was alarmed at his overt outlandishness. Little by little I came to know Stephen well and was duly enchanted by this unique being, often visiting him and exchanging many letters. His were always written in multicolored inks and cobwebbed with sketches. In the late seventies Stephen, not all that reluctantly for a determined recluse, agreed to let me interview him, and David Bailey take a portrait, for Bailey's fledgling magazine, *Ritz*. And a few years after that Henry Pembroke persuaded Stephen to let us film him. In the footage we took, Stephen burbles away as I prod him to an ever more fantastic performance of recollection and self-revelation.

And then there was Nico. One of my earliest Wiltshire visits with

Simon was to an eighteenth-century house with a ravishing ornamental facade near Wilton. Owned by the publisher Michael Harrison and his Latvian wife, Maria, it was called Netherhampton—or, by my school friend Christopher Gibbs, Nether Latvia. There, when we arrived, in the sunniest part of the garden, prone on the lawn, and oiled, lay perhaps the most beautiful girl I had yet set eyes on. Nicolette—Nico—had a wide smile that narrowed her huge eyes, curling the corners of her slightly sulky mouth, yet all the while giving out an air of utter boredom.

Contrary to this appearance, almost anything made Nico shake with laughter. She became an instant friend, and back in London we would go to the movies together, looking, we hoped, like French beatniks in shades and striped sailor jerseys. We would sit for hours in El Cubano, England's first coffee bar, on Brompton Road, giggling, I'm sorry to say, at passersby, in every one of whom Nico could find a mockable defect.

When I was incarcerated back at school, Nico kept up the jokes in letters that were, for the most part, paeans of love to our shared crush, James Dean. One day she telephoned my dame, insisting on speaking to me. Between sobs she managed to tell me that our beloved Jimmy had been killed, mangled in his Porsche Spyder.

During my first year after leaving Eton, Nico was a debutante. It was practically the last official season for that anachronistic procedure when eligible girls were presented to the queen, as part of their preparation for landing an appropriate husband. Though she hated the whole process, it still didn't take Nico long. Barely had the very last deb made the last curtsey than Nico became engaged to the dazzling marquess of Londonderry, my near-contemporary at Eton. Alastair, handsome as sin, had Byronic brooding eyes. Nico, always a bit of a rebel at heart, rather relished the fact that her fiancé was somewhat in the social doghouse, as he had publicly criticized the queen and her family.

Soon after their marriage I went to stay with Al and Nico at Wynyard near Durham, the one remaining of many vast Londonderry estates. Nico sent me a clipping from a local paper showing her and me inspecting some piglets at a local produce show. I look like a fat little blond tranny, but Nico, beside me, is chic and cool as ever; the caption, however, delivers a somewhat backhanded compliment: "If Lady Londonderry continues dressing like this, she may easily become the best-dressed woman on Tyneside."

Alastair's family's town residence loomed on Park Lane, then a narrow street on which had stood many great aristocratic mansions such as Grosvenor, and Dorchester House, all demolished before the war, to be rebuilt as hotels. Now it was the turn of Londonderry House, recently sold to Hilton.

Alastair and Nico decided to give one last great ball, on the night before the wrecker's grabs would reduce to rubble the grand staircase where Alastair's great-grandmother Edith, Marchioness of Londonderry, had stood imperiously, as befitted the descendant of the statesman who had brokered the Congress of Vienna in 1815, and received crowned heads and statesmen for half a century. She was known as Circe for her political acumen, bejeweled evening gowns hid her famous tattoo, a snake writhing up her leg. But tonight, a young, immaculate marchioness and her friends gyrating to the new beat of Alexis Korner, whose hired-in singer, a skinny lad named "Mick something," Min said, pawed drunkenly at her strapless pink satin. Later Alastair's great friend Benny Goodman took over the music, playing into a dawn that would see an epoch bulldozed to the ground.

I MYSELF WAS ABOUT to be bulldozed, by the presence and charm of a second Simon, Simon Hodgson. A would-be (and he *would* become one) aesthete born in Derbyshire ("Holy Matlock, darling"), with long, pushed-behind-his-ears hair and gray flannel suits that evoked the 1920s, Simon was just down from Oxford. I see now he modeled himself on Sebastian Flyte. He was wonderfully offhand, unafraid of offending, and when he frequently did, a sort of explosion of embarrassment swelled inside him, followed by uncontrollable sneezing.

Simon would get Martin Newell, a school-of-Rex-Whistler struggling artist who earned an extra few quid by teaching flower arranging in smart girls' schools, to drive down to Eton fairly frequently. They would bring with them the most fashionable girls of the moment, often the much publicized but somewhat reluctant outré, long-limbed, debutante, Suna Portman, founder member, along with Alastair Londonderry's sister Jane Vane-Tempest-Stewart, Mary Quant, and Alexander Plunkett-Green, of the fledgling "Chelsea Set." Due to her Norwegian mother, Suna was blessed with big blue eyes and streaming white-blond hair, and a penchant for wearing the minimum of clothes.

They brought fearfully sophisticated and unsuitable—for starving schoolboys—picnic food: *mousseline* of artichokes, say, or crayfish in aspic, and lime sorbets. Once, unable to prise open the dry-ice-lined tin that sorbets then came in, Simon petulantly flung it in the river at Datchet, where it fizzed and whizzed wildly about, causing panic in a flock of swans that, hissing menacingly, advanced on the paddling Suna, who hightailed it speedily up the bank. "Darling Su," said Simon over his shoulder. "You'll never make a Leda of men." At another picnic, in Windsor Great Park, all the cutlery had been left behind. Min walked up a drive, rang the bell, asked for—and was given—plates and knives and forks, without any questions.

After these riverine idylls Simon and I sometimes went to a mock-Tudor hotel in Ascot and ordered fearfully dainty doily-encased teacakes, which amused him greatly, and he kissed me, which greatly amused us both. It wasn't till after I left school that we became true lovers, in his room in the seminary attached to Saint Mary's, the ultra–High Anglican smells-and-bells church in Bourne Street, where a slew of other wayward lads of ecclesiastical bent lodged, though it must be said that their use of "divine" was more often preceded by "too, too" rather than followed by "worship." When, a few months later, I went to see Sandy Wilson's magical musical of Firbank's *Valmouth,* I realized I'd been sleeping and feasting with Cardinal Pirelli–like tigers.

Toward the latter part of our friendship, Simon was to meet—and later marry—Priscilla Bibesco, who had inherited a beautiful apartment facing straight up the Seine, on the Vert Galant in Paris. Frescoes commissioned by her parents, the Romanian prince Antoine Bibesco and Elizabeth Asquith, daughter of the Liberal prime minister, from Pierre Bonnard, lined their salon. Sometimes the Hodgsons lived high on the hog, with country houses, country clothes, precious pictures, rare *objets,* and travels in a coffee-colored Rolls-Royce, known as Ro-Ro. When financial turbulence struck, Simon's reaction, slender fingers placed tragically to throat, was typical. "It's *too* unfair. Ro-Ro's *simply* got to go."

MEANWHILE MY EDUCATION at Eton simply had to go on, for another few halves at least. The daunting prospect of Leaving Exams, still quaintly called School Cert, was looming, though far enough in the future that youth sees as endless. "I hope you do not flunk your Tripos," Cecil Beaton had written, even more quaintly, in a letter venting his anger with Hermione Gingold for backing out of the stage version of his spoof Edwardian memoirs, *My Royal Past,* "at the last minute, so we are all rather bitter about her." Flunk? The idea gnawed away in the back of my mind, but my extensive if superficial Simon-imparted knowledge, while probably not what I'd encounter in any exam papers, gave me a kind of mad confidence. I felt I could wing it in history, English, and

French, possibly Latin, but had more or less abandoned hope with any mathematical subjects. All my tutors had long since concluded they couldn't turn this particular sow's ear into a clever boy. Pinning my hopes on making a starry showing in art, I spent most waking and some working hours at the art schools, succored by Wilfrid Blunt, and trying to avoid his deputy Oily Thomas, or the head of the pottery school, Mr. Menzies-Jones, known as Moans. My great friend was Jeffery, the caretaker, a skinny little man always in a long brown overall coat, with a constant drip swinging from his nose. After a lot of negative whining, Jeffery could be prevailed upon to go to Jack's, the frankly rather unsmart "sock shop" on the parade ground nearby and bring back Wagon Wheels biscuits and bottles of Club Orange, which we would devour in the art school's rather scruffy rose garden.

Getting more proficient with oil paints, I did portraits of any friends who would sit, some quite good, one or two even to this day hanging, I'm proud to say, in their houses. Eddie Plunkett, an Irish peer-to-be whose South American mother had passed on her sleek dark Latin looks to her son, was a "rival," and now that he is a major selling artist, clearly a better painter, but it was friendly competition, even though Eddie's tutor thought I was a bit déclassé for him to be friends with. We would meet almost every day to discuss deeply which painters we admired—a fairly standard bunch in those art-book-limited days—and discover how colors and paints interacted.

If I became exasperated by trying to capture an intractable image, I would contact the dramatically Celtic-featured Grey Ruthven, whose love of romantic literature, and penchant for reading aloud his own sonnets were strangely at odds with the desperately hearty house, Mr. Coleridge's, in which he boarded. We would dash down Eton High Street, where Grey, his long-limbed figure a stranger to mere mortals' food, had to manhandle me past the lure of Roland's and a Strawberry Mess, and, crossing the Thames into Windsor ("Oh, *must* you?" Grey would groan when I dawdled to stare at the stills on display outside the cinema), climb up some secret steep stone stairs in the curtain wall of the Castle, of which his grandfather, old Lord Gowrie, was governor.

The Gowries' apartments were in the Round Tower, where there was an amazing library of botany and zoology to pore over and, when bored with that, we'd go exploring endless musty upstairs rooms and corridors, furniture under yellowing dustsheets sewn with the royal cipher—"*GRIV*, 1821," lots of *VRs*, sometimes *VRIs*, and once, heartstoppingly, a damask napkin embroidered with the Russian *N* and *A*, for Nicholas and

Alexandra, clearly a keepsake from some forgotten czarist banquet, which I pocketed. After many of these expeditions we would join Chris Collins, the Goya perfume heir, and my nearest neighbor at Hundridge, for the frequent blow-out teas he would hold in the Gay Adventure (!), a restaurant to outdo—indeed briefly eclipse—the Cockpit, in the High Street. The owner—we invariably called her Mrs. M.—had taken rather a shine to me, and during a previous holiday had insisted on my going to lunch in "proper" London restaurants. She introduced me to such glittering places as L'Écu de France and Quo Vadis; the Ivy, with the dining room then upstairs; and Le Caprice, still all gilt plaster cupids and red velvet banquettes, on the smartest of which we sat next to Vivien Leigh and Laurence Olivier.

Simon Fleet knew a rather louche Russian named Michael Obolensky. At least the name sounded Russian, even if Michael sounded more Greater London than Leningrad. Michael's friend was Kenneth Hume, at the time married to an up-and-coming black singer called Shirley Bassey. They gave bottle parties at their flat in Tottenham Court Road, and at one of these I got talking to Lita Roza. At the time she was hugely famous, her biggest hit, "How Much Is That Doggie in the Window?" already a camp classic. Her girlfriend was snuggled up to Forrest Tucker, an American movie actor who had been in *The Yearling*. I persuaded them all to come to the Fourth of June, an Eton event my parents studiously avoided. I was beside myself with pleasure at parading a genuine film star and the hot singer of the moment around Agar's Plough. We bumped into Anne Purvis, Chester's niece, startling for having the first No. 1 crop in haircutting history, and bleached lint white at that. She was escorted by the season's leading "deb's delights," Toby Jessel and Charles MacArthur Hardy, whose figure-clinging suit trousers had the first flat-front "cavalry" pockets I had ever seen, which I instantly vowed to copy. Delighting debs wasn't seal-sleek Charles's only mission, and a few weeks later we were necking through many a double-bill matinee in the smoke-wreathed balcony of the ABC Fulham Forum, my hands deep in those cavalry pockets.

Another afternoon Anne appeared with two more extremely handsome but highfalutin' young men, clearly lovers, who were "terribly amused" at the decorations of my room. I soon was aware that David Hicks and Norman Prouting were the hot young gay couple in London, becoming renowned as the eyecatchers at Chips Channon's parties in Belgrave Square; they were tall, one blond and the other dark, and pretty additions to his fabulous blue-and-silver "Amalienberg" dining room. But their social mountaineering already had tongues wagging, as, in spite of rather than because of being lovers, neither countenanced the other getting a grander invitation; such as happened when David had been asked, and Norman not, to a reception given by the Swedish ambassador's wife, the very soignée Mme Hägloff, the acme of diplomatic chic. Norman hid in the embassy precincts, leaped out, and laid about David, madly clawing at his hair and ripping his evening *tenue* and—for that night at least—putting paid to David's entrée into such Nordic ambassadorial circles.

David soon started, with Tom Parr, the first ultramodern decorating business in London. Hicks and Parr occupied the ground floor of the fashionable 1930s block of flats off Lowndes Square known, due to its shape, as "the Gasometer." The glamorous summer evening of the opening, with young and old aristocratic London, from Annabel Vane Tempest-Stewart with her fiancé, Mark Birley, to Lady Baba Metcalfe, displayed jaw-droppingly chic unheard- or unthought-of ideas. No one who was there that first evening will forget the twenty-seven metal African lances hung exactly five and a half inches apart, horizontally, on one wall, or the thousand-watt bulbs illuminating, in relief, a vast baroque torso. The spare, sparse energy, the space, the scale, were literally breathtaking. When he moved into Eaton Place, the decor became the cynosure of every eye. Carpets and curtains were banished. Books must be bound all white. Monotones must prevail. Later in life David would have only black or white cattle in his fields, and even maintained that red or yellow dogs were "terribly common."

Tom Parr's refined taste and eclectic eye, combined with David's stark off-whites and earthy buffs, geometric details, and massive overscaling, quickly made them the world's most coveted decorators. At a time when most people were questioning the wisdom of replacing velvet with velvet, and plumping instead for Peter Jones rep, or hemming and hawing over vinyl rather than a linen tablecloth, Hicks and Parr's spare luxury was astonishing. Among their first clients were the Londonderrys, and David remained devoted to Nico all her life. Vere French, no slouch when it came to "the latest thing," also called them in. As she explained, "When Hicks and Parr said *beige,* who was I to lag behind?"

While Tom Parr went on to join, and eventually become the head of, the more conventional decorators Colefax and Fowler, David's most spectacular career move, engineered by Chips Channon, was his marriage to a cousin of the queen, the thus royal Lady Pamela Mountbatten. He unwisely boasted his "grand" engagement to Tony Armstrong-Jones. "Oh,

I don't call *that* grand" was Tony's testy reply. A few days later Tony announced his own engagement to Princess Margaret.

Min had by now left Benenden and was enrolled at the Central School of Art, and I had only a year or so left at Eton. On the many afternoons she drove down to see me, she would describe the various classes she could attend—costume design, photography, book illustration, and sculpture, as well as painting and drawing—and to go there as well as soon as I left Eton thus became my avowed dream. But when, a few months later, I showed the selection committee some admittedly extremely banal theater costume designs I'd done, it remained a dream unfulfilled. However, Min's enthusiasm had increased my determination to leave Eton as soon as possible, and as it was clear as daylight that with my meager academic credentials I would not be going on to university, my parents had no objections. My last half at school was the short spring term, and was largely taken up with cementing the few strong friendships I'd made. I began dismantling the bird's nest my room had become, and finishing off or chucking out paintings at the drawing schools. I also made my leaving photograph—flouting a custom of distributing to most of one's immediate contemporaries, beaks, dames, and staff—a stereotype image of oneself taken by the court photographers, Hills & Saunders, in the High Street, stuck to a white-ribboned white card and discreetly signed. I'm almost ashamed to say that my photograph, taken by Eddie Plunkett and showing me painting at an easel, was pasted onto thick black paper, decorated with a white swansdown bow, and floridly signed in gold ink. I made that last drive back up the A4 with the tingling sensation of being on the edge of a longed-for unknown.

Meanwhile my father, Ralph Hamlyn, and Tony Burney, a somewhat slippery businessman—he "rose" to become chairman of Debenhams—whom Ralph had drawn into his coven, were up to a trick they had of playing gods. Ralph in particular had a habit of manipulating people's careers to his own advantage. This time their intended was John Addey, an aspiring young politician. They had *plans* for him, and I'm sure Burney had his eye on him as well. But John had his eye on something, too: my mother. It wasn't long before John was constantly at Cumberland Terrace, charming the pants off her.

John did have a definite allure: slick-haired, sallow, and slightly Continental-looking. He had a sardonic manner and huge confidence, added to which there was the irresistible, to me at least, glamour of his having recently been at university in California, picking up the slight American accent and mannerisms I pined for. His flat was in Hanover

Terrace Mews, across the park, and was in fact the very one that my father had given to Geoffrey Scott when he first bought 8 Hanover Terrace. I borrowed it from John for a night, and gave my first grown-up party in its garage. The theme was Truman Capote's *Breakfast at Tiffany's*—the book was the current rage—with guests arriving at midnight and dripping jewelry. But John, dressed Yankee-dandy in gleaming white T-shirt and faded blue jeans, stole my eyes. By dawn he and I were lovers.

Now my father began to fret about my obvious avoidance of further education, let alone work. My parents were not overenamored of my ever more glamorous but, as they saw it, useless social life in London. (Mummy had insisted on meeting Simon Fleet—he came to Cumberland Terrace; she adored him, of course, if warily.) A plan was laid that I should, like my brother Michael before me, spend a year in Australia, first working on a cousin's vineyard, Château Tabilk, outside Melbourne, and worse, after that, to be a trainee jackeroo, rounding up on some godforsaken station. Panicked, I set about convincing my mother that she couldn't possibly do without me, going with her everywhere, the soul of filial devotion. It worked, to the extent that my father agreed to let me go to an art school, provided it was *not* in, or anywhere near, London.

I was sent to Corsham Court, a dim establishment near faraway Bath. The fact that my father drove me there, both of us silent in the incessant rain, was a sign that he meant business. The message that I'd better take this next step seriously was implicit. My stomach tightened at each mile, each minute, farther from London. That prize, for so brief a moment in my grasp, was fast receding into the distance. Corsham Court itself, a vast stone Jacobean pile, hadn't seemed too forbidding in the summer sunlight when I'd had my interview. Now the sodden black yews huddling around its wet gray facade, like vultures guarding a bloodless kill, filled me with fear. Worse, I had vile digs up endless worn-lino'd stairs in some dank town straddling a main road nearby. I wrote impassioned letters to John saying, If you love me you'll get me out of this hell.

I was, I knew, Michelangelo and Toulouse-Lautrec rolled into one, and longing to prove myself as such. Instead we did raffia work, made things out of jam jars and corks, and fiddled about with wax crayons. I lasted three weeks, then ran for the station. A train came. I was free, and thinking, I will never be pushed around again. Oddly the reaction wasn't too bad. My father felt he'd tried, my mother was rather proud that I'd made a stand. Either way it was a fait accompli.

The fly in the ointment was John Addey, whose fly-by-night relationships with me, my father, and my mother came to light. My mother was quite happy to give him the push, good riddance, but my father was more prosaic. He told John he had to look after me (financially, was implied), or the *plans* would be summarily dropped. John, already rather cheesed off at finding I was having a romance with his visiting ex-lover, Bart Howard, a San Franciscan songwriter on the cusp of penning his chef d'oeuvre "Fly Me to the Moon," was no fool. He cut and ran. From me. The *plans* led to him standing for Parliament as Conservative candidate in a fairly safe Midlands seat.

It didn't matter to me as much as it might have. I was now in London, and, having tasted the freedom of living away from home that the adventure with John had engendered, I felt it was time to look for a place of my own.

· SEVEN ·

I FOUND A BIG CHEAP BASEMENT in the shabbier part of Chelsea,
Beaufort Street, sharing it with Patrick Rice, another new Old Etonian, whose laconic manner and floppy fringe I had envied when we
became friends during that long-awaited final term. No. 117 was conveniently near the Gothic Box, and thrillingly Samantha Eggar, then in the
dawn of her smoky beauty, and starting out on her journey to Hollywood stardom, lived on the ground floor opposite.

Wearing tight toreador pants, Samantha would sit reading *Photoplay*
on the steps of the house while the setting sun gilded her dark copper
hair, waving encouragement as I fixed a vast poster by Doris Zinkeisen,
a popular set designer, of "Elegant Ladies at the Theatre" to cover one
whole wall, and painted the rest of the room the red of the curtains on
each side of the paper theater's stage.

The independence I had dreamed about was now mine and more intoxicating than I had envisaged. I had, in Min, a soul mate and, with
Bunny Roger, Tom Parr, and Christopher Gibbs, a beloved contemporary at Eton who had left school under something of a cloud a few halves
before, a close group was completed. And above all I had Simon Fleet.
The love shared by all of us for beautiful buildings and deep countryside,
American films, theater, the look and looks of youth beginning to emerge
from the long-lasting postwar hangover, combined with a mutual sense
of humor, melded into a close, special bond. Simon was our champion,
mentor, and protector (in a totally nonfinancial sense). Without any hint
of self-interest he would introduce us to his seemingly boundless circle of
friends. His unusual knowledge and rampant curiosity we plundered
shamelessly. There was no jealousy in any of these friendships, partly,
perhaps, for the reason that none of us was sexually involved with one
another. Min had a sweet boyfriend, most exotically Korean, who lived
in Ennismore Gardens. When they eventually broke up, Min sighed,
"Ennis-no-more Gardens."

Seduced in part by his crisply modern photographic studio with a narrow, banister-free spiral staircase he'd designed and made, I had a very

brief romance with Tony Armstrong-Jones, somewhat one-sided on my part as Tony, who was dazzlingly attractive, had other irons in the fire, especially the flowerlike Chinese actress Jacqui Chan, soon to star in *The World of Suzie Wong*. I found my own thespian in the lean beefcake form of Alfred Lynch, an endearingly monosyllabic young actor who starred in Willis Hall's *The Long and the Short and the Tall*. Deeply in love, I gave him a Maria Callas LP, my most precious possession at the time. Even so sacrificial a present couldn't pry him from his lifelong lover.

Paul Getty's big ball at Sutton Place at around this time was the first really grand party I went to as a bona fide Old Etonian deb's delight. It was in the huge mansion formerly belonging to the dukes of Sutherland that Paul had appropriately filled with tapestries, and refectory tables glittering with an inordinate amount of silver gilt. Tudor portraits hung on the walls, and an enormous marquee provided lavish food and drink, but what most people were fixated on was the fact that Paul Getty was said to be so stingy that he didn't provide cigarettes, and spent much of the evening circling the famous coin-operated phone box, conspicuous in the hall. Chrissy Gibbs decided to get his own back on this perceived tightfistedness by spiriting out one of the table decorations as he left. The trouble was that, with his already extremely discerning eye, he had chosen what turned out to be a very valuable seventeenty-century ewer. The hue and cry that followed actually made the newspapers, and Chrissy rather sheepishly felt it advisable to leave this risky trophy in a phone box outside Woollands, as Harvey Nichols was then, from whence I suppose one of Mr. Getty's agents retrieved it and restored it to the Sutton silver-gilt garniture.

SIMON HAD FOUR QUITE DIFFERENT favorite restaurants. We never went to any others. The Venezia, in a cul-de-sac in Soho, stayed open late—ten thirty!—so if we hurtled from a cinema, we might be in time for their onion-smothered *fegato*. For prematinee lunch or early dinner, there was the Comedy in Panton Street, with what was then thought of as good plain English food. For grander evenings we went to Kettner's, and it was there that Juliet Duff got so cross when Simon unclasped a huge Russian emerald bracelet from her wrist and put it on mine. I say "so cross"— Juliet, who had been brought up never to show emotion, simply said, her eyes darting, "No, Si." The fourth was a brightly lit Formica-furnished cafeteria in the Fulham Road, spitting distance from the Gothic Box. I forget its real name, as it was simply known as "The Smell," probably due to the tinny aroma of every plate slammed onto the clothless tables, none of which cost more than two bob, with bread and butter tuppence extra.

At the Venezia or Kettner's we were often joined by Richard Buckle, one of Simon's closest friends, and a major figure on the ballet scene. He was partly, due to his frequently stinging critical reviews, an enfant terrible, and partly, because of his having been a pallbearer at Nijinsky's funeral, an éminence grise. It transpired that Dicky was the designer of the *Observer* film exhibition where Simon's and my paths had initially crossed, and he had also been the instigator and designer of its precursor, the fabulously beautiful Diaghilev exhibition held at Forbes House a few years before. My as-yet untrained eyes had been sharply focused by its sheer scale and sensuality. One could hardly be surprised that a man of such extraordinary talent would be a friend of Simon's. Dicky lived in a rambling top-floor flat in Henrietta Street, which looked down over both Covent Garden Market—still then in full all-night swing, and the Opera House, nearly nightly in full fig—with innumerable rooms all in a state of permanent chronic untidiness, including plates of food left over from the chaotic dinners he gave almost every evening. He would invite everyone he saw that day; struggling lady artists, handsome young lads, dowager duchesses, visiting Americans—quite a novelty at that time—and the remaining prima ballerinas of Diaghilev's and de Basil's companies would be crammed in among stacks of desiccating rissoles and congealing stews that rested precariously upon rickety finds from the Caledonian Market, and the references, ephemera, paraphernalia, and memento mori of his chosen subject.

Dicky was a brilliant raconteur, and in his slightly dandified voice, which suited the rather-too-tightly-cut clothes that accentuated his pouter-pigeon figure, would enthrall his guests long after the flower sellers below had swept up and the only all-night pub in England had locked its engraved-glass doors.

Added to his piquant critiques for the *Observer*, Dicky wrote the authoritative works on dance, and biographies of several major dancers. His only exception to these was a title-dripping history of his one grand ancestor, a Miss Dawson Damer—a work of deep snobbery that led one exhausted reviewer to write, simply, "Phew!" In contemporary life, however, Dicky preferred the male kiss of a rougher blanket, and thus was hopelessly enamored of a married youth. For one night only Benny had danced on the other side of the footlights, inducing in Dicky a lifetime of histrionics, for which a moment in the mouth had been but fleeting gratification. This agonized yearning made me think that, though I was—and am still, I hope—a romantic, it was preferable not to expose oneself to such masochistic emotions.

It's very hard, from this long distance, to describe the attitude to homosexuality as it was in my youth. I don't think my parents or many of their friends thought it was actually wrong or immoral—after all, so many of their circle were queer, and they tacitly accepted it—but certainly there were those who were appalled at the thought. What was considered bad was finding attractive, let alone having sex with, men (and for that matter women, too, to an extent) outside one's own class.

The enormous shock waves of "the Montagu Case," in which Edward, Lord Montagu, Michael Pitt-Rivers, and Peter Wildeblood were sent to prison on the skewed evidence of two Boy Scouts, and the prosecution of John Gielgud for soliciting, cannot be overestimated. Homosexuals were not then the cozy queens they became later or the ubiquitous figures lauded by the public as they are now.

But its illegality and the necessity of camouflage did make homosexuality more interesting and, I hate to say it, fun. There was that rush of pleasure in discovering someone was queer. Also, then it was rather déclassé to have sex with people immediately, even if you fancied them. There was still a kind of courtship ritual, which has since totally disappeared. Just as in heterosexual relationships of the time, one sent anyone to whom one was attracted a letter, arranged a meeting, went out to dinner, eyes meeting in the candlelight.

I suppose it's almost impossible for people now to believe that there were only a handful of gay—not that the word was used—clubs in London. The best known was the Rockingham, owned by the suave, genial Toby Rowe. Situated in the basement of a grubby tenement in Archer Street, and thus handy for all the Shaftesbury Avenue theater stage doors, the scruffiness of the entrance and stairs gave no hint of the piss-elegance within. All gilt and crystal chandeliers and wall lights, silk drapes and tassels, velvet furnishing and fringes, the Rockingham's decor was like that for almost any play being performed within the radius of a few hundred yards, an *echt* Noël Coward drawing-room comedy.

Which indeed it was, as the Master, mahogany brown with eerily white teeth, would frequently be standing by the piano, Scotch and friends at hand, laughing encouragingly with the extremely handsome pianist, a young South African named Jon Bannenberg. To Noël's immense frustration, Jon was married to the truly beautiful Maggie, a leggy model in the Holly Golightly mold, and went on to become the world's leading yacht designer.

The Rockingham had an impressive membership, which I doubt any club since has rivaled. Simon said he had once taken Anthony Eden. It was there one met the most interesting people of that world: actors, directors, writers, designers, and what were known as "visiting firemen," foreigners, usually Americans, and usually in show business. Among these was Jerome Lawrence, who took me to see Bea Lillie in *Auntie Mame,* the play made from the book that had staunched my tears when sailing away from Raymond Foster and New York.

Not far from the Rockingham was the A & B, a poky first-floor venue overlooking Gerard Street in Soho's Chinatown, which then looked the way I imagined a run-down area of Hong Kong to be and not, as now, self-consciously Orientalized. The main attraction was a brilliantly witty cabaret by the superb drag act Rogers and Starr. On the nights they were appearing, it was literally impossible to move in the smoke-filled room, because for every queen and queen's moll, let alone quite a few straights, this genius couple with their beautifully written songs, hilarious parodies, and wonderful couture dresses were essential watching. They became so popular that they performed at small theaters around London. The newest Rogers and Starr revue was eagerly awaited and never disappointed. I went to one with Michael Duff, who asked them if they would perform for the Queen Mother. Sadly Rogers died before this could happen. The Cake, Michael's nickname for Queen Elizabeth, would surely have loved them.

Bars and pubs alike shut up tight at 11:00 p.m., and at 10:30 p.m. on Sundays. Very few restaurants stayed open till then; public transport began to close down soon after. The streets became practically deserted, but if one saw anyone around Piccadilly, it was likely to be either heroin addicts, like the tiny blond 1930s hangover Brenda Dean Paul, on their way to Boots for a nightly ration, an actor or dancer "relaxing" after a performance, or a club leaver on the cruise. At this time, too, London was often a miasma of yellow-green fog, the infamous peasoupers, which gave the streets a very thrilling atmosphere. People, indeed cars and buses, would suddenly appear from nowhere, wreathed in chiffonlike eddies of fog as they moved, and as suddenly be gone, swallowed into the murky night. One evening we were driving at a snail's pace around Hyde Park Corner in one of the thickest of these fogs with the racehorse-loving and racy Lady Petre, whose languid "Mayfair Cockney" drawl gave her very camp humor an added fillip. We were on our way to one of the first of John Aspinall's "floating" roulette evenings. Gambling was still illegal at the time, and before the laws were changed and John started the casinos that eventually blossomed into the Clermont Club in a magnificent William Kent mansion in Berkeley Square (leasing the basement to Mark Birley for eight pounds a week to start his nightclub, Annabel's), he would "borrow" houses from friends, and the word would be circulated to a small clique of heavy punters for the venue of the next of these top-secret gaming nights.

With the car almost stationary by Constitution Arch due to the density of the fog, a flashlight beam suddenly haloed Peggy Petre's silver blond hair, followed by a helmeted head of the law at the window. Peggy leaned out as the cop bent to address her and, clasping his cheeks in her hands, cried, "Lily, *Dar*ling!" and planted a crimson lipstick imprint on the astonished officer's mouth. Then, foot down, she gunned the car into the curtain of cotton wool surrounding Belgrave Square and John's candlelit illicit game.

Another club, Leon Maybanke's Calabash, was a more amateur affair, in a little studio house off the Fulham Road, its interior as kitsch as the name might imply. The clientele was light-years away from the Rockingham's, consisting mainly of the emergent "Chelsea-look" boys, myself included, wearing narrow black trousers, pointed boots, and tieless white shirts. Leon fancied himself a photographer, even publishing a book containing portraits of his clients such as Anne Bancroft, Victor Spinetti, and Brendan Behan. He included one of Min, which we thought was the height of fame.

There was also Claire's, in the same street as Kettner's, a sleazy dive run by an old theatrical Jewess. It seemed thrillingly naughty to its devotees like myself and Christopher Gibbs and our great friend from Paris, Rod Coupe, for being open, once one had gained Claire's trust, after hours. There, late in the night, some of Claire's less salubrious friends from the East End—gangsters and their flick-knife-carrying boys—would gather to discuss how the evening's extortions had gone.

There was one tiny gay coffee bar, the Mousehole, in Swallow Street, where dark-eyed and curly-haired foreign waiters gathered before and after mealtimes. It was here I met David and Graham, two pretty, amusing boys working in the fashion business who were openly gay and living together, which seemed romantic and brave in so young a couple. With them I would go to the Two 1's, becoming known as the "new" music venue, just up the road in Old Compton Street, where Tommy Hicks, about to be renamed Steele, and Terry Nelhams, soon to be Adam Faith, produced unfamiliar sounds from strange-shaped electric guitars. I fancied Lionel Bart, a stocky Jewish composer, his tight suits as glossy as his close-cut hair, plotting his musical *Oliver* and engrossed in talent or trade spotting. More bravely, I'd go to the two Soho pubs where bohemians gathered, the French Pub or the Coach and Horses, joining writers like Colin MacInnes, no doubt garnering material for his novel *Absolute Beginners,* and Simon Raven, or filmmaker John Sutro and the louche-eyed and lank-haired young Mark Sykes, father of Plum and Lucy, whose famously bad behavior, amusing and even endearing while he was still young, eventually became unbearable and embarrassing. It was a relief when he was shipped out to Australia.

ONE SUMMER, the summer we were all singing along to "Tell Laura I Love Her," a Sunday lunchtime club was started by Patrick Walker in Tachbrook Street in Victoria. Drinking in a garden in daylight with a lot of boys was a novel experience, but a frisson was added to the atmosphere by the rumor that Patrick had pushed a famous astrologer, Celeste, who'd lived on the top floor, down the stairs to get her job on *Queen* magazine. Certainly Patrick became a stargazer, for some time continuing Celeste's column, and eventually becoming highly esteemed under his own name.

Bunny would ask me to join him for lunch in the Spanish Bar, a small restaurant with embossed-leather decor hidden in the depths of Fortnum & Mason, where he went nearly every day. Its largely homosexual clientele treated it almost like a club, and strangers were given swift critical appraisal. Once a very willowy young man appeared on the stairs. Bunny pursed his perfectly powdered cheeks. "There!" he said. "I *told* you I could smell scent." I too became a regular, and often at midday on Saturdays, before it closed, Frank and Victor, a sweet couple who looked like a handsome version of Laurel and Hardy, and ran it, would slip me all the leftover game pies and smoked salmon for my weekend sustenance. It was in the Spanish Bar that I first met the completely charming Liberace. "Please call me Lee," he said when I wished him success in his libel case against Cassandra, the homophobic columnist of the *Daily Mirror,* who had written the then-damning phrase that the world's best-selling pianist was "a quivering fruit-flavored, ice-covered heap of mother-love." Lee did win, striking a mortal blow at such prejudice in the gutter press.

When the Spanish Bar was threatened with a store-replanning closure, Min and I got up a campaign to save it, and we bearded Fortnum & Mason's owner, Garfield Weston, on the shop floor. He was incandescent with Canadian priggishness, but in spite of Nigel Dempster Diary running it, the Spanish Bar was ripped apart. Mr. Weston's daughter recently told me the real reason was not replanning but his hatred of this nest of dirty homosexuals in his otherwise immaculate store. Bunny moved his business to amalgamate with Hardy Amies, and Frank and Victor disappeared, though dear Mr. Lunn, a tiny, blue-rinsed, pink-powdered busybody, naturally known as Sally, because of the dainty Sally Lunn cakes, who was in charge of the grocery floor, managed to escape Weston's cull.

There were no dedicatedly gay pubs, as now, but some were known haunts. The most famous of these was the Grenadier, tucked away behind Hyde Park Corner. Here a fiver would get you a night with an obliging Guardsman. Across the pretty little mews lived the film director Brian Desmond Hurst. Brian's big room was done up in a Syrie Maugham–meets-Tudor style, with dark paneling, gnarled beams, white sofas on white carpets and polar-bear skin. Suits of armor stood in corners, helmets and swords hung on walls. It seemed extremely glamorous, especially as in this Ruritanian setting one was likely to be talking to the major English film stars Margaret Lockwood, Dennis Price, or the exquisitely beautiful Sally Gray, famous for having the Warsaw Concerto written for her in *Dangerous Moonlight*.

It was at one of Brian's parties that I met David Webster, who had recently been made director of the Royal Opera House. This appointment was apparently something of a surprise, as theretofore David had been merely manager of a northern department store, Bon Marché, and thus his nickname was the Bon Marschallin, after the soprano role in *Der Rosenkavalier*. David shared a house, 39 Weymouth Street, with Jimmy Cleveland Bell. Modern, it had an enormous double-height drawing room in which they held open house after the opera, with the major singers attending—it was David who had persuaded Callas to Covent Garden for her legendary Tosca.

David and Jimmy had taken a house on Capri for the summer, and asked if I'd like to go to stay with them. To Capri? Wow. With my mother I'd been sailing at Burnham-on-Crouch or seeing the sights in New York and Paris. With my father I had visited, rather hating being alone with him, the more educational of historic towns: Bruges, Brussels, and Florence. I had never been to the south of France, never seen the Mediterranean. Capri! It was, then, pre–Saint-Tropez, pre-Marbella, pre-Ibiza, pre-anywhere, *the* place to go. Still rather disreputable—Norman Douglas's *South Wind* seeing to that—yet elegant, thanks to the onyx-eyed American beauty Mona Harrison Williams, whose style and chic had been drilled into me by Cecil and Simon. By now she was blissfully remarried to an adoring Count Eddie Bismarck, with whom she had created a house and garden of which guests spoke lyrically. Even in London girls were wearing Capri pants, smart young men were just discovering the skinny flat sandals made in the piazza on the island, and we were all humming along to the hits of the summer, Domenico Modugno singing "Volare" and "Ciao, Ciao, Bambina."

I went by train, alone, to Naples. It cost about twelve lire, took three days, and, *pace* Mussolini, arrived several hours late, at three in the morning. At that hour there were no ferries to Capri. No one to even ask where the ferry went from. In fact, no one anywhere to ask anything. I wandered, half asleep. Where? I remember grass and trees and water on one side, a high wall on the other. I heard a car slow, saw it stop. Two tanned young men, one crew cut, one tousled, both blond, both wearing startlingly white shirts, jumped out. *"Wohin gehen Sie?. . . Wie heisst du, mein lieber Schatz?"*

"I'm Hans," said the crew cut. We drove, not far, just up above the wall, where, in a long garden of orange trees and jasmine, with ice-cold wine and delicious things to eat, we talked. Then, in a cool white room, I slept in Hans's bronzed arms. He took me to the ferry early the next morning. "Give David my regards." He smiled as he dropped me. I turned. "So you know him?" But Hans had driven off.

The ferry, its cargo complete, clanked away from the quay, out into the bay, the famous Bay of Naples that no one should die without seeing ("See Maples and buy," had been the slogan for the furniture store). Above it Vesuvius—*Vesuvius!*—a purple backdrop to the city, a plume above it. Smoke? *Could* it be smoke? Ahead, across a dark blue sea, a glittering white rock; as we drew closer it dissolved into peaks and ravines, then trees and houses, and suddenly, in an azure bay, a jetty, a village, flowers, people. Capri.

Am I making this up? Did Capri then have huge black open cars, with a folded leathery hood behind the passengers? Were they driven to the Quisisana, to Anacapri, to the Blue Grotto, by little bent old men in salt-stained chauffeur's caps? Was it in one of those that I was taken, up those impossibly narrow, impossibly twisty roads, the sea darker and farther below at each heart-stopping bend, to David and Jimmy's house?

At lunch I told about my adventure. "Hans?" said David. "What Hans?" I said I thought his other name was Henser or something.

"*No!* It's not possible!" Gasps of disbelief. My Neapolitan savior was none other than Hans Werner Henze, the most admired young classical composer in the world, whose ballet *Ondine* was about to premiere at Covent Garden.

Hans came over a few days later, but my attention was riveted on Gracie Fields, in whose restaurant, La Canzone del Mare, we were having lunch. It seemed impossible to believe that this quivering-chinned mountain of a woman had been the toast of interwar Britain, though, when she called a command to her latest husband, Boris Alperovici, or leaned over the balcony of her house just above where we were eating to give us an impromptu rendition of "Sally"—"Sall-ee, Sallee, pride of our all-ee" (the memory of Sersee humming it in the kitchen at Hundridge)—the voice still had a piercing poignancy.

That next evening David took Hans and me, in a little fast boat, to the bleaker neighboring Ischia, to visit an older, more reticent composer: William Walton, who had written *Belshazzar's Feast,* and his chatterbox young Argentine wife, Susana. Walton wore clothes appropriate to a London banker, while the most vibrant of Emilio Pucci's prints set off Susana's strong bronzed features and shining dark gray hair, profiled against the purple evening like a Cretan coin. She had just started to create a garden in this dusty earth. Sparse, thirsty-looking plants nestled among the prickly-pear cactus, a labor of love and determined will that has now matured into a positive jungle. Returning on the silver-splashed black water under a melon moon, John Cavanagh, a famous young dress designer, who boasted Lena Horne among his clientele, and whom I had been thrilled to meet, kissed me, tenderly and sedately, on the mouth. I told Jimmy Cleveland Bell.

"What's John's kiss like? Don't tell me, I can guess—it's navy blue, cut on the bias, and has two perfect seams."

Another night, in another restaurant, I was introduced to a hugely fat man in a dinner jacket, his round face topped by a plum-colored fez. It was King Farouk of Egypt, now an exile in Rome, and his nightclub-singer mistress, who continually popped candied fruit into the king's small pulpy mouth. We asked them to join our table, and considering how shoddily the British had treated him, he was charm itself. But not a trace remained of the arrow-thin, aquiline, fair-haired beauty he had been as a subaltern at Sandhurst, just before his marriage to Princess Fawzia, the Shah's sister. This sweet-natured, much-maligned man, the pawn of his mother, wily Egyptian intriguers, and the British High Commissioner, Sir Miles Lampson, though the butt of a million jokes, retained exquisite manners and a certain dignity in the last years of his bizarre, Arabian Nights–like life.

Traveling back to London on the train, I reflected that in almost heedlessly setting out on this summer adventure, so young, so green, so only nineteen, I had reaped a harvest of knowledge, pleasure, and experience that would reward me for years to come.

———

AMONG THE MOST frequent guests at Bunny's dinners were John and Vere French, an endearingly affected but ultimately adorable couple. John, tall and thin as a telegraph pole, habitually dressed in black-and-white-checked trousers and black jacket with a black knitted tie, was the most famous fashion photographer in London. His photographs, featuring a stable of tall *racée*-looking models like Bronwen Pugh, Paulene Stone, Jean Dawnay (who became, in turn, Lady Astor, Mrs. Laurence Harvey, and Princess George Galitzine), Roz Watkins, and Jill Kennington, appeared every few days in the *Daily Express,* at the time the most avant-garde newspaper in Britain. They had a bandbox-fresh sex-free allure, John insisting that his girls always wear hats and white gloves, posing with forefinger pressed to pouting lips as if keeping a secret, or gazing wistfully at a long-stemmed rose.

John had a retiring demeanor and barely spoke above a whisper, as opposed to Vere, whose native and anything-but-lilting West of Ireland brogue had years ago been edged out by a swooping intercontinental inflection during her years as a more mature model in Paris. She would frequently refer to her mentor, "Skap." I was too stupid to realize she meant the great couturiere Elsa Schiaparelli. But where John could seem a touch refined, Vere was always hilariously self-deprecating. "It's not true that when I was a gel, there were green fields round Harrods."

The Frenches, who quickly became close friends, lived in a bijou house off Edgware Road, with an olde-worlde curiosity-shop bow window in the drawing room (and an enormous black poodle), only a few minutes' walk from the flat I had recently found in Marylebone. I would often go for dinner, even if they kept a rather meager table.

"Father," as Vere always called John, "is a very clever carver. He can get six people off a small chicken." Vere once telephoned to say she was cooking "a *splendid* fish," as she had been to Richards, the well-known Soho fish shop. The slogan for a fashion label John often photographed, also called Richards, was "Such Clever Clothes." John asked Vere where she had found something so delicious. "Richards," she answered. John whispered, "Such clever fish."

If the Frenches were frugal nutritionally, they were unbelievably generous with their knowledge of the things that fascinated me—films, music, fashion—and with introducing me to their friends. But in fact it was one of John's studio assistants who was to be the most influential person they brought to my life. One day John invited me to go and watch him work at his immaculate studios in Clerkenwell. There, among the vast rolls of off-white paper that were his trademark backgrounds, the racks of dresses, the models doing their own hair and makeup, the popping, fizzing lamps shielded by black umbrellas, was a trio of lads who dashed about pulling key lights into position, adjusting shutters, preparing cameras, weighting skirts. Eventually, once John had flipped a girl's pageboy, concertina'd a glove, tweaked a collar, and, satisfied, whispered, "Now," one of them would push the button to take the photograph. Of these boys, one was tall and big, with wild black hair. His name was Terence, he said, or Tel, Donovan. Another was slight, his face framed by sandy Napoleonic curls. This was Brian Duffy. The third—stranger, more distant—looked at me from under his thick fringe, his eyes smudged with dark lashes, his look an impudent Mowgli. He was the most junior of the trio, and earning merely three pounds a week. I fell in love with David Bailey instantly. Within a few days we were inseparable.

David was like the Gypsies, or the boys I had noticed manning the carousels and bumper cars at Bertram Mills' Circus that my parents would take me to as a childhood Christmas treat. There was nothing smooth or brought-up-proper about him. He was unruly, though he had wonderful, innate good manners and a sense of style. David Bailey crystallized for the first time exactly the way I wanted to look, though in his earliest portrait of me I seem more like a moth-eaten version of the determinedly underdressed Jarvis Cocker.

David was the archetypal London Mod, and within days my hair was cut like his. I was being fitted for boxy suits by Bilgorri, an Italian-Jewish tailor in Liverpool Street, and taking the bus to a shoe stall in Brixton Market to buy "winkle pickers," the exaggeratedly pointed footwear that, teamed with a checked shirt worn buttoned and tieless, was de rigueur for completing the look.

David seemed to be in constant motion. He traveled light, unlike Simon and his beloved, familiar clutter at the Gothic Box; a satchel and a scooter, and as soon as he could afford it, a camera, were all he needed to start him on his starry ascent. David lived with his parents, Bert and Glad, in East Ham. The East End's bomb-torn buildings crumbled cheek by jowl with the scrubbed steps of the Baileys' terrace. I had somehow managed to cadge the cash out of my father to buy that ultimate accessory for my Mod transformation, a Vespa GS, and together we would zoom up there, igniting in me a passion for the area and its people. He was so utterly different from any of my Etonian friends. The enchanting thing about my friendship with David was that we instantly accepted each other's vastly different backgrounds. While he opened my eyes to pints and pies and Cockney banter, I was longing to introduce him to Simon, whose acquaintance with the East End had so far been divided between visiting Hawksmoor churches and cruising seamen's hostels. Simon was thrilled to meet this bright young Cockney barbarian. With his customary perspicacity, Simon could tell that David was going to be the next big thing.

We would go to the Duraggon pub, where they had drag competitions once a week. The boys were always straight, but they loved putting on their glad rags, dressing as Marlene Dietrich, Rita Hayworth, or more currently, Alma Cogan, "the girl with a laugh in her voice." Their mothers, making a small port and lemon last the whole evening, sat proudly in the front row. Next to them were Brylcreemed gangsters in black-on-black suits and white-on-white shirts. Thanks to some Cockney connection, David actually knew the already infamous Kray brothers, and created a literary sensation by bringing one to Francis Wyndham's soirées.

There were always girls—David was a magnet for the new mascara-eyed, beehived "dollybirds" who had sprung up across the dance halls of the capital. We would smoke endless Capstans while they buffed their nails or took to the dance floor together, dancing to the by-now-commonplace rock 'n' roll, coyly throwing glances across the room to measure the impression they were making. Eventually we would join them to swig a Tizer or, more daringly, a Lemon Hart rum or the pathetic English version of hardly known Coke, Kitty Cola. Rarely, if ever, did we get them on the dance floor, though they would continue eyeing up David all night. But whatever the distractions, David was a steadfast friend. He wouldn't abandon me to get back to the West End alone, even if this sometimes meant I had to snatch a few hours' sleep on the settee in Bert and Gladys's front room. I introduced David to my hairdresser, Vidal Sassoon, at whose David Hicks–designed black-and-chrome salon the heads of all the prettiest people in town were being snipped and shaped into his signature angular style. David photographed Min's jaw-skimming Vidal bob for a Sassoon advertisement.

On one of those evenings in the East End, I'd met a lively Mod boy called Peter Phillips, whose mop of hair tumbled over his jagged features. My scooter was a passport to a somewhat one-sided romance with him—he was, perhaps, my own private version of David. Peter lived with his family in a scruffy street off Caledonian Road, still dotted with the last vestiges of the antique shops where thirty years earlier my father and Geoffrey Scott had found much of the furniture for Hundridge. Waiting for Peter to perfect his all-important toilette, I'd search these by-now-junky shops, having just rented an unfunished upper-floor room near Marylebone High Street from an orange-haired harridan landlady named Mrs. Klass ("Lower," as she was instantly dubbed). Just around the corner was Hinde House, where the author Rose Macaulay, small and pale as an ivory saint, lived in white-bookshelved, cretonne-curtained rooms. I was occasionally asked to the dauntingly learned afternoon parties this literary lioness was famed for holding.

MY FLAT WAS a mere five-minute scoot to my new job at Geographical Projects in Soho. This tiny company, part owned by my father, had the novel idea of publishing 3-D atlases, and my hardly taxing "work" consisted of carving mountains and valleys out of table-size layers and slabs of soap, which were then appropriately colored, photographed, and bound into what were at the time daringly contemporary-looking books. My boss was a very pretty and mild-seeming young redhead named Harriet Cole, married to an even milder young ceramist, though I soon had to be let into the secret of her rip-roaring affair with a much grander potter, the Marquess of Queensberry, great-grandson of Oscar Wilde's tormentor. This was the first illicit romance I had been party to, and I was oddly proud of keeping their secret, which extended to the dramatic pretense of not recognizing Harriet when I saw the lovers in public.

Peter, who, like most boys at the time, was inspired by the heroes of the moment, my friends David Bailey and Terence Donovan, wanted to be, and indeed did become, a photographer. He would hang around in Soho till I could get away from the soap tables, when we would press our noses against the windows of a shop in Shaftesbury Avenue that sold impossibly technical, impossibly expensive Leicas, Hasselblads, and Rolleiflexes. After eating at the Soup Kitchen, a cheap restaurant recently opened by a young entrepreneur called Terence Conran, we would go to coffee bars where earnest young boys played a new sound, skiffle, or to a racy club in Gerard Street, the Condor, which had double beds instead of seats.

In spite of Peter's completely contemporary way of life, he was charmingly intrigued by my older friends like Bunny Roger or John and Vere French, and the old movies that we all loved and discussed ad nauseam. Hearing that Marlene Dietrich was appearing at the Olympia in Paris, Peter, longing to see Paris rather than Marlene, urged me to arrange going to see her. How it happened I don't remember, but we had seats in a box practically onstage, and Marlene would come and stand, kicking out the long flowing train of her white fox coat, within inches of us at the end of each song, sometimes putting her white-gloved, diamond-bracelet-encrusted arm on the rail of our box. I felt I had truly trounced my father for forbidding my mother, on the grounds of Marlene's sexiness, to take me to see her at the Café de Paris. And I had been intensely jealous when my brother Michael's astonishingly rich—from an Australian pig-iron fortune—girlfriend, Barbara Stanley-Smith, had had Marlene *as the cabaret,* if you please, at her lavish coming-out ball. In Paris my first vision of her in the flesh, where I was able to witness the extraordinary professionalism of her act, let alone her breathtaking if somewhat manufactured beauty, ensconced her at the top of my pantheon of idols. I was to see her perform in many far-flung venues, from Puerto Rico to Kingsway, and eventually to meet her, but that evening with Peter at the Olympia remains unrivaled for sheer glamour.

Though the Thayer Street flat was only one room with a bathroom-cum-kitchen (imagine, now!), in which the longed-for monkey, a little gray rhesus, added to the general hygiene, it was my first essay into contemporary decor. I painted the whole place greige, the color my parents called "Elephant's Breath," with white curtains and black floor and furniture. For pictures I faked some big Pierre Soulages canvases, the hot artist of the decade. Even David Hicks, who had clearly inspired it, was complimentary, and indeed, on his first visit, we got immediately into the black bed, which at least "coordinated" with the black rubber suits he insisted we wear. Cliff Richard, "England's Elvis," must have lived locally, as I sometimes saw him from my tiny iron balcony, surrounded by fans as he walked blithely down the pavement signing autograph books.

Bronwen Pugh, the statuesque Welsh television newsreader turned by John French into a supermodel, whom I'd meet at the nearby flat of the quixotic young filmmaker Donald Cammell ("The shit of the desert," as some wag tagged him) and rather fallen in love with, would come for the suppers I was beginning to learn how to make delicious, sometimes bringing her ancient admirer, the scaly archaeologist Sir Mortimer Wheeler.

My friendship with Bronwen became stronger despite her frequent lengthy assignments in Paris as the star for the French couturier Pierre Balmain, who named her, entirely appropriately, Bella. She was certainly the belle of the ravishing high-summer ball that Felix Harbord decorated for his Huntley & Palmer biscuit-fortune-heiress niece at Crowther's, the antique garden statuary dealers with huge premises next to Syon House, the Adam mansion on the Thames. Bronwen and I went together, and whether it had been arranged or was mere happenstance, Bronwen found Bill Astor on her other side at dinner. Pretty soon they were dancing, and for the rest of the evening were never out of each other's arms. A few months after this meeting Bron married Bill, and very soon after that they asked me to stay at Cliveden, Bill's enormous house on the Thames near Maidenhead.

I drove there one Friday afternoon with Peter Coats, who had become much more approachable since the death of his lover Chips Channon and his move from the grand Belgrave Square mansion to a charming flat in the Albany. Peter insisted we visit, on the way, an elderly Australian friend of his, Winnie Portarlington, a name that meant nothing to me, in her house near Ascot. This all sounded pretty dull, but reluctantly I agreed.

Merely the approach to Earlywood, Lady Portarlington's estate, would have been worth the journey. The forerunner of many that it influenced, Earlywood was my first experience of a green, gray, and white garden, the myriad greens of lawns rushing to darker hedges and trees, the gray of foliage, of stone paths studded with pebbles, of plinths bearing urns tumbling white flowers onto beds of white flowers. The house itself, warm stone in a faintly French style, gave no hint of the beauties within, for, at the door, Winnie, herself an immaculate figure in gray linen and cashmere, had varied the style from subtly European to even subtler Oriental. Sofas reflected their subdued grays in polished oak floorboards smelling of the sea, chairs hovered above cubistic Marion Dorn carpets, reflected in tall, unadorned brown coromandel lacquer screens. Pale brown-mauve porcelain cylinders held boughs of white orchids; on low purple-brown tables, bowls of silvery potpourri. It was the embryo of a style of decoration that was to become so achingly clichéd—but not for a half century, which demonstrates the advanced eye of this tiny, thin, chic woman. Years later I would hear famous decorators enviously describe Winnie Portarlington's taste, and feel gratified that, after this initial introduction, she had invited me back to Earlywood, and to her minute but equally stylish mews flat near Sloane Square.

Peter Coats was barely able to tear me away from this magical house, but half an hour later we turned in to the gates of Cliveden. Though certainly impressive in their *richissime,* the grounds, with tumultuously flowered borders rising to ranks of rhododendron, were totally the opposite of Earlywood. We circled a vast fountain, its cavorting creatures carved of meat-pink marble, before the last long stretch of drive to the palatial facade. The new Lady Astor, wearing an unusually shapeless mustard-colored country suit, met us in the vast pseudo-baronial hall. It was strange to see her pouring tea amid tables bearing publications like the *Farmer and Stockbreeder,* and the *Tractor News,* rather than *Jardin des Modes* or *L'Officiel.*

Bronwen introduced me to the many other probably famous weekend guests. I remember only Rory and Romana McEwen. They were a spellbinding couple. Romana, a wide-cheeked beauty with a gurgling, faintly American-accented voice, and a muted tartan sash around her handspan waist; unconventionally long, dark blond hair framed Rory's dancing eyes and smiling mouth, his long legs enhanced by narrow trousers of the same tartan. As one they looked me up and down, from the Vidal Sassoon haircut, the boxy Whitechapel suit, to the pointed Brixton Market shoes. "Look, Ro," said Rory, crying with laughter. "Winkle pickers!!!" They called me Winkle that weekend, and for much of the next year, during which they became close, beloved friends.

However rich the Astors, however grand and gilded the Cliveden salons, however luxe the food served in them, the upstairs arrangements were curiously spartan. Probably Rory and Romana, as relations, had a pale yellow, fringed, buttoned, and tasseled satin suite, but single gentlemen's quarters were narrow bedrooms off school-like corridors, not very near a huge communal washroom, and far above the main rooms. The hard mattress in my room did not, however, stop me having a little rest before dinner. Nor from sleeping. I slept through the dressing gong, through the dinner gong. A footman was sent to wake me, and I hit the dinner table just as an elaborate soufflé was being brought into the astonishing blue-and-gold French boiserie'd dining room. Bronwen motioned me to my place, accompanied by Rory's muttered, "Well done, Wink," and I was relieved to find the soufflé was the entrée rather than the pudding. I hadn't entirely blotted my copybook in this aristocratic, ruling-the-country company. The next morning Bill Astor took us to meet a friend who had a cottage on the estate. His name was Stephen Ward. Within a few months the scandal of his trial and suicide was to bring irredeemable sorrow into Bronwen and Bill's marriage.

· EIGHT ·

Back in London I was starting to go to galleries. One of the most colorful figures of the art scene I was just getting to know was Arthur Jeffress, an American who lived in splendor in Eaton Square, his walls hung with nineteenth-century portraits of aquiline bearded Persian wazirs, whom—had he not been clean-shaven, short, and quite tubby—Arthur, with his big liquid eyes, somewhat resembled. It was considered quite a coup to be asked to dinner by Arthur. Usually all-male parties, they were attended by the minor figures of the art world—the Australian Felix Kelly, or Philippe Julian, a Proust-style Parisian—the kind of painters he showed at his slightly "greenery-yallery" premises in Davies Street.

Up in St. George's Street, Erica Brausen and her small, chic girlfriend ran the Hanover Gallery, where Lucian Freud had his first exhibition. The Hanover girls were the direct continuation of sapphists like Radclyffe Hall, author of the lesbian novel *The Well of Loneliness,* and the painter Una Troubridge. Their set included Madge Garland, then editor of *Vogue,* and her girlfriend, Dorothy Todd. It was said that Osbert Sitwell sent Madge a carved wood garden bench, on the back of which was inscribed in poker-work the legend: "A Garland is a lovesome thing, Todd wot." An early exhibition I saw at the Hanover was Teddy Millington-Drake's first. Teddy, despite being the son of that most prominently upright ambassador, Sir Eugene Millington-Drake, was the prettiest dark-eyed and curled-hair faun with an enchanting lisp, recently released from a short career in the army. His sergeant had shouted, "Youorriblelittlemanwhatsyourname?!" "Teddy, Thir," came the reply.

The work of rather more serious painters such as Victor Pasmore, Ben Nicholson, and David Bomberg could be studied at the Leicester Gallery, while at the Redfern in Cork Street one could see Moore, Hepworth, the naive-genre painter Kit Wood, or that first of the fashionable Australians, Sydney Nolan. This gallery was run by two antipodeans, Harry Tatlock Miller and Rex Nan Kivell. My father had met Harry during one of his visits to his great friend Mari Livingstone in Sydney. Handsome if toothy, he was lively and welcoming, but Rex, round and white, was always said to be a necrophiliac. He had a rather sinister Arab driver-houseboy whom we fantasized looked after such desires.

Knowing it might interest me, Harry would send me information of forthcoming exhibitions. I had already been to one, showing Cecil's sketches of his costume designs for *My Fair Lady,* and had even bought one, the first piece of art I'd ever purchased. A few months later an envelope arrived from the Redfern announcing an exhibition by an artist called Michael Wishart.

A couple of the paintings in the catalog immediately captivated me, especially those portraying little monkeys, some clothed in Gypsy-colored rags, with inquisitive expressions, peering through the silvery white reeds of a flat watery landscape. These images had an astonishing similarity to my memory of the Dumfries organ-grinder's ape, and made me determined to go to the exhibition.

As people arrived I talked to Harry. He pointed out the artist. Michael Wishart, by coincidence, was standing beside one of the monkey paintings, his pale face a contrast to a sheen of floppy black hair and a black corduroy suit. He seemed shy and faintly embarrassed that people were there at all, let alone that they might be genuine admirers of his strange, sad, almost hallucinatory but deeply emotional paintings. I saw him looking at me for a second, his dark eyes darting like lightning, but then he turned away and became merely a silhouette lost in a knot of congratulating friends. I went to look at the other paintings, but the monkeys and their creator were curiously etched into my mind.

THAT SUMMER, with a group of friends, I went for the first time to Saint-Tropez, just beginning its inexorable rise to becoming the preferred destination of the flotsam and jetset, but then still a pretty, unspoiled port. Min was to be there, as her sister, Jane Grinling, had rented a farmhouse in the vineyards, and I knew Suna Portman was planning to arrive at some point that August. As we drove down the old N7, I grew more and more excited as the country changed from lush woods and fields to deep ravines and tumbling rivers to dark mountains and dense forests. When we turned off at Le Luc, following the steep twisting route up to and down from La Garde Freinet, passing the sun-warmed rocks and rosy buildings, the chestnut woods gave way to golden olive groves. Saint-Tropez, despite the fact that we were quartered in a plasticky pension off the backstreets, was a magical mixture of Impressionist vivid color, sun-burnished skin, shimmering water, and film-set fantasy, ridiculously like its film depictions—Brigitte Bardot in *Et Dieu . . . Créa La Femme,* or Jeanne Moreau in *Les Amants.*

Having a ritual *café liégeois* at Senequier after a day at the beach, I saw the longest pair of bare legs ever known sticking up from a passing car. They could only belong to Suna. I yelled. She unwound herself from the backseat, the legs followed by the smallest blue gingham bikini—the invention of Mme Vachon, proprietor of the only clothes shop in the port—and waist-length white-blond hair.

"I'm staying with an artist friend in Ramatuelle, a village up in the hills. Come for a drink tomorrow evening." Suna scribbled a number and address on a napkin. Later she told me she'd casually mentioned the invitation to her host. He'd looked alarmed, and, as he wrote later, replied testily: "You know I dread strangers in my house. Who is whatever-he's-called?"

"Oh, just a boy I used to go down to see at Eton. Says he knows your work. I think you'll like him," Suna had replied.

"I doubt it," was the skeptical response.

I don't remember how I got to Ramatuelle. I can remember changing in the hotel, remember the evening sun sending a blazing reflection off the wall outside, enveloping my miniscule room in its apricot haze. I couldn't possibly have afforded a taxi, so perhaps someone gave me a lift. But I was certainly alone when, after some wrong turnings in the mazelike village, I stepped into the darkening courtyard of a house at its very center.

". . . that evening, at the magic purple hour when my garden assumed an incandescent brilliance in the warm enveloping darkness . . . the youth from the Redfern gallery appeared at my open French windows. Dressed in white, skin tanned, hair burnished, even more seductive than before, he bounced through the dusk like an unpunctual sunbeam, into my room and my life."

These, from his autobiography, *High Diver,* are Michael Wishart's words remembering our second meeting. As he implies, an instant click of recognition made us silent for a several moments. Michael made no special effort for me, hardly glancing in my direction, shutting doors, opening others, moving lamps, bringing glasses. But I would catch his eyes darting toward me, like a dark flash, would see the wisp of a smile break on his face.

There was a clatter on the stairs. Suna, her hair now piled precariously on top of her head, almost fell into the room, carrying a pile of books. "I loved them, Michael, thank you. Especially the Cyril Connolly. Oh, hello—" she gave me a kiss. "Want a drink?" Her long fingers reached around the cocktail shaker Michael had just brought in. "What is it? Oh, yum." She curled her bare legs under a cushion. "Get Michael to show you the view from the roof."

I followed. The doors were open to rooms on haphazard floors, one, a chaos, clearly Suna's; another, bare but for a white bed inside a white gauze netting, had a tumble of bottles and vials on the floor beside the bed. Michael, slightly embarrassed, waved toward them.

"That's Mikey's—you know, Suna's brother. He's in Tangier at the moment." I'd heard of Mikey Portman's reputation for downing every pill he could lay hands on. It was rather thrilling to think that perhaps he did it here, in the house of the man who painted those hallucinatory pictures.

From the terrace warm air spiraled up from the patchwork of roofs the sun had baked all day. Below, outside the village walls, carefully tended fields of vegetables gave way to vines and olives, and thence to the sheer blackness of the forest, pierced here and there by a pale circle of light. Michael pointed. "Somewhere there's the house I lived in with Anne." He sighed. "Let's get a drink." Anne was the wife he had just divorced.

We went back down the shadowy white stairs. While walking on air, I'd failed to pick up three warning signals: melancholy, addiction, guilt.

After more cocktails we were joined by Suna's current boyfriend, Bill Berger, the actor son of Caresse Crosby, an intellectual American woman credited, surprisingly, with inventing the brassiere, and about whom, Michael would later tell me, *Black Sun* was written. They left to go and dine at L'Escale down in the port.

Without either of us expecting it—and I'm not certain, yet, even wanting it—Michael and I were alone. But without asking me, without my needing to be asked, we were walking to his car.

We drove in silence to Gassin, a neighboring hilltop village; were made welcome at its famous restaurant, were led to a table by the parapet of its crowded terrace. Below and beyond, orchestras of cicadas tuned their insistent rasping song, one fading as another took up the theme, each determined to be heard. Beneath a seemingly limitless backdrop of ever-receding mountain ridges, dark valleys fell away to the pewter sea; clusters of footlights edged the distant shoreline.

I looked and listened. The conjuror of this magical vista was talking. "The bracelet is Sainte-Maxime, and then another, which is Fréjus, then a necklace, which is the Esterel, and beyond that a tiara, which is Cannes. That's much too pretty a word to describe such an unpretty town, though there are some amusing bars there. We will go. I dislike tiaras unless they are papal ones. Do you?" he asked.

Until Michael explained that popes' crowns were so called, I had thought of a tiara only as being the thing I'd drawn for my *Breakfast at Tiffany's* party. This was the first example of the esoteric knowledge that threaded all Michael's conversation, and it was fascinating.

Staying, talking, listening till late, Michael insisting on a last bottle of the sepia pink local wine. "The best is made just down there"—he gestured beyond the far side of the village—"by Prince Napoleon, a direct descendant of that little emperor. There's another who lives right out on the Cap at the far end of Pampelonne. We are surrounded by *arrivistes*." I must have looked puzzled, for there followed a succinct explanation of imperial as opposed to royal, French titles. Detailed knowledge of such arcane subjects, of the romantic past, was something I would find increasingly attractive in Michael.

Around midnight Michael hurtled his black Citroën down the ninety-degree bends toward Saint-Tropez. As we came into a flat valley Michael, drunk with the rush of love, I think, as much as with wine, suddenly veered crazily off the narrow road onto the rough grass, weaving wildly between the chestnut trees. I managed to stay calm at this unexpected (and I hoped untypical) display of machismo. When he dropped me at my hotel I thanked him, adding, "Golly, you drive well." Michael later wrote that those words made him feel as though he'd been thrown out of an airplane. He drove, very carefully for the first time in years, back up to Ramatuelle.

A few days later I had to return to London. He wrote me tender and ever more flattering letters that were designed, as he admitted, "to act as a lasso." They succeeded. Within weeks I returned to Ramatuelle, and Michael.

With no good reason to be in London—no soap-carving job any longer—for the next couple of years I was to spend all the time I could in Ramatuelle or Paris or traveling with this godsend of a guide. Michael had lived in the Var for some years while married to Anne Dunn, one of the many daughters of the Canadian metal magnate Sir James Dunn. Both were accomplished artists. Michael had been among the leading lights in the burgeoning art scene of 1950s London, his friends the major painters Lucian Freud, Francis Bacon, and the Scottish duo Colquhoun and McBride. In Paris, which he knew from his early teens, he joined the circle of artists such as Sam Francis and Pierre Tal-Coat, the poet/lovers Jean-Pierre Lacloche and Olivier Larronde, and the famed opium-eating

Denham Fouts, a fatally beautiful man from Florida of whom many diverse characters, including King Paul of Greece, Lord Tredegar, and Truman Capote, and the very young Michael, had been enamored.

In Paris the buzzword they heard everywhere was of the unspoiled beauty of the un-smart part of the Riviera, the warmth and wildness and lambent light of the Saint-Tropez peninsula, for while the port had been lived in and admired by painters and writers as early as the 1800s, the shore and hills remained untrammeled. Michael and Anne immediately fell in love with the area and, taking their newborn son, Francis, moved to Saint-Tropez. Initially renting fishermen's cottages or cramped flats, they eventually found the remote Domaine Pascati hidden in cork-oak forests high above the Plage de Pampelonne, at the time bare of buildings of any kind, let alone the buttock-cheek-by-lifted-jowl plethora of parasols and restaurants of today. Cannes, with its alluring bars and casino, was a day's drive along the endlessly twisting coastal corniche, while dusty one-lane roads led west to Aix-en-Provence and, farther, Arles.

Despite life in these elysian fields, the marriage began to fall apart, not least due to Michael's irregularly controlled intolerance to alcohol, and his desire for opium and the other unchemical drugs he had acquired during his youth in Paris. Divorced, Anne continued to live with Francis at Pascati. To be near his son, Michael bought a house in a nearby hilltop hamlet, Ramatuelle. Almost in the center of a cobweb of medieval alleys, the house lay wrapped around a tangle of garden. Camellias formed a shady canopy, palm trees towered to the sky above, level with the topmost gray-shuttered windows. A cool stone arcade led to low rooms, their rough walls washed white with uneven terra-cotta-tiled floors, the furniture crumbling *provenciale*—the perfect backdrop for Michael's highly charged and deeply romantic paintings. His rooftop bedroom opened onto the distant sea and closer stars, and, as the sky brightened to azure, the wood-against-stone clunk of buckets being drawn from wells in the fields below inexorably woke us from the short sleep we had finally drifted into after hours and days and nights of exploratory lovers' talk. We talked on the port, on the beach, in the sea, in cars, in cafés, in his almost medieval kitchen as I made vichysoisse (my sole culinary achievement at the time, eaten beside the pungent pine fire), in the dark, and inevitably in bed.

We had what seemed an uncanny connection. Much later I would read what Michael had written: "I felt as though some part of me which had hitherto been missing or misplaced was now in place . . . even now it astonishes me that someone ten years younger than I was could have spoken sentences as I was forming them in my head, and anticipated my responses so exactly that I seldom needed to voice them."

And this extraordinary synchronicity went as far back as our childhoods. For him, too, a Gypsy encampment had formed a totem in his earliest memory. I had never before met anyone with so incisive an eye and mind as Michael's. Simon Fleet's fascinating quality was his wildly diverse and not overly intellectual interests. Michael could trace and point out the influences back to the original in a work of art, or the use of language in a poem by, say, Rimbaud. He had very strong opinions about what he felt was excellence—or trash, though that should not imply that he didn't enjoy trashy things. His conversation was a measured flow of information, allusions, associations, and hidden humor, more poetic and subtle than Simon's endearing lighthearted gabble, and thus harder to grasp. You either had to get it or leave it. Nothing was going to be said twice. In a sense Simon was the clown who laughs, Michael the one who cries. Both men had unbounded generosity of spirit, and both were comfortably at home in the romantic past, but where Simon reveled in all things smacking of English quirkiness, Michael was passionately interested in nineteenth- and twentieth-century writers and artists, particularly French and preferably tragic, some of whom he had known, or indeed still knew.

Avant-garde ballet, especially its music by Les Six, the composer geniuses of prewar Paris, or Stravinsky, and decors, particularly by Christian Bérard, enthralled him. Indeed he considered Bébé, as everyone called Bérard, a very great *artist-paintre*. Many of the great Parisian choreographers and dancers, such as Jean Babilée and Nathalie Philippart, were friends, but he was an aficionado of all ballet as much as he was admiring of the bullfight. He followed, especially, the toreros Dominguín and Ordóñez, though I think this was partly because they were both so astonishingly sexy. He was an encyclopedia of the details and subtleties of the surreal filmmakers like Cocteau and Buñuel, and we had to go to *Le Sang d'un Poète, L'Age d'Or, Un Chien Andalou* and *La Belle et La Bête* whenever they were showing at the Pagoda, the gout chinoise arthouse cinema of Paris. He loved aristocrats like Charles and Marie-Laure de Noailles, not because of their grandness but because they had financed many of these films, and facilitated the publication of Raymond Radiguet's *Le Bal du Comte d'Orgel,* an exquisitely written short novel, and Michael's favorite book, not least because its beautiful author, the toast of bohemian Paris, had died—"without knowing it," as Cocteau had written in his biography of Radiguet—at nineteen.

He was determined I should imbibe this intellectual current in Paris, just as much as he wanted me to experience the last halcyon days of his beloved Saint-Tropez. He realized the writing was on its walls; and as he himself put it, "Tourism, after all, destroys the object of its desire." Being superstitious, or rather susceptible to the nuances of superstition, Michael, whose friend Aly Khan had recently fatally crashed hurtling up the N7 from his Château de l'Horizon to tryst with the supermodel Bettina, insisted on going north from Provence by train rather than by car; but I, having myself driven that tiring route fairly frequently, preferred the journey to Paris on the Mistral. We could catch the train at midday, and arrive at the Gare du Sud in time to go to a vernissage at Iris Clert's gallery, the theater, or the ballet, joining Michael's Parisian friends Françoise de Rudder or Princesse Anne de Bavière for dinner, and going on to the great transvestite nightclubs, Le Carrousel with its girl-boys, Le Monocle with its boy-ladies.

On some of these evenings I witnessed the final sighs of a vanished prewar European society, its luminaries on their last legs. Marie-Laure de Noailles, by now a painter herself, still entertained, abetted by the American composer Ned Rorem, in her vast Jean-Michel Frank parchment-walled salon on the Place des États-Unis. At the Palais-Royal lemon-yellow-skinned Jean Cocteau's eloquent fingers traced epigrams in the miasmic amber smoke. Janet Flanner, known for her mannish manner as Captain Jack, gathered in her rooms a bouquet of expatriate journalistic and literary blossoms. Alice Toklas, whose autobiography by Gertrude Stein had recently become *my* favorite book, sat, small and bent, a black velvet Reboux toque pulled down to meet her pale thin nose and dark mustache, lionized by, and sometimes lionizing, the wives of any potential genius. Down on the older, riverine side of the Boulevard Saint-Germain, the octogenarian poetess Nathalie Barney proclaimed her sapphic verses to the last grand lesbian circle, the iambic cadences rising and falling in rhythm with the slaps administered by the music-loving midas Princess Winnie de Polignac, to the shapely white cheeks of Lady Chaplin, soon to be Mrs. James Lees-Milne, and later the designer of Mick Jagger's garden near Amboise.

Back in Saint-Tropez, at warm Christmastides we could take picnics to Pampelonne beach, still without a single building, the pale sun water-gilding its paler sand, beyond which the last perfumed plumes of *lys de mer* (the lily in the French royal arms) stood proud among the huge knots of tough sea grass. When the first stormy waves of spring came pounding in, these clumps would be overturned and lie waving skeletal tangled roots, like vast primeval beetles. By February gardens in Ramatuelle gleamed with the vivid green foliage of camellias, their snail-like buds opening into saucers of red-and-white striped ribbon. In the Place de l'Ormeau the plane trees—the camouflage-like bark of their branches ending in severely pruned stumps—were already sending out the plethora of leaves that would alleviate the heat of summer with their impenetrable canopy. In this dappled shade, wizened old men in faded blue *singes*— overalls so called because the never-tied belt dangling behind looked like a monkey's tail—played aggressive games of boules.

In Saint-Tropez itself, just beyond the Place des Lices, the village gave way to old stone farmsteads and newer villas. Crumbling walls were fragrant with mimosa and jasmine, peppery with the scent of Malmaison carnations. One of the most romantic gardens was that of the novelist Colette, whose pale yellow house lay back from the road to Les Salins, a pine-fringed crescent bay below the half-hidden often-shuttered castle that Wagner had lived in while wooing Cosima. Here the ink blue water was deep and calm enough to learn to water-ski. At the far end of this remote promontory, hanging above the sea, was the four-square, slightly grim residence of old Princess Marie Bonaparte, born in the Greek royal family, married to a great-nephew of the emperor, and a devoted pupil of Sigmund Freud. Lunching with the princess and her entourage of testy old courtiers and acolyte professors could be a drawn-out and frugal affair, as the far from svelte princess was permanently on the strictest of diets and would wave away each dish as it was presented, and also because, before eating, she would have her two boatmen row her half a mile out to sea, where they slung her overboard. Her guests would watch her hefty shoulders, supported by stout rubber water wings, heave bravely against the wavelets, while her boatmen proffered a series of rather salty—one imagined—glasses of fortifying wine.

In the minute community of Tahiti itself lived, in an equally minute bungalow, a formidable couple—real "collar-and-tie-jobs," as the northern comedienne Beryl Reid succinctly referred to those of that persuasion. The larger of these Provençal ladies-of-Llangollen-sur-mer was Ena FitzPatrick, a wild Irish beauty who had been adopted as a surrogate daughter by the Irish-born Princess Daisy of Pless, a romantic attachment of both King Edward VII and Kaiser Wilhelm II. Asked by that gammey-handed emperor at an interminable Potsdam dinner what she would like as a birthday gift, the sharp-witted Daisy replied, "Sire, do not give me anything. Just give Alsace-Lorraine back to France."

Quite why Princess Daisy felt she needed to have Ena as a surrogate daughter was rather baffling, as her youngest son, Prince Lexel Pless, wore more enamel and rouge than his pretended godmother Queen Alexandra, though he could hardly be said to have the total lack of guile and abstemiousness of that Danish beauty.

Ena's girlfriend Margaret was the roaring mouse type, who made sure the gin was locked well away at nightfall. Ena and Lexel, who frequently came to the Tahiti cabana when short of funds after the failure of some particularly nefarious fleecing exploit, would go whooping and banging around to their few neighbors, begging for a nightcap. Ena was certainly the best known of this bizarre community, and indeed had once received a letter forwarded to her from Tahiti in the South Seas. The ire of these long-tucked-up locals at such disturbing revels was made plain, and Lexel would mince off to some remote Prussian estate to think up and perpetrate yet another aristocratic scam.

As well as this handful of year-round inhabitants, many serious artists still spent their winters working on the Tropezien peninsula. Dunoyer de Segonzac drew his feint portraits of friends, his bare wintry vineyards, or a calm bay suddenly whipped into foam-flecked waves by a fierce mistral, at the Chapelle de Saint Anne. Germaine Tailleferre, the only female member of Les Six, made us lusciously thick herb-scented pistou in her little blue-and-white *mas* while her glamorous daughter Françoise de Rudder played her mother's music on a long-stringed *camarguais* guitar. The surrealist poet Paul Éluard, once gratefully divorced from the monstrous Gala Dalí but now a gaunt widower dreaming of his last Nush, shuffled among the fallen leaves of the plane trees in the Place des Lices. Up in Gassin, above the restaurant where Michael had first taken me to dine, George Wakhevitch, the designer of *spectacles* at the Lido in Paris, lit his vast studio with tallow candles in enormous black iron candelabras that dripped a waxy-honey smell into the nights when we would dine there before driving into town to drink *vin blanc cassis* and applaud the dinner-jacketed band at Le Jardin des Licornes, the 1930s white-plaster and plush nightclub on the port. Later we might cut through the whitewashed, arcaded, stone-slabbed market, where fishermen were setting up their earliest catch, to the tiny basement club Ghislaine's, the world's first discotheque. Sometimes I'd be invited to dance a Prez Prado cha-cha-cha with Brigitte Bardot in the infrequent moments she and her costar boyfriend, Sami Frey, whose parents owned the Hôtel de la Ponche, could bear to unentwine their sun-and-salty arms from around each other's perfect bodies.

Other far more energetic dancing took place at Palmyre, an unchanged nineteenth-century *bal tabarin* at the top of the hill above the port. The music came from an ancient mechanical organ, with a repertoire of about twelve tunes, very fast, fast, and slow—or rather, slightly less fast. Polkas, polonaises, gallops, and waltzes wheezed tinnily into the night. Each lasted about ten minutes, and all had different, precisely prescribed steps that had to be perfectly learned before attempting to dance. We sat on a yellow-and-red-painted wooden gallery, watching intently as phalanxes of Tropezien youths, their arms around each other's shoulders, performed these intricate movements. Braving it, knowing that a wrong step could throw the whole line, we would dance till we could hardly stand. There was good reason for that: You had to dance barefoot.

One summer a second discotheque opened in a barn just outside Ramatuelle's walls. Of course it was the thin end of the wedge, but Min and I, and Pascal—an incredibly pretty boy she had picked up who now lived with us—all adored Le Callade. One night I took my 45 of "Itsy Bitsy Teenie Weenie Yellow Polka Dot Bikini" down there. The French owners put it on, and within seconds the place was jumping. Best of all was that they thought *I* was Brian Hyland, and I was greeted with a ritual playing of the song and yells of " 'alo Bri-ann" whenever we went there. Pascal was thrilled at this ersatz celebrity, as he loved to point out all the famous people on the port. There was a rumor that Jackie Kennedy was visiting the town as there had been photographs in the paper of her with her couturier Oleg Cassini, a very good-looking man with gray hair and a pencil mustache. Min spotted him one evening at Senequier—"There he is, that's him!" I looked up, and though indeed it was a handsome gray-haired man, I knew it wasn't Cassini. But whoever it was gave me a half-smile of acknowledgment.

Other Saint-Tropez regulars were the artist Bernard Buffet; the young writer Françoise Sagan, bronzed, sleek-headed, barefoot as publicized, in white Capri pants, drunk with the staggering success of her first novel, *Bonjour Tristesse*. The immense Prince Bertil of Sweden, who wagging tongues said was not allowed to return to Stockholm because of his love affair with divorced Englishwoman Lillian Craig (though after Bertil's death, Mrs. Craig was swept into the bosom of the Swedish royal family and created an HRH), lived in a villa right on the sea at Sainte-Maxime. Oonagh, Lady Oranmore, took the house next door and with her beautiful precocious son Tara Browne—famous for sending back the Bloody Marys at the Paris Ritz when merely six years old—each evening crossed the bay to Saint-Tropez in their white motorboat, both dressed in white, drinking pink champagne. We would meet at Ghislaine's, where one evening there was a great to-do when word came to expect Prince Juan Carlos of Spain any moment. Searching the jukebox tunes for something suitable for his arrival, Ghislaine selected the only Spanish-sounding record. Unfortunately it was Ravel's *Pavane pour une Infante Défunte.*

Oonagh Oranmore lived for nightclubs. Almost half a century later I saw her, aged over eighty, still neatly blond headed and chicly black suited, at the annual dinner for the Queen Mother given by Oonagh's sister Maureen Dufferin. "Ghastly!" she said in reply to my sincere, "How are you." "I'm *so* boring these days. No energy. Last week I flew to Rio for the evening. And, can you believe it, I had to leave the nightclub at 4 a.m."

We knew the building boom that would eventually wreck the landscape had begun in earnest when Gunter Sachs erected his huge striated reddish stone villa in the newly created Parc de St.-Tropez. "Looks like it's made of salami," was Ena FitzPatrick's succinct comment. And a grand new hotel, the Aioli, was created at astonishing expense in the Rue de la Ponche. On the night it opened there was an extremely violent robbery, murder even, and the Aioli shut its golden doors then and there, never to open again.

I FIND IT HARD TO put into words how my relationship was developing. I was certainly becoming aware of Michael's craving for drugs. In a way I found it thrilling, and anyway thought it wasn't a permanent need, but more, that artists such as he just *did* take drugs. I never saw him take them. He never suggested I try them. That had been the role of a charming old Chilean diplomat friend of Simon's, Tony Gandarillas, who was a registered addict and got his gear via the diplomatic bag. He had a flat on the Chelsea Embankment with a full-fledged opium bed, lying on which he'd often let me have a very mild pull on the first burning. Even those made me realize what utter heaven that particular drug is, and how paltry in comparison its derivatives.

I don't think Michael had taken anything since we had first met the summer before, but the wish to do so was certainly present. It was quite a childish thing; he felt he shouldn't deny himself that toy, and I don't think I would have minded. Perhaps getting them would have been better than the ever handy alcohol. When drunk he was never physically violent but could be verbally wounding. This situation worried and puzzled me. I had never in my life been around serious drunks. I began to see why Anne and other lovers had found him difficult, but I was at the age when one thinks one can change people. When the benders ended, I was just so relieved the sweet Michael had returned, and didn't believe for some time that it would be a recurring pattern. His care and love when sober were so strong; he would paint me sleeping, saying he could never make me be still when awake. Cecil Beaton bought one of these sleeping pictures, which made Michael very proud. Not surprisingly, he was a huge admirer of Cecil's, who was in a way the English Bebé Berard.

After painting for several days, sometimes nights, on end (Michael's pictures took shape in his imagination, and were born fully formed, at least in conception, onto the canvas; getting the actual *paint* right was the difficult part), Michael needed to visit the places that inspired him. To reach the most important of these, the Camargue, took well over a day on the often merely one-track main road via Aix-en-Provence and Arles, under the avenues of plane trees the despised Napoleon had planted to shade his advancing armies. The monotonous *thwack!* reverberating against the Citroën's chassis from their all-to-close trunks was as tiring as the blinding shafts of afternoon sunlight between them. The Guinness artist-heiress Meraude Guevara's little whitewashed *mas* on the lower slopes of Mont Ste.-Victoire, with Cézanne's paintings of the mountain outside hanging within, was an ideal place for us to pause, to drink the dark red *vin de Cassis,* for Michael and Meraude to discuss painting or, if her great friend Nancy Cunard had come over from La Mothe-Fénelon, literature.

Arriving at dusk in Arles, the second city of the Roman Empire, we went straight to the bar of the Hôtel Jules César, high in Michael's panoply of romantic tragedy for being where Scott Fitzgerald had stayed while writing *The Crack-up,* a journal of his breakdown, of his wife, Zelda's, madness and its effect on their marriage. However, if there was a *corrida* in the offing, the bullfighting world would gather outside the Nord Pinus, and it was there I saw, for the only time, Picasso, walking through an admiring crowd toward the Arena with Lucia Bose, the beautiful film-star wife of Michael's hero-torero, Luis Miguel Dominguín, who dedicated a bull to Picasso that evening. It was in Arles, too, that we met the great art collector and critic Douglas Cooper, with his handsome, clever, and very funny lover, John Richardson. They lived in a marvelous eighteenth-century sham ruin, the Château de Castille, near Uzès. Built by a Castille for a Rohan, it had CR emblazoned on every surface, appropriate for these particular lovers. While Cooper's unrivaled opinions on the century's art were delivered with a grudging waspishness, Richardson's mocking humor and sexual reputation made him extremely attractive. Hearing that, some months later, he had left Cooper to live in New York, I felt yet another pull to that newer world.

When the Camargue, the sky-wide expanse of salt plains bordered by perhaps the longest beach in Europe, Michael showed me his two favorite towns: Aigues-Mortes, its abrupt medieval walls and muscular towers appearing to rise straight out of the sea, as indeed they once did; and Saintes-Maries-de-la-Mer, the low white houses huddling around their stark ancient cathedral, the pilgrimage destination for Gypsies who come once a year to worship a black Madonna, who in their canon, landed with the white one after the Crucifixion, in a fishing smack on the shores here.

I loved the flocks of carnation-pink flamingos, seeing them now in reality rather than on Michael's canvas, but nothing could coax me onto the equally real white horses of the Camargue cowboys. Michael did coax the distinctive costume from one of them, the dark doeskin trousers and waistcoat, short linen jacket and paisley shirt, all fastened with silver buttons and topped by a shallow-brim black hat. I wore this attire nonstop for about a year. By then cheap imitations were swinging outside the first boutiques to spring up in Saint-Tropez.

Other expeditions took us the other way, to the green baize lure of Monte Carlo. The road wound interminably round the coast and made the drive to Aix seem like flying. At shaded restaurants in La Napoule we ate delicious things new to my burgeoning taste: *champignons à la grecque, nègre en chemise,* or grilled lobster with fried onion at Le Coq Hardi on the *vieux port* in Nice. On the lower Corniche, Michael pointed out the Château de l'Horizon, Prince Aly Khan's iceberg of a house marooned between the sea and the railway line to Italy, where Michael told me that he and Anne had rowed violently following her ritualistic seduction by Aly.

On the cliffs above were the skeletons of cages that in the 1930s had contained the apes of the much-visited monkey-gland supplier, Dr. Voronov. His great rival, Dr. Niehans, had a similar practice in Switzerland. Marlene Dietrich and Somerset Maugham were regular mainliners of Niehans's rejuvenating specialty, sheep glands. Noël Coward noticed a flock grazing in a pasture nearby, among them a huge black ram. "Heavens, business *is* good. He must be expecting Paul Robeson."

Michael was an accomplished and usually successful gambler. He would play only roulette and taught me the refinements of the whole process, of always betting on zero, of leaving part of one's stake on a winning number, how much to tip the croupier. I preferred the Sporting d'Été in Cannes to the grander but breathtakingly beautiful belle epoque rooms in Monte Carlo. And at least I had no trouble getting in, unlike Lord Alfred Douglas, an uncle of Anne's, who at seventy-plus used to boast that he still looked too young for the top-hatted *porteurs* to allow him entry.

We lunched with Graham Sutherland and his somewhat sullen wife, Kathy, at their jungly-gardened white house, unimaginatively named La Maison Blanche, set in a strange, dark ravine behind Menton. Though I admired the work he showed us, Graham seemed less like an artist than a civil servant, dust-dry and persnickety and dainty. "That's a nice trousering," he said of some shorts I was wearing.

The very opposite was true of dinners with the enthralling writer Lesley Blanch at the Casa del Sogno, her hideaway in a hill village above Cap d'Ail. She had been a heroine since Simon had insisted I read her first book, *The Wilder Shores of Love.* Though at this point Lesley was in despair at being left by her dashing husband, the writer Romain Gary, for the young actress Jean Seberg, her romanticism prevailed, exemplified by her passion for Arabia, and the dark arms of a sheikh. To this end her house was decorated as a Bedouin tent, with herself an Ouled Naïl arrayed in jeweled djellabas and heavy silver necklaces, lying on her perfumed couch. One felt one might hear the thunder of stallions' hooves at any moment. Her Paris flat, on the Avenue Mozart, was decked out in the same exotic vein, and perhaps all the more surprising for being situated in a blancmange-like art deco building.

Lesley was also a masterful cook. And once the Circassian chicken had been cleared, and the rose-petal loukoum savored, the stories poured with the Imperial Tokay; of being in Russia, somewhere like Omsk, researching *The Sabres of Paradise,* where at an illicit party somebody played a bootleg forbidden pop record. "What are the words? Please tell us what the words mean," young Russian boys implored. "Well, I couldn't disappoint them by saying it's just, 'Yeah, yeah, yeah,' so I put 'Night and Day' into very basic Russian." Of being sent to interview Anna Anderson, the self-proclaimed Grand Duchess Anastasia, at a cabin in the Black Forest, Anderson elected to speak no known tongue, only grunts. Some tea was brought, and Lesley poured. Suddenly Anna/Anastasia shrieked: "No! No! Milk in first!!" Lesley's utter romanticism erupted. "There! English nanny! Of *course* she's Anastasia!"

Michael had a sweet old friend, a hangover from European courts, the ugly, shapeless Countess Maudina de Montjou, who lived in a many-leveled, potted-palm-filled warren of a house atop La Turbie, the highest village of the Côte d'Azur with a terrifying road. This didn't deter Maudie, who descended every day to "take the sun," though under a parasol, by the Hôtel de Paris pool. She disapproved of Michael and me swimming among the many children. "All those fucking piss-ants," she would shudder—surprising words for this relic of the turn-of-the-century. One year Maudie asked us to join her table for the newly established Red Cross Ball. Sitting there in better-days-spangled-black-net and ragged ostrich plumes she reminded me of Margaret Dumont in a Marx Brothers film. But the plumes were on nodding terms with Princess Grace, who briefly stopped at our table, a vision of Grecian white chiffon cinched by a wide gold kid belt.

FOR MY BIRTHDAY Michael took me to Venice. However well my father knew Italy, it was from Florence south that he lived and loved, and I had never heard either him or my mother talk of going to that most romantic city. Apart from paintings, my only image of the city was from the Katharine Hepburn film *Summertime*, and its bright Technicolor hadn't prepared me for the muted, reflected subtlety of stone and brick of the real thing, the sky shimmering beneath the refracted facades, the sudden, solid green stab of tree and garden. I don't remember how we traveled there—probably by train, as driving would have taken several days. Our hotel was the Gritti Palace, and I can still hear the throaty roar of its motor launch as, speechless, we were transported from the mainland.

Exhausted from the journey and the beauty of its goal, we lay down for an afternoon siesta. Almost immediately a figure wearing brown clothes and a black hat walked quite slowly from the door, past the ends of our beds, and through the wall by the window. Without any alarm, and in one voice, Michael and I said, "Did you see that ghost?" We both had, and looking out of the window, realized that at exactly the spot the figure had disappeared were the stonework remains of a bridge across the small canal to the building opposite. Margot, Lady Asquith, wittily remarked that the trouble with ghosts is that their appearances are against them, but ours was merely restful, and in moments we had drifted back into Venetian dreamland.

Waking at dusk, I saw from our balcony the gondola of my London gallery-owning friend Arthur Jeffress with its handsome gondoliers in their time-honored yellow-and-white livery, propelling their precious cargo, pashalike in the little black armchair, toward Harry's Bar for his regular evening Bellini. Sadly, this ritual was not to last for much longer.

Those handsome gondoliers sneaked to the then-homophobic Venetian authorities about Arthur's preferences. Terrified of the consequences, he fled his beloved city in the middle of the night, and a few days later, in the Hôtel France et Choiseul in Paris, ended his strange exotic life by swallowing the poison contents of a ring he prudently wore for just such an emergency.

Nicolette and Alastair Londonderry had rented the top floor of Daisy Fellowes's palace on the other side of the Grand Canal, beside the wooden echo of the Accademia Bridge. After a morning amid the golden gloom of churches, or accustoming one's sight to the glow of crimsons in galleries and *scuoli,* we would skitter across the lagoon with them to the Lido, Nico's perfectly bronzed limbs as dark as the speedboat's glossy woodwork, her breeze-blown hair swirling around the half-closed green eyes, the laughing mouth. If my eyes were hypnotized by Nico's beauty, Michael was watching deliriously what he considered mine: "Nicky stood at the prow . . . his eyes exactly matched the sparkling lagoon, his golden skin was frosted with sea-salt. . . . I concentrated on the image, printing it on my brain," he was to write. But now the Riva was gurgling gently up to the Giacometti-like jetty, the two rows of striped cabanas stretching away on the colorless sand. During lazy lunches, delighted by strange delicacies, deep-fried courgette flowers or *vitello tonnato,* we would watch barefoot youths plying the wide blond beach bearing straw baskets filled with iced figs, peaches, and grapes. One realized that in the shadier depths of the cabanas of sleek South American millionaires, the transactions took a suspiciously long while. Turning a discreetly blind eye, their *mariage blanc* wives dickered over which emeralds to wear that evening. In the hot late afternoon, disembarking near San Marco, we would drink bittersweet Campari at Florian's, and recount the story of Chips Channon flopping exhausted into a café chair after a tour through the serpentine alleys that link the canals, and declaring, "I don't know about Mary Queen of Scots, but when *I* die, they will find *calle* engraved on my heart."

The most fascinating of Michael's Venetian friends was the art collector Peggy Guggenheim. By turns coquettish or stern, at some moments hideous, at others beguiling, Peggy and her pictures occupied a vast white marble one-story palazzo, the unfinished Vernier dei Leoni. It had been at one time the Venetian home of the exotic Marchesa Casati, whom Simon Fleet had only recently pointed out to me at Hyde Park Corner early one morning, the furred collar of her dusty black coat merging into the serpents of black electrical tape she substituted for false eyelashes.

But unlike that chimeric fin-de-siècle image once captured by Boldini's glittering paint, Peggy was a substantial figure in this city of reflections.

The daily exodus from her baroque marble bungalow for a post-siesta *passegiatta al gondola,* dressed in a caftan painted by Max Ernst, earrings designed by Alexander Calder swinging from her long lobes, the narrow lacquered barque brimming with a batch of shih tzus, was as treasured a tourist sight as any Bridge of Sighs. Her invitations—the oversize erect penis of the Marino Marini sculpture at her water gate steps, screwed into place on her return, signified she was receiving—were jealously coveted. By means of fortune of birth, daring, an intrinsic eye, excellent advice, plus marriages and love affairs with many of the century's leading artists, Peggy had amassed contemporary art of the first rank, and myriad masterpieces hung cheek by jowl above the cubist white leather sofas in the enfilade of rooms in her riverine palace.

It was through one of her many liaisons—despite her lack of physical beauty she had great sexual allure—Peggy had some family connection with Michael, and if this was not actual blood kinship, she considered him as much part of her family as her daughter, Pegeen Vail, who was staying with her that summer. Pegeen, who herself was a talented artist, was also a live-wire of nerves, basically frightened of the human race. She told me she felt safe and happy only when flying. It came as no surprise that not long after, she committed suicide, due perhaps to her ultimate need to be alone, as opposed to Arthur Jeffress's need for company.

Peggy pointed out the famous figures and features of Venice: a Nazi-loving contessa who'd believed "the only trouble with Hitler was that he wasn't nearly fascist enough"; the "stinkin' pink palazzo" of Cole Porter's *Kiss Me, Kate* song; the vastly fat Princess Elizabeth Chavchavadze, with her tiny pianist husband; a morganatic queen of Greece, rumored to have the evil eye because her husband had died of a monkey bite; the haunted Casa dei Spiriti facing the sentinel cypresses of the island-cemetery across the lagoon; violet-eyed Barbara Hutton gazing from the window of her house in the shadow of the Salute. In Peggy's elderly limousine we drove to see the Teatro Olimpico in Vicenza, in her sharp-prowed *motoscafo* we threaded through the reedy waterways of the Veneto to the Malcontenta, that most melancholic of Palladio's villas, though any hint of gloom was dispelled by its rotund, learned chatelain, Bertie Landsberg. Back on what can hardly be called terra firma, every evening at dusk a German gigolo named Kim, said to be the handsomest boy in Europe, would do a circuit of the fashionable bars and cafés recruiting guests for a male couple who gave all-night parties in the Dario, their fifteenth-century palace, unevenly floored, and rumored to be roundly cursed. We went, naturally. In dimly lit rooms, in a fog of incense and smoke, in a musty melange of brocade and crystal, old men and young men danced and kissed, or lay entwined on faded banquettes, while somewhere, somebody scraped Wagner on an untuned violin into the fetid darkness.

It seemed time to say goodnight and good-bye to the world of phantoms.

THOUGH THESE TRAVELS on the Continent with Michael were life-enhancing and mind expanding, the fact remained that I had very little money and had to find a job from time to time. So while Michael retreated to Saint-Tropez to paint for a while, I returned to London and the friends I had often missed even while enjoying such a charmed existence. With his knack for finding fascinating and romance-imbued places to live and things with which to furnish them, Christopher Gibbs had nosed out a treasure of a seventeenth-century house across the river, on its very edge. There was merely a cobbled quay between this building and the water; the area, Bankside, a maze of tiny courtyards and alleys, was one of oldest and least altered in London and, needless to say, soon to be bull-dozed to make way for industrial and office buildings. This house was the actual one Wren had lived in while building Saint Paul's. The thick, old panes in the attic window of Chrissy's room looked directly over the river at the cathedral, sailing stately above its unskyscrapered surroundings. An added picaresque touch was that the room appears, exactly as it was when we knew it, in Henry Wallis's painting *The Death of Chatterton*. The charlatan boy-poet, his face bloodless from the swallowed poison, lies dying in that very window. When I took Michael to see Chrissy's house, he instinctively felt at home in the troubled romance of this room.

Soon 49 Bankside became the central destination for our friends. I'd take the scooter to collect Jane Ormsby-Gore from her parents' flat in Rutland Gate. Jane was the eldest daughter of the politician David Ormsby-Gore, soon to be named ambassador to Washington and created Lord Harlech, and his wife, Sissy Lloyd-Thomas. Jane, and her brother Julian, who had been at Eton with me, had the dark coloring of their Celtic parents, and the fine-cut features of their Salisbury ancestors, and from a nonconformist elsewhere they had been blessed with an entrancing disregard for authority, parental or otherwise.

For these picnic feasts Jane often produced a big basket of food, nicked from the Rutland Gate kitchen. She could balance it on her knee, sit sidesaddle, pin up her beehive, apply her habitual circle of mascara and a pout of pale lipstick, keeping up an incessant stream of chat as we'd sway through the summer evenings to set out our purloined feast under the vast mulberry tree, its gnarled branches propped just above head height by silvery wood staves. Caught, then, in a warp between hooting smoke-blackened boats and the steamy strains of engines hauling out of Waterloo, this ancient candlelit garden was the setting for many nights in our youthful rapture.

One night on my way back from buying some forgotten necessity, I found myself in a pretty little street of small and almost identical Regency cottages. I jumped off the scooter and walked; there were about four of these streets, in a vague grid pattern, the facades varying slightly, but all very small. Except one. This was hardly any bigger, but it was double-fronted, and it too had a garden. More than that, it had a sign: TO LET.

Within a few days, and with Michael's generous agreement, two rooms up, two rooms down, gray brick 23 Whittlesey Street was mine for five hundred pounds a year. Unlike Chrissy's it had no river view, but the estate-village-like conformation, with even a toytown pub and corner shop merely a street away, gave it a unique atmosphere. For the first time in my life, I had somewhere I could stamp with my emerging taste.

I made the dining room into an oval tent of rough brown parachute silk, that staple of old Mr. Afia's material shop in Baker Street. The curtains pulled aside to reveal the fireplace and window, but hid corners shelved for china and glassware. With Gothic chairs and central lantern, I thought it was the bee's knees, but old Mrs. Sykes from the shop said, "Ooh, I'd 'ave all that out," tugging the space-wasting drapery. I painted the downstairs sitting room lacquer red, with tall-as-possible bookshelves from which the two marmosets that had now superseded the monkey would bound, chattering with glee, up onto the curtain rail, or pirouette precariously on picture frames. I said to Michael, "If you call them Nijinsky and Karsavina, what do you expect?"

Michael continued to instill in me a love of ballet, its décors and dancers, and while we were in Paris had booked seats almost nightly for the Kirov's first big tour outside Russia with its young dancers. One evening we were knocked sideways by the technique, yes, but more by the beauty and sexuality of one, Rudolf Nureyev. Michael, instantly obsessed, went to every subsequent performance. Later, down in Ramatuelle, Michael woke up zinc white. "You remember that boy, Nureyev?" How could one forget? "Of course. What?" "I just had a dream he's escaped from the company and wants to stay in the West." Within forty-eight hours Michael's dream proved to have come—typically, given his strange clairvoyance—precisely true. We read the headline in *Nice-Matin* one windy picnic on Tahiti Plage. Nureyev had absconded from the Kirov, and was in hiding in Paris, with rumors spreading thick and fast that his ambition was to go to London and join the Royal Ballet. I could see that Michael would be spending a lot of time in the pretty Whittlesey Street cottage.

FOR ALL HIS PROFESSED love of seclusion, it was habitual for Michael to spend much of his time in his old Soho haunts, though by this time the Gargoyle, his personal nirvana, was no more. After dinner—invariably smoked salmon, Sancerre, and sole Véronique—at the famous original Wheeler's in Old Compton Street—often with Lucian Freud or Francis Bacon—we would end up in the Colony Club. Known to all its regulars as Muriel's, after the astonishingly rude, ugly, impatient, rapacious but totally adorable lesbian who ran it, it was the nearest thing London had to Le Dôme in Montparnasse or Saint-Germain's Deux Magots.

George Melly might be playing the piano, the beautiful Diana Ash, whom he later married, sitting atop it to ensure that her legs looked as tantalizingly long as possible. Henrietta Moraes, then at the apogee of her exquisite Ava Gardneresque looks, with her actor husband, Norman Bowler, would be talking to Bruce and Jeff Bernard. One of Michael's drinking companions was the brilliant but usually plastered photographer John Deakin, and following an afternoon's session in the club Michael and I went back to John's basement flat in Edgware Road for him to take a portrait of me. Proudly wearing my new check tweed Bilgorri suit and winkle pickers, I posed against a piece of Indian fabric that John pulled from under the heap that was the unmade bed and tacked up to form a backdrop. In some of the contacts the pattern behind made me appear to be wearing huge chandelier earrings.

Michael loved to arrange dinners in my tented dining room. Francis Bacon, his hair sleek with a layer of Cherry Blossom shoe polish; Caroline Blackwood, whose astonishing beauty was already fading through her prodigious intake of alcohol; and the *salonière* Sonia Brownell, widow of George Orwell, would endure the bad behavior of the marmosets for the boundless extravagance of Michael's conversation. Among his dearest friends were Pauline Tennant, daughter of the Gargoyle Club's owner and the actress Hermione Baddeley. Pauline had herself played the part of the princess in Anthony Asquith's film *The Queen of Spades*, in which her pale luminous beauty stole the screen. Colette Clark, daughter of the art historian Sir Kenneth Clark, was another. I was immediately enchanted by Celly, by her funny, lazy way of speaking and her scrunched-up blinking eyes.

Sometimes she invited me to her parents' box at Covent Garden. Her mother, Lady Clark, was a terrific snob and out to impress. During a particularly poignant balletic moment, Jane Clark turned to me and, apropos of nothing, whispered loud and clear, "The last time I was reading the Bible was to the king of Sweden." One evening Celly came to Lambeth bringing Tim Willoughby—Lord Timothy Willoughby d'Eresby, heir to the earldom of Ancaster, was a beautiful young Casanova who collected paintings for his many stately homes, as well as girls, and the right girl to run them, among them Min, who deeply loved him. Tim, who owned a house at Eze, then a simple village perched dizzily above Cap Ferrat, was also a friend of Michael's. He was a courageous daredevil and gambler, adoring the gaming tables and the adrenaline thrill of his speedboat *Zero* (named for the winning number on the roulette table whose proceeds had bought it) in equal measure. The boat was to be Tim's coffin. Lost on an ill-judged trip to Corsica—having ignored a weather warning—neither was ever seen again, only a lone mattress bobbing on now calm waves.

THE GARDEN OF 23 Whittlesey Street—in truth more of a yard, as I never seemed to have the time or energy to actually plant anything in the ground—was not very pretty, despite the fact I'd copied Simon's at the Gothic Box with some pots of jasmine and a classical bust on a plinth as an eye-catcher. It was, however, big enough for a party. Most went without a hitch, but for one, on Guy Fawkes Night, we inadvertently reenacted, only slightly downriver from its original setting, the Gunpowder Plot. A spark fell into a huge crate of fireworks I'd gotten from Harrods, where I once heard a dowager cry, "such reliable bombs," and a lot of rather well-known people were saved from being blown to smithereens by the presence of mind of Bunny Roger, who, summoning the strength of Atlas, picked up the fiery crate and pitched it over the wall into the street, where, despite a soaking with the garden hose, rockets attempted droopy shootings, flares fizzed, and Catherine wheels whirled desultorily for the rest of the evening.

Among the nearly immolated guests was Bill Ackroyd, to whom I had been introduced by Bunny sometime before. Bill had a flat in Eaton Place and a big house in the West Country which nobody had ever been invited to as he was famously miserly, despite a Yorkshire carpet fortune ("Yorkminsters," as Chrissy Gibbs called them). Like Bunny, but not to the same elaborate extent, Bill dressed in a dandy style; he was determinedly languid and he stuttered beguilingly. On being shown the full-page picture of the Duke and Duchess of Windsor jumping in photographer Philippe Halsman's *Jump Book,* Bill studied it intently and said, "*They* haven't j-jumped. They've been d-d-d-dropped by somebody."

At one of Bill's rare parties, Noël Coward was the star attraction. I was talking to the Jewish American playwright Leonard Spigelgass, fantastically successful at the time with several plays running on Broadway. Noël came up, extending a limp hand. "Ah, dear, dear Lennie. The *Jewish* Noël Coward." A few nights later I saw Coward again at a cocktail party given by Terence Rattigan. Noël had just been to a matinee of a play about a novice who abandoned her vows, called *I Leap Over the Wall.* "Did you enjoy it?" we all asked. "It deeply strengthened me in my resolve *not* to become a nun." On the other side of the room, an aged little munchkin in a dusty-black dress—who turned out to be Elsa Maxwell, the legendary party enlivener—was somewhat dampening this one by peeing in every chair she sat in. Her long-term girlfriend, Dickie Fellows-Gordon, followed her movements, solicitously covering up the evidence of this forgetfulness with yet another of Rattigan's apricot silk cushions.

Bill's highly respectable mother once found him wearing a satin negligee and marabou slippers. "What *are* you doing?" she gasped. "R-r-r-relaxing," Bill finally blurted out. One imagines Lady Ackroyd kept such information from her husband, as he resolutely refused to go see John Gielgud in a play just after his trial for soliciting, despite her insisting, "But, dear, he's not going to do it *onstage.*"

AND IN THE TIMES when Michael, at this point a resident abroad, needed to be out of England, David Bailey used to spend several nights a week at Whittlesey Street with his gamine wife, Rosemary. She came from the same milieu as he did, and had the same rule-disregarding approach to clothes. She was the first person I ever saw wearing her coat inside out so the lining showed; now, looking back, she seems like an early forerunner of Vivienne Westwood. But it wasn't long before David appeared with a long-legged but clearly conventional girl, with blinking Technicolor eyes and a lazy demeanor called Jean Shrimpton. Initially she hardly spoke in his presence. Surprised by his obvious interest in her, I remem-

ber commenting, really out of loyalty to Rosemary but with extraordinary lack of prescience, "She's a bit placid, David. You'll never make anything out of her." But it only took a few frames of David's first shots of
her to show me how wrong I was.

The Twist had been the dance of the moment earlier that year in Paris.
I'd learned it at a bar in the Rue du Cherche-Midi, and by the time the
craze came to England I was already the acknowledged expert, so much
so that Jack Good, the producer of *Six-Five Special* asked me to demonstrate it on television, dancing with the star of the show, Adam Faith,
and John Leyton, later to turn actor in *The Great Escape*.

Jean's long legs and David's agility in his pointed boots were the perfect instruments for this new craze, and we would dance for hours together to Chubby Checker at the Saddle Room, the smart nightclub in
Park Lane run by Hélène Cordet, famously a former girlfriend of Prince
Philip's. She also had a friendly, well-built Alsatian dog that formed a
very close relationship with Christopher Gibbs, not otherwise known to
his friends as much of an animal lover. Jean's younger sister, Chrissie,
would sometimes join us. One day she came with a skinny young lad
wearing a tight little suit and striped T-shirt. "Who's he?" we said. "Oh,
he's my cleaner—I put an ad in the paper and he turned up. He's a student at LSE." "What's his name?" we whispered. "Mick," she said.
"Funny surname—Jagger." He rapidly became Chrissie's boyfriend and
one of our close friends. With his long hair, wide eyes, and huge mouth,
Mick looked faintly androgynous. But that was not the case at all. In
a restaurant one night the actor Anthony Steele and his buxom, boozy
wife, Belinda Lee, were seated at the next table, taunting Mick about his
looks, saying loudly and rudely, "Is he a boy or a girl?" After bearing it
for a bit, Mick got up, walked around to Tony Steele's table, looked him
in the eye, unzipped his narrow trousers, and slammed his cock on the
table. "*Now* do you think I'm a girl?" he said.

I'D PASSED MY driving test the first time, quite an achievement in those
days when anyone of my age was almost automatically failed. For someone who still has no clue as to the difference between a camshaft and a
carburetor, I had conceived an unnatural passion to possess a vintage car.
With my driving instructor as guide, I made a tour of several garages that
dealt in prewar automobiles, and eventually in one we saw, under a pall
of dust and cobwebs, a white convertible Delage. I'd never heard of this
make, but the garage owners assured me it was the "Bentley of France."

It was certainly, then and now, the most elegant car I'd ever seen. Long and sleek, with a Gothic-tracery radiator grille, it had, somewhat in advance of its time, an automatic gear system operated from a small device on the steering wheel. It had been built in 1939, so I felt an immediate rapport with this beauty of the year of my birth, which I loved even more when later I found out it was the same model Carole Lombard had given Clark Gable as a wedding present.

Restored, buffed, and shining, the Delage added glamour to Whittlesey Street, and knots of people would gather to gaze respectfully at it, the respect turning to near amazement when I had the first version of a record player fitted, a white plastic box suspended from the dashboard, into which one slotted the newest form of record, the astonishingly small 45 RPM. This was likely to be the latest hit of the fabulously handsome Jess Conrad, and with his lookalike—a sullen, Tony Curtis–haired youth called Adrian, whom I shared with young dancer Lionel Blair—we would drive out to Bunny's house in Berkshire for tea, or to Heathrow Airport for breakfast—the then equivalent of thirties debutantes tooling down to Skindles Hotel in Maidenhead, in the trafficless dawn. And later that spring, putting the Delage on the frighteningly basic plane-ferry that flew us across the Channel from Lydd in Kent to an airfield near Cherbourg, I drove down to Saint-Tropez to spend Easter with Michael, my car purring along the roads of the country of its birth.

On returning I found London agog with excitement at the imminent arrival from New York of *West Side Story,* the Broadway hit already widely recognized to have changed the face of American musicals with its theme of racial tension and a jazz-operatic score by Leonard Bernstein. I already knew all the songs by heart, and friends, particularly Dicky Buckle, who had seen it in New York, came back raving about the sensual dances and sexy dancers in blue jeans and leather jackets.

I was hanging around Her Majesty's Theatre late one evening, knowing that within these walls gods were rehearsing. The stage door swung open and, emerging from a shaft of yellow light, there was the taut silhouette of one of them. As the door banged shut, he came toward me with a toothpaste-white all-American smile. After a couple of drinks, we went back to Whittlesey Street, and a night of magic. He was the male lead in the show, and his name was Larry Kert. Over the next few days, Larry took me to rehearsals, introducing me to the cast and to Arthur Laurents, who had written the book of what I had learned from Larry to call simply *Story.*

Arthur was spending the summer in London, staying in a charming little Knightsbridge house with his great American friends the recently retired ballerina Nora Kaye and her husband, Herbert Ross, then a well-known choreographer (though he was at the time working on *The Young Ones,* with Cliff Richard), and later to be the director of many hit movies. All three had the sharpest wit; that quick-fire, camp Jewish humor once typical of New York in general, and showbiz in particular. Arthur, I soon learned, had written several films I'd loved, most recently *Anastasia,* in which Ingrid Bergman played the was-she/wasn't-she surviving daughter of Czar Nicholas.

Arthur had fairly recently broken up with his boyfriend, the film star Farley Granger, and though already in love with Tom Hatcher, a young beefcake actor in California, was having, as a not-unusual antidote to loneliness, an affair with a handsome Norfolk farmer. I was a convenient London squeeze. And all too willing to be one, as I found Arthur extremely attractive, and I reveled in the company of Nora and Herb. Nora had taken a great shine to me, partly because she disliked the farmer and saw me as a preferable replacement. Most nights there would be impromptu dinners, last-minute feasts found by Nora at the conveniently close Harrods, in the house in Montpelier Walk with their friends. One was Lena Horne, then in cabaret at the Savoy, and the most beautiful woman I had ever seen, who appealed to us all to help her fight off the attentions of Nancy Spain, the lesbian panelist on BBC's version *What's My Line?* Other guests were Ruth and Milton Berle; Morton Da Costa, known as Tique, who had had a huge success on Broadway with *The Music Man;* and, for one thrilling moment, Ethel Merman, the crush of all my life, who had come to London to confer with Arthur about a musical based on the life of the stripper Gypsy Rose Lee. Arthur in fact found Miss Merman a nightmare to work with, but loved to tell the stories of her always acerbic and frequently fearless tongue. During her disastrous three-week marriage to the pugilistic actor Ernest Borgnine, the no longer young Ethel had been at a rehearsal. When she got home, Borgnine asked gruffly, "How did it go?" Merman bridled. "Well, they were *crazy* about my thirty-five-year-old face and my thirty-five-year-old body and my thirty-five-year-old voice." "Oh really?" Borgnine said. "And what did they think of your sixty-five-year-old cunt?" Ethel shot back, "You weren't mentioned once."

On warm evenings I would drive with Arthur, Herb, and Nora, all gossiping hilariously in the backseat of the Delage, downriver to romantic pubs like the Prospect of Whitby, usually meeting a couple of Chelsea-set girls, as their plummy voices amused Arthur no end. One lunchtime, he and I were in a King's Road restaurant. I saw a model girlfriend across the room, and waved. "Hi, Sevilla," Arthur corpsed. "It gets better," I said. "Her other name is Glass-Hooper." By now Arthur was almost under the table, and the laugh has lasted. To this day, in whatever Arthur writes, play or film, there is a character called "Sevilla Haslam."

ONE COLD DAWN in November 1960 Simon Fleet telephoned me. I could tell he was in a phone booth. "Can I come to breakfast? There's someone I'd like you to meet." Having been up very late the previous night, I said, "Si, must you? It's incredibly early." But Simon was insistent. Not long after I heard that now nostalgic "tink" of a taxi's flag being flipped, voices, a knock at the door. A woman wearing a raincoat and a Tyrolean hat stood there with Simon, who was grinning from ear to ear. I somewhat unenthusiastically asked them in. The woman said, "Good morning, I'm so sorry we woke you," in a lilting voice, and Simon said something like, "Greta dear," and I suddenly realized it was Garbo. There was nothing I could do, no fanfare, no flowers, no red carpet. Luckily all they wanted was tea—"Black," Miss G. insisted—and, clasping the mug, she explained that she had stayed the night at the Shepherd's Market flat of her old MGM hairdresser, Sydney Guilaroff, but that it was tiny and freezing cold and she was looking forward to getting to "Beatie's lovely warm place in Wiltshire." This was her pet name for Cecil Beaton. Garbo looked at the rest of the house, which took about four seconds flat, pronounced it "convenient," and they left, on foot, for Waterloo station.

It became clear that in the long-running battle for Garbo's affections between Cecil and her Russian fixer and Praetorian guard, George Schlee—whom Cecil loathed and referred to as a "sinister little road-company Rasputin"—Cecil had managed to pry Garbo away. "Fleetie," as she called Simon, was her custodian for the journey to her lover's arms in Broadchalke. A couple of days later, Simon told me that the ticket collector on the train had said, "May I see your ticket please, mum?" Garbo looked up, the perfect profile raised. "Your ticket?" The legend threw off her Tyrolean hat and flung back her famous head, gazing sadly at the conductor as though she were the dying courtesan in *Camille*. "But I *haf* no teecket!" Still oblivious to her identity, the man insisted that she purchase a single to Salisbury. Turning to Simon, he said, "Haven't I seen you before, sir? Nice to see you again."

Gore Vidal told me that Garbo's much-vaunted, "self-imposed" retirement from films after the disastrous *Two-Faced Woman* (in which her stand-in for the skiing shots is the stepfather of photographer Peter Beard) was in fact a myth. Contrary to legend, Garbo was extremely eager to return to the screen when the war ended and the European market, where she had always been a much bigger star than in America, opened up again. The producer Walter Wanger had a script based on Balzac's *La Duchesse de Langeais* for a spectacular postwar "Greta Garbo comeback." But Howard Hughes, then at RKO, vetoed the project saying, "I'm not having that damned gloomy Swede back at my studio."

Gore also said that nobody knew more about the latest movie stars than Garbo. Rising at the crack of dawn in Klosters, where she and Gore spent many summers with the screenwriter Salka Viertel, Garbo strode into the village, awaiting the opening of the newsstand at the little log railway station, returning laden with the latest movie magazines. Hopping back into bed, she would read about Sandra Dee and Troy Donohue with intense interest. The most famous "recluse about town," as Gore once succinctly described her, was a walking encyclopedia about the American teenage idol and singer Fabian. Gore was astonished to find that Garbo religiously watched *Hollywood Squares* on television. I wish I had known such things about the showbiz world at the time, since I was soon to get a job with Anne Edwards at the *Sunday Dispatch,* interviewing celebrities, to go with the other job I had found on the more frivolous end of journalism at *Vogue.*

WHILE AMERICA WAS still my distant lodestar, London felt like the epicenter of the youth-quake that was clearly coming, and whenever I was away I yearned to be part of it. Michael's nature, though, was instinctively peripatetic. And he had a loner side: He never could reconcile his need to be alone, whether for work or for drugs, with his constant need to be with me. The atmosphere between us, which had been so loving, began to seem a little tense. His cravings made him either withdrawn or irritatingly voluble. The magic that he could spin with his knowledge and wisdom could also turn murky with his self-absorption, and I was too inexperienced to handle such changes. The Côte d'Azur, which had been our enchanted playground, began to feel constricting. As he himself described his love for me: "I was particularly insistent that Nicky was too charming to work, and when he received parental reprimands I smiled as he tore them up. It became my vocation to crush any qualities he might delude himself into supposing that he possessed. Not everyone will understand that this was truly a way of expressing my love for him, and a kind of tender trap. . . . It is not as though I were pretending that this love was unselfish."

And so the "lasso" that had initially pulled me to him began to loosen. When Milo Cripps, a young banker, inspired by the dances that, following on the heels of the Twist, were flooding in from America via Paris and Rome, then way ahead of London in music and fashion, suggested that I was the person to start a nightclub for him in London, I was feeling sufficiently independent from Michael's hold to be excited by the idea. It seemed the ideal situation for me—fun plus a salary. I could see how to create an independent future for myself in London.

It wasn't quite to work out that way.

· NINE ·

IN SPRING 1962 David Bailey and Jean Shrimpton had been asked by *Glamour* magazine in New York to go there for three weeks to do a fashion shoot. It was the first time either of them had been to the States—and indeed they were the first of a raft of young British photographers and models who were to cross the Atlantic in ever increasing waves. David suggested I go with them as I already knew something of Manhattan. To be in America with my two best friends, plus a chance perhaps to visit Jane Ormsby-Gore at her father's embassy in Washington, seemed the perfect plan. And it would also be an ideal opportunity to check out New York nightlife if I was to pursue Milo Cripps's venture.

So with the Delage parked outside the door of Whittlesey Street, I turned the key in the door, leaving one or two lights on for the few weeks I was to be away. I met David and Jean and Claire Rendlesham, the most avant-garde fashion editor in London, at the near-new Heathrow Airport. David had elected to dress Jean in his current favorite look—thigh-high leather boots and narrow black dress—the miniskirt had not yet been invented. Jean's innocently beautiful face distracted the beholder from the faintly sinister image the three of us presented, with David and I wearing tight black Mod trousers, black leather jackets, and our pointiest winkle picker boots bought the Saturday before in Brixton Market. Even though Claire was entranced by Jean's absolutely modern look, she was mildly nervous that we might be refused entry into those still very conventional United States.

On the plane Claire and I sat together. She grilled me about what I had been doing and, more specifically, what I wanted to do. I had absolutely no idea beyond "the nightclub." Little did I know that in a few days Claire would alter the course of my life for the next eleven years, and perhaps, in retrospect, forever.

Within a week of landing at Idlewild, I was in the thick of New York. Its society then was a pretty tight one, with a handful of places one went to, and a small group of people. Those whom I was brave enough to contact spread the word among their friends, who were all quite apparently delighted to have a young Englishman in their midst. New Yorkers' generosity and kindness to visitors to their city was legendary, and I was immediately asked to parties; on only the second night I went to one given by the art dealer George Dix, whom I'd seen in London a few weeks before, in his apartment, which was—consciously, I now see—done up to resemble rooms in a Henry James novel. The first person I talked to was Virgil Thomson, the composer of the opera *Four Saints in Three Acts,* with a libretto by Gertrude Stein. I had been fascinated by photographs of the decor, all created from shimmering cellophane by Florine Stettheimer, an extraordinary designer who looked "like a moth that has fed on a gold scarf," as Cecil Beaton said of her. It was thrilling to hear Virgil, a pink-faced, sprightly old man, talk about the team that had created this bizarre opera.

From where we sat I noticed a handsome couple enter the room. They were Speed Lamkin, a very fashionable, and I soon learned, somewhat notorious Southern playwright; he was with his tall, patrician boyfriend, James Davison, whom I instantly thought devastatingly attractive. As a couple, I realized, they represented the most elegant of New York gay society. That night, however, it was Philip Johnson, his gray hair brushed forward around his temples, who appeared to find me irresistible. Aware that he was the architect, with Mies van der Rohe, of the newly finished and greatly admired sepia glass Seagram Building on Park Avenue, I was extremely flattered when Philip asked me to dinner the following week.

The night ended with a group of us, including Alan Pryce-Jones and some of his "Rothschild relations" as he proudly referred to members of his wife's family, going to see Chubby Checker at the Peppermint Lounge on West Forty-fifth Street. Chubby had actually invented the Twist; the lounge was its birthplace, and "Peppermint Twist" his current hit, which he sang that night backed by four slim-hipped, white-suited boys.

The evening of my dinner with Philip Johnson came. "Let's meet in the Oak Room of the Plaza," he'd said. I sat at the bar. After a few minutes Philip was ushered in with much kowtowing by the waiters. Far better looking than I remembered, he was beautifully dressed in one of those immaculate thin black suits only Brooks Brothers knew how to cut, white button-down shirt, and black knit tie. He was extremely attractive. "I was almost sure you wouldn't come, so I came late on purpose," he said as he took his seat. "I wanted to be certain you'd be here already." This was most alluring, and as the evening progressed his transparent seduction was augmented by his palpable ability to give me a crash course in art and architecture—which rooms at the Museum of Modern Art contained the finest pictures, which galleries had the best contemporary art, which buildings he admired—to see in the short time I had left in the city.

After dinner we walked across town to his apartment on Fifty-fifth Street, which was surprisingly small but decorated—if that's the word for minimalism before the term was coined—entirely in white, with an all-too-lifelike sculpture of a burned baby in a high chair the only "color." Philip was going abroad a few days later, but he suggested I use the apartment for the rest of my stay. I went uptown, collected my things from my hotel, and moved in.

"I've been talking to Alex Liberman at *Vogue* about you," said Claire Rendlesham, who, dying to see Philip's apartment, had come for a drink. In her disarmingly direct way, she went on, "I've told him you're talented but waste it, and need a proper job. He wants to see you. Ring him up. Here's his number. Murray Hill 9-5900." How well I was to get to know that number. "Condé Nast Publications. . . ." "Mr. Liberman, please." "Just one moment, putting you through now." I explained myself to the secretary; a pause. "Mr. Liberman will see you tomorrow at eleven thirty."

Though *Vogue* was a major magazine, published in England, France, and America, I had no idea of the scale of the Condé Nast empire. The directory board of the Graybar Building, where I found myself that next morning, had rows of titles under the Condé Nast heading: *Mademoiselle, House & Garden,* and *Glamour* were the most recognizable. "*Vogue* reception, 19th Floor," read the sign.

I took the elevator and stepped bravely out into a new world. As in an Eve Arden movie, greige carpets rushed for miles to greige walls, greige curtains hung behind a greige lacquer desk, at which sat a faultlessly coiffured lady—"girl" is too flippant a word—in a greige suit with white lapels and white gloves, though sadly she was not Barbara Stanwyck, who had begun her career in this very position in the early thirties.

"I'm here to see Mr. Liberman."

"Just one moment." This lady Eve smiled through the whitest teeth, gloved white fingers dialing on a white telephone.

"I have Nicholas Haslam in reception to see Mr. Liberman. Thank you, Miss Slocum. Just one moment, Mr. Haslam, Mr. Liberman's assistant will be with you shortly." A tall preppy girl appeared; I was soon to realize that the high-ranking staff at *Vogue* had high-society assistants, often a mere step removed from the Kennedy White House. Leading me down a hall, she opened a door. This room, too, was greige, but paler. Huge modern paintings in black frames hung on the walls. Black sofas,

A view across the wheatfields of Great Hundridge Manor in Buckinghamshire, where I was born. My bedroom is the first attic window on the right.

My grandfather, the Hon. Arthur Ponsonby, on Isabel, in Wales, ca. 1890

My father in naval
uniform, Rome, ca. 1905

My father, William Haslam (left), and his brother, Robert,
and sisters, ca. 1910

ABOVE: *My father watching my mother with two admirers*
on the balcony above her bedroom at Hundridge, ca. 1938

RIGHT: *My mother's cowboy lover in Reno,*
during her divorce from Henry Marks
to marry my father, ca. 1931

ABOVE: *My grandmother Evelyn Ponsonby playing squaw with two braves, my brothers John and Michael*

LEFT: *Ralph Hamlyn, my father, and Geoffrey Scott at Hundridge in the early 1930s*

By the swimming pool at Hundridge, aged three

My father and Baroness Moura Budberg setting out for tennis at Hundridge, ca. 1955

My American half sister, Anne, on a vacation in England.
She sits between Michael and John, and I am behind with our mother.

I wear my Eton uniform
for the first time, in the garden
of Hundridge, ca. 1953

With Ray Foster at
Tallulah Bankhead's house in
Connecticut in 1953 during
my first trip to America when
I was still at Eton. I am holding
Tallulah's dog.

TOP LEFT: *In my apartment in New York, ca. 1963*

TOP RIGHT: *Simon Fleet at Freya Stark's house in Asolo, Italy, 1965*

ABOVE LEFT: *An unusually tidy interior of Simon Fleet's house, the Gothic Box, 22 Bury Walk in London, 1958*

ABOVE RIGHT: *Christopher Gibbs in London*

FAR LEFT: *David Bailey when I first met him, 1959*

LEFT: *Min Hogg, 1959*

ABOVE: *Michael Wishart painting in his studio, ca. 1957*

LEFT: *I took this photograph of Peggy Guggenheim and her daughter, Pegeen, (far right) at the Villa Malcontenta, ca. 1959, on my first trip to Venice with Michael Wishart.*

I photographed the Queen Mother greeting Margot Fonteyn at St. James's Palace, 1962; I had been sent by Vogue *in New York to cover the opening of Annabel's.*

With the former ballerina Nora Kaye at my house in Montego Bay, Jamaica, ca. 1963

ABOVE: *Dancing with a debutante for a* Vogue *shoot on the St. Regis Roof, ca. fall 1962*

BELOW: *An invitation to one of Cole Porter's dinners in the Waldorf, the year before he died*

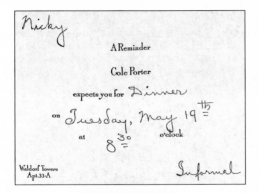

Frugging with Jane Holzer in a New York nightclub, ca. 1963

I am on the right photographing Paul McCartney and Ringo Starr holding Show *magazine, for which I'd just become editor, 1965.*

Mick Jagger at the "Mods and Rockers Ball," I gave for the Rolling Stones and Jane Holzer's birthday at Jerry Schatzberg's studio, summer 1964. Tom Wolfe wrote about the party in "Girl of the Year" in The Kandy-Kolored Tangerine-Flake Streamline Baby.

SHOW

THE
MAGAZINE
OF
THE
ARTS

ONE DOLLAR
NOVEMBER 1964

IAN FLEMING'S
LAST INTERVIEW

THE NEW HUMOR

THE WHITE HOUSE
Palace or Prison?

THEIR OWN
STORIES:
Truman Capote,
Morris West

BALLOT
FOR BEST,
WORST
IN TV

UNDERGROUND MOVIES
How They're Made
(Our cover girl,
one of their stars)

GLORIA VANDERBILT'S
First SHOW Story

GUIDE FOR
PRO-FOOTBALL
"TV WIDOWS"

My most provocative cover for Show,
Jane Holzer by David Bailey

black chairs, a vast ebony table covered in photographs. "Nicholas Haslam," she announced to, seemingly, no one.

A chair behind a black desk swiveled around. A silhouette got up, advanced, hand extended, eyes glittering. "I'm Alex Liberman."

It was the man Min Hogg and I had sat near at Senequier in Saint-Tropez the previous summer, the man she had thought was Oleg Cassini.

After a few minutes' conversation, made easier by the mutual recognition (though it was never mentioned), Mr. Liberman ("call me Alex"—but I never did or dared) sat down, swiveling his chair so that once again he became a silhouette against the skyscraper background. "I want you. Go upstairs."

The door opened, and Miss Slocum beckoned. "Please come with me. We will go and find Miss Campbell. She will figure out your Green Card work permit."

Well, you could have knocked me down with a fender, as Bea Lillie used to say. Nobody had ever offered me a real job, let alone so suddenly and emphatically. But what was the job? What was "upstairs"? Where would I live? And what on? What about Michael? What about Whittlesey Street? What about the white Delage? But as I followed Susie along several miles of corridors, it dawned on me I had just been handed a new life on a dazzling plate.

Mary Campbell, a big, brusque, but motherly woman, took my details. "The Green Card will take about a month. Meanwhile you start on Monday in the art department at *Vogue*. This will be your salary. Miss Gersh"—into a telephone—"please come up and meet Nicholas Haslam. And be so kind as to show him where he'll be working."

Miss Gersh, it transpired, was the secretary to *Vogue*'s art director, Priscilla Peck, whom I was to assist. Dear Gloria. I came to love her, but at our first meeting she had that "I wonder how long he'll last" look. I followed her down to the nineteenth floor—the creative floor of *Vogue*, the twentieth being the executive—past the senior editors' rooms, past their assistants' rooms, past the secretaries' rooms, past the clothes rooms, past the beauty rooms, past the shoe rooms, past the hat rooms, past the fur rooms, past the accessories rooms, past the copywriters' rooms. And then, in a big, brilliantly sunny corner, looking down on the grandeur of Grand Central Station (the Pan Am building had not yet been dumped on top of it), into the art department.

And suddenly staring me in the face was the realization that if I hadn't exactly burned my boats, I'd certainly jumped ship. All at once the past—roots, country, friends, and family—was no longer part of my future. And perhaps one of its hidden benefits was that it perforce ended the painful situation with Michael. In one of our increasingly infrequent telephone conversations, he seemed tacitly to agree. The simple three-week adventure trip to New York with David and Jean was heading toward an uncertain future in a city I'd always felt an affinity with but in reality knew merely superficially.

First of all I needed somewhere to live. My sojourn at Philip Johnson's all-white apartment had sort of hit the skids, marked by some catty remarks by his long-term, if mostly absent, boyfriend, John Hohnsbeen (who was later to become director of the Guggenheim Collection in Venice after Peggy's death). One day, walking down Madison Avenue with Nin Ryan, that daughter of Otto Kahn to whom my uncle Cecil Ponsonby had been sports tutor, we ran into the neat little figure of Franco Zeffirelli, whom I had talked to at one of David Webster's dinners on Capri. He recommended the cheap, old-fashioned, and slightly run-down hotel from which he had just emerged. In a flash I took a room. Due to the fact that its tiny window opened onto a filthy internal space, it gave added meaning to "dirt cheap," and served while I looked for somewhere in Greenwich Village, at that time an excitingly outré part of the city to live in.

It wasn't too long before I found another, marginally cleaner, back room in a semiresidential hotel at 1 Washington Square. It boasted a kind of sub–Bobby Short cabaret singer of Cole Porter–type songs, sung to an excitingly sexy hobo Village audience of both the young and the aged. Djuna Barnes, the author of *Nightwood,* who was living in a pretty cobbled mews called Patchin Place nearby, would drop in. Licorice-thin in black and a bandeau, she would join the singer Libby Holman in her booth, both puffing on the cigarettes that marriage to the Reynolds tobacco heir had surely guaranteed Libby for life. They had given her fine voice the rusty edge I'd always admired in her recordings, especially in "The House of the Rising Sun." One night a homespun-togaed, complicated-sandaled, aquiline old man—skinny as air and slung about with a large goatskin bag containing (I swear) a handmade Aeolian harp—appeared. It was Raymond Duncan, who ran a kind of ancient Greek appreciation seminary up in the high Eighties and was brother, no less, to the legendary scarf-strangled Isadora. I was only faintly interested by the best-known gay bar on Christopher Street, with its brass foot rail made of nose-to-tail dachshunds, and rather more in the rawer encounters with hustlers and johns on Forty-second Street, then in its heyday of seediness. That seminal novel, *Last Exit to Brooklyn,* had just been published, and I wrote to the author, Hubert Selby, Jr., as if from a grateful hustler fan, receiving a most charming, and now lost, letter in reply.

While the furor surrounding the debacle of the opened letters at Eton had faded somewhat, the memory of Ray Foster had not. I had treasured his phone number. I called it, not for a moment believing that it would still be valid or that he, or perhaps—horrors—his mother, would answer. I was astonished when, calm as all get-out, he answered, delighted, and invited me to meet him that evening, and I was thrilled to see that his new image was a Brando-like wild one. This renewal of our relationship opened up the exciting scene of gay leather bars, then an almost purely American phenomenon.

Finally the longed-for card arrived, and I could be salaried. It seemed more appropriate to find somewhere to live near my office in the Graybar Building, and Drue Heinz, the glamorous redheaded wife of the baked-bean king, at that time on the cusp of creating her role as a benefactress of the arts, put me in touch with Teeny Duchamp, wife of the painter Marcel. Teeny had a studio apartment on Lexington in the Fifties that she rented out, and she sweetly made it affordable.

The large uncurtained window faced downtown and practically into my office at *Vogue,* precluding any nudity when descending the staircase.

DYNAMIC AND MODERN AS Alex Liberman was, the actual editor of *Vogue* when I joined was a dusty old party called Jessica Daves. A round little woman invariably dressed in navy blue, with white cotton gloves, she seemed to make no impact on the day-to-day life of the magazine, though perhaps in her office—from which she rarely emerged in daylight—deeply high-powered decisions were being taken amid the Hattie Carnegie suits and Elizabeth Arden evening gowns, designed by handsome young Oscar de la Renta, whom I had admired one day in Tiffany's, and whom I could sometimes glimpse through the infrequently opened door.

The other editorial members of *Vogue*'s staff were far removed from the stick-thin image of fashion editors today. Babs Simpson was the most senior fashion editor, her blue eyes twinkling under her pageboy bob. Dressed with almost Shaker strictness, she had a stunningly simple beach house on the farthest reaches of Long Island. One hot summer night, at one of the barbecues Babs had made Montauk's most coveted weekend event, I again found myself sharing a bench with Libby Holman. At the height of her unlikely affair with Montgomery Clift, she dismissed my gush of fandom with a shrug of her angular shoulder and a stream of smoke, and turned her attention to the just-divorced-from–Marilyn Monroe, and thus rather morose-looking, Arthur Miller. While watching him, I remembered that Simon Fleet's great friends Lord and Lady Drogheda let their beautiful eighteenth-century house, Parkside, set in the woods above Runnymede, to Arthur Miller and Marilyn Monroe while she was filming *The Prince and the Showgirl* with Laurence Olivier. Life at Parkside cannot have been very sunny. Monroe, already fighting with Miller, who would frequently walk out, was often hysterical and indulged in a bout of Freudian territory marking. When the Droghedas returned to their house after the Millers left, they found excrement in every drawer. Babs shared the fashion department with statuesque Chessy Rayner, a Park Avenue princess, known as Little Chessy. Her less tall mother, confusingly called Big Chessy, was married to Pat Patcevitch, a handsome Russian famous for a torrid affair with Marlene Dietrich. Also in this department was Gloria, one of the O'Connor twins, two beauties whose mother had vowed that her girls would make dazzling marriages. (They had been photographed as the originals of the permanent-wave advertising campaign. "Which Twin Has the Toni?")

Gloria had married a banker while her sister, Consuelo, became Contessa Rodolfo Crespi and the reigning beauty of Rome. Gloria's desk was next to that of Count Niki de Gunzburg, the fur editor. Niki had been a dashing figure in 1930s Europe, a member of the close set that revolved around Marie-Laure de Noailles, Coco Chanel, and Elsa Schiaparelli. Rather like his friend the Sicilian jeweler Fulco, Duc di Verdura, Niki had frittered a fair fortune on fancy-dress balls, but now he looked like a Knize-tailored bloodhound: perfect gray flannel suits from the great Viennese tailor, and black silk ties knotted below his liquid, humorous eyes and long disdainful upper lip. Niki had more arcane U and non-U's than my "aunt" Nancy Mitford ever dreamed of. One morning, going up in the elevator with us, Cathy di Montezemolo, a newly arrived *Vogue* editor, said she'd got drunk the previous evening "on red wine." Niki rolled his eyes. "One says," he murmured, "either 'wine' or 'white' wine." He seemed the über-urban man, but in fact he couldn't wait for weekends and his escape to a log cabin lost in the New Jersey forests, where, wearing lederhosen and lodens, he relived his mittel-European past. He was also, I discovered, "the other Niki" whom Simon Fleet had just seen the day we had met in Trafalgar Square.

Next to furs came shoes, a room presided over by big booming beaming Kay Hayes. She was visited regularly by a skinny, spotty lad in black jeans with an artless haircut, short back-and-sides below a wedge of mouse-colored fringe. He carried a sheaf of delicate drawings in a portfolio, the most fanciful designs and illustrations of shoes. Kay was, in effect, the discoverer of Andy Warhol. For, ever since being an unknown student, Warhol had done these illustrations for Kay's pages—and also of scent bottles and other products for Carol Phillips, the beauty editor. Andy smiled easily, a somewhat mirthless smile, and seemed timid, but one sensed a will of steel for which the timidity was camouflage. Until I got to know him—and his nascent boundless talent and ambition—better, I am ashamed to say that in the art department we'd throw away reams of Andy's drawings after we had "statted" his originals to the dimensions we wanted for layout.

The prettiest editors were on "Shophound," the "latest-must-have" page. Chic, cool, and alarmingly critical, Louise Lieberman, a real-estate heiress married to the sexy tennis ace Dick Savitt, worked alongside Afdera Fonda, a volatile emotional Venetian beauty who was in the throes of divorcing actor Henry while having an affair with *Vogue*'s publisher, Ed Russell. Ed's daughter Serena—just to make things easy—sat at the next desk. Serena's upper-class English voice, inherited from her mother, Lady Sarah Spencer-Churchill, was accented with dry East Coast American that I found wonderfully attractive, and we became immediate friends.

One of my most grateful memories is being taken by Serena to meet her great-grandmother, the legendary Consuelo Vanderbilt, Duchess of Marlborough. Mme Balsan, as she became after divorcing the duke and marrying Jacques Balsan—whom she'd loved when a young girl—sat in her pearl gray boiserie salon overlooking the East River amid the most perfect examples of French eighteenth-century furniture. Her face—atop the long white neck familiar from the Boldini portrait that was a favorite picture of Simon Fleet's—turned inquiringly toward one as she talked. With a wreath of blue-gray hair above the delicately drawn features, her weightless body clothed in mauve-gray chiffon down to her pointed satin shoes, she seemed delicate as a bouquet of sweet peas seen by moonlight. I was aware that we were, though in the midst of modern, milling Manhattan, witness to an ethereal echo of a vanished world.

The copywriters were between "Shophound" and us in the art room. The doyenne was Jeanne Ballot, pink and plump as an Edwardian rose, who usually wore black ruffled cocktail dresses to work, and was rumored to have been the mistress of old Condé Nast himself. Rosemary Blackmon was the very opposite, a tall, angular chain-smoker and sharp sentence turner. Annis "Mike" Bradshaw, a funny direct woman, was the mother of John Bradshaw, English *homme fatal* to many girls, and an early boyfriend of Anna Wintour. There were also Edith Lowe Gross and Mary Ellin Berlin, Irving's daughter, and novelist-to-be Joan Didion, who spent most of every morning in tears following a disastrous evening, but by afternoon had put on lipstick and Fleurs de Rocaille, transforming herself into the most desirable, delicious, funny, and perceptive dinner date.

On the corner, overlooking the domes, turrets, and gilded curlicued roof of Grand Central Station, with a seemingly endless view up Park Avenue, was the office of my immediate boss, Priscilla Peck. New England to the core, with her perfectly tailored suits, boyish haircut, and clipped quiet speech, Priscilla made Katharine Hepburn seem as raunchy as Texas "C'mon You Suckers" Guinan. In her youth Priscilla had been a painter of some note, and a member of the set that centered around Joe Carstairs, the flamboyantly tattooed and trousered hermaphrodite Chicago newspaper heiress. Priscilla now lived a rather more sedate life with her girlfriend—appropriately called Marty Mann—who had been the first woman to be cured by Alcoholics Anonymous and was now a big cheese in that admirable institution.

Priscilla was somewhat nervous of Alex Liberman and got very twitchy when word came that he was on his daily visit to our department. However, she bravely showed him my work, which was pretty extreme for the time—I was the first person to put the title of the articles at the bottom of the page, or to use lowercase letters as initials. Liberman would smile thinly at me, nod to Priscilla, and gratifyingly, a month or so later, my layouts would appear in the magazine. Priscilla perked up no end later on when Mrs. Vreeland became editor. I think she was really rather in love with her (it was hard, in some way, not to be), and called her, uniquely, "Dee-Arna."

The head of our department was nominally Woody Pratt, a man of such sweetness that no critical word crossed his lips—words anyway would have had difficulty getting past the constant cigarettes clamped between them. It was due to Woody that I took up smoking, as we waited all night for the couture collection photographs to be flown from Paris. The favored brand was Pall Mall superkings, and I miss them to this day. I still have the gold wire "cage" that the Tiffany jeweler Jean "Johnny" Schlumberger created for me to encase the crimson packets.

There was Jerry, a cheery guy who liaised with production; the rotund Carol Knoblock, who had very little reverence for her employers; and

Gloria Gersh, Priscilla's seemingly comme-il-faut secretary, who with her husband, Martin, had amassed a collection of exceedingly comme-il-faut English walnut antique furniture in their otherwise bare apartment. I soon found that Gloria had a wicked sense of humor and was frequently up for teasing the more pompous members of the staff.

This art department group was joined one day by a perfect-skinned, natural blond if frankly rotund beauty called Karin-Maria Winkelhorn. Half Danish and half Russian—her mother, Sofka (née Kutuzov, granddaughter of the general who had turned Napoleon from the gates of Moscow), had been born at Tsarskoye Selo. Bibi, as she was always called, became my beloved companion on dates and dares, her laughter ringing on the telephone, in taxis, in nightclubs and drive-ins. Many people, Diana Vreeland and Richard Avedon among them, thought Bibi had the most beautiful face they'd ever seen: Dick and I used her as the first oversize model in the issue of *Harper's Bazaar* that we did together a few years later. Thinking of Bibi brings back chicken salad at Schrafft's on Forty-second Street, and, on paydays, Michael's Pub, a fashionable restaurant about ten blocks uptown, which we could just get to and from in our lunch hour, wolfing their corned-beef hash. I remember drive-in movies on spring weekends at her parents' Connecticut house, and hear even now the gruff voice of a Russian grand duchess when I answered Sofka's telephone. I treasure the echo of a summer in Venice, Bibi's constant laughter rocking the boats.

An almost-secret staircase connected our area to the twentieth floor, where the offices of some of the most fearsome ladies on the staff were located. Leader of these was the features editor, Allene Talmey, whose intellectual bent would later frequently clash with Diana Vreeland's frothier approach. Miss Talmey's niece, Pamela Colin, later to marry the British ambassador David Harlech, father of my friend Jane Ormsby-Gore, and Marie-Pierre Colle, the last wife of Pat DiCicco (Gloria Vanderbilt's first husband), were her assistants. Next door, and often on the lavatory with the door open—her unabashed mode of conducting interviews—sat Margaret Case, the social editor. Miss Case was tiny, ugly, exquisitely dressed. All her life she maintained mannequin proportions; couturiers from Mme Lanvin to Paco Rabanne would send her their original creations. Under the dresses and the gruffness she was one of the sweetest people I have ever known. Margaret had been at *Vogue* for forty-five years, an intimate of Mr. Nast, who had guaranteed her a salary—and more important, for her, a position at *Vogue*—for life.

Due to my background and the fact that Cecil was a mutual friend,

Margaret opened the doors on a facet of American society that would otherwise have remained hidden, a New York still faintly redolent of a former elegance, a grandeur, a world still steeped in the long shadow of the so-called Age of Innocence. This stratum of society could, with little difficulty, have stepped from the pages of Henry James or Edith Wharton.

Perhaps the grandest was Elsie Woodward. Tall, with long matchstick-thin legs, she dominated New York society by dint of her birth—she was one-third of the Cryder triplets, all of whom had married American or European aristocrats; Elsie had married the handsome William Wood-ward, scion of the family that had founded the Hanover Bank, among the city's oldest. Elsie had a warmth and wit that embraced young and old alike. At one of her parties she introduced me to a haughty Chicago dowager, who inquired, deafly, "What's your name?"

"Haslam. It's rather an odd name," I answered.

"Not at all odd," she replied. "Old Mrs. Marshall Field's chauffeur was called Haslam."

Elsie's apartment in the Waldorf-Astoria reflected her patrician atti-tude. A quiet, elegant resolve imbued its rooms, exactly as it did their owner. When her son, Billy, was found shot dead, she continued to invite the suspected killer, her daughter-in-law, Ann, to her parties but never again addressed a word to her.

In the same league but perhaps rather more formidable was the ramrod-figured Helen Hull, the first Mrs. Vincent Astor, a determined matron with a taste for classical music and exotic travel. Late in life she proudly recounted her recent visit to Machu Picchu. "Goodness, Aun-tie," said my friend Emily, her niece. "Weren't you frightened on the fu-nicular, and how did you climb up all those stairs?" Mrs. Hull stiffened: "Don't be silly. I didn't get out of the limousine."

Quite a different kettle of fish was Mrs. Gilbert Miller. Kitty liked to keep the decoration of her apartment at 550 Park Avenue right up to date, and Billy Baldwin was routinely employed recovering the silken sofas and Louis bergères that stood assembled under the portrait of Don Manuel de Zuñiga, a coal-eyed child in a scarlet suit. This ravishing painting by Goya was the sole picture Kitty was allowed to borrow (and then only when she was in New York) from the vast collection of old masters given to the Metropolitan Museum by her father, the financier Jules Bache.

However enticing the prospect of having her maiden name on so many galleries in that august institution, Kitty Bache was thrilled to shed it and join the goyim by marrying Gilbert Miller. At the time he was an aspiring Broadway producer, a career Kitty's considerable fortune rapidly advanced. He would refer, in rare flashes of humility, to her as "my incomepoop." For their honeymoon they had traveled to Venice, where Linda and Cole Porter were ensconced, as was their summer custom, at the Palazzo Mocenigo and giving, as they did every year, a fancy dress ball. Gilbert and Kitty Miller, thrilled to be asked, were hanging around the staircase watching the tableaux of arriving celebrities. The Dolly sisters, mistresses to Oxford Street storeowner Gordon Selfridge, swept in, dressed to the eighteenth-century nines in pannier skirts, plumes, with a lamb on a leash. Kitty, versed in artists' oeuvres due to her father's collection, touched a Dolly's lace-gloved arm, and whispered admiringly, "Jenny, you look just like a Winterhalter."

Jenny Dolly whirled around, "Now listen, Kitty Bache, we'll have none of your New York Yiddish around here!"

By the time I met Kitty, Gilbert Miller, a crusty old thing with hair cascading from his nose and ears, was one of theaterland's most prominent moguls, whose own name had been emblazoned on many a Broadway theater. Invitations to the Millers' New Year's Eve party in New York, and their midsummer dance at the Savoy in London, embellished the grandest chimney mantels of several continents. Kitty, though far from beautiful, had turned herself into a minor work of art by becoming totally blue. Carefully curled blued hair—augmented, it was rumored, by blue crayon cunningly applied by the chief restorers of the Metropolitan, National Gallery, or Louvre—trembled above blue mascara'd lids and lashes, blue pearls nestled on lobes; blue diamonds filled the neckline of her blue Mainbocher couture. Rory McEwen's younger brother John-Sebastian, at his first smart party one Eton long-leave, saw this vision and said, "That must be Bluey Mavroleon," never having met the very male Greek shipowner of that name. Kitty's exquisite wardrobe was tended by her beloved ancient maid; when Marie died, Kitty was inconsolable, wailing, "*What* am I to do? She's the *only* person who could get Benedictine stains out of blue chinchilla!"

Kitty's nose for blueness made her a pioneer champion of the Duke of Windsor. The royal-blood connection also greatly impressed Gilbert.

"D'you know what the Dook calls Kitty?" he would ask dazzled listeners. Alert ears and expectant expressions awaited a nickname punchline. "Kitty!!" Gilbert would bellow triumphantly.

Between them Margaret and Kitty arranged for me to be invited to all the grand parties, among them Bill and Babe Paley's coming-out dance for their daughter Amanda Mortimer at their legendarily perfect Long Island house, Kiluna Farm. Placed in a dinner party before it at the nearby home of Edith Baker, hostess-mother of the celebutante Gloria, I sat next to a bubbling blonde, Peggy d'Arenberg, a Standard Oil heiress. She was renowned for never missing a party, flying the Atlantic weekly to attend every lighted candle. Ironically Peggy, who became Duchesse d'Uzes and settled in France, would be killed in a car crash leaving—luckily for Peggy, as someone said, not *going to*—a ball. At the Paley party, which was decorated with hundreds of glowing white moonlike lanterns hung high in the garden's trees, I was pounced on by the distinctly squiffy Irene Selznick; after a few minutes with this determined daughter of Louis B. Mayer, I was happy to be rescued by a very upright lady, Gee Marvel, the former wife of Sonny Whitney.

This rescue developed into a fast friendship, and my going to stay with Gee in Delaware. She took me to a debutante party at the du Ponts' nearby estate, Winterthur, with its famed art collection. Simon Fleet had once told me a story about its assembler, old Harry du Pont. He was showing a student his priceless collection of Early American pottery. She asked if she could hold the rarest piece. "Of course, my dear," he said. She dropped it, whereupon it smashed into smithereens, and she dissolved into tears. "There, there, my dear, don't cry. It's the human heart that matters. Are you all right?" he said, hand around her shaking shoulders. She replied, "Well, I do feel better now, thank you, sir." And then du Pont fainted.

· TEN ·

A FEW MONTHS BEFORE going to America, at dusk one evening in Tom Parr's Eaton Square flat, I had been riveted by a face across the room. I heard the laugh, a laugh of humor, not politeness, saw her throw her head back, saw her hand push her hair away from her brow, laughing the while. I saw only the upturned profile, sketched against the fading day; and then she turned, smiling, full face.

Her glamour was almost tangible. Her whole being seemed to glow, radiating not only humor but that rare quality that says, You and I are going to have good times together. Up close I saw the extraordinary beauty, the kind that is there, not applied. Nothing, I felt, could ever be fake about this woman. Love me or leave me be, was her line.

"Call when you get to New York," she said, handing me a sky blue card lettered in white: Jean Howard.

In the event, I didn't have to. Tom came quite frequently to New York to visit his lover, the jeweler Fulco Verdura. Though born Duca di Verdura e della Cerda, and thus a Sicilian grandee whose grandparents were the role models for Lampedusa's seminal novel, *The Leopard,* Fulco was the least standoffish of people, completely unimpressed by anyone's title or sacrosanct position—even to the point of wanking into the salad whenever entertaining his king—Umberto of Italy, at dinner. Having first designed jewelry for Chanel as a young man, Fulco had known the highest life of Paris, London, and Rome, about which he regaled one with tear-inducing tales and arcane allusions—"Dio mio," he used to say if one asked after mutual friends. "I haven't seen them since the Anschluss!"

During my first few days in Manhattan, he asked me to his apartment, rooms redolent of the Palermo palazzi of his youth, deep terra-cotta-colored-walls and palm trees dramatically lit, like a Caravaggio. "Hi there," said a half-remembered voice from the shadowy corner. I turned and saw Jean's wide, smiling mouth, blond head, perfumed aura.

The allure was, once again, immediate, the bond instantaneous. Jean, in an apartment on East Seventy-seventh Street every bit as gorgeous as its owner, took me into a world of pinch-yourself reality: evenings with all the stars on Broadway, plus painters, poets, photographers, and politicians—not excepting the president. Or suppers for two or three, Jean trying out some half-remembered recipe from Mexico, or making mad drinks last drunk in Bora-Bora. Ice cream flown in from Will Wright's in Los Angeles to guzzle after the movies, bagel and lox at sudden Sunday brunches.

Bit by bit I learned Jean's story, one as twentieth-century American as it could possibly be. Texas-born and beauty-blessed, she had been the youngest and most dazzling dancer in the last Ziegfeld Follies on Broadway. Obviously Hollywood came calling; MGM signed her as a Goldwyn Girl. Then came film roles. But Jean hated the way she looked on film, hated the process, and anyway had fallen in love with the hotshot agent Charles Feldman. Meanwhile she had to fend off the very serious attentions of studio boss Louis B. Mayer, who threatened to jump from his suite at the George V in Paris unless she succumbed. A couple of beefy ladies with whom Jean was traveling managed to coax Mr. Mayer down from the parapet.

Jean married Charlie and presided supreme over two decades of unmarred glamour at their house on Coldwater Canyon. Lady Sylvia Hawks Ashley Fairbanks met Clark Gable at one of Jean's parties and married him the next morning in Vegas; at another Claudette Colbert was shown a good time in the camellia bushes by a handsome lad who turned out to be a lady. Cole Porter played after dinner, Garland and Sinatra sang, Garbo walked down from her house and laughed with Dietrich. Directors Lewis Milestone, Howard Hawks, Billy Wilder, and producer Walter Wanger talked plots around the pool; Ginger danced on the lawn. By the time I met Jean this second time in New York, she had remarried and redivorced Charlie. She still loved him, she said, but knew that one day the heavy things they threw at each other would fatally find their mark. In the meantime they still shared the house on Coldwater, using it at different times. Charlie was in Europe, making *Casino Royale* and had fallen in love with the tall, beautiful French star Capucine, whom some people believed to be a hermaphrodite. The fact that Charlie's rooms in Coldwater were lined with drawings of hermaphrodites certainly added to the possibility. Jean, in her Seventy-seventh Street apartment, was dividing her friendships between Marti Stevens, the cabaret singer/ex-girlfriend of Marlene Dietrich, and the photographer Slim Aarons.

One day she called me. "You're always talking about Cole Porter. You'd better meet him." She arranged a dinner at his apartment in the Waldorf Towers, warning me on the way that we might possibly be alone with Cole, as so many of his friends now found him grouchy, and that, as he was often in great pain, he would probably be rather silent, perhaps thinking about his music, and not make conversation. "That's just fine by me," I said.

Apartment 33A, Waldorf Towers. As the elevator doors opened, we were met by Mr. Porter's lifelong secretary, Madeleine Smith, snow white hair framing a pink face, in a blue-and-white print dress with pearls. She shook my hand and kissed Jean. "You've hit a good day. 'The Little Boss' "—as she always called Cole—"feels pretty well. I think he's quite excited to meet someone new. Go into the library. I'll leave now that you've arrived." I suddenly realized I was the "someone new," but I knew Jean would cover up the nerves now welling.

A manservant took our coats. I looked quickly at the room's decoration, which was by my recently made friend, Billy Baldwin, New York's foremost decorator. I saw its bourbon brown walls, and bronze bookcases surrounding huge stylized paintings of animals and wondered, if perhaps, they had been done for some luxuriant edition of *The Jungle Book*.

After a few moments we heard a discreet cough from the hall—the signal, Jean had already told me, for us to busy ourselves, not to look—as Cole was carried in. In a reflection I could just see his footmen placing "the Little Boss" on a sofa, arranging his damaged legs to appear casually crossed.

"Jean, dear darling Jeannie. I do so love that red Chanel on you. Tell me your news!" His voice, amused and boyish, had a charmingly discordant squawk.

I turned to see a small, immaculate figure, fragile, like a precious object made by Cellini. The eyes in his ivory pale face were shining fragments of jet. His slight body was clothed in soft dark gray. From the lapels, one set with a crimson carnation, down to the razor-edge creases so perfectly arranged, he seemed like an elf sculpted in mercury, his dark tie and glossily shod feet sudden shards of obsidian. One hand gestured, the other needed the reassurance of his stick, his fingers drumming on its gold handle as if he were subconsciously composing a melody.

Jean introduced me. I managed, "Good evening, Mr. Porter." I must have mumbled, for he beckoned me to sit nearer him, saying he hoped I'd like to drink a Gibson with him. This was new to me. I asked. Cole explained it was a martini made with pearl onions rather than lemon peel or an olive. A few moments later it was brought, and I noticed the glass was engraved with the initials of his wife, Linda, whom—though theirs had been a totally sexless marriage—he was known to have adored and clearly still deeply missed.

For a while, as he made the supreme effort to welcome us, it was hard to believe he was in constant pain. However, at dinner, in a pale-green-paneled room hung with Capo di Monte porcelain, even though Jean entertained him with her particular chuckling brand of wit and gossip, one could tell he was getting tired and that his thoughts were elsewhere. She mentioned a mutual friend who had recently turned one hundred. Cole brightened, said he adored her, and hadn't seen her "for a generation." I mentioned that I had just done the layout in *Vogue* for a story we had run on that very person. Cole had not seen it. Next day I sent him a copy of the magazine, the page marked with a red rose, instead of a thank-you letter.

Cole wrote to me, his signature huge, faint, and wobbly under the black type of Madeleine Smith's letter. And then she telephoned asking me to dinner with Cole the following week.

It was the first of several dinners I had alone with him. The ritual of his entrance into the library never varied, nor the Gibson, though that quite often became two. It became almost fascinating to see how little of the delicious food that he insisted on being served he would eat. The mood could change rapidly. For a time he could be bright and enthusiastic; he would be excited with my suggestion of taking him to see, say, Nureyev dance, but after a while he realized he wouldn't be able to manage it. Then his head would sink forward like an old mandarin, and he would shut off. He was amused that I knew the lyrics, let alone the tunes, of so much of his work, including his most recent and, in the event, his last: a television version of *Aladdin* for the actor Sal Mineo, who had starred along with James Dean in *Rebel Without a Cause*. On the grand piano lay a stack of blank sheet music and a silver tub of sharpened pencils, but Cole would never again use them. One night, as he was carried past the piano, he paused. His little hand, simian dark against his pristine jeweled cuff, reached out to the keyboard and played a few notes, smiling at me as he did so. It was one of the most graceful gifts I have ever received.

At almost the same time I met a very funny, snubnosed girl called Susan Hammerstein, married to a struggling actor. Susan asked me to meet her lyricist father, Oscar and, by extension, his musician partner, Richard Rodgers. Amazing as it was to know such legends of the musical theater, whose songs I had sung since my polio years, they somehow were not on a par with Cole. His pathos, his sudden outpourings, sometimes bright and funny, sometimes dark, his consummate style and manners, albeit sitting agonizingly crippled in those memory-suffused surroundings, made him infinitely human and touching compared with his hale and happy peers.

A musical that Cole would probably not have wanted to see was one that Herbert Ross was rehearsing at a theater off Forty-second Street called *I Can Get It for You Wholesale.* Its unlikely, gritty setting was the Seventh Avenue rag-trade world, and its even unlikelier star was the ex-drunk actress Lillian Roth, who had written an autobiography, *I'll Cry Tomorrow,* about her addiction: hardly Cole's idea of glamour. To counteract this somewhat uninviting billing, Herb had given a small part to a girl he and Arthur Laurents had recently discovered called Barbara Streisand. Nora and I would sit in a box, riveted, as Herb shaped and refined Streisand's astonishing voice and equally astonishing temper.

In time the temper would be somewhat cooled by the show's leading man, a gangly tousle-curled boy called Elliott Gould whom she was soon to marry. Wrapping up rehearsal and, not long after, the production itself, which was not a *huge* hit, Nora and Herb seemed to keep open house on Jane Street. It was one of the prettiest in Greenwich Village, narrow and tree lined. But its river view was obliterated by day by the towering steel flank, by night the deck-lit dark bulk of a liner, either of the *Queens,* or the *France,* or the *United States,* startlingly filling the rectangle of sky at its Hudson River end. Evenings in Jane Street were a smooth continuation of those in Montpelier Walk—the laughter, the dinners, and the guests I was so enthralled by in London being all the more vigorous and exciting in their native setting.

Encouraged by Jean, I brazenly telephoned Tallulah Bankhead who, to my astonishment, remembered me from seven years before. She had moved from the brownstone I'd known to an apartment on Fifty-seventh Street, where, in a huge living room, sitting under her life-size portrait by Augustus John she had once given to and then asked back from Noël Coward, we would both get happily crocked on triple-strength old-fashioneds.

This extraordinary performer's final Broadway appearance was as Flora Goforth in Tennessee Williams's *The Milk Train Doesn't Stop Here Anymore.* I sat in agony through the first night as her legion of gay fans greeted every move she made, every line she spoke, with a barrage of cheers. Her distress was evident, her concentration a blur. This caused the straights in the audience to jeer her "poor" performance. It was an evening of pure hell, and the play's almost immediate closure fatally undermined Tallulah's surface self-confidence. Thereafter I spent several evenings in her company, including one extraordinary dinner alone with her and Dorothy Parker in Miss Parker's rooms in the Volney Hotel, but both ladies quickly got so drunk there was no comprehensible, let alone repeatable, conversation.

Raddled from her lifelong excess, Tallulah gave a last-ever performance in a mediocre television play that I watched with her. But if by now she drank the bourbon straight from the bottle, there was still the penetrating wit, the hooded, blinking eyes, the profusion of "Darlings." I was deeply sad when she died, the first truly legendary figure I'd been privileged to know.

One February weekend Jane Ormsby-Gore asked me down to Washington to stay at the British Embassy with her parents, David and Sissy Harlech. Since neither Jane nor I had enough money for the train fare, we planned to leave New York at dawn by Greyhound bus, but the evening before we were taken to Le Club, a new, small, and very smart nightspot in the East Fifties owned by the suavely handsome Olivier Coquelin. Jackie Kennedy, wearing a black dress with very thin shoulder straps and choker of huge pearls, was ushered in with a group of friends and shown to a nearby table, waving a white-gloved hand to Jane as she passed. Jane was too embarrassed to go over and mention our infra-dig journey early next morning.

As we left the club, snow was falling. By the time we reached the bus station it was deep; the bus pulled out into a blinding blizzard. We skidded through Manhattan, slithered into the tunnel under the Hudson. We crawled and lurched along ever more impassable highways. Something went wrong with the heating; through New Jersey we froze. Then it came back, full blast; in Delaware we steamed. Locked in this airless coach, the floor a river, windows opaque, and anyway nothing to see except nothing. "Oh, the heavy, drawn-out loneliness of the American evening," as Sybille Bedford wrote. Endured for fourteen hours, this carriage from a frigid hell turfed us out into the capital's murky daybreak. Struggling, bedraggled, to 3100 Massachussetts Avenue, we arrived, even for the very young and buoyant, totally wrecked. David met us in the embassy's vast hall. "Jackie called. Says why ever didn't you come up with her in the presidential train?"

Why not indeed.

The imposing Lutyens-designed embassy was appropriately treated by the Harlechs as a cheery chaotic country house, and although the ambassadress seemed to show mild, and not unreciprocated, wariness toward me—there was an icy side to Sissy Harlech rather at odds with the gaiety and warmth that David and all their children radiated—daily life at the embassy was great fun and surprisingly informal. At one dinner there was an empty place beside me. Suddenly a figure in heavily embroidered cream satin, with a stiff helmet of glossy dark hair, sat down. "Hello! My name's Lady Bird," said the vice president's wife breezily, extending a gloved Texan paw and a dazzling smile. "Everyone calls me Bird." At another, for diplomats considerably stiffer than Mrs. Johnson or other guests of Her Majesty's representative to the United States of America, Jane and I were determined to get the ill-assorted multinationals to attempt to dance an eightsome reel to country-and-western records. My dreams of being Ethel Merman overseeing "The Washington Square-Dance" in *Call Me Madam* had almost come true as I watched a wizened little cultural attaché from Thailand attempting a do-si-do with the rough hewn wife of an Iron Curtain ambassador.

We were on tenterhooks to see the hottest ticket in town, the White House redone partly by Sister Parish, the doyenne of American decorators, and partly by the great French interior designer Jansen, for Jackie Kennedy, and were asked for drinks with her and the president one lunchtime. The glamour and charm of the Kennedys had swept the world since he was a senator, but only now was Jackie becoming a legend for her unconventional beauty and consummate style.

She had just made a much-admired television special about the changes from the taste of the previous first lady, Mamie Eisenhower, whose taste could be described as lurid tartan or military spartan, or the Midwestern coziness of Bess Truman before that. Jackie was incredibly savvy about each room of L'Enfant's presidential palace, and every picture in them, many of which she had, not unlike Queen Mary, dragooned not only wannabes and climbers but also friends into "donating" to the White House collection. Even Fulco Verdura, normally immune to the most covert cadge, had felt impelled to give her a rare and valuable edition of engravings of portraits of early American Indian chieftains by that marvelous American artist George Catlin.

The Kennedy circle was out of this world: glamorous, witty, healthy, and huge. The tall blond Kay Halle, onetime girlfriend of Randolph Churchill; a molasses-voiced Southerner, Oatsie Leiter; *Washington Post* publisher, Kay Graham. Their conversation was whiplash quick and smart, like dialogue from some 1940s movie, spiced with the latest Oval Office secret; the columnist Joseph Alsop, flirtatiously gay-eyed behind round, black-rimmed spectacles, and recently married to Susan Mary Patten, were the pinnacle of socio-political hosts, eclipsing Gwen Cafritz and Perle Mesta, for whom I had an automatic soft spot as she had been the inspiration for *Call Me Madam;* Gore Vidal, the handsomest and cleverest man then—and indeed now—who shared a stepfather with Mrs. Kennedy; Alice Roosevelt Longworth, the daughter of President Teddy Roosevelt, an extraordinary relic of the century's cusp, after whom a particular color she had worn as a White House debutante, was named. (Sersee used to sing "My sweet little Alice blue gown" as she bustled around the Hundridge kitchen.) In these short Kennedy years the capital was palpably the power base of the world; after a period in the Eisenhower doldrums, intellect and style again infused politics, though the partner-swapping, bed-hopping, incestuous reality of this soi-disant court of Camelot was not to be revealed for several decades.

THERE WAS OFTEN SAID TO have been more newsprint devoted to the Liz Taylor/Eddie Fisher/ Richard Burton/Sybil Burton tangle of marriage and divorce than to the entire Korean War. One of the central figures of this much publicized showbiz carousel was about to become a great friend. Much as I had admired Burton's voice, presence, and intriguingly pockmarked beauty when I had seen him onstage in *Camelot,* I came to know that Sybil was the one who had emerged from this convoluted quadrangle with the most to lose. As a very young Welsh actress, she had married Burton when they were both ingenues at Stratford. They had two daughters and, Richard having become a major leading man, she thought, a perfect life. When he left her for Taylor, she was devastated. Having previously met in London, Sybil saw me, perhaps, as a sympathetic and obviously innocent companion for the first nights and Broadway parties that constituted her world, and thus she and I spent many evenings together. When at last she met and fell in love with the astonishingly handsome actor Jordan Christopher, they started a nightclub, inexplicably called Arthur. It was the coolest place for the young to go, drawing in also Sybil's more intellectual friends like Mike Nichols, Elaine May, and Jules Feiffer, all delighted to be in a place where the music was so loud they didn't have to hear themselves speak, let alone think.

Just starting at this time was the American version of the *nouvelle vague,* which involved making films using utterly unknown, untrained, and very young people in the lead parts. There was a huge buzz about how this was the new thing, the way movies were going, how that success could be copied, and so on. At Arthur one night I had run into and been charmed by the legendary bandleader Artie Shaw, fascinating for having been married to, among others, Lana Turner and Ava Gardner. His current wife was the actress Evelyn Keyes. As her previous husband was John Huston, the Shaws had most of Hollywood under their belt. They also had a screenplay, and for some reason seemed to think I was ideal to star in it. Naturally I was extremely flattered, and spent several evenings in their company, they topping up their Scotches, and conferring about the script, while occasionally appraising me closely across the table. In the end they saw through me, or saw a distinct lack of talent; for nothing came of the project, and I didn't see Artie for years. Then, in Hollywood, at a studio head's table for an Oscar dinner, there he was, a still-handsome man in a black and silver Western shirt and bolo tie.

"Mr. Shaw, you won't remember me, but years ago you wanted to make me a movie star."

He looked up, his eyes, old now, scrutinizing me; then he glanced around the table. "Well, looks like I succeeded, don't it?" he said. One can't ask for more than that in the charm department.

ALMOST THE FIRST TIME I ever heard the word "celebrity" was from Earl Blackwell, the white-wavy-haired fixer who ran a PR company called Celebrity Service. He scanned the gossip columns every day and, seeing my name come up with increasing frequency rather often in the columns of Walter Winchell, Leonard Lyons, and Dorothy Kilgallen, rang me to ask if I would be auctioned at a charity event—"An evening on the town with Nicky Haslam." I was "won" by Susan Weisbart, whose father, David, produced, besides *Rebel Without a Cause,* several of Elvis Presley's movies.

Dining and later dancing with her, I felt by association that I was getting closer to the King, that ultimate celebrity. Being mentioned in these columns also led to what was perhaps the pinnacle of camp fame, being asked by Joan Crawford to be her date for the premiere of *Cleopatra.* I pictured myself on her arm, à deux, as the flashbulbs popped, but Joan (as she didn't ask me to call her) turned out to be accompanied by an overdressed overjeweled tub of a matron from Palm Beach—"my best friend, Mrs. Nate Spingold"—and spent a lot of the evening sending me to telephone Dorothy Kilgallen, with whom she was rumored to be having an affair. Dorothy joined us at the party after the film, dead drunk: "Dorothy's rather *tired,*" Joan very sympathetically whispered, by way of excusing Kilgallen's supine state.

Encountering one iconic gay goddess would have been most people's lot: With Tallulah and now Joan, I had already met two. The third jewel was about to complete the set. I was astonished to find that the woman with wildly mascaraed eyes, rather loose teeth, and a flamboyant purple satin turban, sitting next to me at lunch at Tug Barton's house, was Gloria Swanson. We spoke about Bunny Roger's *Sunset Boulevard* party, and she told me her friend Angus McBean had sent copies of his photographs of Bunny as Norma Desmond. "He was far more beautiful than I ever was," this famously self-centered star said modestly. I had originally met our host with Tony Armstrong-Jones in London before going to America, and due to his passion for show business in general and the ballet in particular, it wasn't long before Tug and I ran into each other. He lived in gaudy splendor in a house in the Seventies off Madison Avenue, where in rooms furnished with mementos of the dance, including several pairs of many prima ballerinas' danced-out pink satin toe shoes lovingly preserved in Plexiglas boxes, he gave many extraordinary parties with some extraordinary guests. I was sometimes lucky enough to be asked to the ballet with Tug, perhaps even to first nights of the Royal Ballet, and seeing Fonteyn and Nureyev in their sublime partnership; it was impossible not to be moved to tears by the no-longer-young Margot's revitalization by, and evident love for, Rudi. After one such performance we went on to supper at El Morocco, where, taking Margot on the floor, I found out that the old adage that ballet dancers have no sense of rhythm was true even in the case of the glamorous dame.

Not all evenings were occasions of such refined elegance. At my Lexington Avenue apartment, I started asking people around to slapdash suppers after work. My old-new friends—David Bailey and Jean Shrimpton on their trips to America, or Julian and Jane Ormsby-Gore—mingled with the new-new friends I'd been making: Ken Lane, a shoe designer for I. Miller, even then nurturing dreams of becoming a costume jeweler. His bejeweled dreams were soon realized, and his ever-expanding talent and corresponding wealth moved him from one fabulously decorated apartment to another; Joel Schumacher, tall and beautiful, at the time a window dresser for Tiffany's, with his eye on a career in fashion and, eventually, directing Hollywood movies; Milenko Blanc, a half-Romanian ne'er-do-well with an intentionally cultivated mittel-European accent, dangerous humor, and a more dangerous tongue, but nevertheless immensely beguiling. His father had been King Carol's corrupt prime minister, the king's notorious flame-haired mistress, Mme Lupescu, was Milenko's godmother, and his idol was the Duchess of Windsor. Vota Blumenthal, his despised American mother, was always referred to as "that drett-ful dyke. My dee-yer, one has to shake the cigarrr ash out of her letters to find the check." Dyke or not, Vota got Milenko one of his few paid jobs as an extra in a film directed by her friend, the intensely masculine Anatole Litvak. Milenko was on-screen for a split second, at a desk, furiously typing—bang-bang-bang, whee, bang bang bang. We asked what he was typing. " 'WallisWindsorWallisWindsorWallis Windsor,' of course! What *else* would I be typing?"

CHUCK TURNER, a young musician, was a friend who lived on York Avenue in the shadow of the Fifty-ninth Street Bridge. We could hear the thump of tires on the steel ramps all night from the cramped top-floor bedroom of Chuck's tiny house. Below, in an equally cramped pitch-pine kitchen, Chuck would cook ambitiously elaborate dinners for his musical friends, Samuel Barber, the gentle and modest composer of *Vanessa,* an opera that I had seen at the old Met; Leonard Bernstein, who, besides being clearly jealous of Chuck's relationship with me, I found unbearably false and conceited; and the wonderfully funny Earl McGrath, a skinny boy with glistening eyes and a drooping Proustian mustache, at the time Gian Carlo Menotti's secretary. Earl's humor gave a whole new meaning to camp: "Tonight I'm going to be Joan Crawford [or Lucille Ball or Hedy Lamarr] all evening."

If Chuck didn't cook, we would get takeout pizza, then a novel form of eating, and go on for a drink at sawdust-floored P.J. Clarke's on Third Avenue, where the by-now Barbra Streisand's "My Coloring Book" or "People" poured almost continously from the jukebox. Hearing them has ever since immediately invoked those stifling New York nights made hotter by the steam from the subway grilles as we crossed the avenues on our way home, the promise of dawn, and the heaven of youth.

MY DAILY ROUTINE AT *Vogue* was about to be dramatically transformed. I had heard about Diana Vreeland, who was the fashion editor of *Harper's Bazaar* (*Vogue*'s only and at that time more chic rival) from Cecil Beaton, who, having worked with her, and admired her unique style for several decades, was a confirmed fan, and also, on our flight across the Atlantic, from Claire Rendlesham, to whom Mrs. Vreeland was an idol. Suddenly a rumor was buzzing around the corridors of the Graybar Building. "Mrs. Vreeland is coming. Coming *here,* coming to *Vogue.*" Sure enough, a day or two later Serena Russell and I received invitations—flatteringly the only two members of staff below the rank of editor to do so—asking us to the party at the Colony Club to welcome Diana Vreeland into the bosom of Condé Nast.

Mrs. Vreeland's appearance was breathtaking. She didn't merely enter a room, she exhilarated it, and all eyes immediately locked on her, hypnotized. Her onyx black hair, sleeked back from a sloping brow, revealed ears powdered terra-cotta red with a hare's-foot brush; her peony pink cheeks, the pronounced crimson lips below a long nose, her cranelike walk and pelvic-thrusting stance had all been described to me, but her actual presence was like a sock on the jaw. You knew you were seeing a supernova. It was not long before I discovered that behind this astonishing exterior lay a much-heralded mind not only of dazzling fantasies (and a sense of history, albeit often reordered to suit them) but of originality of thought, and a carefully shrouded or, rather, disguised loving tenderness.

Her immediate, astounding action on arrival at *Vogue* was to have Jessica Daves's formerly dreary office lacquered shrieking scarlet, and carpeted in leopard skin—"tigre" (pronounced "teegray"), as she called any big-cat markings, whether tiger, leopard, or ocelot. There exists a photograph of her in the room, at her black desk below a vast pinboard smothered with drawings and notes, just visible among them the painted card I'd done to welcome her on her first day. I was to get to know this room well. One of my jobs as a junior in the art department was to attend to the retouching of any fashion photography, a serious matter at that time as, quite apart from there being no question of nudity, we had to touch out navels, such innocent features being then—unbelievable as it now sounds—considered obscene. Each morning, after the ritual of her eleven o'clock entrance, would come the summons: "Send for Rembrandt."

Armed with my layouts, and Mrs. Vreeland with her red wax pencil, we would spend an hour improving on the beauty of those impossibly beautiful girls: Suzy Parker, Verushka, Dovima, Frederica (and before long, Jean Shrimpton and Twiggy), as assistants trundled in racks of clothes for her approval, and hats, shoes, jewels, gloves, furs, cosmetics, wigs, and false hair: "It's not fake anything, it's real Dynel," was a Vreeland remark that became an advertisement. Anything she liked was "diviiine," while "Uuum?" meant *Good God, no!*

In between there would be digressions into the history of costume: "Sewing in a sleeve at that angle was first done in Poland in the 1770s," or "Schiaparelli invented that wrapped skirt in her collection the summer before the war. Couldn't wait to wear it." Constructively critical, Mrs. Vreeland was never bitchy. She also had the brilliant knack of making one think one had just come up with the idea she had subtly put into one's head.

Foreign lands, and especially the then-exotic ones like China, Russia, and Turkey, were a lifelong passion for Diana, due to her supposed birth in France and childhood in England. For Europe she held a special thrall, and she was particularly fascinated by "swinging London" and, by extension, me.

My father had sent me a newspaper clipping of a new pop group from Liverpool. Being from Lancashire himself, he'd been intrigued by them, though he was the least musical of men. I showed this article on the Beatles to Mrs. Vreeland: "They're too *adorable,* get them photographed immediately!" She sent me to England to arrange it. The resulting portrait, taken by Peter Laurie after a gig in Northampton, was the first photograph printed of the Beatles in any American magazine. In those days the fans threw flowers, rather than bottles and knickers, onto the stage. I gathered these up into posies and passed them to the boys. Holding them, these wild young cannibals sat there looking as innocent as Victorian bridesmaids.

Young aristocrats, too, were grist to Diana, and the pages of *Vogue* soon had spreads on Nico and Alastair Londonderry in their David Hicks–designed house in Hampstead; of Desmond and Mariga Guinness with white-blond children at their Gothic Irish castle, Leixlip; or of Peregrine Eliot and his wife, Jacquetta, at Port Eliot, an intensely romantic country house on the edge of the sea in Cornwall—places and people surely as foreign to the American reading public as the inhabitants of Timbuktu. Her antennae being ever on the qui vive, she was intrigued to hear that my brother's Eton contemporary Mark Birley was opening a London nightclub named after his wife, my friend Annabel Vane-Tempest-Stewart. She sent me over to arrange photographs of the unutterably English crowd that would be gathered for the opening night. While I was there, Margaret Case telephoned me in a panic.

"Help," she said. "Main's dying!" Heavens, I thought—had the electricity in New York failed? Then she explained. Her great friend the dress designer Mainbocher was in mortal danger unless I could collect the right pills for him from a doctor in London. I flew with the precious package back across the Atlantic and delivered it to Margaret. Mainbocher recovered and, in gratitude took me for dinner à deux at Le Pavillon. (It's odd that the only two times I dined at Le Pavillon were with world-famous couturiers; the other was Yves Saint Laurent. This time the lights *had* failed, as it was during the great New York blackout.)

Diana's and my working relationship soon became a friendship outside the office. Diana and her husband, Reed, often invited me to join them for Sunday lunch, a fixture of their weekend. The interesting and beautiful young, and especially at this time Italians, were meat and drink to Diana, and one could be sure that girls of the aristocratic calibre of Benedetta Barzini, Verde Visconti, or the model Luciana Pigniatelli would join us. Diana particularly enjoyed evening jaunts to odd things I'd discovered, such as Chinese operetta in a pagodalike theater way down on the East Side, or tango competitions at Roseland dance hall.

We sometimes met for lunch during the week, always in Janssen's, the restaurant on the street floor of the Graybar Building. The most memorable of these was to come about a year later, on the day of President Kennedy's assassination. The first news came on my (illicit) radio in the art department, just as I was leaving to join her. Knowing her family's friendship with Jack, and particularly Jackie, I stayed a few minutes to be able to tell what I heard, and rushed to join her at the booth in the tragedy-oblivious, bustling restaurant. I blurted out, "Diana-the-president's-been-shot-and-they-don't-think-he's-going-to-live." She looked aghast, paused for a moment, and then said only, "My God, Lady Bird in the White House! We can't use *her* in the magazine." Ever the canny editor—though it must be noted that, not long after, she commissioned Horst to photograph Mrs. Johnson wearing Texas-rose yellow in the presidential drawing room.

A few days later we watched Kennedy's funeral on television with Françoise and Oscar de la Renta. We were all deeply moved, but Mrs. Vreeland's eyes remained dry, her voice unusually muted. "He had a golden touch, Jack," she said as we walked down Park Avenue. "The world will get grayer now." I reminded her of this prediction when, an administration later, Nixon was voted into the White House. She shrugged. "What did I tell ya?"

I RETURNED TO WASHINGTON with Diana Cooper shortly after the president's assassination. We again dined with the Alsops in his engaging "cinder-block" house. Now Joe's smokescreen, though all too transparent, of his homosexuality made him nastily wary of me—"He should be so lucky," said Diana later. His sycophancy to her, his ghastly pretended Englishness, and his dismissive air toward his wife were horrid to witness, but his discomfiture when Diana turned her full golden glow on Susan Mary and she became the major star in the room was very satisfying. Susan had been among Duff Cooper's many mistresses while she and her first husband, Bill Patten, were *en poste* in Paris after the war when Duff and Diana ran their embassy with riotous verve. When the affair came to light, in letters published by Susan Mary, Diana telegraphed: "Why didn't you tell me? I would have loved you even more." Diana told me years later that the secret of her long and happy marriage was that she made best friends with all Duff's mistresses ("though most of them had cow's names—Daisy, Lulu, Rosie, Susan, Dolly . . ."), a piece of sensible advice everyone should take on board.

The mood in Washington, not surprisingly, had changed. The Johnson White House was no longer the hot ticket, and as a widow, Jackie was now reclusive in her Georgetown house, ravishingly decorated by my longtime hero, Billy Baldwin. Diana and I went to the newly hung National Gallery. She looked at huge portraits by Velázquez, Hals, Rembrandt, Gainsborough, Reynolds, Sargent.

"Oh, I remember seeing that one at Panshanger; or was it the Palazzo Madama? And that nice old Jew, he was at Lancut. And *she* was in the white drawing room at Trent." (And Syon, and Ferrières, and Wasserleonberg.) Then she said, "Let's get out of here. Too many ghosts." Perhaps she meant the whole city.

LENA HORNE, whom I had been so dazzled to meet with Herbert and Nora and Arthur in London, would often ask me to dinner at the rambling red-walled apartment, filled with paintings and pianos, where she and her husband, the music arranger Lennie Hayton, lived at 300 West End Avenue. Sometimes the other guests would be such music greats as Duke Ellington and Billy Strayhorn; another evening there might be young political writer friends of Lena's beautiful daughter, Gail, who would later marry the director Sidney Lumet. Lena was extremely active in the civil rights movement and, as a result of having recently been subjected to segregation policies in various hotels in the George Wallace–influenced South, extremely angry. Indeed, I was horrified sometime later, spending a weekend in Long Island with Gail, at mutual friends, to witness the fact that the black staff were reluctant to serve her.

I had a sentimental experience in going to the last night of the old Metropolitan Opera, the day before it was due to be torn down. I sat with Lena Horne and Noël Coward in the Diamond Horseshoe. The lights from the stage haloed Lena's impeccable profile, but Noël seemed more interested in leaning over the box to spot people he knew in the audience. I also went with Lena to a Carnegie Hall concert at which Frank Sinatra had arranged to anoint his son as his successor. This might have had a positive result if Frank senior hadn't been knocking back the bourbon while performing, and at the party onstage afterward he somehow insulted Lena, who still had tears in her eyes when the huge body and round black head of Louis Armstrong, with teeth like illuminated battlements, swayed up to embrace her. Even more memorably, Lena then introduced me to Martin Luther King, Jr., and his wife, Coretta. Coretta was immediately charming, with a soft vivacious voice; the sleeves of her radiant white lace dress gleamed against Dr. King's beautiful grape-dark skin as she delicately rubbed Lena's lipstick off his cheek. Lena's devastation at the assassination of this gentle visionary was total, and perhaps in some way triggered her growing desire for seclusion.

But that was some years in the future. One afternoon, shopping with Gail for perfume at Bergdorf Goodman, a voice from across the counter squealed, "Hi, Gail!" We looked up to see a huge cloud of wide blond hair, dark-rimmed eyes, and pale mouth above a long neck, swathed with golden chains interspersed with big baroque pearls swinging over a signature Chanel couture suit. "That," said Gail, laughing—for the luxurious vision simply radiated humor and happiness—"is my friend Jane Holzer." The hair and pearls were now beside us, and immediately Jane's infectious irreverence, her utter up-to-dateness, captivated me. We promised to meet again, but I hardly dared hope that would be the case.

Within an hour I was driving up Madison in the gathering drizzling dusk. On the sidewalk outside the old Ritz-Carlton stood Jane, shopping bags around her Chanel short-skirted legs, Chanel-shod feet, her head a blur as she swung around, trying to hail a taxi. I stopped the car.

"Oh, it's you," she said, as if it were the most natural thing that I should be there, and got in. I drove her to her apartment building on Park Avenue, conscious that a magical friendship was being forged.

My first reaction was to cable Diana Vreeland, who was on vacation in Morocco where her son Frecky was a member of the U.S. ambassadorial staff, with a description of my discovery. With typical enthusiasm she cabled back, DIVINE STOP SOUNDS JUST SORT OF NEW LOOK WE NEED STOP GET HER PHOTOGRAPHED STOP SUGGEST PENN STOP. Jane, hair swirling around her face like a blond tornado, was in the next issue of *Vogue,* and soon her conquests were David McEwen and David Bailey. One evening I took Andy Warhol to dinner at Jane's Park Avenue apartment. He, too, fell for her wacky humor and outrageous beauty, though maybe the fact that this was the first time Andy met Mick Jagger engraved it on Andy's elephantine memory.

I was about to make an interesting conquest of my own. Just before I left London to come to New York, Francis Wyndham had rung me to say that he had developed a fixation on the blond teenage costar of Elvis Presley in a film called *Wild in the Country,* and that I must try to meet her. I remember thinking it was probably the girl's name that intrigued him more than her acting ability, as she certainly had a strange one— Tuesday Weld. Since that first movie she had become a recognized beauty as well as an admired young actress, and Mrs. Vreeland decreed she should be featured in the magazine.

The astonishingly handsome photographer Peter Beard, blond and tanned from a journey to Kenya that would eventually lead to his living—and being imprisoned—there, sauntered into the art department, hung with cameras. "To do a shoot on Tuesday Weld," he said, grinning, in answer to my unspoken question.

"I'm coming," I said.

In the cab we fantasized. At the studio, like all great sex objects, Tuesday fulfilled each of our dreams. To see her curled up on crumpled white sheets, her heavily lashed eyes smoldering behind tousled bangs, her mockingly sensual waiflike allure made Peter Beard's jet-blue eyes glitter with desire. But unaccountably it was I who won this fairest prize. Tu took a liking to me and I fell a little in love with her. We spent some happy nights together, after wolfing her mother's famed chili con carne. Mick reminded me recently that we even said we were engaged. I gave her a dachshund puppy; Tuesday named it Luther.

"So she's intellectual as well. How thrilling," Francis wrote. Too soon she had a film to make in California, then another.

And the least intellectual star in the firmament crossed my path not long after. At a party in Toots Shor's, I suddenly felt someone tugging at the back of my jacket. I turned around to see an extraordinary sight— platinum strawberry curls framed a heart-shaped scarlet mouth and giraffe-like eyelashes. Atop the curls sat what looked like a squashed black kitten—the wearer's idea of a cocktail hat. "Do you have vents?" Jayne Mansfield asked. "What?" I said. "Do you have vents?" she asked again, still holding on to my jacket. "Turn around . . . There," she said to someone over her shoulder. "He *does* have vents. I told you so."

Why she should have been so excited by gentleman's tailoring, having been married for years to a muscleman who wore only swimming trunks, I can't imagine. But she was the sweetest creature, and living at the time with a policeman in Queens. I used to go over there for supper. She could hardly cook but had the most self-deprecating nature, well aware of her camp ultrablond on-screen persona.

· ELEVEN ·

However cheap, practical, and conveniently close to my *Vogue* office, the studio apartment I'd rented from Mrs. Duchamp lacked any semblance of the romantic ambiance I'd started to imagine myself living in. Now ensconced in the safe arms of Condé Nast, I could begin to cast around for something rather more decadent than a run-of-the-mill midtown block, something with a bit of panache, as Mrs. Vreeland put it.

Quite soon it came my way, in a wonderful area just south of Eighth Street on the East Side. Built in the late nineteenth century on land developed by the Astor family, Colonnade Row is one of the few Manhattan cityscapes where one might suppose oneself to be in Rome or St. Petersburg, and it precisely lives up to its name. Emerging from the dim darkness of the Astor Place subway station, you see a facade of vast gray stone Tuscan columns curving gently away into the middle distance, the depth of the volutes giving an unexpected lightness to each pillar's huge scale; and threaded behind them, almost invisible from the street, are steps, entrances, staircases, balconies, and windows of apartments of varying sizes, each laid out on classical lines.

One of these, its mahogany floorboards smelling faintly of spice, its wide white-shuttered windows looking out onto a garden dominated by a massive dogwood tree, belonged to a couple of new friends I had met with Fred Ashton. John Taras, tall and angular, with the lean good looks of his Cossack ancestry, was a renowned young choreographer, creating ballets for leading American dance companies. His opera-studying lover, Frank Rizzo, had the curling dark hair and Florentine features of a Bronzino portrait. While there was intense rivalry among most choreographers, particularly between George Balanchine and Fred—who had been incensed by Balanchine telling Nureyev to "come to me when you get tired of dancing all those princes"—Fred admired John Taras's work, and had taken me to several dance-oriented evenings at Colonnade Row. At one of these I'd formed an instant friendship with the New York City Ballet star Edward Villella and his scatty but acerbic wife, Janet, which led to my being present at the first nights of Eddie's soaring performances in the many ballets Balanchine made for him. When John and Frank decided to spend a few months in Italy helping Gian Carlo Menotti set up the Spoleto Festival, I was delighted when they suggested that in their absence I could rent it.

Colonnade Row was furnished perfectly. The big high living room was calm and comfortable, with low sofas and masses of books on every surface. I only needed to sling my few things into boxes and bundle them onto the Lexington Avenue line downtown. The next morning, on the subway ride up to the Graybar Building, light-headed, giddy with delight at such imposing new quarters, I was astonished to realize that most passengers were wearing hard hats, and a few even had gas masks clamped to their faces. I was embarrassingly unaware that these were the first hours of the Cuban missile crisis.

That particular confrontation, touch-and-go for President Kennedy for several anxious days, passed, and living for those summer months at Colonnade Row, I discovered a part of the Village far rawer, less artfully manicured, than its counterpart over on the west side of Fifth Avenue. While no one then would have dared venture into the Hell's Kitchen–like danger zone below Houston Street, between Astor Place and that downtown limit was a cobweb of cross streets dominated by vast warehouses, in daytime still productive but at night looming black and forbidding, the remainders of turn-of-the-century industrial New York.

I WAS ABOUT TO HAVE my own invasion sprung on me. Michael had telephoned, and we had had a long but tentative transatlantic reconciliation: He would come to New York, but only on the grounds that he would also carry out his promise to go to a drying-out clinic. Before very long I heard he was on a boat crossing the Atlantic that had conveniently divided us. For the remaining few days before his arrival I veered between fury and excitement.

There is thrilling glamour in reseduction, but it's best to be in control. To meet Michael at the Cunard dock, I thought I'd better look tough, moved on from the blond boy in white, my own man now, needing no one. "Disguised as a motorcyclist, in black leather, his face smeared with functional grease, Nicky looked especially touching," wrote Michael later. I'd failed to fool this true romantic.

Underneath the artful grease and leather, though, I still felt rather apprehensive. I was now established in New York with an ideal job and a burgeoning social life, in part due to my being unattached and enjoying my unique identity in the city. Would Michael's presence, his mood swings, his charm, his drugs, his sweetness, his hypochondria, his need to control me, upset this well-balanced applecart? Could the very delicate relationship we had last had, years and an ocean away, be revived in, but not impinge on, the reality of my new, vibrant, self-created, self-sufficient life?

The answers were yes and no. It *was* rather magical for me to be showing Michael New York, introducing him to my friends, taking him to my special places. We revived shared passions when I took him to see Nureyev dance: We would send him victor's laurels rather than flowers; Rudi loved them and carried them onstage for his curtain call. But in some way Michael's innate Europeanness made him slightly alien to the New York that I had created for myself. Intimacy, sharing the daily routine, was easy. It was harder to project that onto a larger screen, and I sometimes used to feel that Michael was slightly *bouleversé* and maybe, sometimes, faintly jealous.

Happy as I was in Colonnade Row, I realized that once Michael joined me, we needed a more permanent place to live. I found, and bravely signed a lease on, a large top-floor walk-up studio apartment in a house on East Nineteenth Street, with, from its roof terrace, a view down to Gramercy Park.

The area had a delightfully schizophrenic atmosphere. Gramercy Park itself, though run down, was still home to a few faded aristocrats and the grand red-brick mansion of Ben Sonnenberg, a silver-haired stocky dynamo of a man who was said to have "invented" public relations. There were shabby hotels; a charming, student-beloved inn; and, as I was to discover, intellectuals from the world of *The New Yorker* and *The New York Review of Books*. Several avenues to the east lay the Bowery, haunt of bums and burlesque queens, both with tragic traces of better bodies. In those days the former were friendly even when fried, as were the latter, who were in addition fat, fair, and well over fifty. In one of the more salubrious of these joints we started a conversation with a couple of young lovers, both male hustlers. Bobby was an artist, hustling to buy the materials he needed to paint his huge, obscene, and witty pop-art canvases. Cecil—which he insisted be pronounced Seesil—was on the game merely to make some money to feed them both.

It was a fortuitous meeting; both these boys had the kindest and most loyal nature, and for several years of my life to come, in New York or the most sophisticated cities of Europe, and even in the desert of the American West, Bobby and Cecil were to be an essential element. After several more evenings in Bowery bars, Cecil became my "major domo."

By now it was clear that the time had come to give up Whittlesey Street, which had been sitting empty for well over a year. Pretty soon its contents were bobbing over the Atlantic. A truck costing many times the sum of that passage brought them the meager mile from Manhattan's docks, and Cecil helped me to uncrate, haul up, and arrange these things. To counteract any nostalgia I hung one of Bobby's biggest and rudest paintings, an over-life-size S-M nude—Bobby himself—on the double-height walls, where it was greatly admired by the ultracritical eyes of John Richardson, whom I had last seen at the bullring at Arles with his then-lover, Douglas Cooper, and Picasso. He was now living in New York, continuing his meteoric career in art expertise. He lived in a black-walled apartment in the Seventies with wonderful paintings and objects, some not very valuable then though worth millions now, for John has an unerring eye for the unconventionally beautiful and rare. (Even then, Picasso's original sketch for *Les Demoiselles d'Avignon,* dedicated by him to John, was clearly priceless.) John also collected the most interesting people into this dark-but-far-from-stygian haunt. One night I found myself next to a girl whose aura seemed very like that of Zelda Fitzgerald. The likeness was likely as it transpired she was born Sayre, as Zelda had been. Nora told me that their forebears had come over on the *Mayflower,* taken one look, and gone straight back to England on the *Mayflower,* reventuring only a century later.

A KEY MEMBER OF John's circle was Bowden Broadwater. Gothic-faced, lank-limbed, his nose twitching for gossip, which he soon hissed, polished and embellished from the side of his mouth, Bowden was an assistant headmaster of St. Bernard's, one of Manhattan's smartest schools, and, of all seemingly unlikely things, catnip to the ladies. Just divorced from Mary McCarthy, author of *The Group,* and having a slew of affairs before his next marriage, he was also an irrepressible flirt with boys; he welcomed me into his academic first-floor apartment up in the East Nineties, around the corner from the school. It was furnished with Amish-like simplicity, but the minds that gathered in it were anything but simple. It was there that I'd meet such luminaries as Edmund Wilson, Dwight MacDonald, and W. H. Auden, who asked me to lunch next day with his friend Chester Kallman and a somewhat severe old lady who turned out to be Willa Cather's "widow."

———

ALONG WITH HANGING Bobby's vast painting on the tall wall of the Nineteenth Street studio, I stapled theater-supply zebra-skin material to the spiral staircase, and placed a pair of huge hurricane lanterns on the shoulder-high mantel of the fireplace that consumed elephantine logs. Rummaging in the junk shops that were then abundant on Third Avenue just below Fifty-seventh Street, I had fun finding dusty overscale furniture and crumbling gilt mirrors, as influenced by illustrations in *The Self-Enchanted,* a biography of the silent movie star Mae Murray, famous for her bee-stung lips. I was aiming for a faded "Hollywood Baroque" look.

It was therefore gratifying when Billy Baldwin was full of praise for the way I had decorated the apartment, and extremely exciting when Camille Duhe, a smudgy-voiced Southern writer for the *Herald Tribune,* asked if he could have it photographed for the paper, which featured it under the not-inappropriate heading "Think Poor." This was my first printed publicity as "the decorator" I would eventually become; that headline, over the text with its gist of "nouveau pauvre" was strangely prescient, as though I have since designed for some of the richest people in the world, I strive to make sure my work looks anything but nouveau riche.

The rather simpler furniture from Whittlesey Street was not the only much-loved cargo to cross the ocean. Min had telephoned with the catastrophic news that Tim Willoughby had been lost at sea.

Risking his wrath for my profligacy, I called my father, and inveigled him into paying the fare of a compassionate flight so Min could join me in New York. For two weeks I had the joy of showing her the city where by now I felt I was an old hand. She stayed in one of the shabby hotels on Gramercy Park, counteracting the mustiness of prewar air conditioners and damp bedding by opening the windows wide to the summer heat day and night, some of which were spent in an unlikely union with my reporter friend Camille. I gave a party at the studio. "Cholly Knickerbocker," the *Journal American*'s legendary gossip columnist, wrote. "An interesting cross-section of Gotham's smart set turned up at Nicky Haslam's jolly party in honor of a lovely young visitor from England, Min Hogg. . . . Sidney Lumet with Gail Jones, Margaret Case, Amy and Milton Green, Bill and Chessy Rayner, Pamela Colin, Louise and Dick Savitt, Mary McFadden." I remember that Ken Lane was embarrassed to realize the girl he ungallantly nicked a taxi from earlier that day on Fifth Avenue was the guest of honor.

Twenty years before she founded *The World of Interiors,* Min was already rooted in decoration. I took her to see Billy Baldwin's faux tortoiseshell library for Cole Porter high up in the Waldorf; to Diana Vreeland's famous red-chintzed "drawing room in hell"; and to Fulco Verdura's "palazzino" apartment, where she and Noël Coward, who was then in cabaret in New York, laughed together at the more ridiculous of modern American expressions.

Up at *Vogue* my editor friends begged her to sell them the quintessentially English short dresses, patent leather shoes, and patterned stockings she wore. Diana arranged for Bill Blass to dress Min for a grand fashion ball, where we were seated at her high-powered table. I tried my hardest to make Min remain in New York permanently, but she was in the throes of setting up her first business as a highly successful photographers' agent in London. However, I felt a great pang of loss as I saw her through immigration at the newly named Kennedy airport.

ONE REWARDING SIDE of Michael being in New York was being able to introduce him to older friends I had already made, many of whom were writers or artists in London or Paris when Michael was there as a teenager. One person he was particularly interested to meet was Bowden, probably to compare notes on the love affairs they had both had with Barbara Skelton, the alluring feline-featured siren married and divorced from Cyril Connolly and George Weidenfeld: a romance with Barbara was de rigueur for lads with literary leanings. Furthermore Bowden was in the throes of a seduction of Caroline Blackwood, Michael's dearest friend, now remarried to the musician Israel Citkowitz. Their Bacon-hung, child-filled, but otherwise unkempt house downtown became a bolthole for Michael and the mutual melancholy he and Caroline loved to indulge in.

Another of my friends who enchanted Michael was the Austrian-born photographer Horst P. Horst. I had met him at work, for since her arrival on the magazine, Mrs. Vreeland had been using Horst with increasing frequency, sending him to Europe to do portfolios of people, some of whom I'd suggested to her. Horst, now sixty, was still film-star handsome, despite a twice-a-day intake of several breathtaking martinis; these probably contributed to his talking to me about his early years, when he had studied architecture in Hamburg and then Paris, apprenticed to Le Corbusier, no less. But Horst's *echt*-Teutonic beauty, straw-thick blond hair, muscular body, and half-knowing, half-innocent blue eyes ensured that he was soon diverted from such solitary study, and he met the Baltic photographer Baron George Hoyningen-Huene, who became his lover, posing him as a near-naked athlete or barely draped god; from this homoerotic harmony Horst, photographer, was born.

Horst's portrait photographs, particularly of women, had captured the most elegant and influential figures of each decade: Mistinguett in the 1930s, the Duchess of Windsor "impossibly thin in a Mainbocher suit" during the war, Coco Chanel, Consuelo Balsan, and a triumvirate of Nancys: Lancaster, Mitford, and Reagan (when she became first lady). For fashion photographs, he developed a distinctive style, favoring such dazzlingly glamorous bright lighting that earlier *Vogue* editors complained that it was hard to see what product was being advertised. For a while Horst's star waned, waiting to dance back into in Diana Vreeland's panoply.

After a photographic session at *Vogue,* Horst often asked me to drive out with him for the night at his house in Oyster Bay on Long Island Sound. Tiffany Acres was a low white stucco building he had designed, influenced by Corbusier, and which he regularly extended, adding more walls to smother with paintings by the major artists of the twentieth century, all dedicated to him, and dominated by his portrait by Bérard, which I knew Michael would covet. Horst shared this house with his lifelong companion, Valentine Lawford, always known as Nicholas, a former diplomat and private secretary to Lord Halifax. Nicholas was now a writer, and the polar opposite of Horst; he was carefully spoken, almost la-di-da compared with Horst's cascading sentences, neatly buttoned up as opposed to Horst's easy elegance. Their relationship seemed an odd pairing to many, and Horst's lifelong rival Cecil Beaton told me, not without a hint of jealousy, "I simply don't understand the caaare-mistry of it." Horst and Nicholas shared the chemistry of a youthful, mesmerizing blond lad they had spotted *langlauf*ing in some remote Austrian *Tal*. Hansi was easily lured to bigger things and brighter lights. But the mayor of Kitzbühel came to hear of this rather more physical experiment, and the oddly paired chemists were thenceforth less than persona grata in Horst's native land. I was delighted, as it meant many more weekends at Tiffany Acres, which was bathed in added glamour when I discovered that Troy Donohue came from nearby, and that his equally good-looking brother worked in the local gas station.

MICHAEL AND I HAD always had a longing to visit the Deep South, so we decided to go to Savannah, which, in a *Gone With the Wind* way, seemed to be the quintessential Dixie town. I drove at breakneck speed down the straight Southern highways to Charleston, where Billy Baldwin had arranged for some good friends of his to have us to stay. Ben and Carola Kittredge owned a beautiful if florally decorated house in the town and a magnificent plantation called Cypress Gardens. It was returning from this plantation one day that I saw an entire porticoed mansion being floated down the river on an enormous barge, a sudden reminder of Hundridge and the panic I used to feel for its fate. We drove on to Savannah on the dusty highways, now frequently being stopped for speeding by policemen, who in those days gave one a gentle warning. Here, at last, was the South at its sleepiest, and we spent several days and nights in its lambent embrace. The grand crumbling buildings and the honky-tonk shanties were stunningly picturesque, whatever the realities of their provenance, and awakened a dormant desire to see those Caribbean islands my grandfather had visited.

IT WOULD TAKE ME another twenty years to get to Barbados, but meanwhile Michael and I had already formed a plan to go to Haiti, partly because, bizarrely, Simon Fleet's brother, Gerald Carnes, was the surrogate bishop there (the real bishop of Haiti had been thrown off the island by the president, and was living in New York), and partly because Michael imagined he had a longing to paint the Haitian landscape. The days in Savannah confirmed our resolve. But the only way one could get to Haiti in those days was via Jamaica, and during our stopover, we got a message from Gerald saying that "Papa Doc" Duvalier had effected a coup. "Don't come," he said. "I hear the president's a perfect beast" (parodying Firbank's famous postcard about the island: "I hear the president's a perfect dear"). So instead we spent ten days in Jamaica as guests of Sarah Russell, her notoriously homophobic father, Bert, Duke of Marlborough, and my Eton-visiting friend Henrietta Tiarks, by now Lady Tavistock. We visited the Piranesi-like ruins of sugar plantations and rafted down the rivers, floating on first-time, for me, marijuana. But whereas I was swept in by the island, the tropics made Michael ill at ease. He said he couldn't paint in Jamaica "despite its extraodinary natural beauty," adding "or perhaps because of it," a line typical of Michael. He was also "stifled by the endless socializing," but I remember even him being amused to realize that the tall suave man we were talking to was the great prewar couturier Captain Edward Molyneux. The next day Michael had flown. I kissed Sarah good-bye and reluctantly followed him to New York.

Perhaps his malaise was more than just geographical. Unsurprisingly his sobriety hadn't lasted, and when he was not drunk he became manically hypochondriacal, visiting every doctor within reach, including Henry Marks, my sister's father, who was my doctor as well, and who would tell me there was really nothing wrong with him. I found myself rather dreading going back to the apartment, not knowing what version of Michael would be waiting there. And no matter how sophisticated and worldly wise I felt myself to be, I was in many ways still the hotheaded boy of those early years, unwilling to compromise my dazzling new life in order to face another's problems. After a few weeks it seemed to me that our relationship really had to be resolved.

Nothing cataclysmic brought this first important love affair of my life to an end, but six months after I had gone to meet him on the dock, Michael would be sailing out of my life again. I could see that I was breaking his heart, and I had never experienced anything like that before; I swung between relief and overwhelming guilt. I have an image of Michael lying on the bed smoking, his hands behind his head. As I started down the zebra-carpeted staircase, I turned to wave. He smiled the smile that reminded me of the first time I had seen him in the gallery, but sadder this time, with a finality in his eyes that told me he, too, had made a decision.

THE CORKBOARD WALLS of the *Vogue* art department had a thousand stats of various sizes and images pinned onto them, but the most important, with carefully maintained space around them, were the "books," as they were called, for the next few issues. Each photograph and article was reproduced in miniature, showing the flow of fashion and features, so that Mrs. Vreeland, Alex Liberman, and Priscilla Peck could switch the pages around at whim during their daily conferences. I usually watched with bated breath in case one of my layouts got praised or axed.

The layouts for August 1962 had an especially interesting run of these tiny pages, bare of pictures or text, but titled, cryptically, in Priscilla Peck's own hand, "The Old Lady." For a few weeks, while the editorial triumvirate would gloat triumphantly over these mystery pages, the whole department was kept in the dark as to this old lady's identity. Eventually during a weekend with Priscilla in Connecticut, I pried the secret out of her.

It was a planned, exclusive "undercover" shoot by Bert Stern of Marilyn Monroe, to be done in Los Angeles, where she was making her next movie, *Something's Gotta Give*. It included—here Priscilla swore me to even stronger secrecy—some in which Marilyn had agreed to pose almost nude. This was typical of Mrs. Vreeland's groundbreaking departures from the heretofore staidness of *Vogue,* where we were still touching out those naughty navels. Priscilla was, I detected, somewhat miffed that Monroe had picture approval, an almost-unheard-of privilege.

There was, at the time, fascinated speculation on both Park Avenue and in the press as to just how many of the Kennedys Monroe was sleeping with. Most people, especially after she had sung "Happy Bwirfday, Mr. Pwesident," lisping in her most tantalizing little-girl style at his Madison Square Garden party, assumed there had been an affair with JFK, but the mill was grinding out the grist that he had handed her over to his brother Bobby, the moralizing attorney general, who was now getting scared about Marilyn's indiscreet late-night telephone calls. Brother-in-law Peter Lawford was another candidate, much to the chagrin of his wife, Pat Kennedy. Though Marilyn was known to be a nightmare to work with, continually late onto—if not for several days absent from—the set, she was at her apogee as America's love goddess, and there was no hint of her rapidly approaching doom.

Huge excitement surged through the corridors of the building when the contacts of the California shoot arrived, by courier, naturally. Only the highest of the high were allowed to see them; Miss Peck's office became as unimpregnable as Fort Knox, the door patroled by a Cerberus-like Gloria Gersh. But they forgot that there was a small secret door connecting Priscilla's room with the art department. One lunchtime, having posted guards, Bibi and I mounted a Marilyngate operation. There, on Priscilla's light box, were a hundred color transparencies of the golden girl, teasing, pouting, winking, smiling, writhing, laughing. And, as had been promised, Monroe was nearly naked. "The Old Lady's" cover had been blown.

A couple of days later, Priscilla called me into her office. She had a very special task for me, and only I was suitable to undertake it. Only I in the department, as she thought, knew the identity of the mystery lady. That evening, at six thirty, armed with a red wax pencil, I was to take the contacts to Marilyn Monroe's apartment on Fifty-seventh Street.

I rang the bell. A small dog barked shrilly. The door opened. The goddess was a foot from my eyes, her bosom closer. She had a greasy face with smudgy lips framed by lank blondish hair. She was wearing a shapeless gray tracksuit with makeup stains around her collar. She looked half awake, almost haunted.

The dog barked again. "Be *quiet*, Maff," she said, her hand half shielding her eyes. I held out the bulging white envelope. "Mrs. Vreeland asked me to—"

"Thank you, honey, but I'm running late." She half closed the door, then looked down. "Are they okay?"

"Yes, they're wonderful. Of course they're wonderful."

"Oh, thank you." The mascara-messy eyes looked up at me, her voice strangely remote. "D'you mind if I look at them right here?" She opened the envelope, held the first sheet of black-and-white contacts against the door, and handed me the others. Chewing on the wax pencil, Marilyn expertly and unhesitatingly circled the ones she liked, X-ed some she didn't and, occasionally sucking her teeth, pushed her nail through anything she hated. Just as we'd started on the color transparencies, a telephone rang in a distant room. Marilyn looked panicked. The grubby, unwashed reality gathered all these extraordinary images of her golden glory in her arms, thrust them at me and, running back along the hall, left me at the half-open door.

I closed it on her vanished image, an image very different from the one I had instantly fallen in love with when, a few years earlier, I'd been taken by the English film critic and screenwriter Paul Dehn to a press screening of *Some Like It Hot*. A couple of hours afterward, Ken Lane told me that the dog was actually called Mafia, and had been given to Marilyn by Joe DiMaggio.

A couple of weeks later Marilyn "committed suicide" in her little suburban house in Los Angeles. I heard the news as I was walking through Grand Central Station and immediately telephoned Priscilla at her house in the country. It was the only time I ever heard Priscilla cry.

THE FAIRBANKS FAMILY, consisting of the movie star Douglas Fairbanks, Jr., and his wife, Mary Lee, lived in New York as well as in their vast house in the Boltons in London (where the ladies' lavatory seats had "Oui-oui Madame" painted on them). Their Manhattan apartment was in the Blackstone, a more-or-less residential hotel on Fifty-eighth and Madison. By this time the eldest daughter, Daphne, had married a Weston, heir to the Canadian ABC bakery fortune, and their youngest, Melissa, was mostly away at school, but Victoria, the gentlest and most stunning of them, who looked very like Claudia Cardinale, and indeed was considered one of the beauties of her time, lived with her parents at the Blackstone.

I often went there for dinner. Doug and Mary Lee were huge fun. He was very entertaining about Hollywood and his marriage to Joan Crawford, and Mary Lee's soft Southern voice was as delicious as the Southern dishes their cook had perfected. Often Doug's mother would be staying there, a slightly spooky, pallid blond woman, who was obsessively concerned with Victoria's well-being. Victoria, with whom I was gently falling in love, could hardly bear to be in the room with her, and immediately after dinner we would hightail it to the new discotheques. If the idea of returning to England to open a nightclub had, by now, clearly gone up in smoke, I certainly had enough firsthand experience of them: from the Upstairs at the Downstairs, where the cabaret was often Mabel Mercer, an elderly Liverpool-born black woman my father was enthralled with, or my mother's friend Greta Keller's club, the Waldorf Keller deep in that hotel, where handsome young Mayor Lindsay was her most fervent admirer, to Shepheard's at the Drake on Park and Fifty-sixth, Trude Heller's, Le Club, or El Morocco.

For a few months Victoria and I were a youthful and, if not quite golden, very colorful couple, and I often now find myself regretting that I never summoned up the courage to make our loving friendship a more exciting union. Perhaps it was the specter of old Mrs. Fairbanks brooding in her bedroom at the Blackstone.

THEN, FIFTY-SEVENTH STREET between Park and Madison avenues was a parade of art galleries, but rather than being upstairs and huge, they were often smallish, intimate, and at sidewalk level. Almost every evening there would be a vernissage in one of them. One particular night Peter Beard and I were leaving one gallery after Jamie Wyeth's opening when we gasped in amazement to see the iconic wild black hair and twirled-up mustache of Salvador Dalí through the window of another. He immediately noticed Peter and motioned for us to come in. The pictures were surprisingly small surrealistic oil sketches, and the crowd, though large, surprisingly drab. Dalí was fascinated by Peter's perfect blond looks; and of course his man-eater wife, Gala, was even more so. For the next hour we seemed to be the center of their world, but eventually the innuendos became clearer, and Peter and I made a timely exit.

A week or so later I was coming down in the elevator of the St. Regis Hotel after visiting a friend. At the eleventh floor the elevator stopped. Señor and Señora Dalí stepped in, both wearing long leopard-skin coats. The bootblack mustache twitched toward me like a fatal spider's love dance, Gala's sunken black eyes glittered greedily. "Come," Dalí said, as we descended. "We are going to the West Side for a séance to raise the ghost of Marilyn Monroe. Come." "Yes, come," echoed Gala.

Innuendo or no, this was too good to miss. I figured I couldn't come to much harm, séances being by their very nature somehow unsexy. And anyway it would have taken a lot of fumbling with those unyielding panels of stiff cat's fur for either Dalí to pounce on our way to this irresistible event.

Outside it was extraordinarily foggy. The normally glittering buildings above us were merely vast black boxes, any light from their windows invisible in the shroudlike grayness all around. A limousine, its headlights seeming no stronger than a flashlight, was summoned to the canopy. With much theatrical twirling of the leopard coat, Dalí ushered Gala and me into its dank interior.

We inched our way across Central Park and turned uptown toward Amsterdam Avenue. In a remote, gloomy cross street we stopped outside a seedy apartment building. Consternation; this all looked far too bourgeois to these leading lights of exoticism. Gala consulted Dalí, who consulted the driver, who consulted a piece of paper. The driver opened the door, nodded to Dalí, who nodded to Gala, and in two shakes of a leopard's tail they shot from the car and into the lobby, apparently forgetting my existence. I caught up with them on the dimly lit stairs, and we stumbled upward to the landing of the bidden number. There they both composed their furs and hats and faces for elaborate effect. Dalí rapped imperiously on the door with his cane.

"*Shhh-shhh,*" came the withering response. "*Shhh-shhh.*"

The door eventually opened a crack, then enough to admit us. Inside, sheer darkness, punctuated by coughs and sighs and squeaks and the odd moan. A woman's irritated voice asked increasingly vague questions into the blackness, which gradually resolved itself into the shapes of figures around a large table. But nothing strange happened, no Marilyn materialized. After what seemed like a lifetime the lights were turned on.

The woman conducting the séance was old Mrs. Fairbanks.

Outside, the fog—and the Dalís—had disappeared. I walked back across the park, thinking of the living Marilyn I had met only a few weeks earlier.

· TWELVE ·

MANY OF THE INVITATIONS Margaret Case issued during my
daily visit to her office upstairs on the twentieth floor were
shouted unabashedly from the open-doored loo. One day she came up
with the most thrilling offer possible.

"Would ya like to have lunch with the duchess?"

The Duchess? Of Windsor? Would I??

"Okay, then, Wednesday, one o'clock, the Colony."

Wallis Windsor was a *Vogue* icon. Only a few weeks before I had laid
out a spread on the Windsors in their Paris house. The photographs, by
Horst, might have been taken, some wag said unkindly, through concrete, so wrinkle-free were the features of both duke and duchess. Her
hard, lacquered head, the scarecrow body in its exquisite clothes—part
Ming empress, part bang-up-to-date modern—totally dominated the
beautiful rooms, the witty eighteenth-century furniture, the Meissen, the
dogs, the duke, with a kind of sexual artificiality that was undeniably in-
triguing. I knew all the drama and anger of the abdication, of course, but
by the sixties the royal family was so safely established that that particular can of worms had somewhat lost its shelf life; the king-and–Mrs.
Simpson business was simply seen as a romantic love story for him or an
understandable career move for her.

But many East Coast grandees were proud of their American royal,
worshiped her drop-dead chic, her sassy wit, her exaggerated jewels, her
perfectionism. To others she was a hardheaded go-getter, a haughty social cipher, cadging her way off two continents. Which?

The totem in the Horst photographs suggested both. The Colony,
Thursday, 1 p.m. Margaret Case, with Kitty Miller and Cordelia Biddle
Robinson, is already seated when I arrive. Our table is the best banquette,
in the farthest corner, affording the longest walk to it, and the best view
from it, in the room. These ladies are the duchess's "set." If she's not natural with them . . . , I think. The commissionaires swing open the doors.
There's a sudden silence: Eyes swivel, forks fall onto asparagus ("Without
butter, Gene, please"). Across the restaurant—cheek-kissing, air-kissing,

winking, waving—comes this minute figure, the flat cubist head made higher and wider by black bouffant hair parted centrally from the brow to the black grosgrain bow at the nape, dressed in an impossibly wide-weave pink angora tweed Chanel suit, concertinaed white gloves, black crocodile bag and shoes. As she approaches, not stopping, not stopping smiling, her eyes greet her friends. Then, "Hi, I'm Wallis," to me, and, "I'll have the chicken à la king, Gene, thank you," to the hovering maître d.

"We call Nicky our Beatle," says Kitty.

"What on earth's a Beatle?" says Cordelia, whose voice, appearance, and mannerisms hadn't changed since the twenties.

(The boys had just hit New York. I had had their first record sent over from England, and taken the cover to Kenneth—my and my sister's and Mrs. Kennedy's hairdresser—saying, "This is how I want my hair cut." Andy Warhol, writing later about the period in his first autobiography, credits me with bringing the English "look" to New York, with my short Italian jackets, pointed shoes, and the curtain lace with which I improvised frilled shirt cuffs under my jackets—I used to stick it on with Speed-Sew glue.)

"Oh, the Beatles. Don't you just love 'em? 'I give her all my love, that's all I do-oo,' " she sings. "Adore 'em. Do you know them? Oh, you are lucky."

Dumbstruck, near lovestruck, I simply listen to the sassy repartee. People . . . Palm Beach . . .Paris . . . until, with a discreet peek at her watch (on a chain tied to her bag, not on her wrist): "Gee, is that really the time? Can you beat it? I gotta go and meet the dook. I've had such fun. Good-bye, good-bye, I'll see you all at Elsie's on Tuesday."

And she leaves, now stopping at some tables, a few words, her infectious laugh as metallic as the clink of spoons in astonished onlookers' demitasse coffees ("No cream, Gene, please").

The duchess was true to her word—as I was to find on several occasions. If she said she would do or send you something, or meet you somewhere, she did. On the following Tuesday I arrived at Elsie Woodward's apartment in the Waldorf Towers. The door ahead of me was slightly open. I listened. No sound, no voices, no music, no merry glugging of martinis. Too early, I realized. I wandered on down the corridor to the elevator, to dawdle and not run into coarrivals. There was a rustle, and I turned. The duchess was also peering through the chink in Elsie's door, equally embarrassed to walk in. She saw me. A silent peal of laughter, and she ran along to me, grabbing my arm and saying, "We must live in the same time zone. You're early too. Let's hide. I live upstairs but the

dook's changing. I know this place like the back of my hand. Here, look."
She opened the door to a housemaid's cupboard. "Quick, come on, we
can go in here and watch till some folks arrive."

We stood shoulder to shoulder in the near dark, talking about our
lunch, the theater—well, musicals—food, friends; what she called "where
we've been and who we've seen," till, "I think it's okay now. Some
frumps have just gone in." She stepped out, bandbox-fresh. "Am I all
mussed up? My hay-er? No? You're so cute to say so. Come." So with her
jewel-appliquéd black-satin-gloved hand in mine, we walked into Elsie's
party.

A couple of weeks later I went to the theater with the Windsors. Our
seats, in the orchestra, necessitated latecomers edging past us to their
places. The duchess would get up, smiling, each time anyone had to pass,
but the duke never would, sitting like a cross little parcel, expecting people to step around him—or step on him, one rather got the feeling. But
no one could have called him humble, except with the duchess, to whom
he was positively servile. The legendary charm had long since faded: His
manner was brusque to the point of rudeness. And at night, after several
cocktails, he would lapse into guttural German, often breaking into Horst
Wessel–type songs, his right arm involuntarily rising dangerously close to
that infamous salute.

At times like these Wallis would distance herself from him with an exasperated "Oh, David." She would melt into a circle of girlfriends and
pretty soon have them cracking up with her wry humor. An example of
this was making the rounds just before I met them. At the announcement
of Princess Margaret's engagement, General de Gaulle, who, like the
Windsors, happened to be in New York, went to the Waldorf to con-
gratulate the duke, saying, "I'm so delighted, sir, to hear the happy news
of Princess Margaret Rose's forthcoming marriage to Mr. Armstrong-
Jones."

"Merci, mon général," said the duke. "How kind of you, and of course
the whole family is thrilled. But I must tell you that, since she grew up,
Princess Margaret has dropped the 'Rose.' "

From across the room, the duchess's usual drawl became a whiplash.
"She's dropped the Rose and picked up the pansy."

It was during this time, it is often alleged, that Wallis was having an
affair with Jimmy Donahue, the idle, rich, charming, and totally gay son
of Jessie Woolworth. Having known Jimmy later, and spent weekends at
his country house, Broadhollow (always known as Boyhollow), on Long
Island, I really can't think he could ever have touched any woman, let

alone one as rigidly undressable as Wallis. Unless she liked trying on the
haute couture drag that New York's leading Catholic priest, Cardinal
Spellman, kept in elaborately constructed closets at Broadhollow, there
wasn't much in the sex line about Jimmy that would have attracted her,
beyond the fact that he was huge fun to be with.

The rumor was that Wallis's real and only attachment was Russell
Nype, a young actor possessing a beautiful tenor voice, who had starred
opposite Ethel Merman in Irving Berlin's hit musical *Call Me Madam.*
My reading of the situation was that, more probably, Jimmy Donahue
had originally caught the eye of the duke, and a sisterly rivalry developed
with Wallis. Years later the duke's proclivity in this area was confirmed
to me from a very different source. A television series, *Edward and Mrs.
Simpson,* had been made, and the day after the first installment was aired,
I was driving to a client's house with my curtain maker, Eddie Page. I
asked him if he had seen the program. "No," he said. "I wouldn't watch
that rubbish." "Why not? Why is it rubbish?" I asked. "They wouldn't
tell the truth, would they?" "What is the truth?" I said, fascinated. "Well,
I'll tell you," said Eddie. "You don't have to believe me, but this is the
truth."

And this is what he told me:

"When I was young, I was very pretty. I was a dancer behind the nudes
at the Windmill Theatre behind Piccadilly circus. As we weren't paid
much, I used to go with the boys to Hyde Park, that bit by the barracks,
which was a great picking-up place for toffs. One day Prince David came
with a friend, who approached me on his behalf. They took me to a queer
nightclub in Seven Dials, run by Elsa Lanchester's sister; I don't remember what it was called. Two of Prince David's brothers were there. The
Duke of Kent—first time I'd ever seen a man in full makeup—Leichner,
he told me, and the Duke of Gloucester, who was wearing Queen Mary's
clothes. He wasn't queer, of course—but the others!! The things that went
on that night, and later. . . . So I know about that Duke of Windsor and
what he really liked. Don't talk to me about a 'love match'—all those
boys ever wanted was Mummy. Or Daddy, more like."

The details, such as "Prince David," the name only his intimates called
him, and "Elsa Lanchester's sister," in Eddie's story gave it a telling ring
of truth.

I was never in Europe at the right moment to witness the duchess going
to Maxim's in sequined hot pants, or the Chantilly races in the latest Rabanne space outfit, but her obsession with the newest and most amusing
that had initially fascinated me, and that I still find touching, was an en-
during one.

Her last tragic years, when she was restrained in bed with her mind almost gone, friends kept me informed of her ghastly condition, gradually shrinking to half her size and turning black like a little monkey. Though they and others tried to help her, they were stonewalled by the terrifying lawyer Maître Blum, who had assumed a total stranglehold over Wallis in life and, eventually, in death. On the day the duchess died, I was dining with David Westmorland, Master of the Horse to the queen, and his wife, Jane. The dinner was for Princess Margaret. I summoned up the courage to ask her what she felt about the duchess. The princess replied simply: "It wasn't her we hated, it was him."

My last contact with the duchess was after her death. I took Diana Cooper—who had initially been a hugely staunch supporter of Wallis's friendship with the king—to see her grave at Frogmore, the royal mausoleum at Windsor Castle. Neither Diana nor I had ever seen this Valhalla erected by Queen Victoria as a shrine to herself, her husband, and her progeny. Lying deep in the park at the foot of the castle, it was then open to the public for a couple of days in May. Diana, always keen on a jaunt, was delighted with my plan for a picnic on a Thames motor launch with some friends before our quest. The spring morning was brilliant with hot sunshine, and as we chugged upstream beneath the castle, we tried to imagine how different the somewhat dour aura that building radiates might have been if Edward VIII had pulled off his madcap marriage scheme, for in 1937 Wallis had commissioned designs, all pale pink and silver, from her friend and mentor Elsie de Wolfe, Lady Mendl, for the redecoration of Buckingham Palace.

Diana, who in her youth had herself been fleetingly considered bride material for the prince, witnessed Wallis's ever-stronger hold on the newly proclaimed king firsthand, especially on a cruise in the Adriatic aboard the *Nahlin,* during which he openly flaunted his infatuation with Mrs. Simpson.

"It was touch-and-go for quite a long time. A lot of people wanted his plan to work, but she never let you feel she thought about it at all. She was embarrassed by all his puppy-dog admiration, but liked the position, of course. I most remember how embarrassingly scornfully she treated him, 'Get my shoes, David' or "You look terrible in those shorts, go and change' sort of thing. But many couples do that. In many ways she was good for him. She made him read papers, meet ministers, keep appointments, which he dreaded. Even used to force him to make regular visits to Queen Mary, which he dreaded even more. It's always seemed odd to me that she, in every way so levelheaded, couldn't make him see the impossibility of it, in the end."

By the time we had left the boat, the afternoon had turned darkly gray. Finding Frogmore was not easy, and many tracks we took ended at various royal dairies or greenhouses. Eventually the mausoleum loomed out of the drizzle, guarded by an ancient retainer who pried open the bronze doors. Inside, in a mosaicked riot of almost Byzantine splendor, a shaft of blue light illuminated the memorials of the great queen-empress and her consort.

"But where are the others, the rest of the family?" asked Diana.

"Outside."

There, in serried ranks, were the memorials to generations of Anglo-German descendents—the Prince Albert Victors, the Prince Leopolds, the Princess Helenas, the Princess Alices. Then a grass-covered mound, flowerless, its headstone inscribed "HRH the Duke of Windsor," and beside it, a tiny plot with the plain legend "Wallis, Duchess of Windsor."

"Not very affectionate," said Diana. "They might at least have put 'faithful companion' like we did for the dogs at Belvoir."

The fate of Margaret Case, who had so long ago introduced me to the duchess, was to be no less tragic. Peremptorily sacked from her supposedly unassailable lifetime position at *Vogue* some years later, she went back to her apartment at 550 Park Avenue. Changing into her best clothes and buttoning her fur-lined raincoat, she went to the window to look down on the city she had known, loved, and chronicled for so long. Then she jumped.

A LONG-AWAITED and promised visit to Jean Howard in Los Angeles came a few months later. Cecil Beaton, there designing the sets and costumes for *My Fair Lady,* had written saying he was "starved in this desert" and that it would be fun if I could get some time off from *Vogue.* I went to California for a fortnight. Now it seems humdrum to fly across that continent; then it was thrilling, watching the day live longer and brighter over a landscape of fact and fable unrolling far below, until the first glimpse of the Pacific marked the shimmering limit of "going west."

The little airliner (this was long before jumbo jets) flew on out over the ocean, then turned in its widening gyre and straightened into the landing pattern. Ahead, beaches and palisades, and soon, closer, highways and buildings, were suffused dark pink by a fireball sun about to slide below the horizon far behind us. As we landed, its last light, refracted in the tall glass windows of a curved terminal, cut a frieze of impossibly high palm trees against a greenish sky. I stood at the top of the towering flyway; by now the sky was almost black, thick, too soon for stars; a pungent tonic of tarry heat and perfume rose from below. I looked down. Drawn up by the last step was a two-door, dark blue Bentley. Jean, a bead-edged sweater over her shoulders, stood beside it.

We went straight to dinner that night, up in the lush though deserted, pedestrian-banned canyons of Beverly Hills with the playwright George Axelrod and his wife, Joan. We laughed a lot, as among the other guests were Lenny Bruce and Mort Sahl, the new-breed comedians invited to meet their master, Groucho Marx. But, amazed as I was to be included in this core of American humor, I could hardly believe my ears, let alone eyes, when Joan Axelrod told me the house was the very one that Elsie Mendl had lived in when she moved to the West Coast during the war. After All, as Elsie had named it, was the setting for an enchanting book about her by Ludwig Bemelmans. Simon had given me *To the One I Love the Best* when I was at Eton, inscribing it "The title says it all." More to the point, that was exactly how I felt about Jean. I don't believe it would have been possible for anyone knowing and seeing Jean at this time not to fall in love with her. As we drove past the porticoed, turreted, half-timbered, sleeping mansions, their occupants dreaming their mad dreams, and upward into the starry dawn hanging above Coldwater Canyon, I knew I was.

The bedroom was cool and dark; shutters at tall French windows held back a hot California morning sky, vividly dismissing that waking-moment panic of skewed location and time. As if by magic a breakfast, concocted from that cornucopia of near-eternal summer, was being quietly arranged on the terrace outside by Gertrude, an angular person of German extraction and Lucullan talent, who, I was later to discover, had a sister who performed the same service for Elvis Presley.

"Miss Howard will come in a moment, and would you like to lunch with the David Selznicks? Meanwhile she thought you would enjoy these." A sheaf of tuberoses, and then, through the swirling layers of heady scent, there was Jean.

"Stay as long as you can," she replied to my fumbling gratitude, "and if you want to go to David and Jennifer's, you'd better get a move on."

It seemed scarcely credible that an hour later I would walk into the home of the man who had produced *Gone With the Wind*. David, whose previous marriage to Irene Mayer, a daughter of old LB himself, had given rise to the quip "the son-in-law also rises," was a big man, round and square at the same time, with a high yet rough-hewn voice.

He immediately took Jean aside, asking her to go and "do something" about his wife, the star Jennifer Jones, who had locked herself in her bedroom all morning, apparently to do yoga, though he wondered why that pursuit needed the accompaniment of a pint of liquor. We went downstairs, past a grotto carved into the rock, housing an Indian deity, to Jennifer's bolted door. Jean called through it, cajoling, and sesame-like the door swung open. Miss Jones was seated cross-legged in the middle of the very cold room seemingly wearing nothing but an expensive fur jacket. An eerie green overhead light lit her face a luminous white, and her lips almost black. Waving me back toward the door, Jean knelt down beside her. As the door shut I realized this was not actually Jennifer's bedroom but the cold storage for furs.

Perhaps the vision-seeing star of *The Song of Bernadette* had been communing with the pelts of clouded leopard or Siberian sable. But Jean's ministrations must have hit the spot; after a few minutes she emerged, teeth chattering, followed by Jennifer, who was wearing, I could now see, a shell pink bathing suit. She ran up the curved staircase, past the grotto, and plunged, a graceful arc, into a heated swimming pool. Selznick died a few months later, and Jennifer moved on to even bigger fur storage, and a fabulous art collection to boot, when she married the billionaire Norton Simon.

"Take the car," Jean had said, heedless of whether I could drive, when I'd mentioned a leather bar downtown someone back east had recommended. In that car, that night, at the corner of Hollywood and Vine, I first heard Bobby Vinton singing "Blue Velvet"; it's remained one of my most poignant memories. "Bluer than velvet was the night," I echoed as I made my way among ranks of gleaming Harleys on the sidewalk and into a long, dimly dark interior. Among the blue-jeaned and black-jacketed boys one vision stood out: Tall, broad, and buff, form-fitted leathers rudely ripped, unruly dark blond hair hiding his gaze, he was the icon of that particular image of sexuality. Transfixed, I gaped, increasingly unsubtly. It took some hours, and several beers.

On the way to bed I asked his name. He told me. "And what do you do?" He told me that, too. He was Peggy Lee's hairdresser.

I telephoned Cecil Beaton at the Bel Air Hotel. "A-a-a-o-o-oh good, it's you, an English voice at last. I'm having te-a-a-r-ribble trouble with that awful George Cukor." I immediately imagined catfights on the *My Fair Lady* set. "Golly, *what,* Cec?" I asked. "He keeps asking me what he should get Juliet Duff for Christmas," he replied.

"Anyway, come to the studio tomorrow, I'll collect you on my way there." "There" was Warner's, a huge sprawling city of its own, hemmed by the drab townships filling in the once-wild San Fernando Valley. Cecil complained all the way. Cukor has no taste, no subtle touch, no class. Rides roughshod over everyone, is making Audrey look tooo hid-eous. "And what's more, my deaaah, he's put the m-a-a-ost gha"—long pause— "stly dream sequence into the film." This was a somewhat surprising critical rant against the great director, legendarily famous for his charm and winning ways with intractable movie stars. Thus it was not so astonishing that Cukor barely raised his head when Cecil introduced me, adding as a sweetener, "He's a friend of Margaret Case."

Perhaps Cukor had made his leading lady look so hideous that day that she was blubbing in her trailer. Anyway, she wasn't on the set, where they were filming Jeremy Brett singing "On the Street Where You Live," so Cecil motioned me to sit in her empty chair, AUDREY HEPBURN stenciled on the back, at the edge of the soundstage. This elicited yet another black look from Mr. Cukor. I was pretty furious myself; why wasn't it *me*, a handsome young Englishman with a perfectly good voice, out there under those lights instead of—well, let's face it, a *very* handsome young Englishman who could really sing. Though in fact Jeremy Brett was dubbed, as he had a poor voice. Cukor did drive me back to Beverly Hills, but I could tell I wasn't his type, friend of Margaret Case's or no. He dropped me at Coldwater Canyon with a discernibly dismissive wave.

One night Cecil took me to dine with the singer Tony Martin and his exquisitely beautiful wife, the dancer Cyd Charisse, whom I had drooled over in the film of Cole's musical *Silk Stockings*. If you wonder why Cyd was thus named, you should know she was born Tulla-Ellice Finklea. The flagstones around the Martins' pool were incised with the names of famous stars, who wrote in a blank book, and then their signatures were somehow transposed to the concrete à la Grauman's Chinese Theater down on Hollywood Boulevard. Cyd brought the book around, to Louis Jourdan, to Shirley MacLaine. I watched Cecil uncap his fountain pen in anticipation. But Cyd passed the book right over his head and on to Paul Newman. Such was the snobbism of Hollywood in those days. But Cecil and I were lucky to even be at the Martins'. Edie Goetz, Louis B. Mayer's other daughter, refused to have anyone to dinner whose name didn't appear *above* the title of a movie.

I'd told Gertrude, Jean's housekeeper, that I longed to meet Elvis. Who didn't? "Can't promise," she'd said. "He's very restless, always drivin' around." A few days later she beckoned me from the kitchen door. "Here," she almost whispered. "Go to this place 'bout eleven tonight." A screw of paper, on it an address high in the hills off Summit Ridge. My head was pounding as the stark black gates opened a crack. I gave the paper to a flashlight-holding hand. Ahead, a vast truck, perhaps a moving van, with its ramp down. "Go on up," said the flashlight. The long dark truck was furnished with some low tatty armchairs, a sofa or two. A few guys, looking like cowboys, were sitting around noiselessly picking at guitars. Others, grouped like a screen toward the back, stood silent, drinking, their bottles and steins glinting from the low lamplight behind them. "Come with me," whispered the now-turned-off flashlight. I followed, wriggling through the screen of young men. Elvis was lying back in a chair, shirtless, his legs straight out, his bare arms dangling over the red upholstery, his eyes shut, a tray of food, presumably Gertrude's sister's, on the floor beside him. He could hardly have looked less restless; but he opened one eye, pushed his hair out of it, waved a hand, mumbled "Howdy," and resumed his rest. Still no one said a word. After a few moments the flashlight appeared and led me back down the ramp, that stairway to paradise, and out those pearly gates. I stood dazed and dazzled by heaven's stars. I had just met their sleepy king.

Michael's old friend, or rather the mother of Pauline Tennant, his oldest friend—the subtly comic actress Hermione Baddeley—was staying at the Chateau Marmont, the famous hotel on the Strip, in those days dingily furnished and barely staffed. Hermione and her companion, a little orange-faced chimp of a woman with the somewhat cumbersome name of Lady Joan Marjoribanks Duff-Assheton-Smith, liked to sit sunning on the balcony all day, a permanent supply of nonvintage "shampoo" at each elbow. Hermione knew all the lesser and therefore much funnier and more natural stars in the town, actors like Hurd Hatfield, who had been typecast as Dorian Gray (and called by everybody, including himself, Turd Tatfield), Kurt Kasznar, and Roddy McDowall, so her sunny balcony was a permanent party. Even her ex-lover, the handsome star Laurence Harvey, came up to visit. "I taught Larry everything he knows," she grumbled when he left. "Gosh, Hermione, *do tell!*" we all said, expecting filth. "Well," she answered. "For a start I taught him to say 'bigger helpings' instead of 'larger portions.'"

Jean took me to lunch at Connie Wald's, widow of the producer Jerry Wald, who is still, in her nineties, among the best-looking and best-dressed women anywhere. We went to drinks with Lewis Milestone, who had come to Hollywood in 1918; rising to director, he made his name with *All Quiet on the Western Front,* to dinner with Audrey and Billy Wilder, or Howard Hawks; to the movies with James Stewart. The hallowed nutritionist Gayelord Hauser lived just up Coldwater amid a plethora of juicers and blenders, and Carroll Righter, tagged "astrologer to the stars" called to tell Jean, who was very superstitious—she had my birth chart done soon after we met—when she could fly to Europe. I begged Jean to ask Dietrich. "She's an awful bore these days," Jean said. "Only talks about herself." I laughed, reminding her of what she had said about Cole, and adding, "Do you think I want her to talk about *me*?" Marlene came to lunch and, true to the predicted form, brought her own LPs, playing us only the applause. Kirk Douglas came to swim and made a pass at Jean and me simultaneously; "threesomes are his thing," Jean explained afterward. Jack Lemmon kissed me as we were searching for a particular record among Jean's massive collection.

Toward the end of the fortnight Jean and I drove out in the evening, right to the end of Sunset Boulevard, where there is no more land to cling to, only the wide and endless sea. As I was buying a beer the barman asked roughly, "And what for your mother?" Blushing and apologetic, I turned to Jean. She was smiling. "Maybe I wish I was," she said quietly.

BACK IN NEW YORK, I was thrust among rather more rudimentary film-makers. Among Bobby and Cecil's more respectable Lower East Side acquaintances were a bunch of wild-haired, not entirely clean guys who played around with the first, and still pretty bulky, 8 mm cameras, making the embryonic form of what would became underground movies. Eventually I was persuaded to let one of them, Jack Smith, whose first film, *Flaming Creatures,* had been banned by the censors because it showed naked women, use Nineteenth Street as a studio. Often I would come back from work to find "stars" like Taylor Mead and Beverly Grant having a relaxing roach after a hard afternoon's filming, sometimes seemingly casually watched by the slight figure of Andy Warhol, his wan face often suffused with either real or feigned surprise.

After several meetings Andy took me to the old Factory on Forty-eighth Street, where he showed me his early paintings. Some were of the Brillo boxes of the scouring pads that my brother-in-law's factories produced—when I suggested to Anne that she buy some of these, she said she had far too many of the real thing. Andy often took me to dinner at his mother's house high up on Lexington Avenue, and in return I began to take him to dinner parties on Park Avenue. Even though people's initial reaction was, "Do you have to bring that funny person?" they would soon be swept in by Andy's compelling combination of weirdness and banality. On the other hand, when I introduced him to Jane Holzer it was love at first sight. That summer Andy and Jane and Taylor Mead and I went to amusement parks at the beach or spent our time following Tiny Tim, the outrageously camp singer with his high-pitched rendition of "Tiptoe Through the Tulips" to theaters as far afield as the Brooklyn Fox or the New Jersey Empire.

Andy asked Jane and me to be in his film *Kiss*—I was a bit reluctant. I knew how drawn out Andy's films, like *Sleep,* were. Later, when we went to see *Empire,* which is simply the camera focused on the Empire State Building for several hours, Jane and I could bear it no longer and had to crawl out on a fire escape, laughing, as the real building towered a few blocks away, instead of Andy's wobbly filmic image. Jane, however, was quite eager. "Sure," she answered Andy, putting on her most Jewish accent. "Anything's better than being a Park Avenue princess."

We did eventually do some filming for the movie. All I can say is that kissing somebody for a full twenty minutes takes a great deal of concentration.

IN ALL THE TIME I had been in America, I'd had a huge advantage in being the young Englishman in New York at the time of the British cultural invasion. I was in a perfect position to be the link between there and London. As well as knowing the next wave of photographers in London, I'd met many of the boys who were the emerging artists, or who would become indelibly famous rock stars. There were many older friends I had met through Simon or Diana who rang me up wanting to see a different side of the city than their staider friends could show them. Or the other way around. Harold Nicolson was determined to go to Luchow's, a German restaurant on Fourteenth Street that he remembered from before the war. This once-famed establishment was my introduction to schnitzel and *Kalbshaxe,* but devilish Harold was more interested in the flesh of the waiters, none in the first flush, and their lederhosen. Even the ancient trembling sommelier sent Harold to seventh heaven. "Look at his *knees,* darling," he'd whisper. "*Look* at his legs."

Enid Bagnold, author of *National Velvet* and *The Chalk Garden,* whom I had met when Diana had taken me to her Rottingdean house the day the Lunts were there, had a new play, *The Chinese Prime Minister,* opening on Broadway. Over lunchtime hot pastrami on rye at the Stage Delicatessen during rehearsals, she told me that it was the first written work for which an author was ever given extraterrestrial rights. There didn't seem much chance that its star, the adorable and gay actor Alan

Webb, would last long enough to re-create his butler role on the moon, as he was already in his eighties.

Colin Clark, the son of Kenneth, and younger brother of Celly, was living in New York, married to the New York City Ballet's French dancer Violette Verdy; they both came to the last-minute parties I gave at Colonnade Row, which were frequently anglophile and balletomane-oriented— sometimes bringing, to our delight, Rudolf Nureyev. One night Colin brought a friend, the eccentric multimillionaire Huntington Hartford. Hunt's reputation preceded him. Multimarried, the first time to Mary Lee Fairbanks, mother of my friend Victoria, he was the heir to the A&P grocery fortune. What with building a theater and artists' colony in Los Angeles, buying the barren Hog Island in the Bahamas (even though renamed Paradise, it took more than Hunt's fortune before it became the glittering resort he anticipated), or having Edward Durell Stone design a museum on Columbus Circle to house his basically mediocre collection, Hunt had made some serious inroads into A&P's coffers. His latest toy was a magazine, *Show*. Subtitled "A Magazine for the Arts," it was a version of *Vanity Fair*, at that time a dormant publication. *Show* had a low but eclectic circulation, its art director, Henry Wolf, was the most respected in his field.

Some weeks after I had met him, Colin called me. "Remember Huntington Hartford? He needs a new art director for his magazine. Wants to see you."

Hunt had a huge apartment overlooking the East River. An inveterate night owl, he was in bed when I arrived at ten, a few nights later. Stumbling around in his dressing gown and pajamas, he gave me a sheet of paper with a printed text, and a pen. "Copy this out!" There was no tone of command in Hunt's voice, more a silky appeal.

He scrutinized what I'd written and wandered off to get dressed. His current wife, Diane Brown, a model about my age, appeared wearing a black-and-white print silk frock that looked sensational with her dark red hair. Eventually Hunt returned, sleek in his habitual gray flannel suit. We all went to dinner, and afterward to a nightclub.

"Dance with Diane!"

She was a wonderful dancer, and we stayed on the floor for some time. I held her close, without talking, but I could feel Hunt's eyes boring into my back and when we turned, saw him watching us intently. When we sat down, I saw with relief that he was smiling. We sat and talked, and at some point he offered me the job.

It was quite a decision to make. I was doing very well at *Vogue,* where there was talk that Alex Liberman had big plans for me. I'd made many friends there, particularly Louise Savitt and Margaret Case; I loved Priscilla Peck and of course Bibi. Above all I was so lucky to be working daily with Diana Vreeland, and the education that entailed, though I knew her friendship would continue whatever I did. On the other hand Hartford had mentioned a pretty substantial salary, I could choose my own staff, and there would be minimal managerial interference. I would be the youngest-ever art director of any prestigious American publication, though there was the tough act of Henry Wolf's reputation to follow.

"Of course you've gotta do it," said Vreeland during our next Sunday lunch. "It'll be diviiine."

Show's offices were the very opposite of the *Vogue* emporium. Hunt had bought and restored the last remaining brownstone on Fifty-seventh Street, between Lexington and Third avenues, and this four-story red-brick, white-shuttered bit of old Manhattan, sandwiched in between high-rises, now looked neat as a newly painted dollhouse.

I soon found out that not only had Henry Wolf departed, but other high-ranking editors had also moved on. Understandably the new team, much of it from a newspaper background, was expected to make the magazine more commercial, to appeal to a wider audience. Up until that point, *Show* had been very New York City–oriented. We were all excited at the prospect of aiming at a pan-American readership.

I interviewed for assistants, eventually deciding on a brilliant guy, Douglas Benezra, to head the department, and, for my PA, Jean Hannon. An accomplished draftsman herself, Jean had a circle of artist and photographer friends whose talent I proposed to use on our pages. In the meantime I had David Bailey or Terry Donovan to take pictures, and Jane Holzer willing and able to be the beautiful model–guinea pig for some of our wilder ideas.

Without too many labor pains, my first full issue came out in September 1964. Diana Vreeland and Priscilla Peck sent congratulatory telegrams; the most cherished came from Henry Wolf.

And when I next saw Alex Liberman, he murmured, with just a hint of irony, "Cher maître."

One morning a small, intense girl with dark eyes glistening—whether due to melancholy or gaiety one was never sure—walked into my office. Sitting on the layout table, she showed me the most extraordinary portfolio of photographs, thrillingly different from the *Vogue* studio staples of Horst and Penn.

I had never heard of Diane Arbus. But a sympathetic spark immediately ignited in both of us. I realized that what this nervous genius offered was that rarest of visual artistic gifts: humor that makes one sad. Diane knew from that moment that she could come to my office whenever she wanted, just hang around, or sleep, or throw out ideas for a future story.

Now world famous as having the *echt*-photographic eye for the grotesque and horrific in the human condition, Diane had, on the surface, a picture-perfect life, being lustrous looking, an heiress to a department store fortune in the Midwest, and married to the most vivacious man, Allan Arbus, himself a photographer with great talent but perhaps less inner turmoil. But of course underneath was a gnawing unhappiness, a desperation and insecurity that would inexorably lead to her suicide.

As my confidence, and *Show*'s circulation, grew in tandem, I used Arbus as much as possible. Perhaps I got the best results when I sent her to photograph the then-forgotten movie star Mae West, living a reclusive life surrounded by an entourage of musclemen in her far from immaculate but once white, all-symmetrical apartment on the ocean in Santa Monica, where, through astute investment, she had become a real estate tycoon.

I'd recalled that my father, usually oblivious to film stars in general, let alone their sexual appeal, had spoken of Mae West's extraordinary attraction, so when I heard that she was still alive, I suggested a story on her to *Show*'s editor. I found out her California telephone number and called it. A soft, slightly accented voice answered: "Miss West's residence."

"May I speak to Mae West?"

I gave my name and my reason for calling. The voice was now no longer soft, or accented. "*Miss* West speaking."

Having apologized and been forgiven my gaffe by the biggest-earning star of her time, I found that Mae's spice became sugar, and she agreed to the sitting with Diane. Before the end of our conversation I felt brave enough to ask for her most famous line.

"Miss West, please will you just say, 'Come up and see me sometime'?"

She did, with all its lusty innuendo. Immediately after this "iconic" statement the line went dead.

Diane's photographs of her are extraordinary, catching this self-absorbed, self-manufactured, supremely camp figure at her ludicrous and yet touching best. Soot black lashes barely attached, mouth a petal pink lipstick smear, canary blond hair piled into a teetering meringue, Mae stands on a box, a spare grimy petticoat tucked around it to give the illusion of height and a train added to her negligee, hand on hips in the ultimate come-on pose. In another sequence she reclines in a white lace bed with her sleeping companions, Toughie and Pretty Boy, who were not her famed musclemen but a pair of apes. A shot from this series was used as the cover of *Magazine Work,* a book on Diane Arbus's work.

The subsequent publicity surrounding the spread in *Show* led to a spectacular screen comeback after an absence of thirty years. She starred, aged seventy-seven, in Gore Vidal's *Myra Breckinridge,* directed by Mike Sarne. (Asked whether Mike had a nervous breakdown during filming, Gore replied: "He handed out breakdowns rather than received them.") Just after this film was made, I was invited to a party at Jules and Doris Stein's house—Misty Mountain, designed by Wallace Neff on top of Bel Air—and finally met Mae West, a tiny blond figure in a knitted claret red cardigan embroidered with flowers. She very charmingly told me the *Show* pictures had revived her career, though neither *Myra,* nor the next and last, *Sextette,* with Timothy Dalton as her leading man, were what *Variety* used to call "boffo."

Another first we achieved for *Show* was getting Miss Streisand. Barbra's reputation as a termagant had grown as rapidly as her stardom, so to pin her down to a shoot wearing clothes by America's hottest avant-garde designer Rudi Gernreich with ace photographer Bill Claxton took the combination of English wheedling and the California pizzazz of Bill's wife Peggy Moffitt; her Kabuki-like beauty and naked breasts had put Rudi's "topless bathing suit" on every front page. We assigned the "Funny Girl" an eight-page spread, and at the last moment I decided to put her on the cover. The presses rolled. Then Madam got on the telephone, whining that she wanted to see the pictures.

Even though it would be too late to pull them, I took the photos over to the Gould residence on Central Park West. Barbra, lying on her bed eating ice cream from a fridge beside it, gave them a cursory glance and went back to ladling in the vanilla nut fudge, hardly removing the spoon when I apprised her of the connection between my mother and the lady whose life she was playing on Broadway. Elliott Gould shambled in, hair all over the place (and his body), and started ranting that we hadn't made his wife look beautiful. I forbore to make the obvious reply, but felt vindicated when Cecil Beaton said he hoped his portraits of "that ghastly woman" would be anywhere near as beautiful as my cover. "You made her look like Cleopatra," he wrote. "I wish I'd thought of that."

Rather more rewarding was a sitting I arranged to illustrate Arthur Kopit's newest play, *The Day the Whores Came Out to Play Tennis,* which *Show* was excerpting. Photographer Jerry Schatzberg drove his black Rolls-Royce onto an all-white set, where fourteen of New York's classiest ladies and demurest debutantes swarmed in, out, and over it, wearing the flimsiest of black lace undress. The resulting photograph of Topsy Taylor, Chessy Rayner, Robin Butler, and Serena Stewart and other friends appeared in the same issue of *Show* as the instantly infamous David Bailey cover of a nude Jane Holzer wearing plastic World's Fair sunglasses and lasciviously licking the shaft of a toy Stars and Stripes flag. This was, in essence, the first pop-art cover and edition of a national magazine.

The odd-looking Liverpudlian group my father had first alerted me to had in the meantime rocketed into stratospheric musical prominence, and by now the Beatles were the talk of New York City. Paul, who had been engaged to my cousin Jane Asher, very sweetly sent me tickets to their concert at Forest Hills. I went to collect them at their hotel, proudly taking them a copy of the magazine. I have a photograph of myself photographing Paul and Ringo holding it up to the camera. While hearing their music live in the open air was exhilarating, the most impressive thing was their leaving the stadium in a helicopter, made golden by the searchlights trained on it, and inside the four black-suited boys waving as it rose up into the dark sky.

On the other hand the Rolling Stones were about to descend on New York. Jane and I were walking down Madison Avenue one lunchtime and ran into Peter Beard. Jane squealed: "Peter, Nicky says these guys the Stones are gonna be bigger than the Beatles." "It's not possible," said Peter. "Nothing and nobody could be bigger than the Beatles." His skepticism was to be borne out when their first concert in New York was not met by huge acclaim. Perhaps they came too soon after the Fab Four—people weren't ready to push the new princes with their pretty melodies aside for a new, grittier sound. However, by the time of their second concert, New York was theirs for the taking, if only they could get some blinding publicity.

Mick would stay with me when he had a free evening, sometimes bringing Keith Richards, who at the time was having a romance with Ronnie Ronette, lead singer of the group whose music became synonymous with the Wall of Sound. There was a big brown velvet sofa below the zebra-print stairs—I remember Mick sprawled on it, his skinny legs topped off by pointed boots, a cigarette in his mouth as he scribbled lyrics. Keith and Ronnie would snuggle up at the other end of the sofa, bodies entwined.

The Stones played a series of now-sensationally successful concerts around New York. To celebrate and propel them even further, I gave an enormous party on Jane Holzer's birthday for them at Jerry Schatzberg's studio. Inspired by our shared Englishness, and the current look of our clothes—mine at the time were ruffled white shirts and a tiger-skin waistcoat and blue jeans—it was nicknamed the "Mod Ball." I found an outrageously camp group, Goldie and the Gingerbreads, four gold lamé–dressed, gold eye-lined teenage girls, at a trashy bar called the Wagon Wheel. And having read about the mods and rockers riots in Brighton, I decided to up the ante by arranging that the leather-clad hulks from all the gay motorcycle gangs should "crash" the party. Which they did, but instead of creating a riot, they were welcomed with open arms by the varied but extremely illustrious guests—including Tom Wolfe, who called it "The Party of the Year for the Girl of the Year" in the following weekend papers, and in the first "salmon light of dawn," Jane, Mick, Tom, and I, followed by Goldie and her girls, took a cab up to "the Brasserie in the Seagram Building for breakfast." Tom later wrote, in *The Kandy-Kolored Tangerine-Flake Streamline Baby,* observing our entrance, "here come . . . four teenage girls in gold lamé, a chap in a tiger-skin vest . . . a fellow in a sweater who has flowing curling hair . . . and then, a girl with an incredible mane, a vast tawny corona. . . . One never knows who is in the Brasserie at this hour, but . . . they will never forget."

· THIRTEEN ·

IN A WAY MICHAEL'S RETURN to Europe was to be a mixed blessing, for I soon began to miss the monogamy that, for better or worse, is my wont. While it was perfectly good fun picking up the face that turned in the street, pretending to be promiscuous in bars, or having a short but successful romance with Jerry Robbins, a less satisfying one with Bill Blass, and a totally unsuccessful pursuit of Joel Schumacher, I felt, however unlikely it seemed then, that I would at some point in the future be with Jimmy Davison.

Since meeting Jimmy at the party George Dix had given almost the first night I arrived in New York, I had seen him on a few occasions and always been struck by his extreme good looks, which combined a patrician elegance with a calm virility. His straight hair broke over a high forehead above alert eyes and an amused expression. He was lithe and tall, over six feet, and usually wore Levi's, still rarely seen in the city, and cowboy boots. Lunching with his lover, Speed Lamkin, I'd said something along the lines of "If you ever get tired of him . . ."

For the moment, such a possibility seemed unlikely. Jimmy and Speed were demonstrably together, living and lavishly entertaining in an apartment on East Seventy-second Street grandly decorated by George Stacey. But nevertheless the unusual circumstance of their union was frequently remarked upon: It was whispered that before Speed snatched Jimmy and his rumored wealth from under her nose, he had actually been engaged to Speed's sister, Marguerite.

These two intensely show-business-ambitious siblings were the offspring of genteel parents from the Deep South decadence of Monroe, a drowsy township on the border of Louisiana and Texas.

On hitting New York, Speed had written an extremely successful play, *Comes a Day,* and for several seasons had been the toast of the town, hailed as "the new Tennessee Williams" or the "natural successor to Faulkner." With his pink, if somewhat porcine features and short near-white curls, Speed could not have looked more different from Marguerite, whose glossy dark bangs, wide-set brows, and pale skin seemed to mirror the image of Holly Golightly, and established her in many people's eyes, and in Jimmy's in particular, as a desirable, funny beauty. But fate, in the form of her brother, stepped in. Instead Marguerite made a brief marriage to the author Harry Brown, which took her to Hollywood, where, due to her perfect if somewhat exaggerated Southern accent, she was chosen to teach Elizabeth Taylor to "y'all" for her role as Maggie in the film of *Cat on a Hot Tin Roof.*

Marguerite, by now remolded as Jimmy's closest friend, had returned to New York, writing "Dear Daisy," a spoof lonely-hearts column in *Glamour,* one of Condé Nast's "younger" magazines, whose offices were on the floor below us. Leo Lerman, the editor of the magazine, was an extrovert, snobbish *echt*-Jewish intellectual with a mischievous wit and a rasp-rough beard. He liked me to nip down with a morning-after report of the previous evening, any especially salty details being rewarded with a prickly hug. (I would have to a give a more sanitized account if Amy Greene, *Glamour*'s chirpy fashion director, wife of the photographer Milton Greene, whose current handling of Marilyn Monroe's career was doing so little to enhance it, or Marguerite, joined us in Leo's room, which, like Diana Vreeland's, was a kind of court.) Marguerite and I would translate my exploits into advice to her lovelorn readers when I'd join her for lunch, often with Jimmy, and usually at the Isle of Capri, on Third and Sixty-first. This restaurant became a kind of club for our friends, and "See you at the Isle" almost invariably followed our "Goodnights."

Jimmy Davison and Speed Lamkin's was an odd union. Jimmy's seemingly ultraconservative banking family, typically educated at St. Mark's, followed by Groton and Harvard—his father had been head of J. P. Morgan—was not the conventional upbringing for a relationship with a flamboyant Southern homosexual, even if Speed had spent a couple of years as companion to the aging movie star and lifelong mistress of William Randolph Hearst, Marion Davies. Speed, given his slightly manic animation and desire to shock with his drawled, name-filled stories, was very clearly a "character," but it was Jimmy's long, languid frame and handsome face, brought to instant life by his deep hesitant laugh, that made him infinitely immediately attractive. I would occasionally run into them at parties. One could not help but be amused by Speed's outré personality, but often my glance would meet Jimmy's, a questioning look in his flint brown eyes, and his quick silver smile more like a statement. I think he knew, as I did, the eventual answer to that unspoken question. The inevitable outcome took several months, but in the meantime Jimmy became part of my circle of friends. He loved Min when he met her, and Jane Holzer and I would often go to his apartment. On a visit to London, Jane and I had been staying with David Bailey. We were all convinced there was a poltergeist in David's flat and had the dopey idea of taking it as a present to Jimmy. We "captured" the ghost in a paper bag, packed it in one of Jane's nine million Vuitton cases, and "released" it in the big room in Jimmy's. The next day two Chinese vases that had stood high up on brackets at opposite ends of the room were lying in smithereens on the floor.

Perhaps this gave Jimmy the idea of moving; anyway, he and Speed parted. Speed was given a ravishing small apartment decorated to the nines by Billy Baldwin, where he amused himself and all New York by introducing elderly grand dames like Kitty Miller to the novel sensations of grass and poppers. Jimmy took over his friend K. K. Kelly's Sixty-first Street duplex. On hearing he was sharing it with a young actor called George Trumbull, I was somewhat distressed, especially as it transpired that this was his new lover. Over the past few months we had seen each other more and more regularly; he had been very open about various problems and passions, past and present, in his life, but not about our new love.

During our conversations we discovered one extraordinarily coincidental link. It was to the Davisons that Dominic Elwes had been sent for the duration of the war. From what Jimmy told me, I understood that he was a product of two very different strata of American society. On his father's side were dour, dyed-in-the-wool Republicans: Fairfaxes from Virginia, Trubees from Connecticut, Endicotts and Peabodys from Salem, that infamously intolerant town. Jimmy's relative Endicott Peabody founded Groton, the ultraconservative private school to which all *Social Register* families aspired to send their sons. Many, including Jimmy, never recovered from the horror of the bullying and hazing that made up everyday life at Groton. Jimmy said his day-to-day fear at Groton was such that he learned nothing until he went to university, for which, bravely bucking the accepted path of Harvard or Yale, with their attendant even crueler induction rites, he chose liberal Stanford in California. I am sure the terror he experienced at Groton accounted for Jimmy's innate tenderness and self-effacing nature. There was nothing of the jock about him. His maleness and sexual allure were very subtle and far ahead of their time, while his mind and conversation were firmly rooted in the romantic past.

Jimmy described the members of his upright family. He told me about

Peacock Point, the Davison estate on the North Shore of Long Island, where his grandmother Goggie, a black-hatted and -coated figure regally progressing around the grounds in her little electric car, presided over the perfectly replicated Queen Anne mansion. Old Mrs. Davison was noted for her thrift. When some local children proudly told her the sand in their Christmas crèche came from Peacock Point's beach, she said they needn't return it. On the other hand all her children and their families lived in various houses she had built for them on the grounds. All, that is, except Jimmy's. His father, until his quite recent death, had lived with his new wife in the city and on Hobe Sound in Florida. Since her divorce Jimmy's mother spent summers breeding Arabian horses on an immense ranch in the Canadian Rockies and wintering in the more temperate climate of Palo Alto, below San Francisco.

This worthy, community-pillar clan had produced an extraordinary wild card, Jimmy's aunt Frances, always called Frankie. Her sister, Alice, was said to have been the mistress of Lord Halifax when he was ambassador to Washington, though it was hard to believe that Frankie's delicious, totally original Americanness, her skylarking humor, and the disregard of authority she shared with Jimmy could have found much in common with Alice's peer, well known for his pro-Hitler sentiment.

Neat as a new pin and vivacious as a swallow, with dark darting eyes, the same deep chuckle as Jimmy, and dressed in the simplest Parisian clothes, Frankie lived in a long low pavilion looking out over the sound, where the lights of fishing fleets merged with the fireflies as, in the after-dinner dark, we sat and sang on Frankie's porch, or watched, from balconies at dawn, the silouettes of returning fishing boats stenciled against the hazy green border of the opposite shore. Frankie dreaded her many demure neighbors, taking me instead to visit less humdrum friends such as Alexandra Moore, a strapping white-haired lady habitually wearing a beige safari suit, who lived in "Chelsea" (so called because the family had owned the Chelsea area in Manhattan, which had once been a farm), a creamy-stone moated castle with many rooms of chiaroscuro frescoes by José Maria Sert, or to see C. Z. Guest, at whose nearby estate, Templeton, with its pedimented pavilion, its perfectly balanced gardens, and its manicured stables of nostril-flaring hunters, she and her Churchill-cousin husband, Winston, had created their idealized Anglo-American lifescape.

Along narrow green lanes near Peacock Point were the astonishingly long gray stone walls enclosing scented azalea and camellia gardens, their closed gates signifying that the owner, Cecil Beaton's "rock crystal goddess," the aquamarine-eyed Mona Harrison Williams, was spending the spring in her rose-pink Capri villa. Locked gates were as nothing to Frankie, who gesticulated to a gardener. We drove toward a strange green hillock, which gradually revealed itself to be various buildings smothered by ivy. "Mona had the main house pulled down. This was the sports wing," Frankie told me, trying the door handle. Even she didn't dare actually break in, so sadly I never saw the vast room, created from the former squash court, which Mona, the daughter of a stable hand from Kentucky, and soon to be Countess Bismarck, had decorated with every color in the rainbow, and carpets from the Old Summer Palace in Peking covering the sprung parquet.

If Frankie was exotic as far as Davison blood went, she wasn't a patch on the women of Jimmy's mother's family. Anne Stillman was the granddaughter of the founder of the First National City Bank, the first man ever to make more than a billion dollars. She had been born in a turreted Gothic mansion, which then still stood on Park Avenue, to a powerful personage named Fifi Brown Potter, whose own mother, Cora Urquhart, had been a turn-of-the-century beauty and acclaimed actress.

Until she married Brown (as in Brown Brothers Harriman) Potter and gave birth to her only child, Cora had proved to possess a fairly catholic taste in lovers, conducting affairs with King Edward VII, who bought her a pretty villa in Cannes; Carl Jung; and Buffalo Bill Cody. Crossing continental America in the company of the colonel and his Wild West show, Cora rode bareback in a three-ring circus, pursued by "redskins."

Cora passed on her exotically flavored lifestyle to her daughter. Fifi's marriage to Jimmy's grandfather James Stillman had produced the required children, Anne and Alexander, and Stillman, true to the expected mores of the time, was by then keeping a Follies girl. Perhaps in retaliation Fifi embarked on a steamy affair with Fred Beauvais, the Native American guide on the Stillman summer camp outside Quebec, by whom she had a son, Guy. In still-prudish New York circles such behavior was considered beyond the pale: Divorce loomed, the Stillmans were shunned. Elderly people I met could remember reports of it being scissored from their newspapers, and Janet Rhinelander Stewart told me that at dinners the guests were often handed typewritten notes reading "Please do not discuss the Stillman divorce" on arrival.

Social pariah or no, Fifi carried on by marrying Fowler McCormick, the scion of the Chicago harvesting family, whose own mother, Edith Rockefeller, had herself been quite an eccentric, believing—even though always wearing a two-million-dollar rope of very material pearls—that in a former existence she had been Ankhesenanum, the child wife of Tutankhamen. In later life she was seduced by two gay European "companions" into building them a whole town, Edithville—bits of it still stand—to decorate, and a zoo exclusively for giraffes. Her husband, not to be outdone, had a transplant of glands from a young blacksmith.

Fifi, by now rich beyond dreams, could indulge her great passion, inherited by her daughter, of breeding Arabian horses. She was among the first to import premier-quality Arab blood into the United States, buying renowned stallions and mares from Lady Anne Blunt, who with her husband, the poet Wilfred Scawen Blunt, owned the legendary stud at Crabbet Park in Sussex. To stable these beautiful and valuable animals, Fifi, perhaps inspired by the Buffalo Bill connection, found a vast acreage of land on the outskirts of Phoenix, the flyblown capital of Arizona, near an adobe village called Scottsdale. She bought the land, then the village. Nearby lived several members of the Hopi tribe. She bought them, too, and created the first—and for all I know the only—private Indian reservation in the now-substantial town of Scottsdale.

Fifi treated her Indians like gods; they could do no wrong. But as is so often the case, the children of such riches are miserable. Fifi kept hers on short financial rations as long as she could, making sure they trembled at her every beck and call, and of course using constant emotional blackmail. Jimmy's uncle Alex, tall and angular like his sister, never married and became a serious alcoholic, reeling between houses in New York and Paris, and the pretty villa in Cannes, his hair in tangled black hanks, his scruffy black clothes hung with enormous pieces of extremely rare early turquoise and silver Indian jewelry. Anne, Jimmy's mother, alcoholic to a lesser extent, fell prey to a female fortune hunter, and for some years after her divorce her children found her company a strain. By the time I met Jimmy the other woman had disappeared, but he was worried by his mother's lonely drinking. One night he called and came down to Nineteenth Street, where he began to cry. By morning the tears were mere memories.

MY RELATIONSHIP with Jimmy had changed; and within a few weeks I had moved uptown. I saw a brownstone on Seventy-seventh between Fifth and Madison with the second floor for rent. It was affordable, and the nouveau-pauvre junk was installed in a darker—I painted the living room coffee brown—setting that somehow made it appear less pauvre and junky. On the floor below lived a young comedian whose name I recognized from Village clubs—Woody Allen. I mentioned how wonderfully quiet a neighbor he was. Woody said, "Yeah, I only play Marcel Marceau records."

Living uptown was in itself an education. Many of the major art dealers were on Madison Avenue, as were some of the best antique shops. The auction house of Parke-Bernet, soon to merge with Sotheby's, was on my block, and opposite was the Carlyle. Outside the hotel one day Jimmy almost saluted in the direction of a nondescript-looking man wearing a plastic macintosh and hat protector. "Good morning, Mr. President," he said, before introducing me to Harry Truman. There was an excellent bookshop, and farther down the avenue, the great men's emporia of Brooks Brothers and J. Press. My apartment was no distance for Jimmy to walk to; he wasn't working at that point, and he loved just wandering around the Upper East Side. Marguerite and I used to joke that if you asked Jimmy what he'd done that day, he'd say, "I went to the bank," or "I had my hair cut." In fact I soon found out he was also visiting jewelers and antiquaires, as with increasing frequency he'd shyly slip little packets into my pocket, which when unwrapped I would find to be a cigarette lighter by Johnny Schlumberger from Tiffany, a seventeenth-century enamel-and-diamond skull, or cuff links from Verdura. These were the proof of Jimmy's intrinsically tender, generous nature. Just as exciting was his knowledge of the city and its less well-known past, the characters and the scandals that had shaped it. Jimmy's evident reciprocation of my love gave me supreme physical and mental happiness. My work at *Show* reflected this self-confidence, which I had never truly experienced before.

This was compounded when one day Jimmy's actor friend locked himself in his bathroom with some fierce wild animal (I seem to recall it being a raccoon). Anyway, he emerged after quite a long time, covered, Jimmy said, with bloody scratches—and raving. That was enough for even Jimmy's compliant nature, and after some frantic negotiations with his family, George disappeared from 116 East Sixty-first Street, never to return.

Almost immediately Jimmy asked me to move in with him, which I did, though I also decided to keep on the Seventy-seventh Street apartment. The only thing I decided to take with me then and there was Claude, a minute Pekingese puppy he had given me, which joined Jimmy's three dachshunds, Lulu, Buster, and Peanut: Jimmy's dogs were almost more important in his life than I was. Luckily they were all better house-trained than George's raccoon, which had run riot throughout the apartment, and we now needed to redecorate. The raccoon lover's quarters became the guest room. The ground floor had a kitchen on the front and a big dark-wood-paneled room with a fireplace and windows giving on to a garden—a yard, as Americans insist on calling it—in which we cut a hatch in the fencing through to the restaurant behind, so for dinner parties we would just go and yell, "Six spaghetti Bolognese!" and the food would appear. It made the kitchen rather redundant.

We quickly went to London to buy furniture, finding a wonderful early-eighteenth-century oak console table at the ultrafashionable antique shop of Westenholz and Mlinaric. On this we placed a huge white Meissen figure of Augustus the Strong. Sofas were covered with brown linen, chairs with yellow-and-brown *point d'hongroie*. The windows' chalk white curtains, a memory of Geoffrey Scott's at Hundridge, made the whole room feel like the painted parlor there.

Upstairs Jimmy's bedroom was all blue and white, with a half-tester bed in which he and I and all the dogs could fit perfectly happily. The bed was in fact so huge that often friends who were staying, like Claire Pelly or young Paul Getty, used to come and join us on it for drinks.

Rory and Romana McEwen were arriving at about this time for the wedding of her half sister Emily Harding. Romana had told me to contact Emily when I first arrived in New York, and she had become an immediate intimate. Their mother, Alice Astor, was the sister of Vincent Astor, the head of the family that owned great swaths of Manhattan, including most of Park Avenue not in the real-estate portfolio of the queen. Their name, expanded to Astoria, became synonymous with grand hotels, as in the Waldorf. Vincent and Alice's father had drowned on the *Titanic,* leaving her a substantial fortune, but it was said that in reality she was the daughter of a handsome Cuban with Native American blood, named Sydney Hatch, whom Alice had never met. A friend decided to put this right and asked them both to lunch at '21.' Alice was, as always, chronically late, but luckily Hatch had not yet arrived either. Finally he appeared, immaculate, though putting in his cuff links. A moment later Alice came in, equally immaculate but screwing in her earrings; all the guests then knew that the rumored illegitimacy must be true. Far more like their mother in looks than was Romana, Emily had the slanted eyes and dark, straight, center-parted hair hinting at the Native American blood Alice supposedly possessed. Emily's long fingers and narrow figure also attested to this lineage. While both sisters had Alice's intrinsic understated elegance, happily neither had inherited her well-known lack of humor. Emily would cry with laughter at the most puerile jokes, while Romana is a deft hand with a pun.

Since Alice's death, rumored to have been murder, Emily, as a young heiress, had the doting eye of her aunt Brooke Astor watching over her. There were regular dinners at Brooke's Park Avenue apartment, after which she would urge Emily and me to go to nightclubs, surreptitiously and sweetly handing me a wodge of dollars as she said goodnight. (On one such night at El Morocco we saw the Texan-booted figure of LBJ on the dance floor.) Sometimes a gangling, shaggy-haired, quick-witted architect would join us. His name was Michael Zimmer, and he was Romana's father's nephew. Emily, stuck in staid New York, had daydreamed of being a member of the dazzling McEwen/Hofmannsthal circle. Her soon-announced engagement to Michael promised both. The wedding, to which all Emily and Michael's mutual Austro-Scottish families were on their way, was to be held at Ferncliff, the upstate, lushly wooded estate of her uncle Vincent Astor, hanging on the banks of the Hudson at Rhinebeck. For the wedding Brooke had added an enormous marquee, lavishly flowered, fabulously victualed, with footmen plying drink that must have induced forgetfulness, for I remember nothing, but possess a postcard from Cecil Beaton: "Terribly funny, your description of the cripples' wedding." What can have been in Brooke's Bollinger?

Alice Astor, besides being "a lunar beauty with wrists that stretched half way up her arm," loved being part of a young intellectual set, and had early on discovered Gore Vidal, and bought him a house called Edgewater near hers at Rhinebeck. By the time I knew him, he had given up Edgewater for Manhattan—which was to my advantage, as with his constant companion, Howard Austen, we would frequently go late-night cruising hustler bars around Forty-second and Broadway, often accompanied by one of the wisest and funniest girls I've ever known, Sue Mengers, soon to become a legendary agent in Hollywood.

One of the many good things that came out of Emily and Michael's wedding was that Rory's brother David, whom I had, probably mutually, loathed at Eton, came with them and decided to stay on in New York. Gum-eye, as he was always known, since waking up was not his thing, was to become the most treasured friend, and, oddly, given his shambolic persona, one of the greatest Casanovas I've ever known. His parentage was romantic—he was supposed to be the son of the Earl of Murray, and was charm personified, even after several of the after-dinner drinks—Katinkas, two parts vodka to one part apricot brandy—that would eventually kill him. He made every man, woman, and dog feel that they had been to bed with him and relished every moment, even if they had only lunched with him. I introduced him to Jean Shrimpton, and they had a lackadaisical affair in between her romances with David

Bailey and Terence Stamp. However, when he met Jane Holzer, the sparks were more electric. If David Bailey was the person with whom I always experienced the newest place, the latest sensation, with David McEwen I had the fun of discovering mutual acquaintances, stories, and gossip of our mutual Etonian halves and holidays. We dined together almost every night, and many weekends I'd rent a Thunderbird and, with Gum-eye, drive to stay with Emily and Michael up at Rhinebeck, or with Lady Sarah Russell, who had the most comfortable house I'd ever known, on the estate of her grandmother Balsan in Southampton.

One summer weekend while Gum and I were staying with Sarah, Consuelo Balsan gave a party to celebrate the wedding of her grandson, Sarah's brother, the Duke of Marlborough, to Tina Onassis. We were dying to be asked.

"Well, I'll try," Sarah said, with her well-known Churchillian snorting laugh. "I'm certain Granny would be delighted, but you know"—snort—"what a stickler"—snort—"Sunny is. I mean, have you brought your"—snort—"white tie?"

David and I promised to spruce up, and Sarah secured us an invitation for after dinner. We must have got too stuck into the Katinkas, and we made our way somewhat unsteadily in the dark across Ox Pasture meadow. Aiming, as instructed by Sarah, for the well-lit front gates, I suddenly saw a nice straight smooth path leading to Mme Balsan's open French windows and the rhythm of Lester Lanin's orchestra. "Quick, Gum," I said, grabbing his arm. "This way." We stepped on the path and sank up to our knees in the Balsans' ornamental water. I managed to scramble out, somehow hauling the cursing sozzled Scotsman up as well. What to do now?

"Do?" said Gum-eye. "Do? We go and get a drink." So saying, he squelched through the French windows and into the glittering throng, his shoes flooding little cascades of pond water onto Mme Balsan's priceless Savonneries.

Sarah's snorts lasted most of Sunday.

Often at weekends we drove up to Yorktown Heights to stay at Haywire, the country house of Pamela Churchill, by now married to Leland Hayward. At one, our fellow guests were Truman Capote, the actor Martin Gabel, and his television-star wife, Arlene Francis. Truman conceived the mad idea that Martin, who was straight as a die, fancied him, and kept squealing all weekend, "Martin Gabel keeps trying to put his howwible wed tongue down my thwoat." As we were leaving, Truman was sitting in his new E-type Jaguar; his red seat belt, then a newfangled device, was hanging out of the closed door onto the ground. "Truman, look out, your seat belt," I said.

He wound down the window and peered out: "Oh my gahd! I told you! It's Martin Gabel's tongue."

This was about a month before Truman was due to give his now-legendary Black and White Ball. But in fact the party everyone *really* wanted to go to was given the night before by Josie Blair. People were vying to get asked, and Josie had thought up a brilliant theme. "Come as your favorite dream" found me going as an American footballer, with the studs of my boots digging into Josie's parquet, and Margaret Case dressed as her true dream, a bride, but wearing the toile of a couture wedding dress by Paco Rabanne.

With all this partygiving in the air, Jimmy and I decided to give one for Rory and Romana on their next visit to New York. Rory was having an exhibition of his paintings. The singing group of the moment—Peter, Paul, and Mary—came to his opening, along with a brace of the president's sisters.

Rory and Romana both still adored wearing tartans, so the theme had to be Scottish. Jimmy and I amused ourselves by conjuring visions of ceilidhs and kilts and bagpipes in the mist. One of Jimmy's most charming traits was his ability to turn dreams into reality: "You find the tartan and I'll find the piper." Not easy, one would have thought, in midtown Manhattan.

By the time I'd bought yards and yards of appropriately plaid material at Klein's, Jimmy had returned triumphant. "I've found a piper," he said.

"What? Where?"

"At the Scotch delicatessen on Lexington Avenue—I asked them, and the girl serving turned out to be a Dagenham Girl Piper," he said. "But what on earth's a Dagenham Girl?"

When, at the end of the dinner, the notes of the "The Skye Boat Song" drifted down the stairs, there wasn't a tear-free eye among the forty people sitting around the dinner table.

Jimmy and his sisters would go every summer to visit his mother at her ranch in Canada. Now he asked me to go with him. I was of two minds about all of this; I hadn't ridden since my various ignominious falls as a child, but I didn't want to let Jimmy down, and I was concerned about what my reception from his mother would be. On the cross-country drive via Chicago and the endless miles of farmlands, the foothills of the Rockies, and over the border into Canada, with Jimmy beside me in his Levi's and boots, I began to rather like the image of myself as a range-roving cowboy.

From Jasper, the Athabasca River tumbles and roars through narrow gorges, flattens out into almost lakelike stillness and then gathers itself and surges on again. The several miles of the Athabasca Ranch it flows through had been the setting for the Marilyn Monroe movie *River of No Return,* and remnants of the set still stood on its banks. Moose and elk stood grazing in some shallow waters; bears and wolves roamed in the heights above. Crossing an iron bridge, we came to the tiny town of Entrance, and there at last were the gates of the ranch. A five-mile drive led to a handful of buildings set in a fertile crescent carved out amid the endless forests of Christmas trees, part of it a new-mown airstrip, its wind sock idling in the summer air, against the snowy backdrop of the Rocky Mountains.

Jimmy's mother met us at the door of the main house, an enormous log cabin designed and decorated in the thirties by her friend Anne Morgan. She was as tall and slim as Jimmy, as fine-featured, but with neat blue-white hair. She dressed from top to toe as a man: cowboy shirt with bolo tie, Western trousers cinched with an Indian silver belt, and sneakers. Contrary to the somewhat fierce impression this gave, she was extremely mild, almost effusive in her greeting. But her steel gray eyes had a tendency to blink frequently, almost as if flinching or warding off verbal blows.

That first summer we had rooms in the main house, Jimmy in his own and I in his brother's, but for future years his mother built us a cabin of our own. Jimmy loved the ranch, and showed me all the special places from his childhood summers: the field where you could watch wolves playing at sunset on a nearby ridge, the Bearbait, a sort of amphitheater in the woods where the foreman would put horsemeat, and grizzly and black bears would come at dusk to gorge themselves as we watched from a thrillingly unsafe platform. He taught me to pistol-shoot, and surprisingly, having never before picked up a gun in my life, I was quite adept. He taught me how to recognize muskegs, the boggy ground that could suck you and your horse down within seconds, and the dip in the Low Field where, after a heavy rainfall, we (naked) could canter our horses through the chest-high water. It stayed light till eleven, but even when night fell we could read by the starlight from the unpolluted expanse above. After a barbecue supper we would saddle the horses and ride on the ridge above the Athabasca, looking across at the little town of Entrance, so named because it was the considered the gateway to the Rocky Mountains. Its few log and stone cabins straddled the route of the Trans Canada Railway. Huge slobbering, steaming locomotives, hooting their way out of Jasper, would suddenly appear from a tall dark chasm cut through the rock, pulling endless flat- and boxcars. These mile-long goods trains clickety-clacked right through, but with a searing scream of sparks the passenger trains halted. If the stop was long enough, the passengers high up in their glass bubbles atop the cars descended to bargain with the Indians who had silently gathered, for any pieces of the miraculously soft, squaw-chewed, tasseled, and bead-embroidered deerskin clothes—gloves, moccasins, waistcoats—that Jimmy and his sisters or I hadn't snapped up as soon as they were made. I commissioned fringed trousers and a jerkin for flower-power summers in London; the outfit was the envy of the King's Road.

The oldest but by no means least sprightly inhabitant of Entrance was ninety-odd-year-old Shand Hervie. He had lived in his tiny candlelit hut up among the pines for seventy of them. Born in Castle Semphill in Scotland, he had been at Eton with a grandson of Queen Victoria and had often been asked to her castle for tea. A youthful journey to the Rockies had lengthened into a lifetime. The strange, almost austere lure of the Rockies had captured his soul. For several years it was to have something of the same effect on me.

MEANWHILE, SINCE MY initial visit to Jamaica, I had returned there often as Sarah Russell's guest. By now she had bought her own house, Content, on a hillside overlooking Montego Bay. About a quarter of a mile away, and slightly above it, was one of the most desirable houses I had ever seen. I coveted it from the moment I saw it. Of course it was for sale. Sarah and I went to see it and immediately hatched a plan to buy it together—I to use the small amount of trust money my father had just released to me. This new Valhalla had been named, by its liquor-loving builder, Drambuie. Because of its magical ninety-degree view of the lushness and blueness of the Jamaican coastline, I decided to call it Skye.

The house stood on a stone parapet and consisted solely of two enormous rooms, a bedroom and a sitting room, opening onto a terrace of equal size, with a swimming pool hidden by a balustrade below a flight of steps. Behind was a kitchen and bathroom, and a guest room in a pink-washed shanty, its veranda overlooking a waterfalled ravine. Sarah smoothed all the paths to furnish it in the simplest possible way, and within a month it was ready for me to return to, this time with Jimmy.

Jimmy had vague memories of a house, which his family, like all Americans of that class, had had in Cuba before the revolution. As a small boy Jimmy remembered the flying boats leaving Long Island Sound on Fridays to land at the Varadero; disembarking, the passengers would be swept by great white, finned Cadillacs to their elaborate beachside mansions. At that point Cuba was one of the most glamorous places in the world, with a highly charged, sensual nightlife. He remembered the ads for the cabaret act of Gargantua, an enormous ape that would perform sexual acts on stage, and, continuing the monkey theme, the stories of old Mrs. Abreu, one of the grande dames of Havana, who would fill the places at her table, if any guests didn't show up, with chimpanzees in evening dress.

With the tropics in some measure in his blood, Jimmy took to Skye and Jamaica immediately. Several of his American friends, Bill and Babe Paley, Henry and Ann Ford with their children, had houses at Roundhill or Tryall, two smart resorts in the valleys below. Skye, anything but smart, was enlivened by two piglets I'd named Weidenfeld and Nicolson that followed us like puppies. Less cute a sight was when the son of our cook, Edith Clarke, slit open his brother's arm with a machete; even now I can see the astonishingly white flesh hanging, like a pale satin curtain, from his black skin.

To many of my English friends, going to the Caribbean in the 1960s seemed far-flung and expensive. But with Skye to stay in, the journey from England was within their reach. Claire and Henry Pembroke came for part of their honeymoon, and Piers Westenholz liked to have fierce Scrabble matches for hours by the pool. Marguerite Lamkin flew down, bringing with her a brilliant English barrister called Mark Littman, clearly besotted by her. To us, he seemed rather stuffy—I remember him saying, "What on earth's pot?"—and Marguerite was of two minds about this sudden admiration from a man she hardly knew. My mother, instead of her usual visits to New York, came to Skye. She brought her cousin Kath Morduant-Smith, as a companion. No great traveler, Kath believed that the cure for all potential tropical diseases, including incipient sunstroke, mosquito bites, and dodgy tummy, was a good slug of rum. Between them they drank the island almost dry.

The greatest joy was when Simon Fleet arrived. From that moment on Jamaica assumed a different aspect. His brother, the acting bishop, came over from Haiti to join us. Unsurprisingly, compared with Simon, he was rather proper and looked most uncomfortable sunbathing in his dog collar and cassock. Simon was determined to see every inch of the island, particularly the "great house" plantations, some ruined and some standing, the grand eighteenth-century buildings in Kingston, the rapids at Ocho Rios, and the private island of Errol Flynn, by now the province of the beautiful Nina Dyer, once married to Sadruddin Khan, who was slowly dying in jeweled seclusion, guarded by two ferocious lesbians.

To help us find the many jungle-clogged ruins, Simon had discovered a man called Colonel Colcannon, a bristly old ex-army type who headed some dim Jamaican tourist board. For reasons known only to himself, Simon decided he had to make a sexual conquest of this unlikely figure, and insisted on sharing his room in all the flea-bitten hotels we stayed in on our journey.

It took about a week to circumnavigate the island, and the same amount of time for Simon to effect his conquest. Perhaps it killed Colonel Colcannon, for we saw neither sunburned hide nor ginger hair of him ever again.

· FOURTEEN ·

I HAD BEEN AT *SHOW* FOR ONLY nine months or so when Huntington Hartford, realizing that, however advanced I and the team there had made it, it was yet another of the pet projects that was draining away his once-huge fortune. He decided to sell. The buyers were a couple of oaflike businessmen, faintly involved with the arts by dint of the fact that they published *Playbill*, the programs given free in every New York theater. So, less than a year after giving up my safe career at *Vogue*, I was suddenly jobless. Marguerite Lamkin, having retired from her "Dear Daisy" column on *Glamour*, as she was now contemplating marriage to Mark Littman, came to my rescue. Through her, Dick Avedon, at the time the most influential photographer on earth, suggested I work as his editorial assistant on the April 1965 issue of *Harper's Bazaar*. He had been asked to guest edit the magazine, the first time this idea had been put forward. He had agreed, provided there would be absolutely no control or direction from Nancy White—the editor of *Bazaar* since Diana Vreeland's departure to *Vogue*—whom Dick thought very provincial and uninspiring. We were given carte blanche to do what we wanted, and Dick said it unquestionably had to be the most modern issue of a fashion magazine ever published.

Having seen a pair of winking-eye spectacles in a Broadway joke shop, I had the idea of using a hologram—not that they were yet called that—of Jean Shrimpton's eye that would wink as you moved, on the cover portrait. Dick was wildly enthusiastic, photographing Jean's sky blue eyes shut and open for hours, but the process turned out to be quite expensive and in the end only first-run copies carried "the Shrimp" winking out from inside a "heavenly pink space helmet by Mr. John." I persuaded the leading pop artists Roy Lichtenstein, George Segal, and Claes Oldenburg to make huge backdrops and sets for Marella Agnelli, Naty Abascal, and Dolores Fürstenberg, the great beauties of the day, to be photographed against, wearing "space age" clothes by the young Pierre Cardin and Paco Rabanne.

In a bar in Chicago, Dick discovered the exquisite, long-limbed Donyale Luna, who would become the first instance ever of a black model being used in a "white" magazine. We photographed her wearing the collection of the American couturier James Galanos. The chief cutter at Galanos, herself a black woman, told Galanos—and us—that she would quit if Donyale appeared in the magazine wearing clothes she had made. Furious, Dick had to capitulate, cropping the pictures so that no telling features above Donyale's long slender neck were visible. (Nevertheless, on publication, hundreds of readers in the South wrote to Nancy White canceling their subscriptions.) Paul McCartney posed in a NASA space suit against a lunar landscape, actually a garbage dump in New Jersey, a toga-clad Ringo was crowned with a victor's laurel wreath.

Dick's portraits of impossibly thin kids like Bob Dylan and the six-foot-seven basketball sensation Lew Alcindor were separated from the ravishingly plump Bibi Winkelhorn and Bob Dylan's wife Sara with a story by Tom Wolfe. Wunderkind artist Jasper Johns and his painter partner, Robert Rauschenberg, were photographed in deep snow outside their West Side studio. I was the stand-in, shivering until Dick deemed the light adequate, at which point these artists momentarily braved the cold to be snapped.

Dick decided to follow up the New York section with a portfolio of "Swinging" London. We took a suite at the Ritz; in those days the boiseried bedrooms were the size of ballrooms, and the marble bathrooms not much smaller. On our first morning, cold and gray and overcast, Dick photographed Winston Churchill's funeral procession passing along Piccadilly below our windows, the spectacle reminding me of watching the coronation from a similar position more than a decade before, while I set up sittings via a single operator at the hotel's antiquated switchboard.

We had hired a studio at the newly built *Sunday Times* headquarters in Gray's Inn Road, and a parade of Mods, some knocking on aristocratic doors, others aristocrats playing, delightfully, at being Mod, poured out of the elevator and into the clothes of young designers like Foale & Tuffin or Caroline Charles: Chrissie Shrimpton; Jane and Julian Ormsby-Gore, now back from Washington; singers Bobby Jameson and Cilla Black, just beginning her rocket to fame; my cousins Peregrine and Jacquetta Eliot; and Lily Langtry's great-granddaughter Lucy Bartlett. After a day of sittings we would dine at the first trattoria to open in England, the Toscana in Soho, before dashing to Brian Morris's Ad Lib Club, high above an alley behind Leicester Square to frug the night away with the same crowd, joined by the Beatles, or Rudi Nureyev with Tessa Kennedy.

Jimmy joined me in London. We had arranged a holiday in Morocco. Getting to the all-white Atlantic coastal town, Essaouira, then more evocatively still called Mogador, with its image of turbaned black princelings, was no picnic, involving several changes of string-baled tin crate, all susceptible to every air pocket. When we finally arrived, I— by that time an extremely nervous passenger—suggested to Jimmy that for the rest of the trip we should rent a car. Once this needle in a haystack was located, we set out for Taroudant. We had, of course, not reckoned with the distances of that sub-Saharan landscape, and endless surprisingly chilly hours later crawled into the thick linen sheets, gently warm from the aromatic logs in the curved corner fireplace, of the Hôtel Gazelle d'Or.

Days spent in the jasmine-scented gardens, reading beside the pool and walking at dusk in the dusty, color-filled village alleys made me aware how much I loved Jimmy, how lucky I was to be loved so strongly by him. He was beautiful, funny, calm, and well read. While I was none of those things, I'm sure he felt, as I did, that we would be together for a lifetime.

Driving up dark pink valleys, passing clusters of round pink mud huts lost high in the ice-capped Atlas Mountains, or slithering on glasslike sandy tracks trying to get to Goulimine, the Tuareg, or Blue Men's, capital of Michael Wishart's romantic memory, or crossing the plain to the Palais Jamaï in Fez, when the full moon hanging low over a rocky ridge was so huge and seemed so close we both felt we'd had a foretaste of a planetary collision, we began to plan our mutual future. Nothing concrete or positive; neither of us knew what we would do or how and why we would do it. But of one thing we were both certain: We wanted to live together, and the sooner the better. In the flush of this romantic decision, Jimmy suggested we take a house for the summer somewhere, so we started to trawl the most desirable European cities we could think of.

From Morocco we flew to Rome, where I heard that my adorable colleague on *Vogue,* Afdera Fonda, had been incarcerated in the Regina Coeli prison for innocently smuggling drugs. Lacking the wherewithal to bake a file into a cake, we sent her an armful of scented flowers. Cy Twombly, using color for almost the first time in those immense *tachiste* paintings that lined the walls of his palazzo, his baroque white-canvas-covered furniture placed as sparingly and sparsely as sculpture, recommended miraculous summerhouses to take, all way beyond even my ever-growing folie de grandeur; he also suggested breathtaking places to look at: the villas Farnese and Lante, the gardens of Bormarzo, the churches of San Giovanni in Laterano and Sant'Andrea al Quirinale, the Piazza Navona. We drank young golden wine from antique gilt-lined silver beakers with Gianni and Marella Agnelli in the Grand Hotel in their velvet-walled apartment, and saw a little castello outside Rome on the Via Appia Antica, which for an hour or so was high on our list of candidates for a summer's lease.

The next destination was Paris. We had the famous "Barbara Hutton" suite on the first floor of the Ritz. Such extravagance may have contributed to the fact that I was the first person ever to be allowed into that hotel wearing blue jeans. Consuelo Crespi introduced me to a friend of both my Dianas, Marie-Louise Bousquet, the Parisian editor of *Harper's Bazaar,* who invited me to her famous Thursday-evening salons at her wonderful apartment in the Place du Palais-Bourbon. The gratin of smart and literary, chic and aristocratic, beautiful and artistic Europe crowded in to be given a single, tiny glass of sticky warm vermouth. Marie-Louise always sat on a small hard chair by the door, intellectually alert, looking like an elderly lemur, and her guests would queue up to exchange the latest Parisian gossip or discuss an unfolding political scandal. Mme Bousquet's tobacco-smoke- and L'Heure Bleue-scented rooms held the distilled essence of the ancien régime: Her weekly salon had remained virtually unchanged since Proust used to attend it. Whether his fabled presence was as riveting as one is led to believe is open to doubt. Kitty Miller, my blue-haired New York friend with no tolerance for bores, answered tartly, on being asked what Proust was like to meet, "Ghastly, darling."

We flew to London, but there seemed no point in even trying to find a house in England due to the ludicrous dog problem (one of the more delightful things about the Duke of Windsor had been his assertion that when he became king he would revoke the stringent quarantine laws). However, Diana Cooper recommended the little Venetian palazzo of her friends Count and Countess Munster, on the Giudecca, just in the shadow of the great church of the Redentore. On condition that Diana would come and spend part of the summer with us, we agreed sight unseen, pausing only to go back to New York to work out the logistics of moving our house- and dog-hold to Europe.

Despite Paul Munster's Hanoverian title, he was for all intents and purposes English, while his wife, Peggy, was decidedly so, being born a ward and a niece of the immensely rich Lord Dudley, father of the man who bought Hundridge from mine. This bloodline had imbued her with a tall frame, angular good looks, a pretty, if conventional, taste in decor— Peggy had plucked John Fowler from chiaroscurity in the painting studio at Peter Jones to join her at the Sibyl Colefax interior decoration firm— and a trait she shared with her husband, an astonishing stinginess. Negotiations, conducted by still-crackly long-distance telephone calls between Sixty-first Street and Bampton Castle, the Munsters' Oxfordshire village, and accompanied by hysterics from operators convinced we were trying to contact TV's monstrous family, were fraught with price-uppings and servant-downings, but eventually, with little good grace, a three-month period, June, July, and August, was negotiated.

We were excited by the idea of our first summer of being together in one place, one house. Jimmy decided to really push the boat out—literally, in fact. We would go by ship, taking two cars, his huge Mercedes and my Jaguar 1.20, three dachshunds and a Pekingese, each in a Vuitton dog carrier, mountains of matching luggage, and, in a last moment of extra madness, Bobby and Cecil, to complement the staff in Venice. So, one May morning, amid much jeering of lusty longshoremen, this bizarre procession was hoisted onto the SS *United States*—the sole liner to allow dogs in the cabin—at New York's Pier 47.

Claude peed on the carpet in my cabin during the entire voyage; I had to keep telling the stewards I'd spilled yet another drink. But at least my eyes were dry, unlike the last crossing I'd made with my mother ten years earlier, when I'd cried for half the voyage because of leaving Ray Foster. Just as at the Ritz in Paris, I insisted on wearing jeans in the boat's smart restaurant, which brought some rewarding gasps of horror from the WASPish covoyagers, but there were, sadly, no stars to ogle. Arriving at Le Havre after a sometimes choppy crossing, we agreed with the prewar hostess Laura Corrigan's famous malapropism, "How nice to be on terra-cotta again." Once the two cars had been shunted out of the hold, we set off across France toward Italy with Cecil, dressed as a musical comedy chauffeur, driving the Merc, Bobby beside him in his self-designed flunky's uniform, white, with lots of gold braid and epaulets, as well as the Vuitton-encased dogs and luggage. Jimmy and I sailed ahead in the Jaguar with only a picnic basket, a cocktail shaker, and the red Michelin guide.

I shudder now to think of this ludicrous juggernaut, but in fact it was idyllic. We took minor roads and avoided major towns, seeing what was a still-rural country at its most vernal. From Normandy, profuse in a blossom blizzard, to the Loire sparkling under the spring sun, and on toward Rocamadour in the wild—people were just beginning to "discover" it—Dordogne, and the Gers, the department that even now retains a faint whiff of pre-Revolutionary France. After a night in austere Carcassonne, the air became hourly more fragrant with lilac and lilies, until we arrived in a rose-riotous Cannes. Jimmy showed me the villa on the Croisette that his somewhat batty uncle, Alec Stillman, had inherited from his grandmother Cora Brown Potter, an actress in several early Somerset

Maugham plays. In one of these, she had caught the monocled eye of the rotund and generous King Edward VII. Hence the villa.

By now scenting our destination, we hurried across northern Italy, arriving in Venice in a cloudburst. Stashing the cars in the labyrinthine garage, we emerged onto a Piazzale Roma almost submerged by the downpour; except for a few water-logged boats, one couldn't discern where stone and sea met. The luggage was tossed into several of these sodden transports, and with tarpaulins around them and ourselves, we set a mournfully stately pace toward the Rialto. Gloomy palace facades like vast grotesque gargoyles loomed from the gray mist, bringing whispered memories of the day some years earlier when I had watched the funeral of Victor Cunard from the balconies of the Palazzo Polignac with Michael, Nico, and Alastair Londonderry.

Under the Accademia Bridge, past Peggy Guggenheim's baroque bungalow, and just before the Gritti, the house that belonged to poor old Arthur Jeffress. Then Harry's Bar. Now we turn into the Bacino, and double back around the Dogana as our damp procession turns and chugs choppily across the Giudecca Canal, tankers and ferries and astonishingly big boats looming across our path, aiming for the elegant and ever-clearer dome of Palladio's Redentore.

And then, finally, landfall at 49 Fondamenta della Croce. Despite this double-digit figure there were only three houses on this canaletto. "Ours"—Casa Munster—with next to it a roseate rococo *palazzina* called Ca'Leone, which we were immediately told by the seemingly affable staff awaiting our arrival was the summerhouse of Signor Il Conte Giovanni Volpi. The house on the bank opposite, apart from the fact that it evidently stood in a huge garden, was a far more modest affair. Its inhabitant's identity was to be for some days shrouded in almost cartoon-like secrecy, eyes rolling to heaven accompanied by exaggerated shrugs and dark mutterings whenever we asked our watery neighbor's name.

Our summer home turned out, even in the rain, to be enchanting. A brown-pink three-sided building with arcaded windows giving on to a flower-and-tree-filled courtyard, above which the Redentore's roofs and dome were suspended in silhouette. Inside, thanks to Peggy Munster's hand and eye, the house seemed more like something in the English counties than the well-known English hospital we discovered it had once been. Indeed Queen Alexandra, on her only visit to Venice, had been taken there, poor thing, to visit the patients—among them, perhaps not surprisingly, the brilliant, if creepy and permanently begging letter writer Frederick Rolfe, Baron Corvo.

"When will the rain stop?" we said on the third day. Fausta scanned the leaden lagoon. *"Dopo domani,"* she announced, a certain satisfaction in her tone. *Dopo domani,* we were to learn, was the Venetian equivalent of *mañana.* "What day does that nice man get the good fish?" "Dopo domani, signori." "Could Guido sweep up the rose petals? Get some petrol for the boat? Post Lady Diana's cards?" *"Si, si, mai dopo domani."* But about the rain she was wrong. That evening the sky turned flame red, the next day azure-golden, and remained so from then on, except for one freak hailstorm. Fausta proudly upgraded it. "Un urrigano. Giaccio grande come melone!!"

Fausta and Guido were also adept, in the time-honored Venetian way, at upgrading the accounts to the baker, butcher, and candlestick maker. Bobby and Cecil's intense Midwestern honesty and sense of honor as former male whores put them on a collision course with any such shenanigans in the kitchen, and several hysterically funny rows could be heard behind the green baize door. The vilest Italian and filthiest American insults rebounded off the tranquil waters outside, until a truce of a kind was achieved through the intervention of the lady of the house herself, no less.

Peggy Munster had telephoned, whingeing about having had a small operation and nowhere to recover. Rather halfheartedly, and purely out of polite sympathy, I said, "But you must come here." And, knock me down with a fender, the Munsters arrived to stay in their own house, but as our guests, almost the very next day. Diana Cooper chortled. "So typical. Paul's nickname isn't Count Everycent for nothing." Nevertheless Peggy "had words" in the kitchen on arrival. Fausta looked rather miffed for a few days, and thereafter Cecil or Bobby would give a reassuring wink if what arrived on the table looked overtly lavish.

The Munsters were fun in many ways, and full of Venetian gossip: Once, when they were on the piazza with the Windsors, the duchess had said, "I'm going to have my hair done; run along, David, and go to a museum." "I didn't know there was anything to see in this town," the duke sulked. Paul, so impressed by wealth, said, when Jimmy was being ultragenerous, "He behaves as if his middle name were Rockefeller." Teasingly I was unable to resist telling him that John D. Rockefeller's middle name was Davison.

The Munsters took us to meet some Venetian grandees: Anna Maria Cicogna, who had an ugly modern house on the Zattere, where my "aunt" Nancy Mitford, chic and brittle as ever, was staying; and a weird homosexual couple who lived amid dainty gloom in the ill-fated Palazzo Dario, Charles Briggs, known, obviously, as the Umbrella; and to Raoul

Carreras, who called Diana "Lady Diana *of* Cooper," upgrading Duff with a particle.

Venetians have always been somewhat hostile to overt homosexuality, as I already knew from the sad suicide of Arthur Jeffress. Similarly, and with scary abruptness, Carreras and Briggs upped stakes for a villa in Nice. The Dario was soon to be bought by rough-trade-obsessed rock impresario Kit Lambert, who came to a very sticky end after a few seasons.

Extraordinary ladies were a different matter. Aside from the most extraordinary of all, *la dogaressa* Peggy Guggenheim, whom I knew from my previous visit, the reigning grande dame was Lily Volpi, the mother of our neighbor on the Giudecca, Giovanni. Lily lived in some state in her palazzo, one of the most ancient, though hardly Volpi-ancestral, on the Grand Canal. She ran a fleet of gondolas, and also a ravishing Hermès-liveried *motoscafo* that idled each evening outside Harry's Bar as Lily ordered her evening cocktail. But this contessa was considered not quite *bien*. Rumored to be Moroccan, and a fortune hunter to boot, she had married the fashionable Parisian jeweler Lacloche before ensnaring Mussolini's right hand in the form of Count Volpi di Misurata, who divorced his first wife for her.

Lily was larger than life, and larger than she should have been, showily glamorous, with a huge lacquered coiffure, and mightily temperamental. At one lunch she fired all the servants in midmeal. They slunk out, knowing the game, knowing they'd be rehired, while we watched Lily order Giovanni to pass around the *dolce*.

Palazzo Volpi was as large and as showy as its chatelaine, with balconies on the Grand Canal the size of small rooms. To sit out there on the brocade banquettes at night and look down on the multitude of vessels glittering to and from the Rialto, and hear the age-old romantic songs of the gondolieri, seemed as near as one could come to previous centuries. A couple of summers later she gave a great ball there for Giovanni's birthday; I was wearing a black velvet dinner jacket, the first ever made, by Rupert Lycett-Green at Blades. A pretty dark-haired young man said, "Ravissante. May I copy?" His name was Valentino.

There was the immensely *raffiné* elderly couple, Paul and Muriel Walraff, who spent summers in their crimson-velvet-upholstered *piano nobile* in a palazzo behind San Marco, stuffed with as many rare treasures and genre paintings as the London flat I would later know. Muriel, ugly but elegant, possessed the fortune, and Paul the eye, for pretty boys and objets d'art, as well as a passion for Pekingeses. She would press her hooked and powdered beak against my Claude's tiny retroussé button, saying, "That's where they keep their thruppenny bits." Paul always tipped our staff when lunching—an Italian, and especially Venetian, tradition, he explained; it was one that impressed Bobby and Cecil, as the lire came furtively accompanied by a telephone number.

Diana arranged for us all to go and see her old friend, the formerly intrepid traveler Freya Stark, now settled in a house atop a hill outside Asolo. Freya talked in her precise Edwardian voice, wearing an Edwardian butterfly collector's outfit of white linen with a white linen hat, with a piece of false hair arranged to hide the scars inflicted in her youth by a piece of machinery that had torn her hair from her scalp. Returning to the flatness of the lagoon, Diana, Simon, and I met Serge Lifar, the dancer-lover of Diaghilev after Nijinsky, walking across the piazza. Still handsome with his Tatar looks and oiled black hair, and a teller of fabulous tales, he entranced us with his stories, true or not, and reminded us that the following day was the anniversary of the great impresario's death. Accordingly, with Cecil Beaton joining us, we chugged in my little *sandolo* across the lagoon to San Michele. Diana and Simon had brought sheaves of bay leaves. With Lifar they placed them reverently on Diaghilev's tomb. I photographed them, four notes from a vanishing melody.

On Diana's birthday we sent Bobby and Cecil out in the boat, and as evening approached, pretended we had gotten a message to say they had been shipwrecked and were lying near death somewhere on some godforsaken island in the lagoon. Diana got very excited, remembering her days as a hospital nurse during World War I, and immediately said, "We must go! I'll go! I know how to give the kiss of life!" By now it was dark, and we all—Dick Avedon, Bibi Winkelhorn, Ken Lane, Minnie Astor and her husband, Jim Fosburgh, June Churchill, and of course Simon Fleet— boarded two *motoscafi* and set out as if in search. We sliced through the starry blackness of the lagoon for several minutes, and then saw in the distance a tiny island with one or two twinkling lights. "That must be them," I said. "Let's go over there."

As we drew closer more lights came on, music could be heard, and as we stepped ashore there were Bobby and Cecil with trays of champagne. They had swagged the whole of the single ruined building with garlands of zinnias. As more lamps were lit, and the music became louder, we could see the table laden with a feast provided by Arrigo Cipriani of Harry's Bar. Diana's disappointment at not being required to administer the kiss of life was overtaken by her sheer and characteristic joy and genuine surprise at this midnight fiesta in her honor. I remember Simon standing over her, in profile, his man-made face a counterpoint to Diana's beguiling beauty, then leaning down and whispering with her. The glinting lights behind them, the profusion of color, brought to mind the first time I had ever met Diana with him at the Gothic Box, and how he had opened a treasure chest that was still producing such lasting jewels of friendship.

This vibrant image was soon to fade into mere shadow. Jimmy and I had been back in New York only a few weeks when Min telephoned me, with heartrending news: Simon had died. Of all banal tragedies, he had fallen down the stairs at the Gothic Box. It seemed to me barely believable that such a force should be so suddenly stilled, that his vigor should be quenched so abruptly.

A memorial service was being arranged, but since Simon was beloved by so many people in America, Jimmy and I thought that instead of flying to London we would simultaneously hold one in New York. I doubt, though, that we had the same music. As a tribute to Simon's flamboyant character and constant innovation, our service broke with the usual mores, the traditional hymns being augmented by music from the ballets Simon loved, and arias from his favorite opera, *Madame Butterfly*. Finally "Experiment," a song from Cole Porter's *Nymph Errant,* the first record he ever gave me: "the apple on the top of the tree is never too high to achieve"—Gertrude Lawrence's adorable Mayfair Cockney voice drifted up toward the blue gold-starred ceiling—"just take an example from me . . . experiment."

The lyrics seemed entirely apt for Simon's loving and bounteous spirit.

DESPITE MY GREAT, and growing, love for Jimmy, I was beginning to be slightly restless, with a certain longing for London. Even if Simon was no longer there to keep whirling his magic into reality, places and people to which he had opened my wide but willing eyes a decade earlier were there, and memories of the past summer in Europe tugged.

After four years of a fascinating life on magazines, I'd begun to think about a different field of work. Decorating my two own apartments, then Jimmy's, and having seen many beautiful places done by great decorators, made me think that perhaps interior, rather than graphic, design was something from which I could make a living.

Added to this I had a sneaking feeling that maybe I *should* go back to London, that my mother might need me more frequently than just the odd visit by her to America, or mine to England. Jimmy understood all these dilemmas, and was prepared to relinquish the quintessentially New

York and Long Island territory of his birthright and find somewhere new and different for us to live. My only stipulation was that wherever that was, there had to be proper tall deciduous trees, the oaks and elms I remembered from Hundridge.

We looked at houses with land, land without houses, farms and follies, and a romantic stone nineteenth-century mansion atop a steep thickly wooded escarpment way above the Hudson River called Teviotdale which we both loved at first sight. I can't remember now what prevented us getting it, but it turned our thoughts toward finding something in England, with the mad idea of getting enough land to import the quarter horses I had so recently learned to ride at the ranch in Canada, along with Western saddles and all the gear. That spring we flew to London, staying with Romana and Rory McEwen in the little cottage at the end of the garden at their Tregunter Road house.

We drove all over the country on our quest; not interested in dainty rectories or mellow manors, we wanted something untypical. We found it in Northamptonshire. Dingley Hall was a crumbling pre-Elizabethan mansion with arches and arcades and towers (on one of which was carved "God Save the King," meaning Philip II of Spain, consort of Bloody Mary) with a wonderful faded *"singerie"* dining room, the painted plaster monkeys leaping from bosky branches to pinnacled ruins all over the walls and ceiling.

Unfortunately, or perhaps in the long run not, the state of disrepair was daunting; also very little land was included in the price. But we both knew we would never find anything we loved as much and, disheartened, decided to abandon that particular dream, and for the rest of our stay I concentrated on introducing Jimmy to more London friends.

We went to dinners given by Cecil Beaton, his house now dressed in Balenciaga chicness. Under black velvet walls perked up by cyclamen pink banquettes mingled a cross-section of the stunningly glamorous from Katharine Hepburn to David Hockney. It was there I met for the first time Lee Radziwill. Princess Lee, Jackie Kennedy's truly beautiful sibling, was then at the height of her sensational success, with men from all continents vying for Lee's exquisite looks and perfect figure.

WE DROVE TO MY cousin Peregrine Eliot's (by now Lord St. German) wedding ball at sea-lapped Port Eliot, where Jimmy fell, firstly, in love with the staggering beauty of Janet Lyle, and then, and forever after, under the glamorous spell of Candida Betjeman. We attended a novel form of gathering, the wine-tasting party. The host proffered a bottle to

Antonia Palmer. "Vouvray?" Hardly glancing, Antonia growled, "Nay-oooh. Open it yourself"—a one-liner worthy of Groucho. We joined a party at Kate and Ivan Moffat's, where the growing distance and determined one-upmanship between Princess Margaret and Tony Snowdon was all too evident. Bored, Tony played with a box of matches, flicking them, lit, at his wife. "Oh, do stop," she said "you'll set fire to my dress." Tony glowered. "Good thing too. I hate that material." Princess Margaret stiffened. "We call it 'stuff.' "

So happy were we with such friends that we were on the cusp of deciding to base ourselves somewhere in England for half the year, the other six months in New York. Then out of the blue, Jimmy got a call from his sister Frankie saying the family hoped he would go to Arizona, where his irascible grandmother Fifi Potter Stillman Rockefeller McCormick lived, hatching convoluted plots to discomfit her nearest though hardly dearest. Jimmy was her favorite grandchild, and it was deemed that only he could pour oil on this troubling situation.

He suggested I go with him. We flew to Phoenix, landing in a hot, dry, dark blue dusk and were driven to the Arizona Biltmore, a massive hotel designed in the 1930s by Frank Lloyd Wright for the tubercular to luxuriate in clear desert air, and surrounded by the bungalows of the American elite. Many of these were camouflaged by papery clouds of bougainvillea, their strident color dimmed by the flood of moonlight. High above, fronds of royal palms swayed rhythmically, making hot, dry music for my first night in this starscape. The next morning it took Jimmy and me about ten minutes to realize that this was where we should live. Jimmy called a Realtor.

By midmorning we were crossing the city from Camelback, joining the highway, which, having wound around downtown Phoenix, gently uncoiled and ran north, ruler straight for many miles, up toward those near-mythical places—TO THE GRAND CANYON, TO THE PETRIFIED FOREST, TO THE PAINTED DESERT, declaimed the signs. I realized, with mounting awe, that these names might become part of my very life, and very soon.

For an hour we passed through infinite desert, bare but for angularly branched saguaro cacti, like surreal signposts pointing the way. Dry, thorny balls of tumbleweed, lifted by some imperceptible current, bounced drunkenly along the shoulders, and roadrunners, the jackass of birds, dashed daredevil across our path, abandoning at the last moment their jerky pecking at blood-furred corpses or tire-flattened rattlesnakes. The day was already hot, a white sun bleaching all color from the land, but after a while hills began to pile up all around, and chocolate brown shadows splodged the rocks with haphazard camouflage. Now the high-way began to rise, twisting among them.

We came to a Next Exit sign. 14. Ours. Black Canyon City, said a smaller one. "City??" exclaimed Jimmy, a note of panic in his voice, fearing trailers and the attendant trash. "We better go look." In a sunless hollow was the "city," consisting solely of an abandoned filling station and a dusty chicken farm (which eventually supplied us, free, with the oversize eggs that wouldn't fit in their boxes). Winding our way back to the exit, we crossed a cattle guard. And stopped, bewildered. Several stony tracks fanned out, identical, unmarked.

By pure luck we chose the right one. It snaked amid taller and now closer saguaros, their elephantine, serrated stems pockmarked with holes, home for desert wrens, and spiny ocotillo trees, skeletal, fanning coral-like above needle-thorned ground cover, which was splashed here and there with the brilliant orange-red tips of Indian paintbrush. Snail-slow, we crossed deep fissures made by some shifting yawn of the iron-hard ground, keeping watch for lethal boulders half hidden by quickshale in the dry beds of arroyos. Above us an arid midday sky, hawks wheeling lazily, loitering for prey; all around nothing stirred in the shadowless heat except white butterflies trembling over nectar-filled cactus flowers. An occasional tire track in the dust was the only sign that anything human had ever traveled this way. I shivered with a strange tingle of expectancy and fear combined.

And then, on the crest of a rocky rise, we turned and saw below a ribbon of tall trees fluttering inky green against warm granite; and before them, on a plateau, an oval of pasture ringed by bleached fences. Beyond, half hidden by shaggy palms, lay a low, reddish brown, and very ugly ranch house.

There was not a soul in sight. Or sound, save for the wheezing of a windmill atop a tall rickety pump among the shivering poplars. But there was the smell: the smell of green, and leaves, and of dark, moist, earth. For beyond the plateau, below these poor buildings, glittering between the ribbon of trees there ran—shallow enough to wade, deep-pooled enough, we would later find, for plump dark trout to lurk—a river, its water the color of whiskey.

I looked at Jimmy, his lanky figure leaning over the ranch's gate, his Stetson pushed back above his brow. I realized that we both knew this strange site, its ramshackle amenities, and its unexpected lushness, this green bouquet set down on an infinite stone table, was our long search become fruitful: and for me, my second love at first sight.

The house, even if distantly hideous, was somewhat better in close-up. A long, deep veranda ran its facade and looked across the pasture, a backdrop of hazy mountain peaks forming the distant view. Two large rectangular rooms, with unexpectedly high, beamed ceilings opened onto this veranda. One had a tall well-built fireplace, the other led into a kitchen. Both were chockablock with the inevitable kitsch of the American West. Once cleared and whitewashed, these rooms could . . . but we were eager to see more. There was a guesthouse, its own little veranda looking down into willows and poplars, and a bunkhouse for cowboys, and a staff house, and stables, refuge for some huge, but not too poisonous, tarantulas. There was a rudimentary swimming pool enclosed by a low wall, an attempt at a garden, and, across the amber river, hidden by cottonwood trees, a log cabin, which was to become my studio.

From here, looking downstream, the river widened, sand gold now, its banks treeless until another distant grove overhung shallows where, evening and morning, cattle would churn the water in their flight from the cowboys' dogs. Beyond, the hills flattened into the sky's dome, framing fairly and squarely a high, flat-topped mesa. On its summit we were to come upon the ruined but still precisely fitting stone walls and chambers of an ancient Indian village.

There was no question. This ranch by a river was to be, was meant to be, our home. We drove down to Phoenix, elated, chattering torrents of ideas, plans. The next morning Jimmy set the acquisition in motion.

AS IS THE WAY of these things, it was to take some time. We would not get possession of our ranch for several months. Besides, that coming summer, we had asked Rory and Romana McEwen to Jimmy's mother's ranch in Canada with their family. But before, in the late spring, Jimmy and I went to Austria, staying with Romana and Arabella's father, Raimund von Hofmannsthal, at his enchanting seventeenth-century castle on the shore of the lake at Zell-am-See, near Salzburg.

This was my initial visit to the country that had been so much a part of my parent's lives, and, thanks to Teresa, mine. From them I'd gathered a smidgen of Austrian city and village life, but the gaunt chiaroscuro of *The Third Man* was my dyed-in-the-mind impression. We left Munich, drove past a silver-shimmering Chiemsee and over a mountain pass into the Salzkammergut.

The first vision of that verdant, almost violent shade of grass, the rising fields of mauve shadows below icy white peaks, creates a landscape of dignity flecked with playfulness; less harsh than the Rockies, etched more sharply on the air than in the Highlands, more jagged than the Arizona mesas. As we descended, the summer cow-byres, set like tables on an emerald carpet, gave way to wood-carved villages smothered blue with forget-me-nots. And, wending though lanes of reeds and bullrushes, we came to the trim turrets of Raimund's home, Schloss Prielau.

Raimund, the son of Hugo von Hofmannsthal, Austria's national poet and the librettist of many Richard Strauss operas, perhaps most famously *Der Rosenkavalier*, was one of the most spellbinding men I have ever met. Not tall, not handsome, he was nevertheless an *homme fatal*, with many of the world's most beautiful women in his thrall. Diana Cooper had adored Raimund's exuberance ever since as a very young man he had attached himself, part clown, part odd-job man, fully love-struck, to the world-traveling circus that was *The Miracle*, a religious spectacle in which Diana played the Madonna. In this group Raimund had met and married Romana's mother, the alluring, somewhat vague Alice Astor. Together they found the forerunner to Prielau—the pink baroque Schloss Kammer, on the edge of the Altersee.

One late-summer evening in the late thirties, Raimund arranged a birthday party aboard a raft on the lake. An orchestra on an accompanying raft played Mozart. Ambrosial foods were served, the champagne flattened as was then the fashion. The sun went down. "Look!" said Eleonora von Mendelssohn, pointing to dancing lights on a distant hillside, "Fireworks! Oh, Rai!" Raimund turned. "But . . . I didn't. . . ." Their voices dropped to ice as they saw that the pattern of fire had become a vast, burning, swastika. Leaning over the side of the raft, Raimund was violently sick.

Among the guests who witnessed this event, signaling the fast-approaching end of a carefree Europe, was Lady Elizabeth Paget. One of the four daughters of Diana Cooper's sister Marjorie Anglesey, Liz had velvet-dark hair with a distinctive silver streak in the center of her brow. Her porcelain skin and perfect mouth, from which came a teasing, languid voice, earned her the reputation as the most beautiful, and eligible, girl in England. But Liz had fallen completely in love with Raimund; they married, once it became clear that the pleasurable and beauty-filled life Raimund had led with Alice had heard its swan song. Alice sent the contents of Kammer to England, which, due to her vagueness, remained miraculously unscathed, on the docks at Dover for the entire war. When the Nazis invaded his country, Raimund joined the American army, and after the war he and Liz moved to New York, where he worked for Henry

Luce at *Time* magazine, and where their children, Arabella and Octavian, were born.

I'd first met Liz and Raimund as part of the kaleidoscope that comprised Simon Fleet's parties at the Gothic Box; they sometimes asked me to dinner in their gaily furnished house in Connaught Square. Liz's beauty and wit captivated all their distinguished guests, with many of whom she was assumed to be having love affairs. Raimund, who would frequently cry with laughter at funny stories, usually his own, before he got to the punch line, had an endearing habit of making malapropisms. "Zey are hand in blouse," he would say, or "She 'as bigger fish to grind." Raimund was intensely sentimental. "Ach, it is like ze old days. Zey haf made Bruton Street two vays again," he told me, blubbing. But he also had a consummate sense of style, and an even greater one of chivalry. He could be very sharp if he thought one was discussing someone, particularly a lady, discourteously.

Now Raimund and Liz were standing in the courtyard at Prielau, waving a welcome, Liz's chiaroscuro looks enhanced by a light summer dirndl. Raimund wore the time-honored gray-and-green Austrian jacket, horn-buttoned, with the prescribed bright pink tie. He gabbled plans and arrivals. "Diana's coming tomorrow, and ve go to lunch viz z' Karajans z' day after. Zen maybe Noël will be here for ze veekend." Coward did indeed come. After lunch we all stood in the courtyard to see him off. "Good-bye, Noël, go with God!" somebody said. Noël paused, his hand on the car door. "I did once, dear. Dis-*aster*".

Our bags were taken in, up to dark, new-mown-hay-scented paneled rooms, the doors still chalked with the Wise Men's initials, a Christmas custom. "Come down for schnapps, then we will go and see Herr Ebster." Ebster was Raimund's tailor in the village, and the answer to my immediate request for the appropriate Tyrolian wardrobe. And I certainly got it, persuading him to make me jackets of the flower-sprigged black velvet used for girls' winter dirndls, along with more a conventional dark blue evening *Trachten,* which I later wore at a restaurant in London. Raimund raised an eyebrow; in his eyes it was just not "done." Despite this gaffe, going to stay at Prielau each summer became a custom in itself, and ended only with Raimund's death a decade later.

· FIFTEEN ·

JIMMY AND I RETURNED TO NEW YORK, where I packed up my rented apartment. We crossed the country to western Canada for the last time. It was exciting to think that in future our route to the Athabasca Ranch would be from the Southwest up through the wild drama of the western Rockies, rather than across the mile upon mile of flat, feature-repetitive farmland that comprises so much of Middle America. On the other hand it seemed suddenly scary to be actually quitting the place in which I had lived so vividly, learned so much, and loved so deeply, even if the love was now sitting beside me.

Any such nostalgic notions were swept away when, on our arrival, there were messages from Romana saying that Arabella, having finally decided to end her marriage, was traveling out with them. The days before they arrived were a whirlwind of deciding which rooms in which houses, choosing and corraling the appropriate horses and ponies, sorting saddles and bridles, making plans for expeditions to distant trout lakes, praying the perfect summer weather would last. The airstrip was mowed, its white-and-red striped wind sock washed; meat was laid out in the Bearbait to encourage their visits: the squaws lolling round the tiny post office at Entrance were encouraged to get chewing on their deer hides with a view to upcoming sales. A hairdryer was found for Romana, no easy task in the Rockies, fly-tying boxes tidied for Rory. It all seemed a very long way from the refinement of our initial meeting at Cliveden.

It was a wonderful month. Rory taught me the rudiments of casting. The Low Field flooded as if on command to make a soft, grassy swimming pool. Arabella had a fling with the handsome young son of the ranch foreman. Elk grazed in the late twilight as we rode on the ridge above the river. We held square-dancing evenings in the saddlery. One dusk the children, hushed, transfixed, saw the bears. A few nights later five-year-old Christabel, now Mrs. Jools Holland, caused pandemonium at the beaver dam. Told to be mouse quiet, she suddenly shrieked, "Pap, why are these animals called tweezers?" *Thurr-ump!* A dozen flat, furry tails slammed the water, diving into their lodges. At summer's end we persuaded Arabella to come down with us to Arizona.

By the time we arrived at the now-renamed Black Canyon Ranch, the high-summer heat was dipping into balmy autumn. The house had been coolly transformed by white paint. Furniture was crossing the country from New York or by sea from Jamaica: Meanwhile there were only camp beds, and makeshift seating on the veranda. We recruited our head cowboy, the astonishingly handsome Jack Denton, who gave me a pup from his round-up dog. Christened Jackson, this wolflike softie loved me from that moment, and took charge of the Pekingese and the dachshunds, teaching them brave desert games with snakes and spiders.

Mrs. McCormick arranged our indoor staff. On hearing we had no chef, she dispatched one of her head Indian's sons. Having theretofore been only a short-order cook in a greasy spoon, Star—unbelievably, his name—became, after a few basic "lessons" from me, a genius in the kitchen within a fortnight. More dramatically, on learning that we had nothing on our walls, Mrs. McCormick sent several squaws with tiny papooses bound tightly in cradles, which they hung on the blank white walls, unhooking them each dusk and padding silently away.

One afternoon an old gray flatbed truck lurched to a dusty halt by the kitchen door. Out got a sunburned, bright-eyed man dressed in faded blue overalls. Though small and slight, he exuded a strange aura of natural power. How, why, he came, we never knew, or where he lived. But Thompson was a godsend. He could do anything: make anything one wanted in the blink of an eye, mend, fix, improvise, carpenter, produce cactus jelly and exquisite patchwork quilts worked by his two spinster sisters, or divine for water.

Maybe he overdivined. One night, robbed of stars, a violent wind awoke us. Palm fronds clattered to the ground, and thunder roared off distant mountains. Then huge raindrops began to fall, lit by regular lightning bolts; we watched them bouncing off the rigid ground. Ah, we thought. A summer storm. In the morning it was still raining, heavily; it continued all day, and the next, and without cease for the next seventeen days. The entire plateau on which the ranch was placed flooded a foot deep, with runoff water crashing down long-dry arroyos to the roiling, muddy river, in which huge branches hurtled downstream like blackened behemoths.

The locals had never witnessed weather like this. Nor had they experienced its eventual aftermath. The desert and hills, as far as the eye could see, burst green with long-dormant vegetation. Forgotten flowers bloomed in droves, the boniest branches grew bouquets of blossom. Birds sang, frogs crooned, brightly colored insects rushed about in metallic formations. Far-off peaks were snow covered for the first and only time. The setting sun flushed them carmine. I wrote, describing all this, to Stephen Tennant. "Oh, Nicky dear!" he wrote back breathlessly. "Pink snow!!! Could you send me some?"

Willa Cather, that most subtle of American novelists, greatly admired Stephen's serious rather than flippant writing; indeed, she commissioned from him the definitive introduction to her collected work. I had recently read her novel *Death Comes for the Archbishop,* set in the Southwest in the nineteenth century, and, with the return of celestial blue skies, I was determined to make the house as much as possible like the one Cather described in that book. The veranda, or more correctly the *portile,* where we would congregate before supper, had an earth-red floor reflecting warmly on the whitewashed walls, which I could only wish had been "finished by the deft palms of Indian women"; the doors and window frames we painted sky blue, hanging two old frayed and faded Indian blankets and, beside the main door, some massive elk-horn antlers, to become the cache for hats, beaded gloves, and silver-wrought bridles. The ceiling was of rough dark beams, their tarlike sap exuding faintly into the warm evening air, as we sprawled below on local palm-wood-and-leather chairs.

Inside, white cotton curtains hung at the doors and windows; in the tall fireplace below a roughly plastered mantel, a gnarled mesquite log warmed three big sofas with its curling aromatic flames. A shabby, pewter-mounted, black lacquer cabinet stood opposite the windows; bookshelves covered the entire end wall, with a high-backed, white-patterned blue linen armchair pulled up to a black-painted writing table.

I would sit there each evening after a day's riding, with a double old-fashioned and the crossword from *The Times* airmail edition that was sent each day from London, printed on tissue-thin China-clay paper. When Fulco Verdura came to stay for the first time he brought us records of his favorite operas, his knowledge instilling in me a new passion. The combination of Canadian whiskey, scented wood smoke, and Callas seemed sublimely sybaritic.

For the dining room we found a big oak Renaissance cupboard, and a dark waxed, refectory table. With no space for conventional seating except for two immense silvery-gadrooned crimson velvet chairs at each end, I had Thompson make long narrow benches, and his two spinster sisters sewed horsehair-stuffed squabs of similar velvet. Thompson also constructed a trestle serving table. The two huge hurricane lamps I'd had in New York stood on it, below a big unframed seventeenth-century Italian painting that Jane Holzer had given us as a housewarming present. The overscale furniture made the room appear far bigger than it actually was.

The bedrooms were, however, truly minuscule. Jimmy's could barely accommodate a double bed and all his dogs, and gave on to an enclosed courtyard. Mine was so small that its simple, dark-stained four-poster, another of Thompson's creations, was hardly wide enough to turn over in. With a blue-shuttered window opening wide onto receding ridges of flat-topped mesas under an immense sky milk-white with stars, this tiny room and narrow mattress seemed like some celestial alcove.

At the same time as we were making the ranch house have some semblance of sophistication and comfort, we began to expand the occupants of the stables, which now proudly bore the brand I had devised. Combining Jimmy's and my initials, and painted in white on the earth-red boards, it looked as if it had been there for ages, but the actual branding of the stock took me longer to get accustomed to. The pain-distracting twitch around the victims nostrils gave them wild, frightened eyes; the burned hair and skin gave off a bitter smell.

We already had three quarter horses, a more practical gift from Mrs. McCormick than the papooses, for riding, but we needed a couple more for guests, and also to choose some Arabian mares to begin the breeding program we were planning.

It was fun for me, got up to the nines in chaps, spurs, and Stetson, to go with Jimmy to the many Arabian breeders around Scottsdale, and get away with my total lack of knowledge of horseflesh by a few grunting comments, as yet another sleek-flanked beauty danced into the showing corral, her tail a quivering question mark, the ears trembling forward, nostrils flared to catch every nuance in the air around them. Like the solid but quick-moving quarter horse, so called for being the fastest horse over the quarter of a mile essential in roundups, these delicate Arabians, some of whom would prance after butterflies that flew near their huge dark eyes, instilled in me a complete confidence when astride their neat narrow backs; so much so that I eventually became competent enough to ride some without either saddle or bridle, using only my heels on flanks and hands on necks to command, as I had watched Jack Denton and the cowboys do. A few months later Jimmy's mother gave us a stallion, a colt of her prizewinning Asdar. Not long after, I watched with wonderment, under a full moon, our first foal being born, overwhelmed at the steaming bloody bundle breaking into intricate, fully formed life. Then Music ate the caul to give her strength, and licked the protective jelly from her offspring's tiny hooves as it tottered shakily to its shivering legs, the still-wet coat glistening in the moonlight.

Though we believed that we had totally moved out of the orbit of a city life by disappearing into the back of beyond, we were soon surprised

by the number of friends who seemed to be circling the skies above
Phoenix airport. Jean Howard came over from Coldwater Canyon,
finding the landscape so attractive that she toyed with buying land
upstream—Agua Fria, (the river's name meaning, coincidentally, cold
water). The novelist Gavin Lambert loved writing in the river cabin; Truman Capote drove across the desert from Palm Springs with two slobbering bulldogs and a taciturn new boyfriend ("in air-conditioning"), to
tell us about the book about his friends he was working on, tentatively
titled *Answered Prayers*. Hope Lange, who was filming *The New Dick
Van Dyke Show* at the Carefree movie studios near Scottsdale, would
come for weekends. In the throes of an affair with Frank Sinatra, she
often flew from Los Angeles in his jet, the first private plane I went on,
with her handsome blond son, Christopher Murray.

From London came Min, from New York beauties like Caterine Mili-
naire and the exquisite Eurasian model China Machado, "a capuchin
monkey in the lap of Genghis Khan," as Diana Vreeland described her,
and my adored friend from *Vogue* days, Louise Savitt with her new husband, Freddie Melhado. John Richardson came to size up a local art collection. Cecil Beaton flew down from San Francisco, twirling girlishly in
the pool with his Californian lover Kin Hoytsma, and making up a thirty-
year feud with Horst and Nicholas Lawford, who were sufficiently mel-
lowed by the near-vermouth-free martinis they glugged from midday on.

Fulco Verdura came with Tom Parr and Niki de Gunzburg. They arrived as I was wading across the Agua Fria after cleaning the cabin carrying a broom, "My dear, she even sweeps the river!" I heard Tom say.
When my father visited, he and I made a pilgrimage up into the Indian
territories north of the ranch, visiting as many places as possible mentioned in Uncle Oliver's letters home of eighty years earlier. For my
brother Michael's birthday we arranged a surprise powwow, forty glossy
young Hopi braves in parrot feathers and bell-hung buckskins stomping
around the astonished cake cutter. We duped Rupert and Candida Lycett-
Green into thinking we had all gotten lost riding out in the desert, only
to turn a corner to find an elaborate picnic, with cold rosé and iced souf-
flés, and Star to serve it, laid out on rugs in a grove of trees. Michael
Duff, and Cecil on a return visit, rode out on an early morning cattle
roundup at the next-door Udall Ranch. It seemed improbable, these two
highly sophisticated utterly English aesthetes jogging along in a cloud of
dust surrounded by whooping cowboys. Judy Montagu came, a journey
of nostalgia for winters spent with Vincent Astor at the Biltmore. We
went to dinner at the Trader Vic's in Scottsdale, where I overdid the fa-

mous cocktails. Driving home I was stopped by a patrol cop. I fell out of the car when he opened my door, and then proceeded to try to steal his hat as he looked at my papers. For some reason—I suspect Judy's hilarious chat throughout—I got away with not even a ticket.

Perhaps the most unlikely guest was Alexander Hesketh. Then in his early twenties, this fabledly rich and eccentric peer, the owner of Easton Neston, was based in San Francisco, working on his substantial family holdings in California. He was awakened each morning by a telephone call from Grace, the doorman at the Turf Club, in London. Alexander came almost every weekend, swanning, to the astonishment of gawping cattlemen, though the airport in ice-cream-pink suits and a floppy white fedora bound with a candy-striped scarf. Fearing for our Thompson-built beds, we would insist that Alexander park his vast bulk in the bunkhouse; likewise forbidden to mount a horse, he exercised by endless lengths in the pool.

It did not take us very long to realize that under his ebullient bravado, Alexander was one of the sweetest, gentlest of people, with as yet untapped knowledge and a marvelous sense of the ridiculous. When he returned to England, Jimmy and I missed his presence each weekend, but in the summer we stayed with him at Easton, and Alexander proved to be an important catalyst in my future.

OUR FAVORITE GUEST was of course Romana, who came several times with her family, and once by herself, to join us on a long-planned journey deep into southern Mexico with Jimmy's cousin Anne Von Ziegeser, for the specific purpose of witnessing a rare total eclipse of the sun. As our journey progressed it became increasingly fraught with unexpected events.

Much as I had read about Mexico, a country I had always wanted to visit, I hadn't quite appreciated its vastness. We boarded a Mexican "express" at the border, and dawdled for two days and two nights through the desert states Sonora, Chihuahua, Durango, featureless, and surprisingly cold. I wondered why it is that the south of countries is invariably warmer than the north of the ones directly below them. Eventually this landscape gave way to hills and valleys, and we trundled through adobe villages while exquisitely beautiful children ran waving beside the train.

At Mazatlán we glimpsed the Pacific Ocean, still and sluggish as a mudhole, on our right; and climbing, even slower now, pulled into the sunset pinkness of Guadalajara, with enough time to buy fresh tortillas off a delicately woven reed tray before the night pulled us toward our destination, Mexico City.

We stayed, I think, at the Hilton. Anyway, somewhere new and tall on that wide main avenida. On our return from seeing the Palace of Chapultepec, where Empress Carlota's beautiful bathroom opens onto a crescent of garden planted with shrubs from Italy, we found a message from Cecil, at the ranch, that one of Jimmy's dogs had died. That night the hotel caught fire, admittedly two floors above us, and not seriously. The next day we saw the chilling ruins of those blood-soaked pyramids and then, to continue our journey south, went to rent a car. It transpired that only I had brought a driving license.

In Pueblo we found a hotel on a wooded park overlooking that city of tiles, every color of colors gleaming from domes in the afternoon sun— that the next day, for several minutes, would vanish, leaving this immense country in total blackness. Experts in eclipses had determined the perfect vantage point to be Cholula, a few miles away. The guidebooks said the town consisted solely of 350-odd elaborate baroque churches, raised by natives on the command of Cortés, to obliterate a massive Aztec temple.

We arrived an hour or so before the sun's rehearsal for its next-day curtain call. We wandered in a haze of golden stone facades, "the colour of biscuits soaked in Romanée-Conti," as one writer so perfectly noted, and then, as we sat on a low shady wall, a wild wind blew up from the dusty ground; the sky turned acrid yellow, then an opaque slate green; bats flew high and away, donkeys brayed a raucous lullaby, dogs howled. After several eerie minutes, cocks crowed the false dawn.

Awed, we returned to the car. At a junction on the desert track, a spiky motorbike skidded into our car. Its rider fell off but got up, limping and whimpering. Jimmy helped me get him into the car, and we drove to Pueblo and a hospital. After a few formalities we left him and returned to the car. Two motorcycle cops were standing beside it, holding the keys.

Within a few moments I was put in their car and being driven, alone, to Pueblo's main police station. During questioning, a reporter with a smattering of English appeared at the table. He helped to translate, talking earnestly to the fleshy, mustachioed officers. Suddenly Romana, Anne, and Jimmy were in the airless, shadowy room. The reporter took them aside, explaining that I was to be kept in prison overnight, with a trial in the morning. He also suggested I should not be put in a common cell, as I would be raped all night. I asked Jimmy for a book and was led away to be locked in a small room with a slight, Indio man younger than I shivering in his thin green singlet. By sign language I established that he was accused of murdering his girlfriend with piano wire.

The Day the Whores Came Out to Play Tennis *was a play by Arthur Kopit that we published in* Show. *Jerry Schatzberg shot this photo to illustrate the article, using his Rolls Royce and some of New York's most fashionable girls: Bibi Winkelhorn, Topsy Taylor, Serena Stewart, Robin Butler, Chessy Rayner, Emily Harding, Jean Hannon, Peggy Claxton, Marguerite Lambkin, Gloria Steinem among them.*

I asked Diane Arbus to photograph Mae West for Show *magazine.*

For her first ever fashion shoot—I had Barbra Streisand photographed for Show *wearing Rudi Gernreich—ca. 1964.*

ABOVE: *Cecil Beaton riding one of the Arabian horses,
Te-Wa, at the ranch in Arizona, ca. 1966*

ABOVE RIGHT: *Fulco Verdura at the ranch in 1967*

RIGHT: *Cecil took this picture of Jimmy
Davison and me at the ranch, 1966*

ABOVE: *Cecil Beaton's photograph of
Jimmy Davison in the stables
at the ranch, 1967*

ABOVE RIGHT: *With my Harley-Davidson
motorcycle (a Panhead 350), taken at the
ranch in Arizona, ca. 1967*

RIGHT: *Jimmy Davison, Truman Capote,
and me by the pool at the ranch, 1968.
Truman had driven from Palm Springs,
where he was writing* Answered Prayers.

I photographed Serge Lifar, Cecil, and Lady Diana Cooper at the tomb of Diaghilev in Venice, 1965.

Writer James Fox at his house in London, ca. 1968

ABOVE: *In my Seventy-seventh Street apartment at the time of my collaboration with Richard Avedon*

ABOVE RIGHT: *Jean Shrimpton on the cover of the April 1965 issue of* Harper's Bazaar *that I worked on with Avedon*

RIGHT: *Diana Vreeland, not in her red-laquered office, 1975*

With Diana Cooper at a ball in the
late 1970s; Margaret, Duchess of Argyll,
behind us, center

Diana Vreeland, Penelope Tree,
Jack Nicholson, and Fernanda Eberstadt
at a party I gave for Diana in the
summer of 1978

Sir Mark Palmer and Min Hogg
at the Vreeland party

Tracy Ward, now Marchioness of Worcester,
at the Hunting Party with its "Tenue de
Chasse" theme. I gave it for my fortieth
birthday at the Hunting Lodge in 1979.

Rupert Everett undressed as a Masai warrior at the Hunting Party

With Joan Collins and Andy Warhol at a party I gave for Andy at Regine's in London

Brian Ferry in military uniform at the Hunting Party

David Bailey, Patrick Lichfield and myself, ca. 1985

ABOVE: *With Queen Elizabeth,
the Queen Mother, at the ballet, London, ca. 1985*

ABOVE RIGHT: *Queen Elizabeth's
dog-grooming table at the Castle of Mey in
Scotland, ca. 1985*

*Princess Firyal of Jordan, Nan Kempner,
Valentino, Judy Taubman, and
Sally Aga Khan at Vivien Duffield's
ball in Gstaad, ca. 1990*

*Paolo Moschino on the lawn at the
Hunting Lodge, 1994*

*Rupert Everett at the height of his
romance with Paula Yates, 1990s*

I'm with my idol, Liam Gallagher, at a party given by British Vogue's *Alex Shulman, ca. 2000*

I took this photograph of Bianca Jagger for Ritz Magazine.

ABOVE: *With Mick Jagger at a London party, 2004*

BELOW: *Romana McEwen (right), with Drue Heinz, at her daughter Christabel's wedding*

I've just introduced the Cockney actress Barbara Windsor to Prince Charles with the words, "Miss Windsor, meet Mr. Windsor," ca. 2003

With Kate Moss at the opening of the play of The Graduate *starring Jerry Hall in London, 2000*

With François-Marie Banier
and Paris Hilton at my party in
Bessborough House, 2008

Parkstead, originally my ancestor's Bessborough House—
where the party was held—which I discovered
almost by mistake by climbing over a wall in
Roehampton, south London

The Hunting Lodge as I first saw it from across the lake

I hope he was as lucky as I was. The next morning, from the back of the paddy wagon taking me to the court, I saw Jimmy at the gate. Desperate, I shouted, "Call Diana Vreeland. She's a friend of Merle Oberon." The film star was at this point married to Bruno Pagliai, one of the most powerful men in Mexico.

Jimmy understood at once. Following me to the court, he found a bar nearby and called *Vogue*. When Mrs. Vreeland finally twigged that I was in danger of being incarcerated for the foreseeable future—the courts closed that day for three weeks—and not on a photo shoot, she called Merle, who called her husband, who called his office in Pueblo, who called their local lawyer. Within twenty minutes he arrived at the court.

Of course it came down to money. Bribes all around, from the judge—a twenty-three-year-old girl—to the little old woman who swept the courtroom. Always travel with three millionaires, I said to myself. Sometime later I was telling all this to Roy Lichtenstein. "What are you doodling?" I asked him. He handed me his drawing: a drowning man with a bubble saying, "Call Diana Vreeland, she's a friend of Merle Oberon." I lost it, as usual.

The eclipse, which passed as we sat at a very late, subdued lunch, had cast more than just a shadow over our perception of this lighthearted but harsh country. Rather than press south to Oaxaca, as planned, we turned north to Mexico City to catch a flight to Phoenix. The coming summer at the ranch was to be full of surprises.

NOT LONG AFTER WE RETURNED I was summoned to meet Jimmy's grandmother. Mrs. McCormick, in an especially controlling mood, was again at loggerheads with most of her children and grandchildren, sending them sharply worded telegrams threatening immediate financial cutoff unless they "shape up." To Jimmy's mother, who didn't need any money, she was cruel in subtler, maternal ways, reducing Anne to the tears that would lead to more alcohol intake than usual. Jimmy had so far escaped Fifi's ire, but we were alarmed to receive the message, or rather command, for me to go to the Scottsdale ranch. Jimmy was wary, but I thought I had better brave it. "After all, she can't eat me," I said. "I wouldn't be so sure" was Jimmy's response. And of course I was eager to see this extraordinary old woman, so scandalously behaved, so self-willed, so determined, so rich, and once so dazzlingly attractive, with my own eyes.

Some hope. I was led by Winston, her Indian majordomo, through several passages, unlit by either sunshine or lamps, until we entered a room with daylight streaming from a big window at the end. Halfway across it were placed white-painted, very intricately carved screens. Winston motioned me to the single chair that stood on my side of the screen, and silently disappeared.

For several moments nothing. No noise, no movement. Then, from behind the screen, came a high, clear, bell-toned voice. "Sit down." Again, quite a long silence. I studied the screens, gradually able to make out indistinct furnishings beyond: a chest of drawers, the silhouette, perhaps of a large cabinet against the window, something low and soft to one side. With a jolt I realized I was in Mrs. McCormick's bedroom.

"Hull-lo, my dear." The voice again, that completely un-American-accented voice of a past generation. I could trace it now. The silhouette in the window was Mrs. McCormick. "Yes. You are very handsome."

This bizarre interview continued for an hour or so. Like some great empress of China behind her high coromandels, Fifi passed down judgments on her family, satisfactory or sinning. Her son Alex, sixty and a gay millionaire, should cut his hair and get a job. Another, Guy, should, or should not, (I forget) divorce his wife. Anne should sell this horse, not that. During this tirade I got accustomed to the light through the filigree. I could make out Fifi's long white hair, once personally attended to by her friend Elizabeth Arden at Main Chance nearby, caught back by turquoise-and-silver combs, the pink-cheeked face sliding into a small mountain of body swathed in white lace. Fifi was frightening in a way, in her tyranny and her belief in her omnipotence. But I could not help feeling that in spite of her self-enchantment, her bank accounts, her pet tribe of Indians on this private reservation, her stables of magnificently blooded Arabians, she was in fact a lonely and strangely touching old woman. On leaving, she had Winston present me with a valuable antique conch belt. Whatever her test, I had passed it.

Not long after, I found myself talking to another woman, softer and younger, but on terms as close to tyranny as Fifi McCormick, in another room in the middle of the desert. Stalin's daughter, Svetlana Alliluyeva, had, some months before, fled to the United States, and had recently married an architect, Wesley Peters. They were staying at Taliesin West, the Arizona home and school of Frank Lloyd Wright, where his flour-faced, copper-haired widow, Olgivanna, sometimes invited Jimmy and me over for some indeterminate meal cooked by lanky students, every dish of which was a greasy orange and sourly spicy, and taken in the angular, ketchup-colored hall. Mrs. Wright, her bony arms protruding from robes of jarring colors, would order Svetlana about like a maid. It seemed impossible that this mild, intelligent person could have a father who had ordered the extermination of sixty million and brought misery to many more; though, as Jimmy observed, if she ever met his grandmother, at least they would have something in common.

WHILE I WAS FILLING MY TRUCK with gas one afternoon, two gleaming Harley-Davidsons roared to a halt on the forecourt. A handsome towhaired young guy in faded blue jeans and a white T-shirt leaped off one, while a slight figure, with a sharply cut profile, who wore a denim jacket and leather chaps, straddled the other. "Hell's Angels, Phoenix Chapter" read the logo on his back. They certainly didn't look dangerous, and their bikes were certainly beauties. I stared at all four of them.

"Hiya," said the blond, holding up his hand in a biker's handshake. "I'm Paul. And this here's Tom Thumb." We shook, and I admired their Harleys. "Wanna come for a ride?" Paul asked. Within seconds we were on the highway, hair streaming back, my eyes squeezed half shut from the wind and the thrill. "You'se better get youself one," Paul said, as we got back to my truck. "Then you can join our club." And actually be an Angel? "Sure. I'll find you a chopper."

So, sure enough, he did. Paul and his brother, who had a moving company called Mother's Truckers, arrived with a dark blue and chrome Harley Panhead 350, which, for a couple of hundred dollars was mine, followed by an induction by Tom Thumb into the chapter. With about twenty other bikers, we met once a fortnight and rode to bars far out in the desert to drink Coors. When I look back, those helmetless, beerfueled, road-hogging trips seem foolhardy, but they embodied the inherent sensation of an older, lawless West.

With Los Angeles merely a day's journey away, I often loaded the Harley, which I pretty soon had repainted with white fish scales and all chrome parts—bar the engine—gold plated, onto the Chevy pickup and spent a couple of nights with friends at Santa Monica or Trancas.

Mark Palmer and Catherine Tennant came to stay en route to the coast, so I suggested we drive there. With "American Pie" playing almost continually on the radio, the roads shimmering with mirage, we passed decaying turn-of-the-century speculating towns with curious names like Love and Salome. In Palm Springs we stopped for lunch with Truman Capote. Naked except for very short, very tight pale blue shorts, a white baseball cap, and a little apron, Truman offered us drinks. "There's anything you want, really." Catherine's eyes lit up. She asked for an Angel's Kiss, or some such complicated mixture. Truman bridled. "Lis-

ten, honey, I may look like a cocktail waitress, but this house only deals
in hard liquor." We arrived heat-bedraggled—there was no air condi-
tioning in my pickup—in Beverly Hills where the cool bliss of Hope
Lange's pool revived us in time to zigzag up the canyon to that drinks
party of Doris Stein's at which we were to meet the tiny figure I had seen
only in the *Show* reportage Diane Arbus had done for me: Mae West.

OUR MAILBOX was up where the highway's concrete gave way to the
dirt track. Anyone coming to the ranch knew to see if the little metal flag
was up, and bring us the post. Given my distance from England, it was
rare to get an invitation to a party there, so I was surprised and excited
when one arrived from Paul and Ingrid Channon asking me to a ball they
were giving for Ingrid's daughter Catherine Guinness. It was to be held
in early June, the most idyllic month in Arizona. Thus I was in two minds
about accepting, but then a letter from Ingrid swayed me.

IN LONDON I STAYED as usual with the McEwens. We drove to the
Channons' Essex house, Kelvedon, recently redecorated by David Hicks,
though that night the guests were eager to see the futuristic design of the
huge marquee by John Stefanidis. As Romana and I entered, I saw the
most beautiful young man I had ever set eyes on. Pale skinned, with dark
smudgy eyes and sardonically curved lips under thick dark hair, he sat
hunched over a table, looking moodily around him. When he saw Romana, he waved, smiling. "Come and meet him," Romana said. "He's
called James Fox. Not the actor," she added.
    Within seconds of talking to James, I was transfixed, not just by his
beautiful face. As we spoke, if only briefly that night, his talk, with its in-
definable accent, was far wiser and wittier than his evident youth suggested. He could have been an eighteenth-century orator and a Romanian
Gypsy rolled into one. In fact he was half American and had left Eton a
couple of years before. We talked for a long time that evening. I walked
on air when he suggested meeting for lunch the next day.
    So began a friendship that lasts till this day. During that far-off sum-
mer James didn't appear to mind or be embarrassed by my evident adoration. If he was flattered he was cool enough not to show it, and kind
enough to include me in his life. In love with, and soon to marry, a curly-
headed insouciant French beauty, Valérie Lalonde, James nevertheless
took me to stay with his family in a mellow rectory below the Sussex

downs, from where we could visit Duncan Grant at nearby Charleston, the farmhouse entirely painted, walls, doors, furniture, by Duncan and his fellow Bloomsbury artists. Or walk through cornfields to chalk white Firle, the great domain of Lord Gage, whom I had last seen reliving the pleasure of "square-bashing," marching, "Hup-two-three-four! Turn-two-three-four!" with the artist Adrian Daintry, on the terrace at Schloss Prielau. There was music too, opera at Glyndebourne, James playing guitar songs he had learned in the Congo, reggae in skinhead pubs, the release of *Sergeant Pepper*. Even now I only have to hear "The Long and Winding Road" and I'm transported to that intoxicating month.

Knowing how much Jimmy would like James, for in many ways they were so similar, I tried to persuade him to come to the ranch later in the summer. But his career as a journalist, and the renowned author he was to become, meant he must stay closer to his sources, and of course to Valérie, with whom he was soon to have a son.

I flew back to Phoenix and was greeted by Jimmy, bursting with the news that our stallion, Riffle, had been selected to compete in the increasingly important Scottsdale Arabian Horse Show. I was determined that he and Bob, his trainer and rider, would be the most glamorously turned out in the parade, and thus combed the city for silks and velvets and plumes; the result was a spectacular sight. We were up against seasoned entrants, and though Riffle did not win, merely being shown among such important bloodstock meant his stud fees could be quite considerable. It seemed that our modest breeding program was beginning to gain ground, and that living in Arizona was to be a genuine occupation rather than merely a romanticized lifestyle.

A MONTH OR SO LATER, Jimmy came back from Phoenix with a hitchhiker he had picked up on the highway. Greg was short legged and square shaped, his head and neck sprouting sun-bleached ginger hair. Freckles covered his flat face and small upturned nose below narrow, strangely yellow eyes. He was wearing the disheveled sweaty clothes typical of kids hitching from coast to coast, clothes that look exactly the same even after being washed.

"Just a night," as Jimmy assured me, turned into several days. Greg made himself useful around the ranch, and his simple intelligence made his presence at meals bearable. His family lived in New Hampshire and, from what he told us, sounded stable. Jimmy knew of the schools Greg had attended. He couldn't ride, and I soon noticed an angry resentment and faint cruelty to the horse as a result. I had also noticed that unless he got his own way, Greg could become sullen, stamping off into the desert. "He's trouble, that boy" was Cecil's summing up. I didn't want to believe him, and was quietly jubilant when, a week or so later, Jimmy drove Greg out to the highway to continue his journey to the coast.

Almost as soon as Jimmy returned I saw a change in him. I could tell he was not really concentrating on his surroundings, or on me, but gazing moodily into the middle distance; our conversation dwindled to the bare minimum. After a few days Greg called him, and within a week he was back.

This time there was an aggressive glint in his yellow eyes. All his at best minimal politeness toward me now all but evaporated, to be replaced by surly condescension. Jimmy tacitly condoned this behavior, clearly under some controlling spell cast by Greg. Whether or not his spell was at this point sexual was hard to tell. Greg clumsily maintained that he was not homosexual, and I found it hard to believe Jimmy could find this grubby, ungainly boor attractive. The scales were to fall from my eyes when we spent a few days in Sedona, the red-mountained valley up toward the canyon. There, away from the territory we shared, Jimmy made it quite plain where his preference lay. As we drove back through the ranch gate, Greg turned and, behind Jimmy's back, put up two fingers, mouthing, "Now fuck off." The gauntlet had been thrown.

I figured, conventionally, that space and time might solve the situation. Surely if Jimmy was left entirely alone with Greg, he would tire of him. I would go to London for a month, Jimmy agreeing that I would join him in Canada in early August.

During that summer in London I stayed with Kate and Ivan Moffat, through them meeting Tatton Sykes, the rail-thin, dark-haired eldest son of the Yorkshire baronet Sir Richard Sykes. One of the most entertaining people imaginable, Tatton, who would soon inherit his famously beautiful house, Sledmere, introduced me to many others, such as Boughton and Chatsworth. Tatton was, and is, catnip to a duchess. To these stately piles we traveled in an enormous yellow-and-black Rolls-Royce lent to me by David Bailey. The duchesses seemed unabashed at this unlikely pair of platform-booted, flare-jeaned, flower-shirted lads leaping laughing from so sedate a conveyance, and these visits certainly took my mind off the problem that had raised its increasingly ugly head in what had seemed, for so long, so happy a union.

The situation was to become even uglier. As soon as I got to Canada, Jimmy went to Edmonton "on business." Of course I knew why, and a few days later he came back with Greg, who now had unbridled license to wreak havoc with our relationship and, by extension, the whole Davison family. At one point he ran around the corrals screaming with paranoia that I had tried to kill him, when in fact I had thrown a can opener at him. Now, however hard I tried to reenchant him, Jimmy was being egged on to treat me with a barely controlled hostility I knew to be completely alien to his normally gentle nature.

At summer's end Greg left to go back east, and as the first snow fell on the mountains, Jimmy and I drove south for what was to be the last time. For some forgotten reason we went by a long roundabout route via the Pacific coast. I thought perhaps the dramatic land- and seascapes unfolding from Vancouver down to San Francisco would improve the knife-edge atmosphere in the car. Instead I saw them though a fog of tears caused by Jimmy's sullen intransigence.

There was little I could do the salvage the situation. On the other hand I still found it impossible to believe that our relationship was absolutely over. Hoping against hope, pinning that hope on time, I hauled the Harley into the pickup, grabbed a few clothes, and took the familiar roads to Los Angeles. The desert that had heretofore stretched away to limitless sunlit horizons now seemed shadowed with dark apprehension.

A somewhat bemused Hope Lange invited me to stay in her cool white house in Brentwood. With children Chris and Patty away at school, Hope said she was delighted to have someone to deflect the constant attentions of Sinatra. I'd practically have telephone sex when he'd ring and instruct me, with part melodious, part threatening insistence, to "tell her Francis called."

Hope's Hollywood was a close-knit circle. Her great friends were Dominick Dunne's ex-wife Ellen "Lenny" Griffin, the actress Norma Crane, the singer Nancy Dussault, and Natalie Wood. These, and more, she handed to me, and their care and lightness carried me through several disquieting weeks. In a telephone call to Cecil, he told me that Jimmy had gone to New Hampshire.

I went back to Arizona. I discovered that Greg, as a parting gesture, had pulled all my papers, including my treasured letters from Cole Porter, and other possessions from the black lacquer cabinet and burned them. Whether Jimmy had encouraged or condoned his behavior, I didn't know, but my feeling of revulsion was so strong that, hugging Cecil, and pulling Jackson up onto the seat beside me, I drove, once and for all, out of the life we had all shared.

· SIXTEEN ·

NORMA FOUND ME A HOUSE almost next to hers, nestling amid oaks on a hillside on Beloit Avenue, just below Sunset Boulevard where it curves through Bel Air. The little Arts and Crafts–inspired 1920s cottage seemed to be the perfect place in which I could forge a life, friendships, an immediate future. While I was desperate to believe that my relationship with Jimmy was not definitely over, and that given time I would rejoin him at the ranch, it was obvious that for the time being I had to come up with a plan.

I had the remains of a small trust from my father but, apart from my work for *Vogue* and *Show,* no credentials that would immediately guarantee an income. And this funny little house, hidden between the mansions of moviedom and the pounding Pacific, seemed as good a place as any to try to search for a career that might interest, amuse, and even reward me.

Immediately friends came to my aid. Jean Howard, who by now had imported Tony Santoro, her Capri–bar pianist—"and goddamn good he is, too" as Sinatra said—to Coldwater Canyon, showed me the archive of her photographs for a book she had long planned; I would love to think I had just the faintest input on *Jean Howard's Hollywood,* her dazzling and touching record of an era. Dominick Dunne, at the time a producer, asked me to be a gofer on the movie *Play It as It Lays,* with Tony Perkins and Tuesday Weld in the leads. But the project was held up when one of the stars, Diana Lynn, died on her way to lunch with me at the Scala Boutique. Jean Vreeland conceived a scheme for making stack-sole versions of flip-flops, which had swept that season's market. We spent hours gluing the strangely unreceptive rubber together neatly and, teetering on our sticky samples, eventually sold a few pairs door-to-door in Jean's apartment building. Alexander Liberman wired suggesting I take some fashion photographs for *Vogue.* I'd never used the proper camera I'd borrowed, let alone read a light meter, but some miracle made the results printable. More important, this assignment led to forming a deep friendship with Eleanor Phillips, the West Coast editor of *Vogue.*

Tall, stately, and classically profiled, Eleanor dressed in pink or turquoise kaftans, the colors gleaming off her upswept silver hair. She wore no jewelry except a fresh flower in a tiny white porcelain vase on a cord around her neck. A native of Los Angeles, Eleanor knew not only the grandees of the movie colony—Mrs. Walt Disney was her closest friend, and her beau was Sammy Colt, the son of Ethel Barrymore—but also the old Angeleno aristocracy, the Pasadena families predominant long before the film industry overtook their community, and who, amusingly, looked down their noses at it, never dreaming of including any of its members in their society.

A scioness of this ultraconservative set was Pasadena's Gwendolyn Rowan. But Gwen, a slender, long-limbed rebel, bucked the system by marrying the handsome, rising young architect Jack Warner. With Jack I would see many extraordinary buildings by Neutra, Wright, and other luminaries of Jack's profession: the subtle elegance of the orchid pavilion of Shirley Burden; the refined rooms of Wright Ludington; the flamboyant movie-star extremes of decorator Billy Haines; the dark, dazzling colors of Ganna Walska's shuttered gardens. And pushing the furniture around the cool airy house he'd built in Santa Barbara was a passion of Jack's that I could share. Doing it with him was pure pleasure, and I began to think again that perhaps interior decoration was what I should concentrate on doing.

This realization was soon reinforced by another of Eleanor's friends. Jay Steffy was a sweet-faced, smiling, shy-seeming innocent. But face value, in Jay's case, was not to be taken. He was wild, wildly funny, wildly opinionated, wildly determined. As a designer he was far ahead of his time, doing sinuous stone and metallic interiors, with massive furniture and vibrant colors. No client was allowed a say, or to interfere. "I'm the star here" was Jay's mantra, and it seemed to work. He insisted the current house he was doing, for John and Sharkey Fink, should have wild animals tethered in the sitting room. Natalie Wood roped me into decorating her living room for a party she was giving to lure back her adored ex, Robert Wagner. I devised a mad scheme of palm trees in baskets held aloft by helium balloons, like some demented Montgolfier rally, under which the likes of Bette Davis caroused. I was elated by this form of "work," and however weird the decor, it seemed to have its desired result, as Natalie remarried RJ, for the rest of her foreshortened life.

Another spur was an invitation to dinner from Tony Duquette, to whom I had been introduced by Cobina Wright, the Hollywood columnist whose daughter Cobina Jr. had been engaged to the young Prince

Philip, on a previous visit to Los Angeles. Anyone who never witnessed the imagination made mortal, the fantasy of mind, eye, and hand that Duquette possessed, cannot comprehend the creativity of this extraordinary man, whom, despite lack of chin and receding forehead, was, due to his constant toothy smile and wonder-wide eyes, extremely attractive. Photographs of his exuberant decors, objects, furniture, or costumes barely approximate the reality. In his youth Tony had been a protégé of Elsie Mendl during her wartime Hollywood years, and later the set designer of many forties and fifties MGM musicals, usually directed by Vincente Minnelli.

Tony and his wife, Beegle, had several romantically situated California houses, but tonight they were entertaining in his "workshop," a deceptively modest-looking building on Robertson Boulevard that decades before had been the private movie studio of early talkies star Norma Talmadge. In the rooms, each a more dazzling baroque panorama, were assembled the crème de la froth of Hollywood. Sitting opposite was the prettiest woman I had ever seen, pouting and flirting with seasoned assurance: Zsa Zsa Gabor.

Next to me was Clare Boothe Luce, author of *The Women* and sometime U.S. ambassador to Italy. Her wan beauty and silk gazar dress, the same faded color as her pale yellow hair, was overshadowed by the dramatic profile of Doris Duke, who had some of the chin Tony lacked, on my right. Miss Duke was the gayest company, and threw up her gloved arms with delight when we discovered mutual friends, whereas Mrs. Luce tended to lecture, reminding me of Lord d'Albernon's observation that those "in society wish to shine, not to be shone upon."

I sidled around the table and persuaded Zsa Zsa, at this point in a rare hiatus between marriages, to let me take her photograph. Her house in Bel Air was done up in *haut* Louis XV–of-Hungary style, lots of tarnished gilt and grubby blond satin, matching its owner and her dog. But in the basement Zsa Zsa had made a nightclub replicating the Parisian set from her most-admired film *Moulin Rouge,* and there, under a single spot, in a gold brocade housecoat, Zsa Zsa morphed into the befeathered Jane Avril, singing, just for my camera, that film's haunting theme song.

I became very fond of this self-created, self-assured, outrageously outspoken, obviously gold-chasing creature, who, when surface scratched, revealed oddly old-fashioned values and an innate kindness. One of Zsa Zsa's lamer ducks was Christina Onassis, living in Los Angeles during her short-lived first marriage to a builder—this was before they became "developers"—named Joe Bolker. At the dinners she gave to cheer this unhappy girl, Zsa Zsa would sparkle with mittel-European if somewhat trite Marschallin-like wit, but Christina's fractured heart needed more than a silver rose, or Zsa Zsa's silver laugh, to heal it. One of Zsa Zsa's early films, *Lovely to Look At,* with exquiste decors by Tony, had been directed by Minnelli.

Out of the blue Mick Jagger called me from a house he had just rented in Beverly Hills. Quite apart from the Stones' infamy, Mick had, since his drug bust with Keith Richards and Marianne Faithfull in England, and his wedding to Bianca Macias in Saint-Tropez, become perhaps the most recognizable man in the world. I had imagined he would have changed, but not a bit. There was the same inquiring mind, fascinated by any detail—historical, architectural, political—and the same grin spreading continually across the now-famous mouth. I met Bianca for the first time, and her deep voice, full crimson lips, and her golden animal languor made her seem a self-composed counterpart to Mick's careless vitality.

They brought with them an apricot-colored bundle, their newborn daughter, Jade, the most beautiful baby I have ever seen, gurgling contentedly in the laps of legions of nannies as her parents took control of the town. Mick opened up thrilling forays into the burgeoning Los Angeles rock scene, introducing me to his black-window-limousined, security-guarded late-night forays to the Whisky À Go-Go, seeing idols like Chuck Berry, Janis Joplin, and The Doors. I could only reciprocate, and also gratify Natalie Wood's amused longing to meet Mick by entertaining them both at Ma Maison, then the ne plus ultra of restaurants. Bianca was the *objet desirée* of the young film and fashion world—and often the not so young. I remember another dinner there with Bianca, Warren Beatty, and Diana Vreeland where it was clear to me that the world's most attractive movie star had eyes only for Mrs. Jagger. I, on the other hand, had eyes only for Cary Grant, when I sat next to him at a film premiere. I studied every inch of his perfect handsomeness and was knocked sideways by his easy charm. On my other side sat Dorothy Lamour, who on hearing I was English, told me she came to England often as, most surprisingly, she owned several knitting mills in the North Country. A *Road to Rochdale* hardly conjures up a saronged siren.

I had good friends, and had made several new ones. I loved my little house, the freedom to drive up to Jack and Gwen Warner's in Santa Barbara, or take a bike ride out to friends in Santa Monica and Venice. I even loved the much staider group over in Pasadena. But . . . I had not met anyone who could replace Jimmy. I had been away from England for more than a decade, and if I didn't exactly miss my parents, I did feel that being as far as possible from them was overdoing it. With the odd exception, not many friends from England came to Los Angeles with time to stay as often as they had at the ranch. Could I believe what was happening to me? Was I, who had spent almost all my life in thrall to America, actually homesick?

DICK AVEDON had once told me that however much one was attracted by the idea of living in Southern California, in actuality it eventually palled because of the unrelenting sameness of everyday life. No seasons, and the only change from constant sunshine being bouts of drenching rain, for which no city is less prepared, and in which no landscape looks less appealing. Dick had also added "no real arts and no real friends," and though I had many of the latter and the former were on the upward path, there was something debilitating about that febrile climate that wore one down with its promise of eternal dawn. And unless one was directly involved in the process of moviemaking, there was little gossip or fun, let alone intellectual stimulus.

It was not so much a question of being bored—more that there was something nagging at one's soul. Perhaps being at that limit of the Western world unconsciously turned one's mind back, sent a message to retrace one's path, reinhabit former houses. Nathaniel Hawthorne wrote, "The years have a kind of emptiness when we spend too many of them on a foreign shore." Or, as Joan Didion more crisply put it, something brings the realization "that it is distinctly possible to stay too long at the fair."

Suddenly, contact from Jimmy: He suggested we meet in New York. I could read into his words that there was unlikely to be a change of heart, nevertheless hope sprang. I stored the Harley in a garage, left the keys of the house with Norma next door, took a flight. The next day we met. It was lashing with freezing rain. Jimmy was wearing a neckerchief I'd given him at the ranch. It was known as "the blue string."

There was no hope. He repeated, in that remembered disembodied voice, all the conventional phrases for "It's over," adding, strangely, that he had no money anymore, as if that might explain the fact that he was about to take a bus to Maine. Clinging still, though knowing the uselessness, I went with him to the bus depot. As he boarded, he turned, unknotting the blue string. "Keep this for me." I watched the gray bus sloshing out of sight into the hard gray rain, glacial shards melding with hot tears. The clock had struck. It was time to go home.

I TOOK A STUDIO in South Kensington. Only one room, so the rent was bearable. The bed was on a platform up a steep ladder. A torn, crackly, and increasingly intractable Holland blind flapped against the grubby glass of a window that took up most of the opposite wall, with meager means of cooking and washing tucked behind another. Giving some character was a leggy iron stove improbably installed between twisted marble columns that supported a tall brass canopy. From this imposing contraption I was incapable of coaxing a flicker, though a decade earlier it had warmed the ardor of John Osborne, who'd conducted his love affair with the beautiful stage designer Jocelyn Rickards, my landlady, in its sultry glow.

I slung in a couple of browbeaten sofas, a basketwork chair, and a pockmarked pine kitchen table, after which I wrote to Jimmy asking him to send what was left of my Greg-rifled belongings, my furniture, and above all my records. Some months later, in a dank suburban warehouse, I pried open the crate containing those remnants of that sunny life. Now there truly was no turning around.

There was, however, a very urgent need of income: Here I had some possibilities. Alexander Hesketh, admiring the look of the ranch on each of his many visits, had bolstered my confidence in thinking that decoration might be something I could be good at, when he'd asked me to work on his house, but he had sold it before work started and now lived in the splendor of his inherited estate, Easton Neston, in Northamptonshire, a picture-perfect palace built for Fermor-Hesketh forebears, and adjoining their private racecourse, complete with its regal "royal" box, at Towcester. There was a buzz in the air about the look of American design due to the publication of a new magazine, *Architectural Digest,* a sleeker rival to staid *House & Garden,* and due to my decade in the United States I had acquired a more comtemporary taste than the older school of decorators, who were mired in the swagged-and-dragged school derived from such masters as Nancy Lancaster or John Fowler, and exemplified by the many peach-and-chintz merchants that then lined Sloane Street.

But there was also an equally urgent need for companionship, passion, even love. Probably I had been too young and naive to understand the sophistication of Michael Wishart's passion, and I had certainly been scarred by Jimmy's sudden abandonment, but so far my liaisons hadn't put me off the idea of a relationship; though I was capable of putting on a bright social face, time was passing.

The most fashionable and successful restaurant was San Lorenzo in Beauchamp Place. Its owners, Mara and Lorenzo Berni, had some years before introduced to London the varied pleasures of Sardinian peasant

cuisine, importing the handsomest of that island's youth to serve it. However, the more stimulating place to eat was a clothes shop in the Fulham
Road at its junction with Sydney Street. Owned by a Belgian designer,
Alain Mertens, the shop was named after his lover, Piero di Monzi. Tall,
shaking a slice of ebony fringe out of his ember eyes, Piero had, naturally, been a waiter at San Lorenzo, where Alain had discerned in him a
singular talent for choosing and selling the fashion of the moment. Narrow black or plum corduroy jeans, open-neck white shirts, velvet jackets,
and tasseled loafers worn sockless became the coveted uniform (a look
described by Dominic Elwes as International Bobble-shoe Fun-folk), and
lunch in the shop's garden a coveted invitation.

I knew many of the team of girls who were ostensibly employed to
help shift the merchandise, but were really there just to make Piero and
Alain laugh. This troupe of salesgirl jesters, Janet Wolfson, Victoria Man-
croft, Giancarla Forte, and Jane Leveson, would sometimes be augmented
by a rogue male such as the teenage Rupert Everett or Ricardo Pavoncelli,
and, in that first hot summer month, a golden-skinned, auburn-mopped
boy who sat opposite me one bucolic lunchtime. His nose wrinkled whenever he laughed, which was gratifyingly often, and long lashes would
sweep down over his oriel gaze with appealing diffidence.

I gradually gathered that this bashful imp was, improbable as it
seemed, the budding twig of a Welsh-treed family; Roddy's brother was
the dark, svelte, handsome lothario Dai Llewellyn, his father Colonel
Harry of show-jumping fame and foxhunting memory, and his uncle the
very beacon of a Brecon baronet. By the end of the afternoon Roddy and
I were firm friends. And he told me, as our friendship advanced, how he
longed to meet Princess Margaret, whose marriage was now reportedly
on the skids. It seemed a more interesting ambition than Lloyd's or the
Foreign Office, and one that I might be able to nudge him toward. And
the fact that Roddy, like Tony, was small, red-blond, slim, and Welsh
would make this fantasy possible. When he showed me a horrid little flat
he was thinking of buying, I expressed my doubt. Roddy said, "In that
case I'll have to live at your studio for a bit." He did, and together we
gave scrappy, music-blaring, drug-dabbling dinners to my, Dai's, and
Roddy's friends.

In the mornings, half awake, I would squint from my platform as
Roddy climbed unsteadily into a rumpled pinstripe, jamming on a hated,
hair-flattening helmet, and scootered off to the Royal College of Arms,
where he had craftily wheedled a job out of Sir Anthony Wagner, the
head Garter. There, amid dusty archived shelves and the scratch of quills

on parchment, the first seeds of Roddy's vocation for gardening were germinating; to cultivate them, at weekends we would drive with Min to any garden within range of the Porsche 356 I had rashly bought from James Fox.

It was not long before Violet Wyndham, whom I had made aware of Roddy's princess-pine, brought off her constitutional coup by arranging for him to stay with her cousin Colin Tennant in Scotland. With a brief stop-off in Edinburgh to buy skimpy swimming trunks, he was trawled into the unhappy gaze of the diminutive princess; Roddy and she fell instantaneously in love.

At the same time Tony Snowdon was having an affair with my friend Jacqueline Rufus-Isaacs, the long-limbed, sardonic granddaughter of a former viceroy of India. The telephone at the studio crackled with breathy, infatuated yet imperious messages for Roddy, or late-night commands along the lines of "Get your friend out of my wife's bed" for me. As the Snowdons' marriage deteriorated, Roddy became a more permanent fixture in Princess Margaret's life, eventually bringing her many years of happiness, a situation that changed only when she selflessly encouraged Roddy to marry and start a family; and it was not long before Tony met and fell in love with Lucy Davies, a soft-spoken, liquid-eyed Irish girl who possesses, James Lees-Milne noted, that rare quality of becoming even more beautiful close up. Lucy had first married the filmmaker Michael Lindsay-Hogg, always rumored to be the son of Orson Welles, but it was his mother, the dazzling actress Geraldine Fitzgerald, whom I found more fascinating. Lucy's marriage with Tony produced one child, their exquisite daughter, Frances, who with satisfying neatness has become the wife of Rodolphe von Hofmannsthal, grandson of Raimund and Liz. Jacqui and I were the ones left out in the cold. When I asked one of the princess's ladies-in-waiting why her boss was now rather cold toward me, the answer was probably because I'd had a relationship with Roddy before Margaret had. Oh dear, I thought. Wait till she finds out about my earlier one with Tony.

ONCE I HAD TAKEN the bull by the horns, if one can use so bullish an expression about the profession, to become an interior designer, I had to learn about setting up a business. In this I was helped in the first place by both Tom Parr and David Hicks, by now no longer partners but running world-embracing design companies, éminences grises of the trade. And in the second by the funny, beautiful Victoria Warrender. She had inherited a flair for stylish decor from her Yugoslavian mother, Tania Bruntisfield, and volunteered to be my first assistant. My first sight of Lady Bruntisfield's London drawing room, its walls a glassy, whiskey-colored lacquer, and near-transparent white silk curtains surrounding shell-pink-linen-covered furniture, was an instant lesson in subtle color and texture. Victoria was passionate about pansies, both the flowers and the fellows, so between her, and Tania Bruntisfield's *haut-européen* set, schemes for commissions, small at first, began to clutter the pine table in my studio.

Stalwart supporters at this initial stage were Tatton Sykes, for whose grandly furnished flat I made an all-mirror mantelpiece, and for the Belgian baroness Meriel de Posson, a drawing room walled in emerald-green corduroy. Within a few months, the kohl-eyed, jet-tressed Louisa d'Abo joined, enabling us to handle more ambitious projects; a minuscule modern Pimlico flat for huge Nicholas Soames, and a bigger one in a 1930s building on Berkeley Square for some Texans. This was the first time I had been given carte blanche, and on seeing the bare white spaces was immediately inspired to use "makeup" colors, powder pinks, lipstick reds, eyeshadow blues. The owner of the building asked to see the finished result. Standing in my cosmetic-colored rooms, he wondered if I'd known to whom the flat had originally belonged. No, whom? His answer: Helena Rubinstein.

A MAJOR COMMISSION FOLLOWED. This was a large mansion flat in the very block in Kensington my mother had moved to after selling Cumberland Terrace. David Davies had an important collection of contemporary American art that needed the appropriate setting. It was my first, and thrilling, experience of actually changing the shapes of rooms, knocking through walls to create better spaces to display the paintings, and installing sophisticated electronic systems along with an appropriate mélange of traditional English with a New York edge. It was the first example of my work to be featured in *Vogue,* and still, four decades later, the photographs show its fresh, inventive elegance.

This project, too, had a codicil. The mirror-image apartment across the hall was owned by a Libyan, the nephew of Colonel Gadhafi. Appearing at David's door one day, he asked if I could re-create it, exactly, for him. I did. The furnishings were easy, but Gadhafidam had no paintings. With Tom Bell, who had recently come to work with me and is now a much-collected artist, I spent a frantic weekend stretching canvas, and painting the Stellas, Rothkos, Dines, Fontanas, and Warhols required.

With the work and staff expanding, I rented a larger studio on the river at Chelsea. Our assistants now included Tina Moore, the sister of my friend the writer Susanna Moore from Los Angeles. Both were now in England, Tina as a breather during an intense affair with a California carpenter called Harrison Ford, and Susanna as the companion of Michael Laughlin, a film director I had known in Hollywood when he was married to Leslie Caron. Tina was succeeded by Annabel Ferguson, so sleepy after hectic nights on the town she could hardly lift a telephone to her flawless white cheek, let alone open her cornflower eyes to muster the organizational skills she now displays as Countess of Portsmouth.

Having a workplace separate from Roland Gardens meant less frantic tidying up for the singsong supper parties that were becoming a weekly event. A new recruit to these evenings was Margaret, Duchess of Argyll. This milk-skinned crimson-mouthed relict of thirties glamour and fifties scandals knew each note and word of every popular song of her times, and would arrive with rare 78s. When I played one by the huge-nosed Jimmy Durante, Margaret, well known for liking things big, sighed "Ah, Schnozzle! I should have married him!" Sometimes Margaret and I would go to dine and dance at the restaurant at the top of the Hilton hotel. Other diners clapped in awe as we fox-trotted or samba-ed in perfect Victor Sylvester–strict step. On being handed the bill by a kowtowing maître d', Margaret would blithely tear it up and sweep out.

The business became more visible. Mark Shand, one of the world's best-looking young men, asked me to decorate his sunny bachelor pad, in which to juggle his attachments to Jane Leveson, Marie Helvin, Lee Radziwill, and Caroline Cushing, among many, with the emphasis being on a much-used bedroom. Without knowing that India was soon destined to become a major influence in Mark's life, I chose Mogul-inspired eighteenth-century printed cottons, and combined them with linear metal furniture, designed and handmade by a teenage Indian art student who had just joined the company. His name was Anish Kapoor. Anish also made carefully wrought pieces for the art deco–inspired house I was simultaneously working on for the actor Peter Eyre.

A GROWING CONFIDENCE and more commissions were making my life financially more rewarding, and a growing circle of friends both in England and Europe was making it fun. I had met Betty di Robilant when we were both staying with Rory and Romana in Scotland. Originally from Virginia, she had come to Rome as a model in the early fifties, where her astonishing beauty made her the heartthrob of the Via Veneto, and soon the wife of the elegant young count Alvise di Robilant. Their apartment nestling below the Pincio gardens had modern pictures above classical consoles, and their country *villino* at Porto Ercole, near their great friends Tatiana and Cy Twombly, was decorated with painted furniture on whitened floors. At night candlelight glinted off nuggets of rock crystal hung on iron lanterns as we dined at Betty's octagonal marble table in an orange-blossom-scented gazebo.

Porto Ercole was then still a small village with a marvelously diverse cross section of Italian aristocrats, playboys, artists, and writers, and some eccentric English expats. The Corsinis and the Borgheses ruled the social roost, but Betty's preferred friends were Donald Ogden Stewart, son of the American playwright, and Alan Moorehead, best known as the author of *The White Nile* and *The Blue Nile*. Rosie, the sailor wife of Taffy Rodd, my godfather Francis Rennell's brother, often had a salty retort. "Why did Evelyn Waugh once say he didn't find you a lady?" said a friend. Rosie replied, "I never *once* asked Evelyn to find me a lady." Each evening at sundown I'd cross the lagoon with Betty to Orbello, to eat an ice in the piazza of that perfect water-circled town. And to watch the *passeggio* of dark-haired, dark-eyed, bronze-limbed youths, dreaming.

That summer we drove north to stay with Gianni and Marella Agnelli at Villar Perosa, their nineteenth-century villa set amid the lushest of Italianate-Edwardian gardens above Turin. Inside, amid the silvery-green rococo furniture and porcelain towers of tuberoses, the rare paintings and the simple wines, the phalanxes of gloved footmen pointing the way to whichever monkey-frescoed *salone* Marella had decided we should dine in, I most remember a white fruit salad. White strawberries, white raspberries, white everything was served in a rock-crystal-like bowl formed entirely of ice. Such subtly contrived simplicity seemed a minimalist counterpart to the theatrical sumptuousness of Juvara's royal palace for the Savoys at nearby Stupinigi, to which Marella, no doubt for the umpteenth time, gallantly shepherded her guests the next morning.

It was then that I began to understand the attraction Italy held for my father, a passion his generation had inherited from earlier romantic northerners, from the grand tourists, from Goethe and Heine on down to Henry James and Edith Wharton. Italy's charm, "akin to falling in love," as Stendhal described it, was working its spell. I would go there as frequently as I was able, to Rome, Naples, and especially to Sicily, with its golden honeycomb of baroque bravado. For my first visit to Palermo,

Fulco Verdura made me a handwritten guide to the beloved if bomb-depleted city of his birth, detailed directions to out-of-the-ordinary marvels from Norman to 1910, which I still use. He also arranged an introduction to his Niscemi cousins; his grandparents—their great-grandparents—had been the inspiration for Tancredi and Angelica in *The Leopard;* it was however, the Niscemis' mother, a canned-meat heiress from Pittsburgh, who'd kept the roof on the gilded salons of their ancestral villa close to the Palazzina Cinese, the exotic Far Eastern creation of Queen Maria Carolina, sister of Marie Antoinette, for her enforced exile from her throne at Naples.

I recall especially one room in that balconied, tin-bell-trimmed building, the bedroom of the queen herself. Its walls were pale blue moiré, over which was a scrim of once-white broderie anglaise, standing proud, and all this masked by a dusty film of pleated voile. Though it was recently, and even sensitively, restored, I fear those ghostly layers will have been swept away.

· SEVENTEEN ·

ONE EVENING, ONE SPRING, I had dined with Tatton Sykes and a young friend of his from Yorkshire. Slightly built and alertly intelligent, with mocking dark eyes, Cavan O'Brien had trained as a doctor but had switched professions to art dealing, one in which he was deemed to go far.

He was certainly attractive, though seemed entirely self-sufficient, almost aloof, and in that short meeting gave no hint of wanting any kind of liaison, with me or anyone else. But a day or so after I had returned from a visit to Italy, we bumped into each other in Piccadilly, and in his intense yet rather teasing conversation I detected the spark of admiration.

The line had been cast, and I was hooked. Cavan resisted for several months, but when he finally acquiesced, I was to embark on a happiness that turned to misery over a decade. Through Cavan's wide knowledge, my eager but meager appreciation of painting grew, as he was the dealer for Henry Moore, David Bomberg, and Leon Kossoff, among many British and Australian artists. He shared with me his interest in architecture, medals, plants, gardens, books, furniture, cities, and landscapes, and traveling with him was instructive; living with him was not so harmonious. What I took to be bouts of verbal abuse and moody introspection, I gradually came to realize were evidence of Cavan's schizophrenia. It took me longer to recognize that he was also an alcoholic. When finally he had to be taken for treatment, I somehow felt guilty that, given my experience of Michael Wishart, I had not read the signs correctly. And in the last years of his young life, in a self-induced vodka-fueled exile, he could still wound me with torrents of crazed communications. Was it my fault? I asked myself. Had I brought this on him? Had I been uncaring, or overweening, in my love? Counseling told me not: and it wasn't till after Cavan's death that dark hints of a childhood experience emerged.

Initially, however, our liaison ran comparatively smoothly. We decided to keep our separate flats in London and idly fantasized about finding an architectural gem in the country. Astonishingly, this happened. Arabella von Hofmannsthal had remarried and now had two engaging daughters, the youngest my godchild, Jessica. I drove Diana Cooper down to Devonshire for the christening. On the way a stone shattered my windshield. Diana's head and clothes were covered in nuggets of crazed glass. "That *was* fun," was her typical reaction as we brushed them off. Later, at dinner, I was electrified to overhear Charles Farrell, a high-up on the National Trust, saying to Diana that it was proving difficult for the trust to find the right tenant for a tiny "Gothic" folly, the Hunting Lodge, which the decorator John Fowler had bequeathed on his death.

I'd seen many photographs of this fabled pink brick, ogee-arched, lattice-pane-windowed facade, its triple gables topped with flamboyant stone urns. And though aware of Fowler's demise, I had assumed that it would surely have been immediately snapped up. I could hardly believe my ears, my possible luck. "What about me?" I managed to squeak. "Well, why not try?" answered Charles. "I'll give you the number of the land agent." I drove up the potholed lane to the Hunting Lodge on my way back to London. Across a lake, its gables a gold-pink in the late sun, the ravishing vision beckoned. By Monday morning the wheels had been set in motion, and a few endless-seeming months later the lease was signed.

IT IS RISKY TO EULOGIZE one's own home, but to me the Hunting Lodge is quite simply the prettiest small house in the world, and "small" is the operative word. None of the rooms in the Tudor core, behind the circa 1720 "pretend Jacobean facade," as Pevsner puts it, is more than twelve feet square; the doorways are correspondingly, head-bangingly, low. Slightly larger rooms, clad in silvery wood, had been sympathetically added behind the original frontage, which looks out over a garden, reclaimed from heathland by John Fowler and laid out in an eighteenth-century Dutch style. A terrace of matching brickwork leads into a lawn bounded by pleached hornbeam trees "on stilts." The Hunting Lodge has a history as romantic as its appearance. During the eighteenth century it had been built as one of several eye-catchers to ornament nearby Dogmersfield Park, the near-palace-size seat of the immensely rich Mildmay family; and it was they who added the Jacobean facade. However, its original incarnation was a simple hut in which to take a breather from the hunt, and, in those times it stood in the vast swaths of royal lands that stretched from Windsor to Winchester.

Documents show that Queen Elizabeth I visited on one of her numer-

ous "progresses," being entertained by a mock sea battle at nearby El-
vetham, and the Hunting Lodge is by tradition the spot where Prince
Arthur, son and heir of Henry VII, following some ancient royal custom
of meeting in forests, first set eyes on his future wife, Catherine of
Aragon. On Arthur's soon and sudden death, his widow of a few weeks
married his brother, Henry VIII.

The digging of the Basingstoke Canal, the second oldest in England,
which passes just south of the house, cut the Dogmersfield estate in two;
many of its follies were pulled down or fell into ruin. The Hunting Lodge,
while suffering the Victorian indignity of being painted white with pillar-
geranium-red trim, survived, eventually being occupied, along with chickens and gin bottles, by an old lady called Mrs. Fox-Pitt, from which state
John Fowler rescued it.

The house had been empty in the years since John Fowler had died,
and bare of furniture, but the walls were still as painted by him; the sitting room, with its toughly carved white fireplace, was, is, a subtle
brown-pink, achieved by mixing bull's blood with distemper. Another
room had Fowler's signature shadow paneling. Here and there some cobwebbed curtains and faded carpets made mincemeat by mice; bird's nests
blocked the chimneys, bats swooped blackly in the shadows. None of
these mattered. It was a paradise. This beautiful little building, its garden,
its pavilions, and vista down to its lake, and the prospect of living there,
offered exactly the emotional and physical stability, and responsibility,
to fix me in England. No nostalgia, no backward glances, no greener
pastures.

An extraordinary bonus was that in the only other house visible, a tiny
cottage by the lake, lived the great actors Michael Redgrave and his wife,
Rachel Kempson. It was because of their daughter Vanessa's ties with the
area that her husband Tony Richardson had used the Hunting Lodge
as her English home in his film *The Charge of the Light Brigade*. On
summer evenings Michael would come whirling up the lawn, arms flail-
ing, the involuntary movements of some inner dance; or we would see
Vanessa, a sculpted, violent beauty striding down to the water. One
learned not to approach her. She invariably asked for money for her ob-
scure causes.

That first summer I trawled the junk shops for furnishings, the house's
voice in my head, telling me what was appropriate. My mother, at the
same time moving flats, had a few things from Hundridge that were exactly in the spirit of the Hunting Lodge, and my father, his taste in art
suddenly and unaccountably going "modern," gave me some of the

charming pictures he had bought with Geoffrey Scott so long ago. But before the house became too organized, and with a fortieth birthday in the offing, I decided to give a party; clearly it must have a hunting theme, one that would reflect the Continental, eighteenth-century style that had inspired Fowler when laying out the garden. A much-loved part-French friend, Fiona Montagu, suggested "Tenue de Chasse," and with that wording, five hundred invitations for June 16 were sent out.

A marquee for dancing, flowered with huge baskets of buttercups and cow parsley from the meadow, was to be erected by the lake, over which silver and violet fireworks would be sent up after midnight. In front of the house's floodlit facade, the cushion-strewn lawn and pavilions, for sitting out, would have gentle 1930s music, while couples who wandered into the forest could canoodle to lilting pastorales and birdsong. There would be supper in the garden room, and breakfast at dawn.

To my despair, it rained for a week. Then, the evening before, it ceased; like the transformation scene in a ballet, misty light suddenly suffused the air like a cloth of gold, slowly darkening into a field of stars, made brighter by my gratitude. Many guests, among them, Evangeline Bruce, Nico Fame, Janet Lyle, and Bunny Roger, wore beautiful variations of hunting costumes over the centuries, and many of the young and very lithe were animals, birds, or insects. Some interpreted the theme more imaginatively. Bindy Lambton came wearing a rubber diving suit, complete with flippers and snorkel, though Mary Soames, as a Victorian butterfly catcher, was easier to dance with. Mark Shand was one of a gang of *Clockwork Orange* boys; David and Martha Mlinaric were cat burglars. I spied Cecil Beaton, Proustian in a black cloak, whispering with Liz von Hofmannsthal in rainbow chiffon—Dorothy Parker's remark that Verlaine was always chasing Rimbauds to the life. Diana Cooper, holding court in her bedroom overlooking the scene, was dressed as her Greek namesake, the huntress Artemis, in white robes, a gilded wreath circling her forehead, and Henry Pembroke leered as a top-hatted fortune hunter. At ten the next morning the last dancers fell asleep on the bank under the willows. I, too, was exhausted; the night had been an exuberant conclusion to a decade that for me had begun with so much emotional battering.

My personal euphoria was shared professionally by many of my colleagues, who welcomed Margaret Thatcher's premiership. Continentals, and more especially Americans, were flocking to Britain, buying properties that needed designing, and thankfully they embraced the role and point of using an interior decorator. My company and staff expanded;

William Yeoward persuaded me into more prestigious premises off Sloane Square, where we were joined by Cath Kidston and Adam Sykes. Princess Alexandra's handsome and self-effacing son, James Ogilvy, drove the company's van, and before long Kirstie Allsopp arrived, her effervescent laughter preceding her through the door.

Among the decorating commissions was the Paris apartment of a huge and hearty-laughing Dane with the endearing name of Wum. Finishing a meeting one evening, we went for a drink with his fellow Dane, our mutual friend Erik Nielsen, or Erikino, as he was called by the international set that so adored their tiny, faultlessly dressed, twinkle-eyed playmate. There was a rumor that Erik had been a steward on a transatlantic liner and had pushed his immensely rich protector through a porthole. Now Erik loved mixing all sorts in his exquisitely decorated salons in the Rue du Cherche-Midi, his taste as subtle as his wit. Stavros Niarchos once greeted him, "Erikino! I haven't seen you for years. I thought you were dead." Erik smiled "But I was never married to you, Stavros," he said to the tycoon whose two wives died in suspicious circumstances.

Erik was showing me some engravings he'd just hung in the hall when the door opened, and David Bailey came in with a gaggle of fashion folk. I recognized one of them as Pierre Bergé, the partner of Yves Saint Laurent; with him was an actor I had fantasized about since watching him in Visconti's *The Damned,* in an Arizona cinema with my father. Now, across that room, Helmut Berger was even better looking, his dark blond hair slicked back from a honey-colored brow, his mouth sensual and eager, his slate-blue gaze level and inviting. We spoke, briefly but intently; Bergé was not happy when Helmut and I left, returning to Wum's apartment. Later I found that that honeyed brow gave way to skin the color of almonds, the texture of finest suede. I would thereafter see Helmut, when he was all too infrequently in London, meetings in my studio being preferable to the Savoy, until he went to California and a disastrous role in *Dynasty.*

Another less fulfilling Parisian *coup de foudre* began at Isobel Goldsmith's exotic debutante ball, where all the girls were instructed to wear *tête fleuriée.* Next to me at dinner a towering tiara of flowers encircled the head of a rather pretty blonde named Marie-Christine. We danced frequently, and suddenly she held me very close, whispering that this moment was all she had dreamed of, waltzing with a handsome young Englishman; she would like it to last forever, and even hinted at something more permanent. Somewhat alarmed, I asked Isobel the name of this forthright friend. I was even more alarmed to learn she was a princess of Belgium, daughter of King Leopold III and Mme de Réthy. And within a few minutes I was bowing to that supremely elegant woman, who was clearly giving me the once-over. I failed her testing eye. But not, it turned out, entirely. A year or so later, at Patrick Lichfield's wedding to Leonora Grosvenor, there again was *ma princesse,* with the same intentions; so much so that I was asked to spend that night at Cholmondeley Castle, where she and Mme de Réthy were staying. I declined, I hope politely. Later I rather proudly told the story to Tom Parr. "Good God," he said. "Just *imagine* being the Tony Snowdon of Belgium."

Soon after, flower-strewn Isobel herself married the breathtakingly daredevil and handsome Arnaud de Rosnay. She asked me to help with the huge apartment they'd bought on the Left Bank. But after several nights of being driven by Arnaud, at hair-raising speeds, in the teeth of traffic, across red lights, at policemen, along pavements, and once actually *into* Le Dôme brasserie, I felt that proximity to such a maniac was not propitious. Nor did it take long for Isobel herself to come to the same conclusion. Her father, Jimmy, meanwhile, sent me down to the Dordorgne to look at a château he was dickering with buying. By the time I came back he'd gone off the idea, but included me in a lavish dinner at a restaurant he'd discovered, L'Ami Louis in Les Halles. During it he declared that anyone who had any spare money should buy water; it would become one of the world's most valuable commodities. Prescient, for the late seventies; though I doubt he had in mind anything as rural as the little water-lilied lake beyond the garden gate of the Hunting Lodge.

DESPITE THE MINIATURE SCALE, this sublime house could sleep, in a pinch, nine guests; thus most weekends those first summers the house was frequently chockablock. Claustrophobia and hunger were staved off by two wonderfully generous sets of neighbors. Mary Soames, her ever-youthful beauty belying her age as Churchill's daughter, and her huge, teasing husband, Christopher, were the parents of my near-first client Nicholas, the eldest of their three equally huge sons. Though Castle Mill House was a good two miles away, I swear we could hear this noisier-than-life family's booming badinage, and Mary frequently asked us all to join them for the erudite wines and earthy dishes like *oeufs à la tripe* she'd perfected when she was Britain's ambassadress in Paris.

In a very pretty village just outside Soames shouting range lived the former minister of war John Profumo, married to the actress Valerie Hobson. Valerie, her wondrously white skin and red red red hair illuminated their white-painted house, bright with yellow trim, its garden neat as the exquisitely mannered, faultlessly dressed, spit-and-polished Jack. His high-flown parliamentary career had been ended, entwined in the poisoned tendrils of the Stephen Ward scandal. The infamous dalliance with Christine Keeler, and his lying denial, had very nearly toppled the government. Jack's consequential cold-blooded rejection by the Conservative hierarchy gained him some sympathy, and he was thereafter widely admired for having paid his dues in his selfless work with the Toynbee Trust in the East End of London, and for his devotion to Valerie. I would meet Jack in the local hardware shop; with his tweeds cut close to his slight frame, his shoes with just the right amount of shine for the country, he was the exemplar of that faintly derogatory word "dapper."

Jack and Valerie were certainly a venerated couple, and though, whenever he and Valerie came into a room all conversation immediately died for a noticeable moment. And then, one evening at a dinner party given by Maureen Dufferin for Jack's great friend and champion the Queen Mother, he was sitting between Her Majesty and Maureen's exceptionally beautiful seventeen-year-old granddaughter Ivana. Not far into the first course, as Jack talked to Ivana, I watched her pale complexion turn crimson. It transpired that Jack, not standing on ceremony, had whispered to her, "Ever been fucked by a seventy-year-old? No? You should try it." Shocking as such lechery should seem, I couldn't help admiring Jack for unabashedly retaining the old, wicked satyrlike side of his gentle personality.

Another fascinating neighbor lived nearby in stately Hackwood, a lovely wooded estate with a tumbledown eighteenth-century theater in a clearing; for some reason I'd retained a mental picture of her ever since Johnny Gallier had taken me, not long out of Eton, to a party given by Sir Edward Hulton, proprietor of the *Picture Post*. Indicating a tall, angular woman with an amusing face, Johnny asked, "Do you want to meet the mother of God?" I was nonplussed, but Johnny explained to me that Joan Aly Khan, whose hand I was about to shake, had been the wife of Prince Aly Khan before Rita Hayworth, and was the mother of the young, handsome god to millions, the Aga Khan.

Now in her seventies, Joan, still with the same nervous darting smile and the same narrow hips encased, invariably, in tapered dark velvet pants, was chatelaine of Hackwood, and the longtime lover of its owner, Seymour Camrose, a debonair, dandyish Welsh peer whose family controlled the *Telegraph* newspapers. Both Joan and Seymour were the fount of hospitality, asking me to any or every meal I wanted, each weekend,

where in Hackwood's vaulted dining room I could never fail to be dazzled by Joan's fin-de-siècle approach to catering. Even if we were no more
than four, pyramids of lobsters reared up from silver dishes, crayfish
clasped in their claws, prawns in theirs. Snipe and woodcock flew low
over toasted brioche spread thick with foie gras, tenderloins quivered *en
gelée*. Encouraged by Joan's unique entreaty to "Box on!" I would gorge
on these Lucullan pleasures, imagining myself at some last great Edwardian banquet. In a sense one was; daughter of an 1890s music-hall artiste
who eventually became Duchess of Leinster, Princess Joan, with her three
sisters Countess Cadogan, the Duchess of Bedford, and Lady Ebury, was
a lovable and loving last echo of the Edwardian swansong.

Lord Camrose had a far more complicated nature. His incisive mind
and retentive memory, Celtic profile, thick dark hair, and perfectly cut
clothes disguised a lifelong insecurity. It was said that his not being the
match for such brilliant youthful contemporaries as Brendan Bracken or
Randolph Churchill had also added inferiority, and this led from time to
time to his going on a roiling binge. He was as ghastly drunk as enchanting sober, the torrents of vitriol pouring from his fury-contorted
mouth would afterward be unremembered by him, and so, too, by those
who loved him. Joan would pretend not to notice when Seymour reeled
around Hackwood, and never let on if she knew he had been taken, in-
capacitated, to rooms kept for just such times in the Dorchester Hotel.

I was guiding Seymour through to dinner one evening during a mild
binge when he fell heavily back onto a table piled high with glasses, he
and they crashing to the floor with a chaotic cacophony. As I pulled him
up and brushed the needlelike splinters off his hair, Seymour, eyes intense
and beseeching, his expression a childish plea, whispered, "You won't
tell Joan, will you?" No, of course; but she couldn't *not* have heard or
not seen the chaos. She said not a word; her Edwardian manners for-
bade it.

Besides these elaborate productions at Hackwood, there were summer
voyages on Seymour's charmingly old-fashioned yacht, which, flying the
coveted White Ensign, signifying membership of the yacht squadron,
ensured us near-royal respect at even the grottiest anchorage. With him
and Joan, we explored Neapolitan palaces and the temples at Paestum,
Philip's golden hoards in Macedonia, and the fleshpots of Sardinia, where
Joan's son, married now to my beautiful friend Sally Crichton-Stewart,
had created his glitzy khanate.

Never drunk at sea, Seymour was a wizard with times and tides, shoals
and stars, the appropriate burgee whizzing up the pennant-fluttering

masts to signal yet another luscious lunch Joan had conjured from the miniscule galley. These marvelous treats, seaside and landlubbing, were to end too soon, when Joan, bereft at Seymour's death, gradually retired from Hackwood, and the world, until her own.

AT THE SAME TIME as I was beginning to find my feet, and new roots were starting to form, my mother was beginning to feel hers slipping away. She had been having, for several years, an affair with her Canadian poet-professor, George, who, when a glamorous young Canadian Air Force officer, had been billeted at Hundridge during the war; their eventual affair was as sexual as it was romantic. "Darling, he puts his thing in my mouth," she coyly told me. George was now back with his wife in Ottawa, and Diana was at that not-uncommon stage of giving possessions away, in her case often "Indian-giving" style: one frequently had to return the gifts. She most unnecessarily talked herself into going to a home, partly, I think, as she envisaged a captive audience to enchant. She tried several, the friend-recommended ones, the jolly-Irish-staffed ones, the town ones, the country ones, eventually coming to rest handily near the Hunting Lodge.

I decorated her room with rose-splashed chintz the blue of her eyes, and the pictures and furniture from her last London flat. Unlike most people of her age and class, she made no "ghastly common people" comments, and, adept at making a wall talk, cajoled lives and stories from the other inmates. She ate little and drank a lot, never embarrassingly but enough to pass the time. I'd visit her, or occasionally she would come to me, and I'd take her for drives, once to Stansted Park in Sussex, the house her Bessborough cousins had bought when they had quit Ireland for good. As she looked at the classical facade from the car's open door, a telltale tear veiled her eyes; not of envy, certainly, or even sadness; but, possibly, at some fleeting vignette of her Victorian childhood.

MY FATHER, ON THE CONTRARY, was going very strong, playing squash until a few weeks before his death at ninety-nine. His flat in a gloomy Whitehall block was a surprising mélange of trusted dusty treasures and youthful contemporary paintings, and given the fact he was incapable of making even tea, Brook's, the Garrick, and the Beefsteak, the three clubs he frequented, were a handy stone's throw from its door. He seemed not to mind the deaths of his siblings or old friends, not even of Ralph Hamlyn, who had gone on to boss God about some years before; maybe it was a relief after a lifetime of Ralph's belligerent company, though I certainly never dared tell him I had once come across the sanctimonious ogre in a louche club plying himself, on a banquette, surrounded by sprawled young men, with copious alcohol.

Perhaps it was a godsend that my father died before a tragedy that would most certainly have shattered him. My brother John—who, partly for never blaming our parents for his malformed feet, or displaying an iota of self-pity, shared a special bond with them—took his own life. Fairly unhappily married, with exaggerated financial worries, John had put a shotgun to his curly blond, normally smiling, temple. His two extremely handsome, sensitive sons, Timothy—so named by John for the child my parents had lost at a few weeks old—and Augustus, coped valiantly with their devastation, telling my mother that John had died of pneumonia. With a mother's intuition, she knew the truth.

A FEW YEARS PASSED before I felt ready to visit New York again, remembering only those last days. But the call of siren Bianca Jagger's birthday party at Studio 54 proved irresistible, and once again I flew into the unpretty airport that had still been called the far prettier Idlewild on my initial arrival.

On the surface, the city had changed greatly; the ethnic cleansing of the more colorful aristocrats, with their fading WASP grandeur, was fast approaching, to be replaced by the boom-boom-boom of moneymaking. In the decade since the end of the draft, an avalanche of youth, mostly boys, all looking, thinking, and dancing alike, aimed only toward a hedonistic Xanadu of drug-fueled sex snorted to ceaseless rock. Underneath this new surface, some pockets remained, clinging to a raft of memory and manners.

Diana Vreeland gave a lunch at Mortimer's, a restaurant so successful it had knocked Le Pavillon and the Colony for six. Owner Glenn Birnbaum had sussed exactly who would want to eat what, with whom they wanted to eat it, and whom they wanted to watch while eating. So Mortimer's, with its rustic floors and café tables, became a club you were lucky to be welcomed into. Vreeland, since her unceremonial sacking from *Vogue,* was now the Queen D of the Costume Institute of the Metropolitan Museum, her wildest fantasies showcased in three dimensions rather than on the flat page. These exhibitions incurred many visits to the farthest-flung gulag of fashion, usually with London as their starting point. Each of DV's regular check-ins at the Dorchester was reason for a party, one in Kenneth Turner's newly opened flower shop. Inspecting the dinner earlier laid out in the basement, I realized rats had been gnawing. A few judicious dollops of mayonnaise repaired the damage, and Vreeland and her date Jack Nicholson were none the wiser, or indeed sicker.

Andy Warhol was king of both these castles, his realm vastly widened and financially enhanced by Fred Hughes's very public relationships with the "New People," though Andy's faux-innocent act remained unaltered. After lunch à deux, we blinked into a blizzardy Sixty-third Street where two nuns were shoveling snow. Andy raised the ever-ready camera. "*No!*" the nuns squealed, black-sleeved arms up to their starched wimples. Andy was amazed. "Gee," he said. "If I was a nun, I'd love to be photographed."

I wrote my *Ritz* column sitting at the *Interview* desk in the now-patricianly furnished new Factory, and Fred's fertile PR brain came up trumps, giving a dinner at his home, in the house I'd previously known as Andy's mother's, for "someone I think you'll like." That someone was Bryan Ferry, and it was the beginning of a deep friendship that lasts till this day. Then at the outset of his heady romance with Jerry Hall, the red-gold-headed rose of Texas, Bryan was racing toward lustrous fame due to his beauty and style, poetically crafted lyrics and bittersweet music, plus the visual dazzlement of his band Roxy Music; as the affair with Jerry faded, we spent much time in each other's houses, and a summer later he met Lucy Helmore at Rory and Romana's Ayrshire house, Bardrochat. This produced four extremely good-looking sons; Otis, the eldest and bravest, is my godson.

Diana Vreeland had asked the interior designer Mark Hampton to join us for lunch. Mark was America's ultrafashionable decorator of the moment, but that cliché belied his encyclopedic memory for the fascinating minutiae of his profession. His fingertips clicked with which architect built every great New York apartment building, with the color of the piping on Wright Ludington's daybeds in Montecito, with the stuccadores of Ireland, with the width of the stripes on La Fiorentina's awnings. I had never met anyone who literally breathed, alas for too short a time, that rare air that Nancy Lancaster believed hangs between two perfect colors. Mark's imparted knowledge and generous praise buoyed me beyond the clouds as I flew back to London.

In the slipstream of Mick Jagger's staccato stage persona and Bryan Ferry's sleek glamour, a weird phenomenon now imploded like some fascinating fetid stink bomb onto England's music scene: punk rock. Tom

Bell had befriended its early-warning missile, an angry-looking cherub, the bleached-blond Billy Idol. This led us to the door of Vivien Westwood and Malcolm McLaren's foul-mouthed, antifashion shop up the King's Road, where ripped, pinned, and acid-drop-Mohicaned weedlings lolled around spitting and snarling. Loving a rebel, I was amused by this gang of rule breakers, and if the sound was frankly unbearable, their mindless performances were electrifying. Susanna Moore felt the same way, the robotic, swaying tattooed torsos reminding her, perhaps, of her native Hawaii. I'd watch her dark cascade of hair, her high wide cheekbones and languid eyes, dancing among the gobbing, yobbing wraiths at the Vortex in Wardour Street. And afterward, almost nightly, Susanna would fold her mile-long legs into a booth at Mr. Chow's in Knightsbridge, whose fried seaweed, vast-scale contemporary artwork, and lily-pale wife, Tina, were the essential ingredients of that decade's dining.

A CONTRASTING CALM to any rowdiness could be found when staying with Candida and Rupert Lycett-Green. Their different personalities, Rupert lean and sport loving, Candida luscious and literary, seamlessly combined to make successive homes, each one more colorful and informal, each setting lovelier than the last. From a color-filled, countrified, kitchen-oriented villa in a stuccoed Notting Hill terrace, via a misty Cotswold cottage, they moved to a small mansion, the pilasters of its mellow stone facade dappled by golden lichen, the facade itself propped up by a magnolia tree bearing blossoms the size of Ascot hats, facing downland reflected in a sleepy river. Staying with them that first Christmas, I made two huge console tables for their hall of massive oak trunks topped with feather-faux-marbled planks, which passed even her father's aesthetic eye: John Betjeman was the co-guest of one's dreams, rocking at jokes, laughter quivering his gap-toothed, shabby bundle of a body. He was always ready for an outing, and when he was on one, his boundless knowledge would be imparted with sometimes querulous, sometimes childlike behavior: Back by the fire his appetite for stodge and Horlicks was endearing, his devotion to the arcane captivating: "Never say 'The New *Forest*.' Say instead 'The *New* Forest.' Sherwood was the old," John insisted. "What are the O colleges at Oxford? The ones to which you go 'Oh' when people say that they were at them." John was intrigued that my playboy-architect uncle Robert had been apprenticed to one of his idols, Voysey; we made plans, unfortunately never realized, to search Bognor for Robert's arts-and-crafts-y relics.

Sometimes Candida's mother, Penelope, would appear, having riskily driven many miles from a tiny cottage lost high in forests among the Welsh mountains. Her flat staccato voice would be heard—Had her granddaughters braided their ponies properly? Had Rupert collected the new cob? Had the missing waterproofs arrived from Simla?—long before, terrier-preceded, she entered the room, the steel gray twenties bob that brushed her nut brown cheeks swinging with her horsewoman's waddling stride. Perhaps it was Penelope's radiating energy that had made the more-relaxed John leave her, but their relationship—like my parents, they had never divorced—was still very strong; Penelope's sardonic quickness was still the foil for John's somewhat simulated bumbling, and her adventurous spirit the counterpart to his true nostalgic vision. Penelope's books on her journeys in India, where she had been brought up, stressed a more human and humorous aspect of the country that had been the scene of such bloodshed in my youth.

· EIGHTEEN ·

I N 1976 DAVID BAILEY, never one to hide his key light under a bush, decided to start a magazine. Not a blatant copy, but along the lines of Warhol's *Interview*. Andy's canny amalgam of buttering, and sending up, the new world of money and celebrity, as well as that of the established and jaded, had created a entirely new social scene in New York. *Ritz,* as Bailey and David Litchfield called their version, was to be equally iconoclastic, concentrating on emerging fashion and talented futures, as well as paying homage to our glamorous or eccentric past.

They asked me to write for *Ritz.* I was both elated and nervous, but can still remember pulling over my car to read, again and again, incredulous at seeing my words in print, the first interview I'd done. It was with Norman Hartnell, the couturier who had dressed all the three English queens of my lifetime for many decades. He had told me the much admired—even by the French—"mourning" crinolines he had created for Queen Elizabeth's state visit to France in 1938 were in fact the suggestion of her husband George VI. Seeing Queen Elizabeth's tightly corseted figure exuding loving support of the nerve-racked king, the Parisians wittily dubbed her Le Soutien George, *soutien gorge* being old-fashioned French for "bra."

More interviews followed. I was amazed to find how many people who liked to be thought of as highbrow, or to give the impression of being a "recluse," were eager to be questioned and quoted in such a flippant publication. Sir Harold Acton was delightfully indiscreet about Virginia Woolf, "so hideous, with that *maddening* overdone enthusiasm for the slightest thing"; and he remembered reading, in the unpublished diaries of Bernard Berenson's wife, how Winnie de Polignac would saddle up and ride Alvilde Lees-Milne around her Paris salon, "*using* the whip, which might interest that lugubrious writer on the restoration of country houses." Harold praised the book of my father's great friend Geoffrey Scott, *Architecture of Humanism,* as "one of the most perfect of the century," but dismissed Gertrude Stein as "a monumentally massive monster, dressed by Balmain. It was *no* credit to Balmain."

Other interviewees could be hilarious. I'd met the fabled Broadway director-producer Josh Logan when I lived in Manhattan. In the *Ritz* interview he told me stories about many people we had both known. Of Fulco Verdura saying, when friends were describing their latest toilet, with a fan and pipe that removed all smells immediately, "Oh dear, that takes away the only fun of going to the lavatory." Or how, in the forties, Josh was Marlene Dietrich's dialogue coach for *The Garden of Allah*. "Marlene had trouble with her *r*s, kept saying "Sahawah" and "widing," and how the scwipt was twash, which it was, but the other day, when she read that story in my book, Marlene rings a friend and says, "Josh makes me sound illitewate!' "

PERHAPS THE ODDEST ASSIGNMENT was being sent to interview Michael Wishart in 1977, when his autobiography, *High Diver*, was published. I'd been apprehensive of what he might write about me, but on reading his exquisite book I was deeply moved, let alone flattered. Nevertheless the interview promised to be emotional. But now Michael's obsession had moved on to others; I was less critical and hotheaded. The meeting led to gentler, occasional contact, and some very moving letters from him, lasting till he died.

Despite Stephen Tennant's proclaimed need for solitude, he readily agreed to be interviewed, and I suggested Bailey should take Stephen's portrait. Driving to Wilsford with David's wife, the supermodel of the time, Marie Helvin, I tried to prepare them for the house, for Stephen's bizarre originality. "It's a kind of ever-ever land, a land of dreams. And in the house you will find Beauty, perhaps not sleeping, but certainly resting," I said as we knocked on a front door almost impenetrable with bolted foliage. The butler, Mr. Skull, opened it. "Mr. Stephen's upstairs, resting. He says please go up."

The hall took our breath away. Pink velvet swags covered what walls weren't painted with gold stars on powder blue, a gleaming silver ceiling, turquoise fake fur rugs over polar bear rugs over fraying Aubussons. We passed white-and-gilt carved rope furniture upholstered in white leather and draped with fringed Chinese shawls and American Indian blankets. A fuggy light struggled from cracked crystal appliqués; hollowed shells layered with cobwebs cast Gothic traceries.

On the staircase each low, wide tread displayed clusters of objects, casually, artlessly, carefully arranged. Broken lacquer fans, glass bowls of face powder, playbills, topaz-and-ruby bracelets, lengths of ribbon and swansdown, sheet music of soubrettes' songs, ropes of pearls, empty boxes of Cadbury's chocolates, cheap colored postcards of sunsets and black-and-white ones of 1920s boxers, matinee idols, actresses, and football players. Although we trod gingerly, dust swirled.

"Stephen?"

"I'm in here, dear, in my room, do, do come in. I'm resting, a touch of neuralgia, I think. I got it in Bournemouth. Do you ever go there? Such *lovely* shops. Yes, do come in and sit down. So sweet of you to come. But I'm afraid I shall have to lie here and be quite, quite, quiet. I *do* think that after a certain age one should stay quite quiet."

Stephen lay fully dressed on what was not only an unmade bed but also his surrogate desk and drawing board, piled high with the many books he constantly read, reread, and referred to. Some were by him, such as his ever unfinished and unpublished novel *Lascar,* and *The Vein in the Marble,* which he had written with his mother; his poems, *My Brother Aquarius,* dedicated to—of all unlikely people—Barbara Hutton. There were photographs and postcards and prints, travel brochures and movie magazines, the talismans that made his reclusive memory and imagination soar to fantastic realms and places. He had seen the world, seen *through* the world, from here. His surprise at its beauty and fallacies was undimmed.

I introduced David and Marie. "What *pretty* names. You both look as if you had a touch of the East about you. Have you, Mr. Bailey? Perhaps the East End too? *So* much more mysterious. Oh, you were born in India—how exciting—the Orient. And you, dear Mrs. Bailey? Hawaiian and Japanese? *Too* thrilling. I must show you my paintings of Hawaii. No, I've never been there. But I can see it all, the sunsets, the coral reefs, the palm trees. I adore palm trees, don't you? I've planted several in my garden, but I'm afraid they go brown very quickly. Rather like me. I'm brown from this wonderful summer we've had."

He stopped his resting, gathering up the various bags and shawls, books and photographs he always carried, piling up his waist-length red-tinted hair, selecting rings from the glittering recesses of several jewelry cases, neuralgia gone with the whirlwind of talk—with our, and his own, company.

"What have you been doing, Stephen?" I asked.

"I've been looking after some *lizards.* Do you like lizards, Mr. Bailey? You look as if you did; we must see them after tea. Mrs. Bailey, I used to be beautiful like you, can you see that? I used to be *so* beautiful, like you . . . it's a thing we can never stop being, can we? You must never stop, and I will never stop: We'll be beautiful always"—adding with a stage wink—"but we won't inquire about each other's ages."

Stephen opened a crested album. "Look at this photograph of me. It's a dress I had made all of gold ribbons, loose from the neck to the hem, so when I danced, the ribbons formed a gilded cage around me. We used to have ballets there on the lawn. And this photograph, me when a young man, a mere boy. How boyish the young look, don't they? I had my mother's pretty chiseled nose . . . but I get so weary of my dreary face and we *all* look better with a little makeup, a little *banana* makeup. I saw a pantomime not long ago and all the actors wore banana paste on their faces. I thought it too *lovely.* And we all need the dye pot as well, but of course it has to be *beautifully* done.

"My tea has gone ice cold as usual. My friends tell me I do nothing but sit drinking ice-cold tea . . . so funny of them. Yes, please look at those paintings, they are quite recent ones, and they are selling *very* well. Isn't it silly? I'm just going to fetch something which may amuse you all. Yes, *do* look."

The paintings covered the floor, and every surface of the furniture. Original, unique in style, in colored, iridescent inks, smolder-eyed Marseillais sailors with mouths like crushed roses, or lubricious soubrettes in vast hats, glowed among exotic flowers and night-sky stars, the names of which—Vega, Orion, Cassiopeia, Venus—delighted Stephen's poetic eye, were written in his voluptuous hand.

Stephen now rejoined us, changed into an electric blue shirt and some voluminous but very short shorts. His legs, mahogany in front, were milk white at the back. "Aren't they a good color? Just that cream, Ambre Solaire. Nothing else. I've Mistinguett's legs. Second to none!" He pulled out some tangled string netting. "Now, this, *this,* is Mexico! A hammock from Mexico! Look at the color . . . much better than my legs! And look, my turquoise ring, *that's* Palm Beach. I can't understand how I've never lost it. I lose everything. Or they disappear in other ways. My nanny used to say, 'If you have lovely things, you can't expect people not to covet them.' Do you like this pink scarf, Mrs. Bailey? May I give it to you? It looks lovely with your coloring. We must give and we must receive. Sarah Bernhardt said that it's only by spending that you gain anything. It's *very* profound—she was a mystic, there's no doubt. Look at this brooch! '*Tendres pensees.*' Only the French could make that, couldn't they? They are comic, the French people, really. They shock and amuse one at the same time. Come along."

The momentum gathered as we followed Stephen—now burdened

with album, hammock, rings, ice-cold tea—into another room, the theme of which was black lace over white satin. "That rock crystal. It's the largest ever found in the *Alps,* so funny. And Syrie Maugham put this white rope round the cornice. Doesn't it go well with the Tudor paneling? She used a lot of color in this house, *most* unlike her. She said color in the country made the silence sing, and I do so agree with her."

As we followed him from room to room, exclaiming at each exotic vista, at the dining room ceiling covered in shells, we urged him to continue his flow of unique conversation, but Stephen pressed his fingers to his lips. Like all good givers, he knew when to stop. "And now I must rest my throat. Silence. I want to be a mystery to you. All beauties should be mysterious. I wish I could ask you all to stay the night, but I expect you are busy. I must rest . . . this horrible neuralgia, it makes me so dull, so dull to be with. I loved you bringing dear David and Marie; I'm sure they are difficult to pin down, always traveling. That's the *trouble* with the nicest people, they're always traveling. Thank you for giving me so much pleasure. Thank you, thank you. . . ."

His voice floated down from the darkness above the stairs. The front door closed behind us. Outside it was cold and wet; we instinctively realized that Stephen wouldn't notice weather. After all, it doesn't rain in dreamland.

MY DOING THESE INTERVIEWS FOR *Ritz* led the editor to suggest that I write a gossip column. It sounded fun; for my nom de plume I combined the names of the two most entertaining American gossip writers, Maury Paul on the East Coast, and Louella Parsons on the West, into Paul Parsons. The trouble was that, unlike them, and though being lucky to be able to retain most of what I've read, I simply cannot remember what somebody has told me half an hour ago. So the "gossip" was more a social overview of London at the time than titillating tattle. But primarily the column was a platform for me to think up the most complicated puns. Describing the Anglo-American Diana Phipps's Opera Ball, I wove in "Rocker fellers and Carmen'd rollers." Lines like that, or "Italian newspapers are full of the news that Jackie Onassis will marry that curious Prince Johannes Thurn und Taxis; but of course she knows that every Kraut has a silver lining," seemed to amuse my friends as much as myself. It was also great fun to parody famous songs. Watching Margaret Argyll meeting a supposed sex-change relative, I wrote, "With a song in her heart, Marg beheld an adorable face. It may be a her to you

and me, but it sure is a him to Her Grace." After I'd written several issues for *Ritz,* Beatrix Miller, the editor of *Vogue,* asked me to transfer the
column to her pages; the puns continued, if on a less convoluted level.

THE ANNOUNCEMENT THAT Prince Charles was engaged to Lady Diana
Spencer meant a cousin would become Princess of Wales and, it followed,
the next queen. Our family relationship was fairly distant. Though her
uncle Robert Spencer habitually addressed my mother as "Cousin Di,"
this was due more to jocular old-fashioned manners than familial closeness, and my mother's by-now great age, and Diana's extreme youth put
them generations apart. Until I saw the see-through skirt photographs I
was hardly aware of her existence, though I had come across her sisters
Sarah and Jane.

Suddenly this enchantingly awkward girl, with her shy, downward-
lashed smile, badly cut hair, and hopelessly unchic clothes was thrust into
a limelight glare stronger than anyone before her had had to endure.
Sometimes reveling in her Georgiana Devonshire–like position, sometimes rabbit scared in the headlights, she made her virgin way to royal
status with no one to guide her, no one to ask, only a set of contemporaries who treated her new position with either unmasked envy or mild
derision. A few, perhaps necessarily aristocratic, older women were wise
to the danger looming. Joan Aly Khan, herself married too young to a
handsome prince, believed the age gap to be exactly wrong; that if
Charles had been older he would have been *bouleversé* by her youth.
Diana Cooper, perhaps remembering attempted matchmaking with a former Prince of Wales, and slightly put out that "Lady Diana" no longer
signified exclusively her, was rather appalled by the determination of her
friends Queen Elizabeth and Diana's hard-bitten grandmother, Ruth Fer-
moy, to force the marriage. She was, however, entranced by her namesake's poignant allure; when that one breast peeped innocently from
Diana's silken décolletage, she observed to me, "Well, wasn't *that* a dainty
dish to set before a king?" And of course there were coded asides about
Mrs. Parker Bowles, waiting patiently in the wings, while her husband
carried on an affair with the prince's sister.

The preparations for the wedding included me insofar as David and
Elizabeth Emanuel, the young and green couturiers Diana had selected to
make her dress, asked me to decorate their salon as an appropriate setting for the many fittings this would entail. We draped yards of cream silk
on the walls and trailed it over the windows, David constantly flapping

his hands to indicate a need for "another zhush, another bow." As the end result had more zhushes and ruffles than the Emanuels eventually managed to cram onto the dress itself, it must have been difficult, at the final fitting, for Diana to tell where my decor ended and her frock began.

A few days later those yards of silk tumbled out of the coach as Diana drew up at Saint Paul's. I had watched the procession from the balcony of the old *Daily Telegraph* building on Fleet Street, sitting among many newspaper grandees, a prime position engineered for me by its owner, Seymour Camrose, and his power-behind-his-Fleet-Street-throne sister-in-law Lady Pamela Berry. There were, naturally, oodles of champagne and lashings of foie-gras, but the most delicious taste was left by the beauty of Princess Michael of Kent, in a hat and dress of palest lilac, like a twilit swan, passing along the cheering crowds in the Strand below. One understood then and there why the family she had recently married into might resent her style and looks as much as they had those of her equally beautiful mother-in-law, Princess Marina.

Once the cavalcade had passed by on its return journey, its leader a near-child on her way to a tongue-tied honeymoon, there was a scramble to leave for the party the queen was giving to celebrate her son's marriage. In order that important wedding guests would not experience any let-down, she had decided that her party should begin directly after the palace balcony appearances. And thus at 5:30, I changed into black tie and walked into the anteroom at Claridge's, to the most extraordinary sight imaginable. Sitting in a semicircle, their eyes glued to a hastily erected screen, were the major participants in the ceremony, watching themselves on film that Liza Shakerley had somehow spliced together in less than an hour. Besides the entire royal family, and every king and queen regnant or exiled, there were Nancy Reagan, Princess Grace of Monaco, the Empress of Iran, the Crown Prince of Japan, archbishops, archimandrakes, princelings, and potentates. "You know the Queen of Romania, don't you?" David Hicks said at my elbow. "Anne dear, may I present Nicky Haslam?" A slight, unassuming woman in a floral printed dress held out a jewel-less hand. Now David was in his element. "And look, there's Alexander Romanov—with the old infanta. And just behind them is Maria del Gloria, Dom Pedro of Brazil's eldest. Such a nice girl," he added.

This extraordinary mélange, these remnants of foreclosed kingdoms and endless lineage, sat cheek by jowl with the few who had survived, watching that film of a real live fairy tale. One could catch sotto voce comments. "Ach, vot *has* happened to poor Alfonso? . . . How *could*

Dagmar have worn that? . . . Lilibet does things *so* well. . . . Ma chère, the *size* of Karim. . . . Only Carol Price can carry off green lace. . . . The 'Elephant' should be worn on the *left* breast." Mrs. Reagan, a neat figure in a column of red jersey, cupping her face in her hands, her dark eyes shining with tears, turned to whisper to her Hollywood contemporary, whose fairy-tale wedding I'd watched, enthralled at Grace Kelly's golden beauty, on the flickering set in Teresa's attic room. Now the screen bride extended her white neck to meet her new husband's shy cheek: the kiss! again! and again! The sound track roared; then the film flickered and dimmed. Lilibet stood up, beaming. "Supper!" she said, and led the way into the ballroom, where Lester Lanin's orchestra, the one that had played for every coming-out dance and cotillion across America for the past half century struck up a quickstep-rhythm rendition of "They Say That Falling in Love Is Wonderful."

ALL THIS TIME my humdrum London base had remained the studio in Kensington. There was a moment of excitement when the volatile tenant above me, Francis Bacon's erstwhile boyfriend George Dyer, was lugged down our staircase after one of his frequent attempts to look as bloodlessly flayed as his portraits by Francis; I went through a curious, and never-to-be-repeated, chiaroscuro period, deciding to redo the studio in ultracontemporary style, all black and steel and mirrors. It looked stunning but was a self-taught lesson that unless you live like a robot, that sort of "design" looks a mess with merely a piece of paper left around. The bleakness made me yearn for the room's former reassuringly higgledy-piggledy comfort. I began to look for somewhere different, a bit larger, which I could decorate in a more comforting and comfortable way.

I could practically have touched my next flat, in Drayton Gardens, from the studio. It was just one street west, and the stucco houses cheek to cheek with redbrick mansion-blocks lining it had always seemed charmingly ungrand, if nevertheless unaffordable. Nina Campbell, a well-known decorator who lived there, had told tell me the flat below hers was coming up for sale.

THE ENTRANCE TO NO. 53 was covered by a welcoming, iron-pillared portico running from pavement to broad steps, its pointed glass roof haphazardly reflecting a tall, wide-windowed facade above. Brass-furnished oak doors and brown-painted Lincrusta gave a solid, almost military air to the hall; with reason, as buildings of this style and date were often concieved as apartments for Victorian officers and gentlemen. And as I walked around the lovely bay-windowed rooms, the image of that most romantic painting *The True Blue* swam before my eyes. The gallantly mustached, tightly uniformed Captain Burnaby Atkins, lounging long-legged on his flower-printed chaise longue, among his black-framed engravings and and regimental portraits, was the clue for how my new home must look. I maintain that houses and rooms quietly tell you how to decorate them. One must listen to those whispers, not fight them, or sooner or later, sure as eggshell's eggshell, the room's soul will kick against the pricks.

The building's voice spoke through much of the way I decorated Drayton Gardens, though I imagine Captain Atkins might have been mildly surprised at my creating an octagonal ruined mirror dining room, with silver paper, masquerading as cracked, smoke-blackened glass, rising up to painted dilapidated walls under a stormy trompe l'oeil sky. Lighted entirely by candles, this theatrical fantasy was the setting for many parties; dinners for Natasha Richardson after her wedding to Robert Fox; for Joan Collins prowling between husbands; for Dominick Dunne; for Lee Radziwill and her husband, Herbert Ross; for Jean Howard on her last ever visit to Europe, and before her tragic descent into a Baby Jane–like madness; for Jimmy, as now the scars were healing, and besides I was curious to meet his latest successor to Greg; and memorably, for Princess Diana, though I should have registered her suggestion of lunch, "because then he doesn't come," as ominously early in the marriage.

I moved into Drayton Gardens at about the same time as the birth of a magazine that would give a terrific boost to the profession I was now fully practicing. Within a few months of Min Hogg's initial meeting with Kevin Kelly, an audacious Irish publisher with a face as merry as a grig, their mutual brainwave *The World of Interiors* was flying high onto, and off, newsstands. Min's instinctive taste and perception, her retentive memory and eye, ensured that from the start they published not only the smart and new but the old and shabby as well. Almost overnight the magazine lifted people's attitudes to interior design by showing that the profession was not merely airy-fairy whim but one employing a vital grid of artisans, specialists, and craftsmen. One of the earliest of *Interiors* featured the Chelsea flat I had recently decorated for Bryan Ferry. At one site meeting we heard the news of John Lennon's murder. During our shocked silence I thought how long I'd known John, and however much I'd originally disliked him for his aggressive attitude, and later, all that rubbishy

Yoko stuff, he was a dear old wuss. I was brought down by Bryan more pragmatically saying he would immediately record "Jealous Guy."

With several ever-more-stylish issues of *Interiors* appearing under her editorship, Min put together a book with her choice of its very best articles. The party to celebrate the publication took place at Drayton Gardens, and noticing the alacrity with which the kultur mavens pounced on *The World of Interiors: A Decoration Book,* I saw the the possibility of doing, someday, something along the same lines about my own work. In fact this was not to happen for another decade, when I brought out a book of my most elaborate decoration, which, as an antidote to the all-too-prevalent minimalism, I shamelessly entitled *Sheer Opulence*.

But before that, a different idea for a book suggested itself.

I HAD BEEN ASKED BY Princess Michael of Kent to paint watercolor views of their rooms in Kensington Palace, a house containing some of the furniture and objects originally collected by Prince Michael's parents for their house in Belgrave Square. His father, Prince George, preferred eighteenth-century engravings, porcelain, and painted furniture over anything overtly grand or gilded, though the greater part had been dispersed when his mother, Princess Marina, had been forced to send them to a saleroom.

Marie-Christine has very strong original ideas, having had her own professional interior design business before her marriage to Prince Michael. She had used his inherited gems as the bones and backdrop for her decorations, mixing in, much as she does in her conversation, iconoclastic dollops of mittel-European verve, color, and humor. Looking at these rooms so intently, I began to wonder if there might not be a book on the subject: photographs and a bit of text, not necessarily of just the Michaels' but of current "royal interiors" in general.

I put this idea to my cousin Geoffrey Shakerley, the blue-eyed boy of the royals on account of his shy charm and wit, as well as his marriage to the Queen Mother's niece, Lady Elizabeth Anson, sister of the photographer Patrick Lichfield. I also felt that because Geoffrey is extremely subtle and nonintrusive when he works, he would be the ideal illustrator for the project.

Geoffrey was as keen as mustard: "I think it's a great idea. I'm sure we could get Daisy Denmark. And Trixie Holland. She's just redoing Huis ten Bosch. Apparently it's divine. Maybe Sophie Spain too. I'll have a think and get back to you."

About a fortnight later Geoffrey rang. "About the book, I've been doing some spadework, and you'll never guess who has agreed to be the guinea pig." He sounded pretty excited.

"Who? Do tell."

"Queen Elizabeth. The Queen Mother." I was speechless. It seemed just too good to be true.

"No, I promise you," Geoffrey went on. "She says we can do the Castle of Mey. It's never been photographed. She's going there any minute and wants us to fly up for the day, have lunch, and bob's your uncle."

Before there was any chance of a queenly change of mind, Geoffrey and I, all his equipment, but no assistant—that was my role—were on a very early flight to Aberdeen. From there we changed to a four-seater prop that took us up to Thurso. It was a dazzlingly clear morning, the landscape less mountainous than I'd expected, the sea silvery glass, with myriad islands scudding, like reflected clouds, now flint dark, now sunlit, across it. Wild, almost desolate moors were made luxurious by extravagantly green valleys, their rivers rushing brightly to the shore.

Queen Elizabeth's very spruce but clearly not very new Land Rover, with an equally spruce uniformed army driver, was waiting on the grass landing strip. He bowed, briefly.

"Her Majesty"—I'd forgotten this bit—"apologizes for not being here herself. She expects you'll need this." A basket, cups, a flask. The cups were paper, the flask malt whiskey. "It isn't too far," he continued. "We should get you to the castle by eleven thirty."

Geoffrey looked at his watch. "May be able to get some shots in before lunch. At least, before the drinks before lunch."

The coastline in close-up was much more rugged, the hills behind now seemed far higher. It was astonishingly isolated. We sped across marshes, around shimmering bays, across stone bridges, through groves of wind-bent oaks. We passed a couple of kirks, about ten bothies, and fewer humans. Our driver slowed for a bend, then ahead, we saw a large pinkish gray toy fort standing on a rocky plateau, seemingly rising from the waves. As we drove closer, the toy gradually transformed into a real-life stone castle, white-windowed, wide steps up to an arched doorway. We stopped. The door opened, and William Tallon, Queen Elizabeth's much-loved page, wearing a black bum-freezer jacket buttoned in silver, glided down the steps to supervise the unloading of Geoffrey's cameras.

Inside, stairs led steeply to a landing. Off this, doors opened to a high-ceilinged drawing room, its main window, larger and high up, giving, it seemed logical to assume, onto the sea; but in fact, on the other side of the glazing, with another window beyond it, the main staircase crossed this window diagonally, creating a stagelike effect. There was a fireplace on the opposite wall, and because this had been the central room of the castle's ancient keep, doors in each corner.

Geoffrey said, "I'm going to scout. You stay here." I looked around. An unlit fire. Big dark portraits in simple frames, one slightly crooked. Some very-low-seated, one might almost say saggy with comforting use, sofas covered in a floral cretonne, and several armchairs done in a plain rep. A radio, with LPs scattered on the floor all around it, *Me and My Girl* uppermost. Magazines dedicated to the more rural pursuits, the *Radio Times* in a tooled leather cover. Under the window a long table, and on it, odds and ends, toffees, a jigsaw in progress, a jumbo box of Good Boys dog treats, a geranium in a cachepot, and family photographs, Tony Snowdon's iconic portrait of Princess Margaret the most immediately recognizable. Between two doors stood a tiered, wheeled, crazed-glass-shelved and bamboo-edged hostess trolley, with a fifties plaster vase holding a few orange gladioli.

Geoffrey reappeared, saying there were some wonderful shots, come and look, but at that moment William and another page came in bearing trays groaning with bottles, which they transferred to the gladioli trolley, along with a few rather small glasses, a tiny ice bucket, and some Twiglets on a saucer. William gestured toward this plethora of drink. The bottles, many less than half full, contained every single aperitif known to man. Dubonnet, naturally, but also red and white Martini, Punt-e-Mes, Fernet-Branca, Amer Picon, Cinzano, Crodo, Campari, Ricard, all of which I happen to love. As we were choosing, a rotund figure crossed the window, a theatrical silhouette descending the stairs. The figure was holding a glass, in which the gin was bluer than the sky beyond.

There were mumbled "Yes, Majesty . . . Of course, Majesty" from the hall, and then "Oh, dear, I *am* so sorry to be *quite* so late. I can't *think* why. . . ." The wide, stumpy-teeth-revealing, glittering smile, head slightly on one side, the voice trailing. "Dear Geoffrey! *How* well you look! Have you got a drink? That's good. And you?" She waved her hand toward the tray. "Oh, *do* you? Stickies? Me too. Yes, it *is* a lovely day to do pictures, *aren't* we lucky? But after lunch. . . . In a minute, William, yes? Oh, good . . . I'm afraid it's very humble, just some sea trout. . . . Oh yes, this morning, actually . . . no, I didn't catch it, just rivers for me these days. Come along, fill up on the way."

We followed our imperial hostess up and down more steps—the castle is on many levels—and into a pine-paneled dining room; several large, modern, and very colorful landscapes hung on the panels. The windows looked onto a lawn enclosed by ramparts, the Atlantic horizon beyond.

Nodding to me, she waved a plump hand to her right. "Would you like to sit here? Geoffrey's family, after all . . . thank you, William, it looks delicious. . . . Oh, those paintings? By my son-in-law."

I blanked. She saw. "Prince Philip. Don't you think he's getting rather good? Do have a tiny bit more. . . ."

Lunch, with much Alsatian wine and a treacle pudding, lasted longer than it should, as we started singing the cornier of American musicals, "Oh, what a beautiful mornin' " stuff. Geoffrey looked anxiously at the passing afternoon. Queen Elizabeth read it. "Now, you two, get on. Tell me if I'm in the way."

Oddly enough, she often was. The Castle of Mey is not big, and due to its layout, the Queen Mother was frequently on the wrong side of a door. Geoffrey used natural light. "No, ma'am, don't come out, not for a minute. No, no, not yet, ma'am. Now. . . . Oh, but we were *just* going to do your bedroom, now the sun's off it. Well, if you wouldn't mind, ma'am. I'll be quick, ten, fifteen minutes max."

I could hear—and often see—all this, as I stealthily went to each room, snapping details with my idiot-proof camera. On the Queen Mother's desk, the unwieldy black Bakelite telephone, with its long case and many buttons marked "Lilibet . . . Bedroom . . . Balmoral . . . Home Farm . . . Sandringham . . . Windsor . . . Royal Yacht" and oddly, "London," rather than "Buckingham Palace." The downstairs lavatory was particularly touching. It housed a jumble of macs, fishing rods, nets, sou'westers, rubber bootees, waders, an old wooden croquet box stenciled E.R.& I., and a little table dedicated to her dogs' grooming: practically toothless combs, near-hairless brushes, chewed collars, muzzles, thermometers, flea powders, more Good Boys, tick sprays, and toys, all almost burying a fearsome-looking little iron instrument bearing a bright blue label inscribed in huge black letters HER MAJESTY QUEEN ELIZABETH THE QUEEN MOTHER.

You couldn't make things clearer than that.

I found Geoffrey upstairs. By this time he'd dragooned Queen Elizabeth into being his assistant. "If you could hold that blind *juuust* a little higher, ma'am. That's right; no wait, hang on, I'm getting your foot. No, other one. Tiny bit back, there, that's it; stay absolutely still while I reload."

A clock struck. She patted her hair. "Goodness, is that the time? I had *no* idea. I said I'd go and help the ghillies hacking back those *maddening*

rhododendrons, the horrid wild purple ponticums. They are simply taking over, the brutes. I must go and get tidy. Willl-iam!"

"Majesty?"

"My things, William. I'll be five minutes."

"Majesty."

We left at the same time, in opposite directions, us in the Land Rover,
Queen Elizabeth in a buggy and brandishing a slasher. "Thank you,
ma'ams" from us, and "I *have* so enjoyed its" from her. As we bumped
away I secretly wondered if she really understood the plan to publish
these very intimate records of her private life.

In the end we didn't. Though Geoffrey was cock-a-hoop with the photographs, and the publishers thrilled with the dummy, one of those world-
shattering things happened—an American invasion in the Caribbean?
a war in Israel?—that for some unfathomable reason gives publishers
the jitters. The project just fizzled out, never to raise its head above the
battlements.

Not long after, I saw a headline in a downmarket tabloid: KILLER
PLANTS STALK QUEEN MOTHER. It was a story on how ponticum rhododendrons were invading and strangling the woods around the Castle
of Mey. The *brutes*.

A FEW MONTHS AFTER that unforgettable encounter with the last empress of India, I had a chance to visit the subcontinental ("Why is it always a subcontinent?" Diana Cooper wondered. "It always seems big
enough to be a full one.") part of her former empire. By a somewhat
roundabout route, I have an Indian relation: Uma Morvi, daughter of a
maharajah of that state in Gujarat. I'd decorated an apartment for her in
London. Working with Uma was like walking through a looking glass, revealing the fantastic and unconventional on the other side. She wanted
the decor to resemble a fading Indian palace, and the Victorian state portraits of her forebears and their concubines she shipped from their house
in Bombay, which was said to be bigger than—but certainly as ungainly
as—the Victoria and Albert Museum, spurred me to dizzying excesses of
ersatz Raj-erie. Uma asked for the tallest bed imaginable, swathed in silk
dyed the Morvi princely colors, and she cried with laughter when one of
the huge heavy turbans I'd made to crown the posts plummeted down
onto the expansive tummy of her sleeping husband.

Enthralled by Uma's sense of fun, I was excited when she asked me to
spend Christmas in Morvi "and bring a friend . . . or several." Luckily,

about a month before leaving, I met the ideal traveling companion. Dai Prichard was a young SAS officer, the first soldier to be sent to the Falklands to reconnoiter the terrain before the invasion. More male than anyone I'd ever met, and extremely good-looking, Dai took over the preparations for our trip, totally disregarding civilian regulations and appearing in my office with mimeographed buff forms to be signed and lethal-looking syringes of anti-all-sickness injections straight from the SAS HQ.

Taking off from the Dubai stopover, the jumbo shuddered most alarmingly. Dai laid a reassuring hand on my arm. "Don't worry, Nick, I can fly these things." For the next month I would have no qualms, even on inter-India flights.

For our arrival at chaotic Bombay airport, Dai wore his army uniform, smothered with ribbons that immediately gave coded messages to officials, getting us through the chaos in a trice, through the beggars, the halt, and the maimed, and on our way to Uma's seaside bungalow. I watched Dai swim like an otter in a bloodred, sunset-reflecting Arabian Sea.

The next day we traveled up to Morvi. There were two palaces—an official city one, 1840-ish, all turrets and terraces and towers. Nearby was the palace in which the family now lived, built, furnished, and decorated entirely in art deco a hundred years later. Saris embroidered in Paris by Balmain for Uma's grandmother still hung in her bedroom, their detail echoed in the stitching on the borders of the linen napkins we used at the sumptuous banquets of calm northern Indian dishes—spicy food being, in Uma's book, rather common—or the elegant Parsi cuisine prepared by her husband's many chefs.

Several of our friends were guests, among them Alexander Hesketh's younger brother Bobby, recently married to the beautiful but chronically unpunctual Jeanne. Before any expedition Bobby could be heard shouting up the staircase, "Hurry, Jeanne!" Over the days I noticed the Indian servants shrink away whenever Jeanne appeared. At last it dawned. *Harijan* is Hindi for "untouchable." At a candlelit party Uma gave on the city palace's rooftop, Dai, wearing his form-fitting dress uniform, was anything but untouchable to the troupe of exquisite dark young dancing girls Uma had laid on.

Dai wore his uniform again to take a letter from Uma to the neighboring maharaja of Wankener. We trundled through jungle in the Morvi private train, a toy engine puffing two rickety ivory white carriages, to be met by a bearer standing by an ancient Rolls-Royce with the entertaining license plate of 1 Wank. The maharaja, his wife, and his son were all deeply educated, speaking perfect Oxford English, and reading the latest erudite books in this quaint time-untouched backwater.

From these smaller states, warranting only a nineteen-gun salute, we went to a twenty-one-gunner, Jaipur. Apart from the fabled pink, and the palaces, and the size and glorious color of the carpets within them, I was singularly struck by watching Aysha, widow of that most glamorous maharajah, Jai Jaipur, and herself still exquisitely lovely despite several months in prison at the command of Prime Minister Indira Gandhi, cross the wide lawns from Lilypool, her cool, flower-filled bungalow, to the Rambagh Palace where she had lived with Jai. As she walked amid a wave of saried women, many of them would fall to kiss her robes, her feet, even the ground she'd trodden—a goddess on earth. The only other time I've witnessed such obeisance was in Moscow, where babushkas did the same to Prince Michael of Kent, due to his near-identical family resemblance to their revered last czar, Nicholas II.

That it was then against the law for tourists to drive didn't faze Dai. He commandeered a jeep to drive me to see the great masterpiece of urban architecture, Edwin Lutyens's vast complex at New Delhi. I sat in the back swathed in a mauve shawl feeling like Lady Willingdon, the vicereine of Cecil Beaton's time. As they drove though a throng of beggars, Cecil wrote, Lady Willingdon nodded to her ADC: "Distribute the largesse." I had no need of an ADC, as the moment guards or officers caught sight of Dai's uniform and ribbons, arms jerked to a rigid salute, gates opened, ropes fell.

We crested the Rajpath, and before us lay Viceroy's House, more imposing and bigger—beyond belief bigger—than I had ever imagined. I was reminded of Lutyens's witticism, after being forced to concede the battle of designing the flanking pavilions to Sir Herbert Baker, his rival, that he'd met his Bakerloo.

Viceroy's House is one of the few buildings that have made me cry; Dai didn't seem to mind. A few days later, in Amber, we were told it was tradition to ride on an elephant up to that mirror-mosaicked marble mansion. Dai took me aside. Would I mind if we went up in the jeep instead? No, Dai, why? "Because I'd feel such a cunt on an elephant." The juxtaposition of those two words still makes me weep, but with laughter. On our return to England, it was fun to watch Dai cut a swath through the prettiest girls in London. He especially loved Charlotte Soames's dancing energy, or Sophy Cavendish's semaphore gestures and languid wit inherited from her Mitford mother, Deborah Devonshire. At a dinner in Sophy's tiny flat, we were discussing people with charisma, then a fashionable word. I said, "Surely, Debo, Hitler must have had huge charisma to a crowd?" "Well," she answered. "The thing is, I never saw Hitler"— pause—"in a crowd." One Sunday both Dai and Lee Radziwill came to lunch at the Hunting Lodge. Unfortunately Dai had driven down in a car so open it hardly had a windshield, and his suggestion of whizzing the stiffly coiffed Lee back to London fell on stony ears. Lee asked me to drinks at Claridge's the next evening. During the day I saw the Duke of Beaufort in the Mall, so beautifully dressed that I copied his pinstriped chic to a T for Lee's drinks. Proud as punch, I walked into her suite. The only other person in the room was the Duke of Beaufort.

· NINETEEN ·

THE MONTHS FOLLOWING Cavan's breakdown were infinitely distressing. My initial sense of relief gave way to guilt that our relationship, while increasingly unbearable due to his alcoholism, had ended with his sudden removal. His possessions, which I alternately hated and treasured, remained all around. It seemed callous not to leave them untouched, were he to recover. Even the dark torment of rambling and abusive calls seemed to pale by morning. Surely his demons would likewise fade.

Or were they my fault? Had I brought this schizophrenia about? Attending Al-Anon showed me that the problem was far from unique, counselors would tell me exactly what would happen next. But knowing the pattern only made me feel I should be able to alter it. One night I decided to go to Yorkshire the next day and face the hideous discord. The telephone rang. Fearing the usual, yet hoping for change, I was bound to answer. It was Rupert Everett, suggesting I meet him—in twenty minutes, okay?—at a new bar across the river.

As soon as my eyes got attuned to the room's murkiness I was aware of an oddly familiar presence. Not Rupert, nor anyone I knew. A tall lithe figure, the contours of his head defined by curled dark hair; his strong-featured profile only occasionally looking up from the drink he held, he was the exemplar of the youths I'd so often admired at a Tuscan *passeggiata*. I watched him, transfixed, not daring to move closer. And then something almost incredible happened. He came over to me. He was Italian. His name was Paolo. And he came from Orbetello. I fell in love then and there.

Paolo was to be in London for a month studying English. He moved into Drayton Gardens from his student digs in Elephant and Castle three days later, and by the end of the following three weeks we both knew he was not going to return to Italy. He showed me his portfolio, photographs taken when he was modeling in Florence. In them he was conventionally handsome, but what I found irresistible about his looks was their originality. That slanted profile, his bold nose set below earth brown eyes, his mouth pale against his dark-shadowed cheeks; naked, his lean body recalled black-outlined figures on red Etruscan beakers. Dressed, he wore the clothes he could then afford with innate elegance.

When his English course ended, it was clear that he needed to find a job. As he was interested in fashion, I asked the clothing mogul Joseph Ettedgui if there was a place somewhere in his empire. As I spoke, I surreptitiously changed Paolo's surname from Moschini to Moschino, as clearly that would play better on the fashion stage. He was a salesman born and swiftly rose in that position. However, he had told me his dream was to have his own boutique, and seeing how quickly he was able to assimilate my taste and style, I began to think he should be dressing houses rather than people. So, some months later, when my business expanded to a larger building, he joined the company; the Holbein Place premises became the Nicholas Haslam shop under Paolo's aegis.

Meeting Paolo had effectively doused any remaining embers of my torch for Cavan, and calls from him suddenly stopped. I wondered if perhaps previously I'd wanted them to happen, in a strange way had wished for them as a desperate link, but now, had my newfound joy sent out an unwritten message? And Paolo's enraptured first sight, one red-gold autumn day, of the Hunting Lodge in a stroke obliterated any stigma it held for me. We would go every weekend, Paolo shrugging with bafflement at the vagaries of English country customs, and I trying to speak what little Italian my father had taught me. But Paolo begged me to stop, saying my construction was so old-fashioned he couldn't make head or tail of it, though I gradually learned a bit more modern lingo from the compatriots who flocked around him, and from visits to and from his family in Tuscany.

For the next ten years my happiness with Paolo was boundless. I'd found someone I loved completely, or rather, more fully and sensibly, than anyone I'd loved before. Here was someone I admired both physically and intellectually, whom I could amuse, enthuse, inform, and offer any knowledge, taste, and friendships I'd formed. And I believe that love was reciprocated. Paolo was caring, wise, tender, strong, quick to understand, and quick to learn.

After I'd received an irresistible offer for the Drayton Gardens flat, we lived in several different places. Progressively, in each of these—bar a glamorous house lent us by Janet de Botton, where masterpieces of the contemporary art Janet was soon to donate to the Tate Modern as the nucleus of its collection, hung in such profusion that no other decor was needed—I could witness Paolo's eye forming, his taste growing, his sense of color developing. At one point we rented Cecil Beaton's house in Pelham Place. This was a lesson in decoration for both of us, as by some extraordinary quirk of luck, all of Cecil's furniture, the black velvet walls, the shocking-pink-and-orange banquettes, the Jean-Michel Frank bed and lamps, were still in situ, exactly as I remembered from seeing Cecil's transformation of the house in the late 1950s. Only the pictures had gone, replaced by minor modern muck. Paolo and I solved that problem by covering them with swaths of violet silk. This achieved a soothing backdrop for the many lively parties we gave there, including an intimate dinner for Shirley MacLaine, with like-minded flying saucer fanatics, and a whopper for the publication of the first volume of John Richardson's definitive Picasso biography.

Meanwhile my work was getting more and more recognition, with important commissions in Barbados, New York, New Orleans, and the Far East added to many in London and the country. I rediscovered the fun of designing parties, the planning and buildup to produce something ravishing that lasts a mere few hours. I created lavish balls for Simon and Laura Weinstock in London, for Jennifer and Simon Murray in Somerset, and built an entire, huge rococo opera house, with a floor large enough for five hundred Chinese debutantes and their escorts to dance a presentation waltz, in three days in Hong Kong. At the Royal College of Art I re-created the epitome of glamorous supper clubs, El Morocco, so vivid in my mind's eye since my Manhattan nightlife, for the twenty-first birthday of Evelyn and Victoria de Rothschild's daughter, Jessica. Tiers of blue and white zebra-print banquettes shaded by white plaster palm trees ringed a dance floor onto which, at midnight, the Gypsy Kings erupted. For the Prince of Wales's Trust I decorated the immense White Rooms, built by Empress Maria Theresa in the royal castle in Prague for a lavish banquet, enhancing their snowy splendor only with crimson velvet, and in London an all-greenery (gathered, permission of the forest ranger, from Windsor Great Park) Christmas lunch for Charles and Diana. It was the last event they would give together.

I ALSO REDISCOVERED THE JOY, missed since Arizona, of owning a Pekingese, bucking the trend in this country of Labrador lovers by still far preferring dogs with flat faces, and particularly that breed, which continually makes one laugh. Before long Paolo, too, was a Peke freak, and litters of puppies no bigger than your thumb became a regular event at the Hunting Lodge. Adept at planning any trips abroad around canine pregnancies, we went to Rome as often as possible, to rococo Vienna and Budapest with Min, to Long Island, to the Caribbean, and most frequently of all, to Istanbul. Kirstie Allsopp had introduced me to the unstintingly generous Cigdem Simavi, a woman in full beauty who, as far as I could tell, quite simply ran Turkey. Keys to kiosks, passes to palaces, patient chauffeurs, spices, and speedboats, yachts, and yallahs were at our fingertips, the sights our oysters. Hagia Sophia and the Cistern, Topkapi and Chora, pearls all, but paling before the magnificence of Suleiman's mosque, with his turban, and that of his beloved Roxanne, still on their tombs. Aysha Nadir gave dinners in her oval, frescoed pavilion. Set in a Roman ruin on the Asian Asian side of the Bosporus, the Saddulah Pasha, surely one of the most sensual eighteenth-century houses in the world, would suddenly leapfrog into the twentieth, by Aysha, at dawn, clapping her hands to summon a boatman to ferry us to Europe, to the nightclub on the opposite shore.

During one memorable stay, Cigdem's eldest son, Mustafa Koch, was married. Amid a ballroom swirling with couture dresses and *parures* of emeralds swayed the tall black toque of the Greek patriarch, the beribonned miter of the bishop of Gibraltar, the diadem of the archimandrake, while Ottoman diamonds trembled on the breast of Princess Nezlijah, granddaughter of the last sultan, and the last person of imperial blood to have been born within the Seraglio. And during another, the airport customs held up the things I had designed for Cigdem's Decorative Arts Fair. "Those damned gumrugs can be *so* obstructive," she said. Hours passed, no one, nothing, came. Then Cigdem called out, "Look! Gumrugs!" A trio of very young men sidled sheepishly toward her. "Put out your hands." Three hands were apologetically proffered. "You are naughty, naughty, naughty gumrugs," said Cigdem, giving each a good hard slap.

So many such shared experiences made Paolo and me laugh, stare in wonderment, revel in new friendships. We had so much that we mutually enjoyed—homes, towns, landscapes, work, food, fun—that I basked in the safeness of our ideal relationship. I was totally unprepared when, in the drear of a Frankfurt airport hotel bedroom, after having missed our connection to St. Petersburg, Paolo said he was leaving me.

I CRIED AS I HAVE NEVER cried before or since. Paolo lay on his bed, a light somewhere throwing a golden edge onto the outline of his head and shoulders. He looked so young and beautiful and desirable, dark against the white sheet, just as he had one night, not so long before, on a balcony of a hotel on Elba. We had gone there that summer by chance, by day taking peaches and prosciutto in a tiny boat to silvery rocks, falling alternately into the sea or asleep, later dining in mountain villages; and then the balcony, with its one particular, perfect night. Now it would all be gone. Ten years of happiness reduced to mere memory.

I pleaded, but knew it was no use. Paolo is not a Taurus for nothing. I reasoned, but saw there was no point; there was someone else. For some time I indulged in stupid talismans—if I get the right key the first time things will work out.

Looking back now, I can see that my naturally outgoing persona may have been overwhelming, and conversely my withdrawn feelings about physical sex, my tenet that its very intimacy can degrade a relationship, must be extremely disheartening. My "Don't shatter the crystal" mantra is probably better left behind along with roses, moons-in-June, and candlelight. But one can't change one's animus any more than one's personality. And now for the first time in many years I had no emotional attachment. The situation called for thought about the structure of my life. I had shaped someone else, now it was time to concentrate on re-shaping myself. Now I was a free agent, with no one to irritate or embarrass, and time was passing. As Min Hogg had once perceptively remarked, "After all, one's only middle-aged once." I was now well beyond that moment. Some form of repair was in order, I wasn't prepared to take up Stephen Tennant's dictum about getting older: "We all look better with a little banana-colored makeup." A few laugh lines were acceptable, but baggy eyes and saggy jowls were not.

I VOTED LABOUR IN THE 1997 election for the first and probably only time in my life, largely because of the increasingly fascistic attitudes of Conservative Party henchmen—especially Jeffrey Archer. I heard his chilling words on the radio as I drove over the New Forest, that anyone who didn't vote for his party "would be remembered." An unspoken "hunted down and shot," hung in the misty air. Five years on, my switch seemed justified; even though Tony Blair's meddlesome government was manipulating almost every aspect of urban, and increasingly, rural life, the economy was thriving. More and more money poured into the City; young American bankers imported their families, even younger fund managers importuned models, and though the Arabs visited less and less, Indians and Chinese were taking their place. And the astonishing wealth being mined by new metal and oil oligarchs in Russia was just beginning to be channeled into the tax haven that New Labour was deftly creating.

The arrival of this golden hoard had created a new and exciting climate, and though the conspicuous spending of it wasn't quite yet the order of the day, my occupation, and those affiliated with it, was given a shot in the arm. Old Money was still there but playing dead. The vivacious New Money brought with it not only the necessity to democratize the social stage, but, following the still unconvincingly explained (I believe) death of Princess Diana, a need for the media to find a replacement icon. This was a tall order, given the gamut of beauty and pathos Diana ran, but the press and its photographers applied their pens and lenses determinedly, and before long there was a raft of substitutes with, as its figurehead, Tara Palmer-Tomkinson. Tara's father had been at Eton with me, and her family were among Prince Charles's intimates, but she had a sulky classlessness, a self-deprecating humor and lack of shyness, the latter perhaps drug induced, that made going anywhere in her company, with the attendant paparazzi flashes, undeniably exciting. In many ways it brought back the spirit of the early sixties in New York, with Jane Holzer in the Tara role; even the very label "It Girl" that the media instinctively slapped on Tara and her clones had been around in America for ages, from silent movie star Clara Bow through to prewar debutantes Brenda Fraser and Gloria Baker.

I COULD SEE THAT along with Blair's pan-inclusive policy, its pretty new people and its shiny new cash, would come the need for a platform where both could coalesce; the latter would be delighted to entertain the former provided there was plenty of publicity attached. Suddenly half one's friends turned into PR agents, the daughters of "good" families tearing out their hair to get the required tally of footballers or minor television personalities to be photographed at sponsored events, with a slew of magazines launched to feed the appetite of the new beast in town. And there they were in livid color on those pages—young, good looking, some bland, some ambitious, some even talented, and they were everywhere. Where they ate: at Nobu, naturally. How they scored their drugs. What they drank at the Met Bar, why Meg Matthews bought thousand-pound jeans on Bond Street, where the Beckhams shopped on Sloane Street, which car she arrived in, which watch he wore. These mindless stories, running under even blander headlines about a whole new milieu, were the only ones anyone seemed to want to read. This celebrity-led culture rapidly transformed London's social landscape. It became rare not to see the paparazzi at a party, private or product publicizing, in fact they seemed naked without them. The traditional bastions of the elite, such as Ascot, which had anyway long since lost any aristocratic standing, became yet another photo op, wedding guests videoed bridal couples from the pews, and as nobody seemed to want privacy, that prized possession began the sad slide to its demise.

I'M NOT SURE I recognized that at the time. The technological gadgetry that enabled such a culture to function seemed miraculously modern and the results amusing to witness. I knew I must be attuned to this culture of Cool Britannia, in which young friends such as Marc Quinn, Damien Hirst, and Tracey Emin were creating art that no one was sure was art, where enviably bony boys with shaggy hair were making music no one could truthfully say was tuneful, albeit catchy. I had a bit of a crush on Alex James of "the boy group" Blur, at the time hiding his brooding intelligence under a woolly hat and massive intake of alcohol; one night in Soho House he gave me his woolly hat, a bearlike hug, and then passed out in a heap at my feet. Irredeemably fickle, I switched my allegiance to his rival group, Oasis, and in particular Liam Gallagher, whose looks and clothes I was, in the not-too-distant future, to ape unrelentingly. I think Liam was quite flattered at my slavish attempts. A year or so later I ran into him in the Ritz in Paris. "What's happened, Nick?" he said. "You don't look a bit like me anymore."

Well, I certainly had tried. Liam's looks were the calatyst that made me aware of my dissatisfaction with my own, his energy the spur to summon up what was left of mine, energy I would need if I was to ride this new wave, share this different vigor, be part of, in fact *be,* the zeitgeist of the time. The past had been wonderful, sad, difficult, memorable. Now it was time to fashion myself to a future and what I could make of it.

In a desultory way I had made appointments with plastic surgeons, one in New York, one in Paris, and a couple in London, but I hadn't been at ease with their too-polished premises and their too-smooth approach. Petanguy, the great Brazilian master carver, rumored to have lifted Nan Kempner's knees when miniskirts came back, offered me a freebie if I got myself to São Paulo, but it seemed foolhardy to attempt something so potentially risky in so distant a location. I'd almost given up the idea and, having a horror of Botox, relied instead on a few jabs of Restylane from time to time, when the jabber, whom I noticed pronounced it "re-stylin'," said, "Why don't you go and see my colleague upstairs?"

From the moment I walked into Bryan Mayou's surgery I was reassured. For some reason the somewhat disheveled figure sitting behind his slightly chaotic desk immediately convinced me I'd found my man. He asked me what I wanted done. "Oh, just a few little tucks here and there," I indicated with an airy gesture. As I said the words, I saw Bryan write on a pad, "N. Haslam. Full face-lift."

It was the beginning of a very intense relationship. My belief is that if one is going to entrust someone with something so deeply personal, one just has to do it with total conviction. Thus, three weeks later, during which I'd had more detailed discussions, studied diagrams of proposed incisions, and had Bryan very gently point out that what I wanted done he could do in his sleep—it was the guys who'd had their faces shot off in wars who were the challenge—I was wheeled into surgery. As the anesthetic took over I remember murmering, "Bryan, do more than we agreed."

I awoke at three in the morning. My head hurt, but of course I was grateful that I was alive to feel it; besides, the pain, caused by my swollen face inside the bandages was not actually unbearable, and by morning was almost gone. A few hours later those bandages were removed, a mirror brought, a cautious glance. The huge, round, smooth bruise-free melon staring back had not the faintest line on it. Bryan must have done "the more" I'd groggily suggested; I half hoped it would stay that way.

The next morning, at home, I was lying in bed telephoning. I telephoned Bryan. "I'm lying in bed telephoning, Bryan. Is that okay?" His answer made me get up then and there. Putting on a big hat and even bigger sunglasses, I went straight to my office. Then came the way I wanted to dress. I'd long ago decided I wasn't going to grow old even faintly gracefully, and dreaded the thought of looking "distinguished." I'm rather ashamed to admit it, but I think many episodes of my life have been predicated by wanting to look the part. Who *hasn't* longed to be a cowboy? Who didn't want to dress like James Dean? Or Presley? Go punk? Or look like Liam? Since the early days of Carnaby Street, and later the King's Road, I'd always preferred the immediate and up-to-date rather than the traditional and tame, and tended to imitate the look of people I found attractive; and even though Bunny Roger, who did the same, had pointed out years ago that it was the surest way *not* to attract them, I saw no reason to stop now.

Having had white hair since the Arizona sun bleached it, I needed no encouragement when my friend Hilary Alexander, the *Daily Telegraph*'s daredevil fashion editor, suggested we darken it "just a scrap, mind you," for a photo shoot. The result was perfect. "Don't touch it, darling." Not a hope. Over a few months I went gradually darker, till I was, eventually, Elvis raven. These seemingly capricious changes may have appalled some people, but on the whole they were amused. I certainly was, and so was the press. My appearance and attitude upheld my theory that of all professions, interior design is the most enjoyable. Each and every day one's eye receives information; even in my sleep I see memorable, or remembered, shapes and colors that, while not exactly dreams, can be turned into realities. The other advantage is that there is almost no boundary between the work and the leisure. Every moment is informative, any journey potentially an education, any relationship with clients or craftsmen potentially inspiring, and perhaps they felt we would have fun together. To my already solid client base I now added several bona fide celebrities; it was certainly fun to be doing a penthouse in London, and after that rebuilding and redesigning from scratch a country house, for Ringo Starr, or decorating Rod Stewart's rambling mansion in Essex, even though the helicopter I had rashly hired for a site visit managed to cover his snoozing parents with a soggy pall of grass cuttings as it touched down. I worked on several other projects in England, on the Continent, apartments in New York, and that most mysterious of American cities, New Orleans.

· TWENTY ·

WITH SO MANY MORE PROJECTS, I was regularly expanding the space suitable for a growing number of designers and assistants. I eventually found the ideal offices on Pavilion Road, a mewslike street lined with former coach houses, running from Knightsbridge to Sloane Square. The building accommodates up to twenty-five people, which, to be certain our designs remain individual and original, is the maximum I like to employ. Most of these people are young, with little previous experience and no predictably banal formal training, but who possess flair and zest. Humor and good looks are also essential in such intimate surroundings. I can teach almost anyone how to draw in a fortnight and how to decorate pretty soon after, but I can't make them beautiful.

This rule, though, can misfire. In the early eighties I was asked to do an apartment on the river in Chelsea owned by Barbara Black, then married to the Canadian tycoon. I took an assistant, a truly ravishing Swede. Barbara and David liked our ideas, it was all on track, and then nothing. I called: What was wrong? Barbara said very sweetly that if I thought she would ever let so pretty a girl as Marianne anywhere near her husband I was completely insane.

Barbara became a good friend, though sadly not a client; maybe she is the exception that proves the rule, as many of the closest friends I have, I originally met as clients, and a handful now count among my most beloved. Of these, I have known Janet de Botton the longest. Janet is the granddaughter of Lord Wolfson, an impressively astute tycoon, and the only person besides Jesus to have a college named after him at both Oxford and Cambridge. We met just after she and Michael Green, the father of her two clever, beautiful daughters Rebecca and Catherine, had divorced, and she would soon marry the financier Gilbert de Botton, a partner of our mutual friend Jacob Rothschild.

Janet's appreciation of art is echoed in her deep though not-uncritical loyalty, her outspoken wit, her wild sense of humor, and due to the precision of her mind and memory, her prowess at any intellectual game. Woe betide the unwary disposed to challenge Janet at Scrabble. And she's a world-class bridge player, with her own private team, as impressively rare a possession as old Mrs. McCormick's private Indian reservation, though happily Janet never subjects one to a lecture, or even mild discussion of past hands, except in the column she writes on the game in the *Spectator* magazine.

In the rooms we have made together, I constantly learn from Janet's eye for the finest eighteenth-century furniture and rare objects, which she mixes with an iconoclastic eye for the best contemporary art. On her walls, canvases confected from colored elephant dung vie with the Weisweiller commodes below, Picassos, Bacons, and Freuds hang above damask fauteuils, Julian Schnabel's shattered plates above fragile bouquets of porcelain flowers.

But perhaps Janet's most sensational creation is Pradelles, an ancient bull-breeding farm transformed into a sensuous house set in vernal grass prairies under the bone-bleached crags of Les Baux. From its wide terrace one looks down, astonished, on the achievement of her initial intent: a massive maze, and in the foreground, three fountains, three plumes of frothing white water. The plumes soar high, unfurl, and fall, spraying the air with a rainbow veil; beside them, fish-scaled centaurs, frozen in honeyed stone, gesture with tridents to distant statuary.

In an arcaded garden, vines entwine with roses, and a dozen varieties of strawberry warm in trugs on shaded seats. While white peacocks flaunt their tails in hummocks of lavender, Oh Hell! is being played for highish stakes beside an infinite pool. These are spring and summer's alchemy; by winter firelight we laze and wonder which shade of silk velvet, ashes of violet? *gorge de pigeon*? should cover the ceiling of her library in London. Janet demands only the finest feast for the eye, but her precision somehow prevents ostentation. This is personified by her spontaneously agreeing with my suggestion of lugging two massive, lichen-covered stone dolphins from the garden and placing them in the dining room, a contrast to the panels of ravishing eighteenth-century *papier peint* that Susan Gutfreund had found for Janet.

Two incomparable friendships came about through a rare circumstance. There is a house in Kensington that I had worked on for three successive owners. Each one allowed me to improve on what I had done there previously. I eventually fulfilled my vision of it in a fourth incarnation, when it was bought by Carol and Reinhard Winkler. At the time Carol, then better known as Carol Galley, was the brilliant chief executive of Mercury Asset Management. Reinhard was also a famed financier, but as he owned his own private bank, he could maintain a less demanding schedule than the Wonder Woman of the City, who, because of her steel-cool nerve, was nicknamed The Ice Maiden. Thus it was Reinhard, with his effusive personality and his faith in my taste, as well as his (all too rare) ability to understand scale and read a plan perfectly, with whom I met and discussed my ideas more frequently.

Sometimes I was at the house when Carol was able to come back early from the City. Quite apart from her calm, clear intelligence, I was struck by her quietly expressed happiness at what she saw, and by her intuitive understanding of the process of decoration. Aware that there are several layers that have to be applied before the final effect is achieved, she would never make a judgment until its completion. Most of all I became increasingly aware of her warmth of heart and generosity of advice. Anyone less icy than Carol is impossible to imagine.

Most spring and summer weekends, Reinhard and Carol flew to the south of France, to "a funny little house" they had bought several years before. The pleasure we all shared in working together was self-evident in our growing friendship, and when Egerton Place was finished they asked me to come and look at "our funny little" house in France. With their typical modesty, it turned out to be anything but funny or little. Le Mas Notre Dame stood four-square atop a leafy hill, the silver rocks of the Alpes-Maritimes its dramatic backdrop. The lawn overlooked terraced hectares of garden and orchard, a smudge of sea glistening beyond. "Nothing too radical, let's just change the Provençal wallpapers and tidge up the paintwork," we all decided. But Reinhard dearly loves a project, and within a few weeks plans for an almost total reconstruction were drawn up.

This construction went at such a pace that it was suddenly critical that the re-sited staircase I had designed, a three-storied elliptical stone spiral, should now have its railings installed. I had taken the drawings for them to a blacksmith I'd come across with Janet in a village near Pradelles. M. Aiello was a throwback to the *ouvriers* in Ramatuelle forty years ago. Squat, square, mahogany-faced, he wore the same faded blue overalls, their untied belt making *le singe* tail. The heat of his smithy blurred into the already stifling day as we spread the drawings on the yellow earth, refining curves and solving gradients.

Responding to my urgent summons, M. Aiello drove up to the *mas* in a ramshackle, rattling camion out of which clambered a seemingly backward lad and Mme Aiello, an equally squat, coal-black-curled figure dressed, surprisingly, like Jane Russell in *The Outlaw*. "It's obviously going to take a few days, so he's brought the family along," I replied to

Carol's raised eyebrows. How wrong I was. While Jane Russell's unharnessed cleavage jiggled as she moved about on her cork wedgies, her husband and the silent boy deftly welded the panels of scrolled iron into place, brazing the joints with flame and rasp, a sound and smell reminiscent of Uncle Oliver's workshop at Cairngill. By nightfall the staircase was finished, every arabesque and banister perfectly positioned. Witnessing such an ancient skill deployed entirely by hand, with not a single element factory-made, was deeply moving.

A few weeks after this, a chimney we had moved from one side of the salon to the other resolutely refused to draw. Stonemasons came and chipped, tilers came and added hoods to the stack, builders scratched their stomachs, the architect dodged the telephone. The hearth still billowed smoke. Then somebody mentioned a hippie living in a hut high up the hillside who could mend anything. "Let's ask him," I said. A messenger was sent, and an hour later one of the most beautiful people I have ever seen sauntered through the French windows. Extremely tall and lean, naked under khaki dungarees, Gordon had the pale blond hair and dark almond eyes that revealed the German-Chinese blood I'd just been told he possessed. After a brief inspection of the recalcitrant chimney, Gordon asked for a bucket of water. He slapped some cheesecloth dipped in plaster up into the flue, and soon, hey, presto! no more smoke.

While watching this miracle, Carol and I were talking about Gore Vidal's recently published memoir, *Palimpsest*. I joked that as Howard Austen, one of the main characters, is Gore's lifetime partner but never his lover, the book should have been called *Pal Incest*. Gordon looked around.

"Gore's my godfather."

"What?"

"Honestly," he said.

I called Gore to tell him the unlikely tale; his response was unexpectedly terse. "He is. Send him!"

So a month later, Gordon, near-naked now and gold-bronze, his hair to his waist, bareback on a small gray horse, leading a donkey clanking with cooking things and followed by a string of dogs, rode from the Alpes-Maritimes to the towering, blue Amalfi coast and reached the narrow path to Gore's eyrie. Near the house the film director Wes Anderson was shooting a scene as this cavalcade appeared. I was told that his star, Anjelica Huston, fainted at the sight.

I went to see Gore and Howard during that summer, almost their last at La Rondinaia, their house perched against the mountainside, its balconies flying above a dizzying plumb line dropping hundreds of feet, and ahead an uncompromising view straight out across the Mediterranean to, had one but eagles' eyes, Africa. Better to stay inside, in the chalk-cool rooms lined with immense, inky quattrocento paintings in dull gilt frames tarnished by these two old boys' lifetime of nicotine, sink into the book-encircled sofas, be lulled in belle-lettristic security. But one had to keep on one's mental toes or that security would most surely be shattered. Gore, aided by several bottles of Scotch, is the master of iconoclasm. His every idol, one eventually learns, has at least one clay foot. As even, perhaps, does he; for if, in old age Gore's glorious all-American handsomeness is giving way to the pronounced features of his Vidal ancestry, his universally deprecatory view of the present has outweighed any youthful hope he had of its salvation. More fun to talk about his subverting the homophobic Charlton Heston's *Ben Hur* script, the young Paul Newman, dinners by the pool with Princess Margaret, or how Winston Churchill wrote the dialogue of *That Hamilton Woman,* using Napoleon's threatened invasion of England therein as a coded warning to Hitler. As I drove down from this nest of learning, my head reeled with the facts, the fictions, of Gore's conversation. They remained with me as I swung off the autostrada to visit the vast palace at Caserta, where, at the top of the monumental staircase, I marveled at the camply extravagant mauve and silver *salle de gardes.* Here, indeed, Lady Hamilton, the divine Emma, had sparkled. Only later, at dusk, eating sweet tiny vongole beside Cy Twombly's pale castello at Gaeta, was Gore's convoluted brilliance replaced by the calm of Cy's rooms, which, though containing myriad exquisite things, are as pale and pure as his most serene paintings.

By the time I had finished the *mas* in the Alpes-Maritimes, Reinhard had found another project. With his uncanny flair for nosing out potentially incomparable property, he bought a chalet in Klosters, the smallest and least chi-chi of Swiss skiing villages, despite its being the bolthole favored by Garbo and Gore, and the favorite winter sports destination of many old-monied English families, the Prince of Wales foremost among them.

Reinhard's new discovery stood on a clover-covered hillside, its nearest building a farm; the muffled toll of cowbells echoed the bright chimes from the church tower nestled among the houses below, a panoply of mountains, their peaks blue and gold at sunrise all around. The only snag was the chalet itself; conceived in the hacienda style, with thin plasterboard arches and a wealth of red roof tiles, it would have been more at home in Orange County. But of course it could be made lovely. Easily. In no time. We can just take away that corner fireplace, and perhaps *not* have the bathroom opening off the entrance hall.

But Carol and Reinhard never settle for second best, and as the next winter approached the hacienda was a mere memory. Springing from stone foundations, the new chalet's wood-clad walls were soon roofed, a pine-scented shell noisy with buzz saws and strung with yellow lights, momentarily blinding after the whiteness outside. Stomping our snowy boots, we would see divisions chalked on concrete become identifiable rooms, stone and oak floors laid. Come the spring, it was time to install the decorations, and a growing army of carpenters, plasterers, uphol-sterers, and curtainmakers carved and molded and measured and pinned. Carol and Reinhard asked me to stay for their first Christmas. There were cozy evenings over claret by an aromatic fire, and while they skied, I wrote much of this manuscript.

FROM ANOTHER WORLD, there was my friendship and work with Tina Brown. When she was the editor of *The Tatler,* she had often asked me to contribute articles. When she moved to New York and was editing *Vanity Fair,* she had commissioned me to design the party for the maga-zine's London launch. With her usual flair for the unusual, Tina had found a little-known building for this event, the Baltic Exchange in the City. Behind a brave neoclassical facade, the immense marble-columned trading floor was lit by huge stained-glass windows. How to humanize this monumental space, make it as lighthearted as the words vanity fair imply, occupied my thoughts in the many hours I spent measuring, sketching, planning. Then, a few weeks before the event, the Baltic Ex-change was bombed, wrecking the building and killing three people. Tina felt too upset by the tragedy to consider even the most low-key party. To make magic for her, I had to wait until she progressed to the editorship of *The New Yorker,* when she entrusted me with transforming the pub-lic baths in Paddington into "Backstage" at the Royal Court Theatre, the rebuilding of which the magazine was supporting. I found props, chairs, birdcages, plaster statues, hip baths, tents, guns, and rosebushes that were then hauled up on ropes into the rafters among bagged-up chandeliers; canvas backs of scenery flats, lettered with which famous production at the Court they were from, were layered around the walls. Tables with "first-night" bouquets in scenery-painting pots were lit by beams from klieg, key, spot-, and floodlights. Though Tina observed that it would have been cheaper to move the Royal Court to Paddington, in many ways this party symbolized the zeitgeist of the nineties, the power of new money, the newly powerful celebrities, the mix of old guard and young talent.

Another commission took me to Cape Town. Apart from several visits to Morocco, which in some weird way doesn't seem to count as part of the continent, I hadn't been to Africa since the late seventies, having gone on safari in the Serengeti and Masai Mara before going to rough it in the then almost undiscovered Lamu, Kenya, an ancient trading village, far-flung on a virgin coast, with few modern conveniences. From the cockpit of a hiccupping biplane, the sight of the wonky, squared white houses, seemingly two-dimensional, and pasted, childlike, into a jungly background, looked exactly like Celesteville, the capital in the Babar books, if rather less luxurious. As we skidded to a stop on the skittery dirt landing strip, the radio crackled with information that some elephants were on the rampage nearby. We stared through the fly-encrusted windscreen in excited anticipation of a trumpeting tusker. Instead, Jackie Kennedy appeared and, stepping lightly into a rather sleeker craft than ours, taxied smoothly away.

Now the overnight flight landed in Cape Town. In the early, misty, dawn I felt that the city and its undeniably dramatic setting would be better seen, perhaps I mean viewed, from a distance. There was something frightening about that mountain, rising, steely cut-out, hard, wild, and oblivious, reaching up to pull the sky down to its level, as it loomed over the dense grid of the capital city sprawled at its inflexible base. It was a feeling that remained while under its shadow. But from a distance, from a sudden curve on the highway, the sight of that flat lilac brushstroke zinging against infinite blue stops the heart. And there is perhaps no more idyllic view of it than from the lush wooded uplands beyond Stellenbosch, above the phalanx rows of vines. Among these hills and ravines, at the top of a long, rutted drive, stands a crumbly gate-piers topped with acanthus plants, their gray arms akimbo. There is a sign: "Beware! Giant Apes, Fierce Dogs, Wild Agapanthus!" It is no idle warning. Dogs rush and pant, baboons squeal and scatter across the sky blue ground as one approaches this stone-flagged, tree-shaded farm, the last home of that most adventurous spirit Patricia O'Neil.

Pat was brought up at La Fiorentina, in its heyday the most exquisite of all Cap Ferrat houses, made so by her mother, Lady Kenmare, a delicately lovely Australian. Despite this fragility, Enid was rumored to have done in several husbands, thereby earning the nickname of Lady Kilmore from their neighbor Somerset Maugham. However murderous Enid's intentions toward her two-legged companions, they were compensated for by the care of the many exotic quadrupeds she collected, going so far as to have Vuitton make giraffe-shaped cases in which to transport her baby giraffes, regardless of quarantine, to London for her seasonal sojourn at Claridge's. Pat inherited this love of animals and thus lived for many years in Kenya. When the atmosphere of the country became unbearably threatening, Pat packed up her camp and trekked her entire menagerie of not exactly wieldy pets, including a large lion that habitually slept in her bed, the torrid three thousand miles to South Africa, to this sheltering homestead, Broadlands.

Tall and long necked, with pale blond curls and blue eyes, Pat is nanny to any orphaned creature and runs an enchantingly comical nursery. Her airy pink-and-turquoise rooms swarm with tiny ape children wearing nappies; even smaller furry things clamber onto Pat's dining table to nuzzle her ear, cubs tug at her fingers as she feeds them, a foal skitters stiff legged along the polished floors.

She is also an author, and possesses an acute eye and flawless memory for worlds far removed from this sanctuary. When I ask her why she thought the Duchess of Windsor might have been a hermaphrodite? "Well, because you see, before the war, at La Fiorentina, the Windsors would come to dinner. I was too young to join them, but I would sit with the gossiping maids—people always took a maid when they went out in those days—and they would all bring sewing. One night the duchess's maid looked at the crepe de chine underwear my mother's maid was mending. "What lovely things *your* lady has," she said. "*My* lady's things always have a urine stain in front." It seemed a telling, if not particularly pretty, detail in the puzzle of that odd couple's relationship. I remembered Capucine, the actress who was one of Charlie Feldman's affairs during his marriage to Jean Howard; Cap had the most ravishingly beautiful face, but her large physique fueled speculation. I can understand the hermaphrodite's allure. Years before I had watched the sculptor Fiore Henriques, her tall figure neat and lean in jeans, a tartan shirt defining her small breasts, as she stood listening to Ravi Shankar play a raga with Rory McEwen; her leonine head, with hair like burnished granite and mouth of carved marble, she was one of the most sexually alluring people I have ever seen.

THE VERY OPPOSITE of an enigma was the subject of a meeting that occurred barely a hundred yards from my office in London. I had often seen a tiny, intensely feminine figure, a knitted cap pulled down around her lined but beautiful face, her bird-fine frame pin neat in silvery brown pants and jacket, being buffeted about by even the mildest breeze as she strolled around around Sloane Square. One day Adam Moore, a young lawyer friend with an encyclopedic knowledge of showbiz, and I found ourselves next to her in the local café. With a beckoning smile, she introduced herself. Luise Rainer. Luise Rainer? Alive? The Luise Rainer who had made Hollywood history by being the only nominee to win the Oscar for best actress two years running? The Luise Rainer who had famously torn up her contract with Louis B. Mayer and walked away from her stardom? The Luise Rainer who had married the communist playwright Clifford Odets?

The very one. Now nearly a hundred years old, she was a personality so powerful, with a mind so illuminating about the great intellectuals of her past, and a memory for the grand and the trivial events of her extraordinary life. "Mahler, darling? I knew him well. And Alma, too, after she'd left Franz Werfel. And Strauss, of course. Bertolt Brecht? Horrid little man, he wrote *Caucasian Chalk Circle* for me, turned it down, I couldn't bear him. But Frank Wedekind, he was so charming." That world of 1920s Vienna, the writers and painters and musicians, leaped to life as Luise talked.

"I knew your grandfarzer, darling," she said to Lucian Freud, who had just told her the first film he saw was Luise's *The Good Earth*. "*Die Gute Erde, Die Gute Erde,*" they cooed together. Marty Scorsese, even Harvey Weinstein, paid homage after the premiere of their film about Howard Hughes. "Dreadful man, darling." Alone, quietly, Luise told us about going to Los Angeles, to stardom.

"Artur Schnitzler, Chaliapin, and the violinist Mischa Elman were on the *Île de France* with me. On my birthday, the menu was printed, 'In honor of Miss Luise Rainer.' Me! I was so embarrassed; I mean, those great artists! The voyage took five days; no one to meet me at the pier in New York; three days alone in a hotel, then five across the country, thinking I'd be raped by child-eating Negroes, but luckily I was befriended by George Kaufman and Sam Behrman. Even so, no one at Pasadena station. I sat on my luggage, swinging my legs. No one. I took a taxi to the Beverly Wilshire Hotel. No one. I called the studio, saying I wanted to go back home. But they said no, you are to do a test for *Escapade*, as Myrna Loy's been sacked. Myrna Loy! I insisted on doing a scene from Cocteau's *La Voix Humaine*, very rash of me in that dumb town. They saw it, said I would start filming next day. By the end of shooting I was a star."

Luise came to the Hunting Lodge that New Year's Eve. We ran her masterpiece film, *The Great Ziegfeld*. During the famous telephone scene, she craned closer and closer to the screen, studying her technique, perhaps, or being moved at her own perfect performance as the ravishing, tragic creature flickering on it? When it was over, she stood up, hands on hips. "Gott, I was so FAT."

I gave a dinner for Luise on her ninety-eighth birthday, asking only men, so she could flirt, and only men with some connection to the arts of Luise's Viennese circle, the Czechoslovakian-born Tom Stoppard and Stefan Ratibor, the definitively handsome Austrian prince, among them. But the person who intrigued Luise most, the youngest there, was Rodolphe von Hofmannsthal, grandson of Raimund and Liz, from both of whom he inherited utter charm and good looks mixed with a certain idiosyncratic streak. A year before his hair had been a tangle of dark copper dreadlocks, his aura a bohemian troubadour. Now slick and polished as a new coin, his poetic wanderlust transformed into extremely successful art dealing, he was to marry Frances Armstrong-Jones, the porcelain-pale daughter of Lucy and Tony Snowdon, only a few days thence. They have produced a perfect fat smiling boy, Rex, who is, I imagine, the last and best child to whom I am godfather. I hope Rex meets Luise, that their Austrian birthrights mingle in a loving cup. An entire century unfolds between their two births.

THOUGH I WAS IN Los Angeles a lot during my time at the ranch, it was Graydon Carter's *Vanity Fair* Oscar parties that brought me back in touch with friends from that time. Being asked to the star-studded dinners gave one a wild sensation of being part of Hollywood's elite. I was next to Hilary Swank one year, Oprah Winfrey another.

Graydon insisted on good old-fashioned Yankee food, and for many years encouraged cigarettes, subversively putting a logoed silver lighter at each place, though most people seemed to prefer table-hopping to either eating or smoking. Though the party has now moved to the art deco Sunset Tower Hotel—where Frank Sinatra and Bugsy Siegel once had apartments—it used to be held at Peter Morton's renowned Los Angeles restaurant, which was transformed with astonishing speed and skill by Basil Walters, and brilliantly lit by Patrick Woodroffe, who every year created, seemingly out of nowhere, an ever bigger space to accommodate the ever-swelling guest list.

At these memorable parties I could see friends and heroes I had known when I'd lived in Los Angeles: Angie Dickinson, whose crinkly smile has haunted me ever since I knew her as Mrs. Burt Bacharach; Warren Beatty; Tony Curtis; or George Hamilton, always more charming, more unfairly handsome, and funnier than ever. Lately I've taken to rounding off an evening at Paris Hilton's black, gold, and fuchsia house high in the hills, with its huge fridge filled with every form of cookie and doughnut one would imagine forever forbidden to the pearl-complexioned Paris. The most special treat is breakfast with Sue Mengers. Long ago, long before she became Hollywood's most powerful agent, Sue and I would cruise the seedier bars of Broadway. Now her setting's more pastoral. Jutting into a wedge of forest just behind the Beverly Hills Hotel, her house has the aura of an eighteenth-century pavilion reworked in the mid-twentieth. Though professing now to be almost a recluse, Sue, a twenty-first-century oracle, sits amid towers of scripts and layers of swirling smoke, knowing and commenting on every scrap of gossip, intrigue, and career of everyone in the "industry." Except one. When *Vanity Fair* ran an article about me, she telephoned. "Honey, I didn't know you'd done all those things. I thought you were just a cute kid!"

AFTER A RECENT OSCAR PARTY, I was flying from Los Angeles to Miami, to make the connection to Barbados, where Anthony and Carole Bamford, hearing that the deadline for my manuscript was looming, had offered me ultimate seclusion in the Pink Cottage, a refuge of luxury that belies its simple name, on their estate at Heron Bay. My eyes flickered with anticipation of shaded coral terraces, of the sea's shell-strewn tide line, of Heron Bay's vistas, Palladian facades rising above lantern-hung branches of ilex and oak, palm-shadowed paths sloping down to a baroque-bridged waterway. The tropical vistas, Piranesi engravings colored by Douanier Rousseau, drifted into dreams.

"On our left, you can see New Orleans." The pilot's voice, adding somberly, "Or what's left of it." Awake now, I looked down though the blue haze to the evidence of Katrina's deadly path far below, the pall of disaster still lying over its devastated bayous.

I closed the blind and my eyes, recalling the first time I went to that most mysterious of American cities. All Louisiana, but New Orleans especially, must, I knew, exude the spectral shadows and pungent essences of its Franco-Spanish past and a Mafia-esque, menacing present, though both impressions were somewhat spuriously based on Bette Davis in *Jezebel*, and *A Walk on the Wild Side* with Laurence Harvey. Even earlier, from childhood, I had a vivid memory of a novel, *Dinner at Antoine's,* in a bookcase in my father's study at Hundridge, its title enticingly and deliciously foreign in ration-booked Britain. How I came to know that Antoine's was in New Orleans, or even a restaurant rather than a Parisian hairdresser escapes me, but naturally I went to Antoine's my first night in the French Quarter, being introduced to a bittersweet sazerac, the original cocktail, and their famed Oysters Rockefeller, before going to hear the jazzier members of the famed Marsalis family playing on Bourbon Street. Next day, we lunched at Galatoire's, it's décor unchanged for more than a century, merely row upon row of brass coat hooks on magnolia-painted anaglypta walls. Until quite recently, the maître d' told me, in order to to get a table, even the oldest families would send a Cajun footman to queue outside. In addition, it was preferable that the footman be a dwarf.

My second visit there had coincided with Mardi Gras, when, quite as much as the exotic drag that the majority of its participants couldn't wait to wear, I was fascinated by the krewes, societies unique to Louisiana, and the polar opposite of England's madly modern Cool Britannia. For a week I went to extraordinarily elaborate pageants where jewel-crowned kings of each krewe, wearing cloth of gold, presided from golden thrones; debutante cotillions; presentation ceremonies; and white-tie balls—the whole rigmarole part hokey, part twentieth-century glamour, part fairy tale, and part legend of the French court from long before the Louisiana Purchase. I learned that to the New Orleans elite, it still really matters that one's grandmother had been a queen of the krewe, perhaps Comus, and had married the son of a duke of, say the krewe of Proteus; I remembered thinking this exclusive clique mirrored the other society America had invented, that of the city I had so recently left, those dynastic marriages woven among the offspring of filmdom's founding fathers, the Mayers and the Mannixes, the Schenks and the Warners, the arranged liaisons and pretended passions between the stars that made the make-believe believable.

Skimming over the cluster of shanties that borders the runway, the plane descended in strong winds into Barbados. "Bonsoir!" Jerome, gleaming in white T-shirt and shorts, guided me, through snaking queues of the arriving and departing, to a jeep. Installed on its white slipcovered seats, we wove through fields shoulder-high with sugarcane, and, dropping down through a grottolike gorge, turned in to the gates of Heron Bay.

In the early 1990s I had been asked to decorate another pavilion nearby, and nearly, in its builder Oliver Messel's whimsical baroque style, as beautiful; one night we put on gala scarlet clothes and drove down to

Heron Bay's pillared portico, for Carole and Anthony, who had bought the house from the widowed Marietta Tree, were giving a magnificent Red Ball.

I thought back to the time I had first seen this perfect building, this amalgam of Palladio's villas in the Veneto. Built after the war by Ronald Tree, of lustrous coral stone set by a coral shore, its one huge *salone* high in the columned facade giving on to a jungly outdoor drawing room around which curved wings terminating in frescoed gables embraced the turning tides, it was a bold last statement from the man who had created, with his former wife Nancy Lancaster, "an earthly paradise" as Debo Devonshire wrote of Ditchley Park in England.

Heron Bay had been the talk of sixties New York. "Staying with Ronnie and Marietta" was the acme of social elegance, topped only by an invitation from Bunny and Paul Mellon. Marietta, famed for having given Adlai Stevenson the kiss of life when he collapsed on the steps of the American Embassy in Grosvenor Square, was Jimmy's cousin. Both of us were faintly unnerved by her highbrow, somewhat arch intensity, though Ronnie, with hair shiny as molasses topping his tall, faultlessly dressed frame, had an erudition and generous charm that enslaved one for life. Many years after, I was at the same lunch party as Nancy Lancaster. She was deeply upset at Ronnie's last illness; advancing blindness, she said, made him unable to see his bridge hands clearly. By an extraordinary coincidence, I'd just bought, for some decorative scheme, two packs of double-sized cards. Nancy took them to Ronnie's bedside that afternoon.

Hence a friendship, ever strengthened by Carole's faultless eye for that rarest of traits, simple extravagance, began, and has been continually abetted by Anthony's boundless generosity, whether at Daylesford, their country house they've restored to the heyday of its builder, that romantic nabob of eighteenth-century India, Warren Hastings, or their boat, or their blue-and-white villa outside Hyeres. But now, at Heron Bay, and the pale cool of the Pink Cottage, unseen hands have placed my laptop in quiet shade, sharpened pencils, left dictionaries at elbow, put cold pink wine a hand's reach away.

But I had another reason to be in Barbados at that particular moment. A few months earlier I had been telephoned by an architect with a view to meeting a client of theirs who had recently bought some houses, one in London, another on Cap Ferrat. Such introductions are a fairly standard procedure, and often lead to a good working relationship, but not many lead to something deeper, to a friendship that has become as close and dear to me as any I have.

Natasha Kagalovsky was born into relative poverty in Leningrad. Blessed with outstanding numeracy, she excelled at college and immigrated to the United States in 1979. After studying at Princeton, she became a banker and married her politically ascendant husband Konstantin. Now they had decided to return to Europe and were looking into buying a house in London.

At our first meeting Natasha's discerning humor, judgment, and adaptability had been evident, the last a relief, as I'd insisted on a restaurant I'd heard was delicious and comfortable but turned out to be a basic student café. During lunch, Natasha gently disabused me of my over-romantic view of Russia and Russian, "a wonderful country now full of awful people," and shrugged gently when I said I was enjoying working in Moscow. "It can't last," she said, smiling. "You'll see."

She was waiting, as the sun fell into the sea, by the hotel pool, still smiling. Her face was lit with an excitement, which I knew meant she had a secret, not secret for long. "I think we've found the perfect house. But before you can get your hands on it there'll need to be a year or so of repairs and reconstruction." But even before that, another beautiful building would manifest itself, in real life, just as it had for many years in my subconscious.

A long time ago in Sotheby's I'd seen a watercolor of a classic porti-coed country house, set in a wooded park with horses and deer, and in the foreground, a silken couple stroll under an umbrella, while a gardener rakes leaves. It was just the sort of picture I like anyway, but something about this very typical eighteenth-century scene especially intrigued me. Its catalog entry read, "Bessborough House, in Roehampton, Surrey; now called Manresa House." I remembered my mother talking about that family land across the Thames and a house, probably long gone like so many others, gambled or given away, burned or abandoned, its possessions dispersed. I was determined to bid for this poignant painting, this evocative relic of ancestry. Luck was with me, for though the picture was by a named artist, Luke Sullivan, it hadn't attracted any serious attention, and at underestimate, it became mine.

I studied maps of the area: no sign of any Manresa House. Driving around the area raised my hopes: I found Duncannon, Ponsonby, and Bessborough roads; but my enthusiasm dimmed when these blind alleys led only to hideous high-rises or petered out in scarily run-down council-estates. Bessborough, or Manresa, House had surely been demolished in some postwar wave of destruction.

For several years I forgot the place had ever existed; but more recently, and usually on the way to Gatwick, I'd tell Nash, my driver, that some-where around there might be a former home of my ancestors. Nash would shrug, and I could feel him thinking, Yeah, right. Then one spring evening, when I'd flown in from Moscow, he could bear it no longer. "You got an hour to spare? Let's find your bloody house." For a time we drove the same roads I'd done those years before. Same dead ends, same blanks drawn. But Nash's adventure blood was up. "Come on, let's walk it." We left the car, heading far into the bowels of sink estates. Anyone we asked looked blank, noncomprehensive. Dusk was imminent, sudden cold wind swirled plastic and paper. Nash called to a group of hooded boys slouching by a wall. "Hi! Is there a big old house somewhere near?" Of course they knew. "Other side of this wall, 'n through the hedge." They helped me scramble up, over. I pushed through bramble-clogged hawthorn. From almost exactly the point where my picture had been painted, I saw Bessborough House, in all its eighteenth-century perfec-tion, washed by a watery sunset.

IT SEEMED ALMOST miraculous the building should have survived the wholesale cull of such postwar "white elephants." Though the fifth Earl of Bessborough (my mother's grandfather) had left it for his Irish seat in the early 1800s, and Sir John Soane was the principal buyer at the sale of its antiquities at Christie's soon after, something in the house's soul made successive owners treat it with respect. Even the Jesuits, who had the place for a century, added sympathetic wings and stables to form a large rear courtyard and a substantial Gothic chapel, where their most fa-mous novitiate the poet Gerald Manley Hopkins worshiped. Since the 1950s, when the estate was joined to the University of Roehampton and its affiliate, Whitelands College, the third oldest in the country, it became the domaine of the college rector. I learned all this while being shown the interior by Gilly King, the archivist.

As miraculously intact inside as out, every room had chimney-pieces and plasterwork as immaculate as they were the day Sir William Cham-bers, the architect of this little masterpiece, had installed them in 1760. And there was more. Gilly King told me that there were temples by Chambers on the grounds, one of which had recently been found, dis-mantled but complete, in a pit. They wanted to re-erect it but didn't have the necessary funds.

In a rush of enthusiasm, I heard myself tell Gilly I would raise the nec-essary £100, 000. We set up the Ponsonby Temple Appeal. Due to the instant generosity of relations, friends, and trusts, the Prince of Wales and his duchess first among them, within six months we had enough in the kitty to haul the first of the numbered hunks of stone out of their dank tomb and into their designated position.

IT SEEMED ONLY APPROPRIATE to give a party to celebrate the rebuilding of what I soon thought of as *my* temple: small, of course, and probably in the early evening. It didn't take very long for the idea of this simple gathering to become far more elaborate. After all, I would, all too soon, enter my eighth decade. And while that was hardly a cause for festivity, I thought I could cloud the issue by asking Janet de Botton, whose devotion to the bridge circuit has almost eliminated what little appetite she has for social life, if I could give the party in her honor.

On getting Janet's agreement, I started planning and assembled a thirty-strong team; naturally at each meeting the plans became more elaborate and fanciful. While the eighteenth-century rooms needed merely dramatic lighting, enormous candle lanterns made from white swansdown would hang in profusion over the staircase hall down to the inner courtyard, which we decided to turn into a huge surreal rococo ballroom, its décor based on that of a film by my Hollywood friend and hero, Tony Duquette. The walls and ceiling would be red, with a gigantic chandelier and chinoiserie figures of white plaster, all seemingly opening onto an ethereal landscape of white trees against a china blue sky. There were banquettes on a raised tier on all three sides, while Janet's sensational contribution, an eighteen-strong band from Paris played, spotlit, on a fourth. My special request, that the dance floor should revolve, took some tactful negotiations. But on the evening, it was the added surprise to an already astonishing setting, the one that gives a party a unique fillip.

Having planned the look of the evening, I now had to send invitations to fulfill it, and boldly started at the very top. As the queen had given, on the evening of Prince Charles's wedding to Diana, the greatest party I have ever been to in my life, I wanted to reciprocate by asking her and the Duke of Edinburgh. Their reply regretted they had a previous engagement, but sent their hopes and wishes for a wonderful evening. This refusal was followed by the most romantic one from Lady Antonia Fraser, who wrote that she always devoted October 16 to mourning her heroine Marie Antoinette "who was murdered on that day, so no dancing." Reading it, I recalled Bunny Roger once insisted a guest leave his house for having said that Marie Antoinette spent too much.

A year later, nine hundred people drove through the hideous high-rises and into the university campus, where banks of students cheered them on. Turning in a wide gyre around the lawn down to Richmond Park, guests arrived at a candlelit avenue that led them up the floodlit facade, alighting to climb the double stairs up to the portico where Janet and I met them. Supper was laid out in the enfilade of rooms that Chambers had designed with this exact purpose in mind: bucolic revelry, drinking, and dancing.

Then the many revelers were Georgiana Devonshire, Charles James Fox, Caroline Lamb, and Prinny, the acme of eighteenth-century Whig society. Tonight there were many descendants of that society but mixed with a worldwide cross section of friends from my past, Lucian Freud, Paris Hilton, Lee Radziwill, Jacob Rothschild, several Greek princes, Clarissa Pilkington, Tracey Emin, Emanuele di Savoia, Keanu Reeves. It was extremely gratifying to show the ballroom to Denise Hale, once married to Vincente Minnelli, who directed the Tony Duquette film that had inspired it. "Of course, it's *Ziegfeld Follies*!!" she exclaimed. Three months later, Chambers's temple, now proud on its plinth, felt a mantle of snow on its honey stone for the first time in a hundred years.

BACK IN CHELSEA, the tarpaulins enshrouding Stanley House and the gangways of scaffolding behind them were about to be taken down from the house that Natasha and Konstantin Kagalovsky had bought. It was ready for the interior decoration that I'd been planning for many months, encouraged and inspired by Colette Anthon, a brilliant young Canadian designer who had joined my company shortly after the move to Pavilion Road.

When I first saw the building I got that jolt, half delightful, half alarming, of déjà vu. I realized it was the same dilapidated mansion, looming forlornly behind a high nondescript wall that I had passed so frequently, and I had in fact been to a party there, as it was once possible to rent its scruffy big rooms, but now that it was restored, the scale and mellow brick walls immediately reminded me of Hundridge. And the more I saw and learned of the house, the more that impression was reinforced. First built as a manor, Stanley House had stood in fields and orchards, beyond Chelsea, on the King's Road, the highway made by Charles II as his direct royal route from St. James's to Hampton Court. It was almost exactly the same date as Hundridge, and in original size and plan echoed it to a T. Inside, with an intricately banistered pine staircase on the selfsame wall, doors led to paneled rooms the shape and height of my father's study on the right, and the parlor on the left; the dining room was in a similar position, with a kitchen beyond as big and bright as Sersee's. Upstairs, all the rooms, including the tiny attic rooms, were uncannily familiar. There was a difference, though, between what I saw and my memories.

Stanley House had for decades been a council school, each room painted and overpainted in those garish and, at the same time, milky solid colors preferred by administrators of such institutions. Some of the original paneling had been crudely ripped away, shutters nailed up, floors boarded over, window latches and doorknobs wrenched off long ago.

Astonishingly, one large room that had been added a century or so later, in the almost identical position to the Long Room at Hundridge Clough Williams-Ellis had put on for my father in the 1920s, remained virtually intact despite having the Parthenon frieze, enticingly pot-shootable to unruly schoolboys, of casts of the Elgin Marbles around its walls. Why? It transpired that the house had belonged to Lord Elgin's secretary, William Hamilton, and the casts had been made the moment they touched the ground, the minute they had been prised off the ancient temple. When designing this room, I instinctively decided on low white bookcases against the walls, adding white overdoors surmounted by white busts. My presentation drawings included one for the picture-hanging scheme, showing, arbitrarily, a small one propped on the fireplace mantel. Later I was told about the existence of a detailed water-color of the room, done two hundred years ago by Hamilton's sister. We found it, and Natasha bought it. Not only does it show white bookcases, doors, and busts, but also a small picture propped on the mantel. Looking at it still gives me a frisson.

I TELEPHONED THE PRESENT OWNERS of Hundridge. I knew they had taken pride and pains to keep the house authentic. Would it be possible to send my team to look at, make notes on, and photograph many remembered details? Would they mind if we replicate the ironwork and wood-turning, copy the pattern of floorboards? Charles and Georgina Mullins were the epitome of accommodating generosity, fitting in with any time that suited my team. In the event, heart-in-mouth, I went too. I had hardly seen Hundridge, certainly not been inside the house where I'd been born, since my father sold it during my first half at Eton. I'd heard of the changes made by successive owners, but I still retained the memory of deep woods, hazed with the ghosts of bluebells, carpeted with damp brown leaves noiseless to my footfall, of the stubbly fields strewn with flints, of the deep green hillside dotted with mushrooms the size of saucers, and cowslips, and under a blackthorn hedge, the badgers' sett. I couldn't expect to see such things as these, I knew, but I wondered, as I got up that morning, if perhaps a sudden view, a muddy scent, the creak of a hinge might manifest childhood's mirage.

WHAT HAD SEEMED, in that childhood, a day's journey from London, with stops for carsickness, was child's play that day, taking barely an hour. But nearing the house, the roads seemed no wider, just as tree-dappled, and at the banked hedgerow's only gap, the huge oak overhanging a stile, from where one caught a momentary glimpse of the house across the fields, had not been felled. But just a little way beyond, the drive, dipping through the woods, was now announced by two imposing closed gates with many electronic instructions, its surface, ridged and rough-rutted in my parents' day, now smoothly cambered and a breeze to climb.

On the crest, a swirling wind was blowing fleeting dark airwaves into the summer wheat. Beyond this flying green carpet, a pattern of russet and gray fused into a frame around glinting panes, windows into far-away rooms. Closer now, the random shapes of outbuildings spreading from the house, the barns, the differing reds of roofs tumbled into place on memory's blueprint. An antique magic hung in the air until the distance between past and present contracted.

Inside, change was more acutely obvious: some previous philistine foreigner had stripped the unique, madly painted rooms. There were necessary additions sensitively carried out, but the top floor was hardly altered. I found my attic bedroom, its door latch making the same double click as it rose and fell back. Stepping inside I saw the two sloping corner walls, one with its small bright square of window; I lifted its curled iron handle. It caught the wind and swung wide.

Piled-up, billowing clouds scudded away across the sky; not far below, on tall apple trees, last leaves clung to spiny branches, quivering like fish in a pool. Each sudden gust released a new shoal, which rose and tumbled and rose again high over the fields, past the line of elms, glinting and flashing, an airborne semaphore that compelled the eye to follow, beyond, and on, toward the distant heath . . .

And in memory's free fall I saw the plume of blue smoke, smelled the scent of fiery ashes, saw phantoms running in rust-gold summer bracken. Somewhere in the low chalk woods, rooks cawed, heralding winter. I closed the window.

Index

Ackroyd, Bill, 140–1
Acton, Sir Harold, 279
Acton, Sir William, 23
Addey, John, 99–101
Africa, Haslam's visits to, 311–12
Aga Khan, 272, 273
Agnelli, Gianni and Marella, 224,
    226–7, 264
Aiello, M. and Mme, 307–8
Alexander, Hilary, 304
Alexandra, Queen, 82, 83, 87, 229
Allen, Woody, 215
Alliluyeva, Svetlana, 248–9
Allsopp, Kirstie, 270, 299
Alsop, Joseph and Susan Mary, 167,
    174
Aly Khan, Joan, Princess, 272–4, 284
Aly Khan, Prince, 126, 132, 272
Amies, Hardy, 109
Anderson, Anna, 133
Annabel's (London), 107
Anne, Princess, 284
Anthon, Colette, 321
Arbus, Diane, 204–6, 250
Argyll, Margaret, Duchess of, 263, 283–4
Arizona, Haslam's home in. See Black
    Canyon Ranch
Arliss, George, 80
Armstrong-Jones, Frances, 261, 314
Armstrong-Jones, Tony. See Snowdon,
    Tony Armstrong-Jones, Lord
Arnstein, Nicky, 29–30
Ash, Diana, 139
Asher, Jane, 207
Ashley, April, 69
Ashton, Frederick, 78–9, 83–5, 87, 178
Aspinall, John, 76, 106–7
Astor, Alice, 84, 216, 217, 238
Astor, Bill, 117, 118
Astor, Bronwen Pugh, 79, 116–18
Astor, Brooke, 217

Astor, Vincent, 216, 217, 244
Auden, W. H., 181
Austen, Howard, 217, 308–9
Austria, Haslam's visit to, 237–9
Austro-Hungarian Empire, 27–8
Avedon, Richard, 157, 224–5, 232, 258
Axelrod, George and Joan, 197

Bacon, Francis, 123, 139, 286
Baddeley, Hermione, 139, 200
Baerlein, Di, 46
Bagnold, Enid, 88–9, 202–3
Bailey, Bert and Gladys, 113, 114
Bailey, David, 92, 113–14, 115, 141–2,
    148, 152, 170, 176, 204, 207, 211,
    217–18, 252, 270; Ritz and, 279,
    280–3
Bailey, Rosemary, 141–2
Baker, Edith, 160
Baker, Nanny, 10, 13
Bakst, Léon, 87
Balanchine, George, 83, 178, 179
Baldwin, Billy, 158, 163, 175, 182, 183,
    185, 211
Ballot, Jeanne, 155
Balmain, Pierre, 116
Balsan, Consuelo Vanderbilt, 155, 184,
    218
Bambi (performer), 69–70
Bamford, Anthony and Carole, 315,
    316–17
Bankhead, Tallulah, 64–6, 165–6, 169
Bannenberg, Jon and Maggie, 105
Barbados, Haslam's visits to, 315,
    316–18
Barber, Samuel, 171
Bardot, Brigitte, 121, 128
Barnes, Djuna, 152
Barney, Nathalie, 126
Bart, Lionel, 107–8
Bartók, Béla, 33

Barton, Tug, 169, 170
Bassey, Shirley, 97
Bath, Henry, 91–2
Beacon school (Chesham), 40, 45, 48
Beard, Peter, 177, 189, 207
Beatles, 173, 192, 207, 225
Beaton, Cecil, 75, 77, 82–3, 87, 88, 95,
    109, 120, 131, 145, 149, 157, 171,
    184, 196, 198–9, 206, 212, 217,
    232, 234, 244, 246, 252, 253, 269,
    294, 298
Beatty, Warren, 257, 315
Beaufort, Duke of, 295
Beit, Randlord Alfred and Clementine, 14
Bell, Jimmy Cleveland, 109–11
Bell, Tom, 262, 276–7
Benson, Sir Rex, 61
Bérard, Christian (Bébé), 125, 184
Berenson, Bernard and Mary, 6, 23, 279
Bergé, Pierre, 270
Berger, Bill, 122
Berger, Helmut, 270
Berlin, Irving, 18, 194
Berlin, Mary Ellin, 156
Bernard, Bruce and Jeff, 139
Berners, Gerald Tyrwhitt-Drake, Lord,
    22, 23, 77
Bernstein, Leonard, 143, 171
Bertil, Prince of Sweden, 129
Bessborough ancestors, 25, 319
Bessborough House (Surrey), 318–21
Betjeman, John, 277, 278
Betjeman, Penelope, 278
Bibesco, Prince and Princess Antoine
    (Elizabeth), 95
Bibesco, Princess Priscilla. *See* Hodgson,
    Priscilla.
Birley, Mark, 56, 98, 107, 173
Black, Barbara and David, 305
Black Canyon Ranch (Arizona), 235–7,
    241–5, 250; decor of, 241, 242–3,
    259; stables at, 243, 251; staff at,
    241
Blackmon, Rosemary, 155–6
Blackwell, Earl, 169
Blackwood, Caroline, 139, 183
Blair, Josie, 219
Blair, Lionel, 143
Blair, Tony, 300, 301
Blanc, Milenko, 170
Blanch, Lesley, 133

Blass, Bill, 183, 209
Blumenthal, Vota, 170
Blunt, Anthony, 61
Blunt, Wilfred, 61, 96
Bobby (male hustler and assistant),
    180–1, 182, 201, 228, 230, 232
Bogarde, Dirk, 47
Bonnard, Pierre, 95
Borges, Jorge Luis, 20
Borgnine, Ernest, 144
Boscawen, Simon, 57
Bose, Lucia, 131
Botton, Janet de, 297, 305–6, 307, 320,
    321
Bousquet, Marie-Louise, 227
Bowler, Norman, 139
Boxer, Mark, 85
Bradshaw, Annis "Mike," 156
Brando, Marlon, 72
Brausen, Erica, 119
Brett, Jeremy, 199
Brice, Fanny, 29–30, 64, 65, 66, 206
Broadwater, Bowden, 181, 183
Brown, Horace, 54
Brown, Tina, 310
Browne, Tara, 129
Brownell, Sonia, 139
Bruntisfield, Lady Tania, 262
Buckle, Richard, 104, 143
Budberg, Moura, 13
Buffet, Bernard, 129
Burney, Tony, 99
Burra, Edward, 78, 81
Burton, Richard, 168
Burton, Sybil, 168
Byron, George Gordon, Lord, 25, 56
Byron, Nora, 54, 55–6, 58

Calabash (London), 107
Callas, Maria, 103, 109, 242
Call Me Madam, 18, 167, 194
Cammell, Donald, 116
Campbell, Mary, 151
Campbell, Nina, 286
Camrose, Lord Seymour, 272–4
Canada, Haslam's visits to ranch in,
    219–21, 237, 240
Capote, Truman, 100, 124, 218–19,
    244, 249–50
Capri, Haslam's visit to, 109–11, 152
Capucine, 312

Carnes, Gerald, 185
Carter, Graydon, 314–15
Caruso, Enrico, 23
Casati, Marchesa, 76, 135
Case, Margaret, 157–8, 159, 173, 182, 191–2, 196, 199, 204, 219
Cassandra (columnist), 108
Cassini, Oleg, 129, 151
Cather, Willa, 242
Catlin, George, 167
Cavanagh, John, 111
Cecil (male hustler and assistant), 180–1, 201, 228, 230, 232
Celeste (astrologer), 108
Cézanne, Paul, 131
Chadwick family (Forres), 48, 49
Chamberlain, Houston Stewart, 27
Chambers, Sir William, 25, 319, 321
Chan, Jacqui, 103
Chanel, Coco, 50, 154, 161, 184
Channon, Chips, 75, 83, 97, 98, 117, 135
Channon, Paul and Ingrid, 250
Charisse, Cyd, 199
Charles, Prince of Wales, 284–6, 287, 298, 301, 309, 320
Checker, Chubby, 142, 149
Cheney, Frances, 212–13
Christian, Linda, 32
Christian Science, 41
Christopher, Jordan, 168
Churchill, Pamela, 60, 218
Churchill, Winston, 86, 225, 309
Churchill, Winston (grandson), 60
Cicogna, Anna Maria, 230
Clark, Colette, 140
Clark, Colin, 203
Clark, Lady Jane and Sir Kenneth, 140
Clarkson, Gerald, 71–2
Claxton, Bill, 206
Cleopatra, 169
Clermont Club (London), 106–7
Cliveden (near Maidenhead), 117–18
Coach and Horses (London), 108
Coats, Peter, 75, 117
Cocteau, Jean, 125, 126, 313
Cole, Harriet, 115
Coleridge, Samuel Taylor, 71
Colette, 77, 127
Colin, Pamela, 157
Collins, Joan, 287

Colonnade Row (New York), 178–9
Cooper, Artemis, 76, 77
Cooper, Diana, 75–7, 85, 86, 87, 88–9, 92, 174, 195–6, 202, 238, 239, 267, 269, 284, 292; in Venice, 227, 230–3
Cooper, Douglas, 131–2, 181
Cooper, Duff, 76, 174
Cooper, Sally, 65
Cordet, Hélène, 142
Corfe Castle, 49–50
Corrigan, Laura, 228
Country Life, 8
Coupe, Rod, 107
Coward, Noël, 86, 88, 89, 105, 132, 141, 165, 175, 183, 239
Craig, Lillian, 129
Crane, Norma, 253, 254, 258
Crawford, Joan, 65, 169, 189
Crespi, Consuelo, 227
Cripps, Milo, 147, 148
Crosby, Caresse, 122
Cuba, Davison's memories of, 221–2
Cuban missile crisis (1962), 179
Cuffe, Lady Sybil, 23
Cukor, George, 198, 199
Cunard, Nancy, 84, 131
Cunard, Victor, 229
Cutting, William Bayard, 23

d'Abo, Louisa, 262
Daisy, Princess of Pless, 127–8
Dalí, Salvador and Gala, 189–90
Damer, Miss Dawson, 104
d'Arenberg, Peggy, 160
Daves, Jessica, 153, 172
Davies, David, 262
Davison, Anne, 214, 219–21, 237, 243, 247, 248
Davison, Frankie, 235
Davison, James, 149, 209–16, 219–22, 233–8, 240–54, 287, 317; country home purchased by Haslam and, 233–4, 235–7, 241–5; family of, 211–14, 235, 247–8, 249; Haslam's breakup with, 251–4, 257, 258, 259; Haslam's New York home with, 215–16; traveling in Morocco and Europe, 225–33
Deakin, John, 139
Dean, James, 90, 93, 303
de la Renta, Françoise, 174

de la Renta, Oscar, 153, 174
Dempster, Nigel, 108
Denton, Jack, 241, 243
Devonshire, Deborah, Duchess of, 294, 317
de Wolfe, Elsie (Lady Mendl), 195, 197, 256
Diaghilev, Sergei, 86, 104, 232
Diana, Princess of Wales, 25, 284–6, 287, 298, 301, 320
Didion, Joan, 156, 258
Dietrich, Marlene, 50, 78, 114, 115–16, 132, 154, 162, 201, 280
di Montezemolo, Cathy, 154
Dior, Christian, 77
Disney, Walt, 66
Dix, George, 149, 209
Dolly sisters, 159
Dominguín, Luis Miguel, 131
Donahue, Jimmy, 193
Donovan, Terence, 113, 115, 204
Dors, Diana, 80
Douglas, Kirk, 201
Douglas, Lord Alfred, 133
Douglas, Norman, 109
Drogheda, Lord and Lady, 154
Duchamp, Marcel, 18, 153
Duchamp, Teeny, 18, 153, 178
Duff, Lady Juliet, 84, 86–8, 198
Duff, Michael, 75, 87, 106, 244
Dufferin, Maureen, 130, 272
Duffy, Brian, 113
Duhe, Camille, 182
Duke, Doris, 256
Duncan, Raymond, 152
Dunn, Anne, 122, 123, 124, 130, 132
Dunne, Dominick, 253, 254, 287
Dunoyer de Segonzac, André, 128
Du Pont, Harry, 160
Duquette, Tony, 255–6, 257, 320, 321
Dürrenmatt, Friedrich, 88
Dyer, George, 286
Dylan, Bob and Sara, 225

Eddy, Mary Baker, 41
Eden, Anthony, 106
Edward II, King, 11, 50
Edward VII, King, 127, 213, 229
Eggar, Samantha, 102
Egremont, John, 44
Eisenhower, Mamie, 167

Elgin Marbles, 322
Eliot, Jacquetta, 173, 225
Eliot, Peregrine, 173, 225, 234–5
Elizabeth, Queen Mother, 22, 83, 85, 87, 106, 130, 272, 279, 288, 289–92
Elizabeth I, Queen, 267–8
Elizabeth II, Queen, 6, 8, 22, 61–2, 93, 279, 320
Ellington, Duke, 175
Ellis, Dick, 46–7
Éluard, Paul, 128
Elwes, Dominic, 14, 33, 260
Elwes, Simon and Golly, 13–14
Emanuel, David and Elizabeth, 284–5
Emin, Tracey, 302, 321
Eton, 51–2, 53–61, 63, 65–8, 71–2, 77, 89–90, 94–7, 99, 102, 137, 153, 221, 250, 301
Ettedgui, Joseph, 297
Everett, Rupert, 260, 296
Eyre, Peter, 263

Fairbanks family, 188–9, 190
Faith, Adam, 107, 142
Farouk, King of Egypt, 111
Farrell, Charles, 267
Fath, Jacques, 46, 73
Fedorovitch, Sophie, 73
Feldman, Charles, 89, 162, 312
Fellowes, Daisy, 85, 135
Fellows-Gordon, Dickie, 141
Ferguson, Annabel, 263
Ferry, Bryan, 276, 287, 288
Fields, Gracie, 110–11
Fisher, Eddie, 168
Fitzgerald, F. Scott, 131
Fitzgerald, Zelda, 131, 181
FitzPatrick, Ena, 127–8, 130
Flanner, Janet, 86, 88, 126
Fleet, Simon, 73–8, 82–9, 91, 93, 97, 100, 102–5, 109, 114, 125, 130, 133, 135, 145, 154, 155, 160, 185, 197, 202, 222–3, 232–3, 239; Bury Walk residence of (Gothic Box), 73, 74–5, 90, 113, 140; death of, 233; Haslam's first meeting with, 73–4
Fonda, Afdera, 155, 226
Fontanne, Lynn, 86, 88–9
Fonteyn, Margot, 78–9, 83, 170

Forbes, Anthony, 56
Ford, Henry and Ann, 222
Forres (Swanage, Dorset), 48–51, 55
Fortescue, Lady, 81
Fortnum & Mason (London), 77–8, 108
Foster, Raymond, 64–6, 106, 153, 228
Fowler, John, 227, 259, 268
Fox, James, 250–1, 261
Fox, Robert, 287
Francis, Arlene, 218
Franz Josef, Emperor, 28
Fraser, Lady Antonia, 86, 320
French, John, 79, 112–13, 115, 116
French, Vere, 79, 98, 112, 115
French Pub (London), 108
Freud, Lucian, 86, 119, 123, 139, 313, 321
Frey, Sami, 128
Frogmore (Windsor Castle), 195, 196

Gabel, Martin, 218, 219
Gabor, Zsa Zsa, 256–7
Gadhafi, Muammar al-, 262
Galanos, James, 225
Gallagher, Liam, 302, 303
Gandarillas, Tony, 130
Garbo, Greta, 145–6, 162, 309
Garland, Madge, 119
Gary, Romain, 133
Gaudier-Brzeska, Henri, 8
Gaulle, Charles de, 193
Geographical Projects, 115
George VI, King, 22, 50
Gernreich, Rudi, 206
Gersh, Gloria, 151, 157, 187
Getty, Paul, Jr., 76, 91, 103, 216
Gibbs, Christopher, 93, 102, 103, 107, 137, 138, 141, 142
Gibbs, Reginald, 17, 40
Gielgud, John, 105, 141
Gingold, Hermione, 95
Givenchy, Hubert de, 75
Gladwyn, Jebb and Cynthia, 14
Glamour, 210, 224
Goalen, Barbara, 79
Goldsmith, Isobel, 270, 271
Good, Jack, 142
Goode, Sir William, 27, 28
Goodman, Benny, 94
Gorky, Maxim, 13

Gould, Elliott, 165, 206
Gowrie, Grey Ruthven, Lord, 59
Grace, Princess of Monaco, 134, 285, 286
Gramercy Park (New York), 180
Granger, Farley, 144
Granger, Stewart, 79
Grant, Cary, 257
Grant, Duncan, 14, 251
Gray, Sally, 109
Greene, Amy, 210
Grinling, Jane, 120
Gross, Edith Lowe, 156
Grosvenor, Lady Leonora, 271
Groton, 211
Guevara, Meraude, 131
Guggenheim, Peggy, 135–7, 152, 229, 231
Guilaroff, Sydney, 145
Guinness, Catherine, 250
Guinness, Desmond and Mariga, 173
Gunzburg, Count Niki di, 154, 244
Guthrie, Robin, 8, 14

Haile Selassie, Emperor, 61
Hale, Denise, 321
Halifax, E. F. L. Wood, Lord, 212
Halsman, Philippe, 141
Hamilton, William, 322
Hamlyn, Dora and Rachel, 34
Hamlyn, Ralph, 24, 30, 31, 33, 34, 37, 41, 46, 48, 67, 69, 77, 99, 274–5
Hammerstein, Oscar and Susan, 164
Hampton, Mark, 276
Hannon, Jean, 204
Hanover Terrace (London), 5, 25
Hansen, Vagn Rees, 83
Hapsburgs, 28
Harari, Philip, 58
Harbord, Felix, 75, 79, 82, 116
Harding, Emily, 84, 216–17, 218
Hardy, Charles MacArthur, 97
Harlech, David Ormsby-Gore, Lord, 59, 137, 166
Harlech, Sissy Ormsby-Gore, Lady, 166
Harper's Bazaar, 157, 171, 224–5, 227
Harrison, Michael and Maria, 93
Hartford, Huntington, 203–4, 224
Hartnell, Norman, 279
Harvey, Laurence, 79, 200, 315
Haslam, Agnes (aunt), 21, 35, 37

Haslam, Augustus (nephew), 275
Haslam, Diamond Louise Constance
    Ponsonby (known as Diana)
    (mother), 6–8, 11–18, 22, 25–33,
    37, 38, 39, 50, 52, 53, 56, 68, 100,
    101, 116, 134, 189, 206, 222, 228,
    233, 237, 257–8, 262, 268, 275,
    284, 318; admirers and romantic
    affairs of, 46–7, 68, 70–1, 274;
    Austrian sojourn of, 27–8; as
    Brice's assistant, 29–30, 64, 65, 66;
    decline of, 274; events leading to
    second marriage of, 27, 28, 30–1,
    69, 71; family background and
    upbringing of, 25–7; fashion sense
    of, 71, 78; first marriage and
    divorce of, 30–1; London homes
    of, 52, 67, 262; personality of, 30,
    71; physical appearance of, 26;
    separation of, 67; son's education
    and, 55, 99, 100; son's
    homosexuality and, 105; son's
    travels with, 45–6, 56, 63–6,
    68–70, 109; spiritual practice of,
    41
Haslam, Dolores (aunt), 21
Haslam, John (brother), 10, 14–15, 46,
    53, 67, 275
Haslam, John (grandfather), 20, 25
Haslam, Judy Browne (sister-in-law),
    67
Haslam, Mary Heywood
    (grandmother), 20, 21, 24, 25
Haslam, Michael (brother), 10, 11, 13,
    14–15, 53, 55, 56, 67, 77, 100,
    116, 244
Haslam, Mildred (aunt), 20
Haslam, Nicholas: ancestry and family
    background of, 20–31, 318–19;
    birth of, 8–9; childhood of, 3–19,
    32–67; drawing and painting
    abilities of, 60–1, 96, 99; early
    homosexual experiences of, 50,
    52–3; education of, 40–1, 45,
    48–52, 53–61, 63, 66, 77, 89–90,
    95–6, 97, 99, 100; employment of,
    115, 137, 146, 150–1, 153–7,
    171–4, 186–8, 203–7, 224–5, 233,
    254, 259, 279–84; family home of,
    4–19. *see also* Hundridge Manor;
    as interior designer, 90, 116, 138,

    182, 233, 242–3, 255, 259, 261–3,
    269–70, 286, 287, 288, 297, 298,
    304, 305–10, 321–2; midlife
    makeover of, 302–4; as party
    designer, 298, 310–11, 320–1;
    religious upbringing of, 41;
    stricken with polio, 3, 9, 18,
    37–44; as writer, 276, 279–84,
    310
Haslam, Oliver (uncle), 20–1, 35–7, 42,
    51, 244, 308
Haslam, Robert (uncle), 20, 21, 277
Haslam, Timothy (nephew), 275
Haslam, William Heywood (father), 6,
    9, 10, 12, 13, 14, 16, 18, 20–5, 30,
    33–4, 37, 38, 39, 41, 46, 47–8,
    50–1, 52, 61–2, 77, 90, 99, 100,
    101, 109, 113, 115, 116, 119, 134,
    173, 189, 205, 207, 237, 244, 254,
    257–8, 264, 268–9, 270, 297;
    ancestry and family background of,
    20–1, 24–5; diplomatic career of,
    22–3; education of, 21–2; events
    leading to marriage of, 27, 28,
    30–1, 69, 71; Hundridge Manor
    and, 4–5, 7, 11–12, 25, 67, 114,
    321–2; later years and death of,
    274–5; London homes of, 5, 25,
    67; personality of, 24; physical
    appearance of, 23–4, 71–2;
    separation of, 67; son's education
    and, 45, 53, 54, 55, 99, 100; son's
    homosexuality and, 105
Haslam, Winifred (aunt), 20
Hatch, Sydney, 216
Hatcher, Tom, 144
Hatfield, Hurd, 200
Hawkhurst Court (Sussex), 51
Hawthorne, Nathaniel, 258
Hayes, Kay, 154–5
Hayward, Leland, 60, 218
Hearst, Randolph, 13
Heinz, Drue, 153
Hell's Angels, 249
Helpmann, Robert, 84, 85
Helvin, Marie, 280–3
Henriques, Fiore, 312
Henze, Hans Werner, 110–11
Hepburn, Audrey, 199
Herbert, A. P. and Gwen, 14
Herbert, David, 91

Herbert, Henry. *See* Pembroke, Henry
	Herbert, Earl of
Herbert, Lady Diana, 91
Hersee, Miss (Sersee) (cook), 9, 16, 17,
	43, 45, 52, 55, 111, 168
Hesketh, Alexander, 245, 259, 293
Hesketh, Bobby and Jeanne, 293
Heywood, Elisabeth Shawcross
	(grandmother), 24–5
Heywood, Robert (great-grandfather),
	20, 24–5
Hicks, David, 97–9, 114, 116, 173,
	250, 261
Hicks, Tommy (renamed Steele), 107
Hilton, Paris, 321
Hitler, Adolf, 13, 27, 212, 295, 309
Hobson, Valerie, 271–2
Hockney, David, 85
Hodgson, Simon and Priscilla, 94–5
Hofmannsthal, Arabella von, 237, 239,
	240, 266–7
Hofmannsthal, Raimund and Liz von,
	237–9, 261, 269, 314
Hofmannsthal, Rodolphe von, 261, 314
Hogg, James, 67, 68
Hogg, Lady Polly, 68
Hogg, Min, 67–70, 89–90, 94, 95, 99,
	102, 107, 108, 114, 120, 129, 140,
	151, 182–3, 211, 233, 244, 261,
	287, 288, 299, 300
Hogg, Sir Cecil, 68
Hohnsbeen, John, 152
Holman, Libby, 152, 153–4
Holzer, Jane, 176, 201–2, 204, 207,
	208, 211, 218, 242, 301
Hope, Lord John and Lady Liza, 91
Horne, Lena, 111, 144, 175–6
Horst, Horst P., 174, 183–4, 191, 244
How, Fred, 54, 55, 58, 61, 66, 90
Howard, Bart, 101
Howard, Greville, 59–60
Howard, Jean, 89, 161–4, 165,
	196–201, 244, 254, 287, 312
Hoyningen-Huene, Baron George, 184
Hughes, Fred, 276
Hughes, Howard, 146
Hughes-Hallet, John, 50
Hughes-Hallet, Richard, 50, 52
Hull, Helen, 158
Hundridge Manor (Buckinghamshire),
	4–19, 26, 32–5, 44, 46–51, 71, 77,
	111, 168, 185, 216, 234, 268, 274,
	316, 321–3; description of, 6–12;
	effects of war at, 12–13, 15;
	gardens and grounds of, 5, 11–12,
	17, 34; Haslam's recovery from
	polio at, 3, 9, 18, 39–43; Haslams'
	sale of, 67, 227; history of, 4–5, 6;
	staff at, 16–18; visitors to, 13–14
Hunting Lodge (Hampshire), 12,
	267–9, 295, 297, 314; furnishing
	of, 268–9; history of, 267–8;
	neighbors of, 271–4
Hurst, Brian Desmond, 109
Hutton, Barbara, 156
Hyland, Brian, 129

I Can Get It for You Wholesale, 165
Idol, Billy, 277
Imokilly, John Ponsonby, Lord, 25
India, Haslam's trip to, 292–4
Ingram, Sir Bruce and Lady (Lily), 45
Istanbul, Haslam's sojourns in, 299
Italy, Haslam's sojourns in, 6, 23,
	134–7, 226–33, 263–5
I Tatti (Florence), 6, 23

Jagger, Bianca, 257, 275
Jagger, Mick, 126, 142, 176, 177,
	207–8, 257, 276
Jamaica: Haslam's first trip to, 185;
	Haslam's home in, 221–3
James, Alex, 302
Jansen, Maison, 167
Jeffress, Arthur, 119, 134–5, 136, 229,
	231
John, Augustus, 91, 165
Johns, Jasper, 225
Johnson, Lady Bird, 166–7, 174
Johnson, Lyndon B., 175, 217
Johnson, Philip, 149–50, 152
Jones, Gail (later Lumet), 175, 176, 182
Jones, Inigo, 91
Jones, Jennifer, 197–8
Juan Carlos, Prince of Spain, 130
Julian, Philippe, 119

Kagalovsky, Natasha and Konstantin,
	318, 321, 322
Kahn, Otto, 28–9, 152
Kai-Nielsen, Wum, 270
Kapoor, Anish, 263

Karsavina, Tamara, 84–5
Kaye, Nora, 144, 165, 175
Kelly, Felix, 119
Kelly, Kevin, 287
Kenmare, Lady Enid, 311–12
Kennedy, Jacqueline, 129, 166, 167, 174, 175, 192, 234, 283, 311
Kennedy, John F., 89, 167, 168, 174, 179, 187
Kennedy, Robert, 187
Kennedy, Tessa, 225
Kenneth (hairdresser), 192
Kert, Larry, 143
Keyes, Evelyn, 168–9
Keynes, Maynard, 14, 22
Kidston, Cath, 270
Kilgallen, Dorothy, 65, 169
King, Gilly, 319
King, Martin Luther, Jr. and Coretta Scott, 175–6
King's College, Cambridge, 22
Kingston, Gertrude, 26
Kirov Balley, 84, 138–9
Kittredge, Ben and Carola, 185
Kivell, Rex Nan, 119–20
Knickerbocker, Cholly, 182
Knoblock, Carol, 156
Knollys, Eardley, 91
Knox, Caroline, 44
Kopit, Arthur, 206–7
Korda, Alexander, 13
Korner, Alexis, 94
Kray brothers, 114
Krug, M. (champagne maker), 10

Lalonde, Valérie, 250
Lamb, Lady Caroline, 25
Lambart, Julian "Legge," 55, 57
Lambert, Gavin, 244
Lamkin, Marguerite, 209–10, 215, 222, 224
Lamkin, Speed, 149, 209–11
Lamour, Dorothy, 257
Lancaster, Nancy, 259, 276, 317
Lane, Ken, 170, 188, 232
Lane-Roberts, E., 8
Lange, Hope, 244, 250, 253
Laurents, Arthur, 143–5, 165, 175
Laurie, Peter, 173
Lawford, Peter, 187
Lawford, Valentine "Nicholas," 184, 244

Lawrence, Jerome, 106
Lawrence, Jonathan, 51
Lee, Belinda, 142
Lees-Milne, Alvilde Chaplin, 126, 279
Leigh, Vivien, 97
Lemmon, Jack, 201
Lennon, John, 287–8
Lerman, Leo, 210
Leverson, Ada, 85
Lexel, Prince of Pless, 128
Lezzard, Hilda, 43–4
Liberace, 108
Liberman, Alex, 150–1, 153, 156, 186, 204, 254
Lichtenstein, Roy, 224, 247
Lifar, Serge, 77, 232
Lillie, Bea, 106
Lichfield, Patrick, 271
Litchfield, David, 279
Littman, Mark, 222
Litvak, Anatole, 170
Llewellyn, Roddy, 86, 260–1
Lloyd-Thomas, Sissy, 137
Lockhart, Bruce, 13
Loeb, David (nephew), 63
Loeb, Diana Marks (known as Anne) (half sister), 14, 30, 31, 33, 47–8, 63, 66, 192, 201
Loeb, John (brother-in-law), 63
Loeb, Virginia (niece), 63
Logan, Josh, 280
London: celebrity-led culture in, 301–2; galleries and art scene in, 119–20; gay clubs and hangouts in, 105–9; Haslam's childhood visits to, 32, 39; Haslam's flats in, 102, 116, 138, 140, 181, 259, 286–7, 297–8; Haslam's return to, 233–4, 257–9; New Money in, 300–1; restaurants in, 103–4, 108, 259–60
Londonderry, Lord Alastair, 93–4, 98, 135, 173, 229
Londonderry, Lady Nicolette (née Harrison), 92–4, 98, 135, 173, 229
Longworth, Alice Roosevelt, 167–8
Loomis family (Boston), 29
Los Angeles, Haslam's sojourns in, 196–201, 253–8
Losch, Tilly, 75
Lovat, Shimi, 78

Lowndes family, 5
Lowry, L. S., 20, 67, 72
Luce, Clare Boothe, 256
Ludington, Wright, 255, 276
Luna, Donyale, 224–5
Lunt, Alfred, 86, 88078
Lycett-Green, Candida, 244, 277–8
Lycett-Green, Rupert, 231, 244, 277–8
Lydig, Rita, 82
Lynch, Alfred, 103

Macaulay, Rose, 115
MacDonald, Dwight, 181
MacInnes, Colin, 108
MacLaine, Shirley, 298
Maclean, Donald, 89
Mainbocher, 173, 184
Mansfield, Jayne, 177
Margaret, Princess, 8, 22, 83, 86, 99,
    193, 195, 235, 260, 261, 290, 309
Margot, Lady Asquith, 134
Mariano, Nicky, 6
Marie Antoinette, Queen of France, 25,
    265, 320
Marie Bonaparte, Princess of Greece
    and Denmark, 127
Marie-Christine, Princess of Belgium,
    270–1
Marina, Princess, Duchess of Kent, 61,
    83
Marks, Anne. *See* Loeb, Anne Marks
Marks, Henry, 30, 31, 186
Martin, Tony, 199
Marvel, Gee, 160
Marx, Groucho, 197
Mary, Queen Consort of George V, 43,
    87, 167, 194, 195, 279
Mary, Queen of Scots, 81
Maudina de Montjou, Countess, 133–4
Maugham, Somerset, 77, 91, 132,
    228–9, 311
Maugham, Syrie, 91, 283
Maxwell, Elsa, 141
Maybanke, Leon, 107
Mayer, Louis B., 162
Mayou, Bryan, 303
McBean, Angus, 79, 169
McCartney, Paul, 207, 225
McCormick, Fifi, 213–14, 235, 241,
    243, 247–8, 249
McDonald, Hector, 81

McEwen, David, 176, 217–18
McEwen, John-Sebastian, 159
McEwen, Rory and Romana, 118, 216,
    219, 234, 237, 240, 245, 250, 263,
    276, 312
McGrath, Earl, 171
Mead, Taylor, 202
Melly, George, 139
Mendelssohn, Eleonora von, 238
Mengers, Sue, 217, 315
Merman, Ethel, 18, 40, 59, 144, 167,
    194
Messel, Oliver, 75, 83
Metcalfe, Lady (Alexandra) Baba, 98
Metropolitan Museum of Art (New
    York), 63, 275–6
Mexico, Haslam's trip to, 245–7
Mey, Castle of, 288–92
Michael, Prince, Duke of Kent, 288,
    294
Michael of Kent, Marie-Christine,
    Princess, 285, 288, 294
*Milk Train Doesn't Stop Here Anymore,
    The,* 165
Miller, Alice Duer, 77
Miller, Arthur, 154
Miller, Beatrix, 284
Miller, Gilbert, 158–9
Miller, Harry Tatlock, 119–20
Miller, Kitty, 158–9, 191–2, 211, 227
Millington-Drake, Teddy, 119
Milnes-Gaskell, Lady Constance
    "Puss," 43
Minnelli, Vincente, 256, 257, 321
Mitford, Nancy, 14, 69, 154, 184, 230
Moffat, Kate and Ivan, 235, 252
Moffitt, Peggy, 206
Molyneux, Edward, 185
Mom Chow Skon, Prince of Siam, 22
Monroe, Marilyn, 59, 154, 186–8, 190,
    210, 220
Montagu, Judy, 244–5
Montagu, Lord Edward, 105
Montgomery, Bill, 59
Monzi, Piero di, 260
Moore, Adam, 313
Moore, Susanna, 277
Moore, Tina, 263
Moorehead, Alan, 264
Moraes, Henrietta, 139
Morduant-Smith, Kath, 222

Morgan, Anne, 220
Morocco, Haslam's trip to, 225–6
Mortimer, Amanda, 159–60
Mortimer, Raymond, 91
Morvi, Uma, 292–4
Moschino, Paolo, 296–300
Mountbatten, Lady Pamela, 98
Mullins, Charles and Georgina, 322
Munster, Count Paul and Countess
　　Peggy, 227–8, 229, 230
Murray, Christopher, 244
Murray, Mae, 72, 182
My Fair Lady, 196, 198–9

Nash (driver), 319
Neff, Wallace, 206
Nelhams, Terry (later Adam Faith), 107,
　　142
Newell, Martin, 94
New Orleans, Haslam's memories of,
　　315–16
New York: Haslam's apartments in,
　　152, 153, 178–9, 180, 182,
　　214–16, 240; Haslam's departure
　　from, 233–40; Haslam's move to,
　　148–53; Haslam's visits to, 63–6,
　　275–6
New Yorker, 310
New York Herald Tribune, 182
Niarchos, Stavros, 270
Nichols, Beverley, 77
Nicolson, Harold, 22, 86, 202
Niehans, Dr., 132
Nielsen, Erik, 270
Nijinsky, Vaslav, 84, 87, 104, 232
Nixon, Richard M., 174
Noailles, Marie-Laure de, 125, 126,
　　154
Norman, Archie, 68, 70–1
Novello, Ivor, 73, 86
Nureyev, Rudolf, 83, 84, 138–9, 170,
　　178, 180, 203, 225

Oberon, Merle, 247
Obolensky, Michael, 97
O'Brien, Cavan, 266, 296, 297
Observer, 74, 77, 104
O'Connor, Gloria, 154
Ogilvy, James, 270
Olga, Princess Paul of Yugoslavia, 83
Olivier, Laurence, 97, 154

Onassis, Christina, 256–7
Onassis, Tina, 218
O'Neil, Patricia, 311–12
Oranmore, Lady Oonagh, 129, 130
Origo, Iris, 23, 51, 62
Ormsby-Gore, Jane, 59, 137–8, 148,
　　157, 166, 167, 170, 225
Ormsby-Gore, Julian, 59, 137, 170, 225
Orpen, William, 80
Osborne, John, 259
Oscar parties, 314–15

Paddick, Hugh, 53
Page, Eddie, 194
Paget, Lady Caroline, 87
Pagliai, Bruno, 247
Pahlmann, William, 63
Paley, Bill and Babe, 159–60, 222
Palmer, Antonia, 235
Palmer, Mark, 249
Palmer-Tomkinson, Tara, 301
Paris: Haslam's childhood visits to,
　　45–6, 56, 58, 68–70; Haslam's
　　decorating commission in, 270–1
Parish, Sister, 167
Parker, Dorothy, 165, 269
Parr, Tom, 77, 98, 102, 161, 244, 261,
　　271
Parsons, Paul (Haslam's nom de plume),
　　283
Pavlova, Anna, 84
Peacock, Kim, 41
Peck, Priscilla, 151, 156, 186–7, 188,
　　204
Pelly, Claire, 216
Pembroke, Claire, 222
Pembroke, Henry Herbert, Earl of, 91,
　　92, 222, 269
Pembroke, Mary, Countess of, 90–1
Pembroke, Sidney Herbert, Earl of, 91
Petre, Lady Peggy, 106–7
Philip, Prince, Duke of Edinburgh, 142,
　　291, 320
Phillips, Carol, 155
Phillips, Eleanor, 254–5
Phillips, Peter, 114–16
Picasso, Pablo, 131, 181, 298
Pilkington, Clarissa, 321
Pinsent, Cecil, 5, 6, 11, 23
Pitman, Raine, 92
Pitt-Rivers, Michael, 105

Plunkett, Eddie, 96, 99
Plunkett-Green, Alexander, 94
Poiret, Paul, 77
Pol, Poppet, 91
Pol, Talitha, 91
Polignac, Princess Winnie de, 126, 279
Ponsonby, Cecil (uncle), 28–9, 152
Ponsonby, Evelyn (grandmother),
    18–19, 25–7, 28, 39
Ponsonby, Honorable Arthur
    (grandfather), 25–7, 28
Ponsonby, Iris (aunt), 27
Ponsonby, Judith (aunt), 26, 47
Ponsonby, Sir Frederick, 26
Ponsonby Temple Appeal, 319
Portarlington, Lady Winnie, 117
Porter, Cole, 59, 136, 159, 162–5, 183,
    199, 201, 233, 253
Porter, Linda, 159, 163
Portman, Mikey, 122
Portman, Suna, 94, 95, 121–2
Posson, Baroness Meriel de, 262
Potter, Cora Brown, 213, 228–9
Poulenc, Francis, 75
Power, Tyrone, 32
Pratt, Woody, 156
Presley, Elvis, 169, 176, 197, 199–200,
    303, 304
Prichard, Dai, 293–5
Priestley, J. B., 68
Profumo, John, 271, 272
Proust, Marcel, 227
Prouting, Norman, 97–8
Pryce-Jones, Alan, 149
Pugh, Bronwen, 79, 116–18
punk rock, 276–7
Purvis, Anne, 97
Purvis, Chester, 28, 68–9, 70, 97

Quant, Mary, 94
Queensberry, Marquess of, 115

Radziwill, Lee, 234, 263, 287, 295, 321
Rainer, Luise, 313–14
Ralli, Figi, 77
Ranfurly, Lady Hermione, 16, 43–4
Ranfurly, Lord Dan, 43, 44
Rattigan, Terence, 75, 88, 141
Raven, Simon, 108
Ray, Johnny, 65
Rayner, Chessy, 154, 182, 207

Reagan, Nancy, 184, 285, 286
Redfern Gallery (London), 119–20, 121
Redgrave, Vanessa, 268
Reeves, Keanu, 321
Reid, Beryl, 127
Reinhardt, Max, 76
Rendlesham, Claire, 148, 150, 171
Rennell, Francis, Lord, 14, 23
Rice, Patrick, 102
Richard, Cliff, 116, 144
Richards, Keith, 207, 257
Richardson, John, 131–2, 181, 244,
    298
Richardson, Natasha, 287
Ripon, Lady, 86, 87–8
Ritz, 276, 279–84
Rizzo, Frank, 178, 179
Robbins, Jerry, 209
Robilant, Alvise di, 264
Robilant, Betty di, 263–4
Robinson, Cordelia Biddle, 191–2
Rockingham (London), 105–6
Rodd, Peter, 14
Rodd, Sir Rennell, 22, 23
Rodd, Rosie, 264
Rodd, Taffy, 264
Rodgers, Richard, 164
Roger, Alan, 80
Roger, Lady, 79–80
Roger, Neil "Bunny," 77–81, 102, 108,
    109, 112, 115, 140, 141, 143,
    169–70, 269, 303, 320
Roger, Sandy, 78, 80
Roger, Sir Alexander, 80
Rogers and Starr, 106
Rolling Stones, 207–8, 257
Rome, Haslam's sojourns in, 226–7,
    299
Rorem, Ned, 126
Rosnay, Arnaud de, 271
Ross, Herbert, 144, 165, 175, 287
Rosse, Lady Anne, 83
Roth, Lillian, 165
Rothschild, Jacob, 57, 305, 321
Rowan, Gwendolyn, 255
Rowe, Toby, 105
Royal Court Theatre (London), 310–11
Roza, Lita, 97
Rubinstein, Helena, 262
Rudder, Françoise de, 126, 128
Rufus-Isaacs, Jacqueline, 261

Russell, Ed, 155
Russell, Lady Sarah, 185, 218, 221
Russell, Serena, 155, 171
Russell-Cooke, Mel, 14
Ruthven, Grey, 96
Ryan, Nin, 152

Sachs, Gunter, 130
Sackville-West, Eddie, 91
Sackville-West, Vita, 6, 22
Sagan, Françoise, 129
Saint Laurent, Yves, 77, 173, 270
Saint-Tropez, Haslam's sojourns in,
    120–30, 143, 151
Santoro, Tony, 254
Sarne, Mike, 206
Sassoon, Siegfried, 91, 92
Sassoon, Vidal, 114
Savitt, Louise Lieberman, 155, 204, 244
Savoia, Emanuele di, 321
Schatzberg, Jerry, 207, 208
Schiaparelli, Elsa, 112, 154, 172
Schlee, George, 145
Schlumberger, Jean "Johnny," 156
Schratt, Katharina, 28
Schumacher, Joel, 170, 209
Scotland, Haslam's childhood stays in,
    35–9
Scott, Geoffrey, 5–6, 7, 8, 22–3, 100,
    114, 216, 269, 279
Seberg, Jean, 133
Selby, Hubert, Jr., 153
Selznick, David, 197–8
Selznick, Irene, 160
Sersee. *See* Hersee, Miss
Shakerley, Elizabeth "Liza," 285
Shakerley, Geoffrey, 288–92
Shand, Mark, 263, 269
Shaw, Artie, 168–9
Shawcross, William, 25
Shearer, Moira, 8
Sheer Opulence, 288
Shelburne, Charlie, 56
Show, 203–7, 215, 224, 250
Shrimpton, Chrissie, 142, 225
Shrimpton, Jean, 89, 141–2, 148, 152,
    170, 172, 217–18, 224
Simavi, Cigdem, 299
Simpson, Babs, 153, 154
Simpson, Wallis. *See* Windsor, Wallis,
    Duchess of

Sinatra, Frank, 162, 175, 244, 253, 314
Sitwell, Edith, 77
Sitwell, Osbert, 119
Sitwell, Sir George, 23
Six-Five Special, 142
Skelton, Barbara, 183
Slocum, Miss, 150–1
Smedley, Oliver, 51
Smith, Barbara Stanley, 116
Smith, Jack, 201
Snowdon, Lady Lucy, 261, 314
Snowdon, Tony Armstrong-Jones, Lord,
    77, 83, 98–9, 103, 170, 193, 235,
    260, 261, 290, 314
Soames, Mary and Christopher, 271
Soames, Nicholas, 262, 271
Soane, Sir John, 319
Somerset, Frieda, 50
Sonnenberg, Ben, 180
South, Haslam's travels in, 184–5
Spain, Nancy, 144
Spellman, Francis Cardinal, 194
Spencer-Churchill, Lady Sarah, 155
Spigelgass, Leonard, 141
Stacey, George, 209
Stanley-Smith, Barbara, 116
Stark, Freya, 232
Starr, Ringo, 207, 225, 304
Steele, Anthony, 142
Stefanidis, John, 250
Steffy, Jay, 255
Stein, Doris, 206, 250
Stein, Gertrude, 126, 149, 279
Stein, Jules, 206
Stern, Bert, 186
Stettheimer, Florine, 149
Stewart, Donald Ogden, 264
Stewart, Janet Rhinelander, 28–9, 213
Stewart, Rod, 304
Stillman, Alec, 228
Strachey, Lytton, 22, 23
Streisand, Barbra, 165, 171, 206
Sunset Boulevard, 79, 169–70
Sutherland, Graham and Kathy, 133
Sutro, John, 108
Swanson, Gloria, 78, 79, 169–70
Swope, Herbert Bayard, 30
Sykes, Adam, 270
Sykes, Mark, 108
Sykes, Plum, 108
Sykes, Tatton, 252, 262, 266

Tabilk, Château (Austria), 100
Tailleferre, Germaine, 128
Talmey, Allene, 157
Taras, John, 178–9
Tatler, 310
Taylor, Elizabeth, 168, 210
Tennant, Catherine, 249–50
Tennant, Colin, 261
Tennant, Pauline, 139–40, 200
Tennant, Stephen, 92, 242, 280–3, 300
Tennant, Toby, 56
Teresa, 3, 10, 15, 16, 17–18, 37, 38, 41,
    42–3, 47, 50, 237
Thatcher, Margaret, 269
Thomson, Virgil, 149
Thorpe, Jeremy, 56
Tiny Tim, 202
Toklas, Alice, 126
Tone, Franchot, 65
transvestism and drag, 69–70, 106, 114,
    126
Tree, Ronald and Marietta, 317
Truman, Bess, 167
Truman, Harry, 215
Trumbull, George, 211, 215–16
Tucker, Forrest, 97
Turner, Chuck, 171
Twiggy, 172
Twist, 142, 149
Twombly, Cy, 226, 264, 309
Twombly, Tatiana, 264
Tynan, Kenneth, 82

underground movies, 201, 202
Uniacke, Robie, 56

Vail, Pegeen, 136
Valentino, 231
Valois, Ninette de, 84
Vanderbilt, Gloria, 157
Vane-Tempest-Stewart, Annabel, 98,
    173
Vane-Tempest-Stewart, Jane, 94
Vanity Fair, 310, 314–15
Venice, Haslam's sojourns in, 134–7,
    227–33
Verdura, Fulco, Duc di, 73, 154, 161,
    167, 183, 244, 265, 280
Verdy, Violette, 203
Victoria, Queen, 23, 26, 79, 195, 196,
    221

Vidal, Gore, 145–6, 167, 206, 217,
    308–9
Villella, Edward and Janet, 178–9
Vogue, 146, 150–1, 153–7, 164, 171–4,
    176, 177, 178, 183, 184, 186–8,
    191, 196, 203–4, 224, 254, 262,
    275, 284
Volpi, Lily, 231
Volpi, Conte Giovanni, 229, 231
Von Ziegeser, Anne, 245
Voronov, Dr., 132
Voysey, C. F. A., 21, 277
Vreeland, Diana, 156, 157, 171–4, 176,
    177, 178, 183, 184, 186, 187, 188,
    204, 210, 224, 244, 247, 257,
    275–6
Vreeland, Jean, 254
Vreeland, Reed, 173

Wagner, Richard, 83, 127
Wagner, Robert, 255
Wakhevitch, George, 128
Walker, Patrick, 108
Walkling, Mary, 16–17
Walraff, Paul and Muriel, 231–2
Walton, William and Susana, 111
Wanger, Walter, 146, 162
Ward, Stephen, 118
Warhol, Andy, 155, 176, 192, 201–2,
    276, 279
Warner, Gwendolyn Rowan, 255, 257
Warner, Jack, 255, 257
Warrender, Victoria, 261–2
Washington, D.C., Haslam's sojourns
    in, 166–8, 174–5
Watson, Sydney, 56
Webb, Alan, 202–3
Webster, David, 109–11, 152
Weiler, Paul-Louis, 76
Weisbart, Susan, 169
Weld, Tuesday, 176–7, 254
Wellesley, Gerry, 22, 23
Wellesley, Lord Gerald, 22, 23
Wells, H. G., 13
West, Mae, 205–6, 250
Westenholz, Piers, 222
Westmoreland, David and Jane, 195
Weston, Garfield, 108–9
West Side Story, 143
Weymouth, Alexander, 92
Whalley, George, 71

Wharton, Edith, 22
Wheeler, Sir Mortimer, 116
White, Nancy, 224, 225
White House (Washington, D.C.), 167
Wilde, Oscar, 85
Wildeblood, Peter, 105
Wilhelm II, Kaiser, 127
Williams, Mona Harrison, 109, 213
Williams, Tennessee, 165
Williams-Ellis, Clough, 5, 6, 15, 322
Willoughby d'Eresby, Lord Timothy, 140, 182
Wilson, Colin, 75
Wilson, Edmund, 181
Wilson, Sandy, 95
Windsor, Duke of, 141, 159, 191, 193–6, 227, 230
Windsor, Wallis, Duchess of, 67, 141, 170, 184, 191–6, 230, 312
Winkelhorn, Karin-Maria "Bibi," 157, 187, 204, 225, 232
Winkler, Carol and Reinhard, 306–10
Winwood, Estelle, 65
Wishart, Francis, 124
Wishart, Michael, 121–7, 130–7, 138–40, 143, 146–7, 151, 152,

200, 226, 259, 280; drinking and drug use of, 124, 130–1, 179, 186, 266; Haslam joined in America by, 179–80, 183, 184–6; Haslam's breakup with, 186, 209; Haslam's first meetings with, 120, 121–3; Haslam taken to Venice by, 134–7, 229
Wolf, Henry, 204
Wolfe, Tom, 208, 225
Wood, Natalie, 253, 255, 257
Woodward, Elsie, 158, 192–3
Woolf, Virginia, 279
World of Interiors, The, 287, 288
World War I, 27
World War II, 9, 12–16, 22, 32, 48, 79, 87, 88, 211, 238–9
Wright, Cobina, 255
Wright, Frank Lloyd, 235, 248, 255
Wyndham, Francis, 85, 114, 176, 177
Wyndham, Violet, 76, 85–6, 261

Zeffirelli, Franco, 152
Zimmer, Michael, 217, 218

ILLUSTRATIONS

The illustrations reproduced in the text have been provided with the permission and courtesy of the following:

FIRST INSERT:
WWD Archive, Condé Nast Publications Inc.: In my apartment in New York
Copyright © Terence Donovan Archive, courtesy Diana Donovan: David Bailey
Bruce Davidson/Magnum Photos: Danced with a debutante
Getty Images/Michael Ochs Archives: Frugged with Jane Holzer
© Apple Corps Ltd.: Photographing Paul McCartney and Ringo Starr
© Jerry Schatzberg: Jagger at Mods and Rockers Ball
© David Bailey: Jane Holzer cover for *Show*

SECOND INSERT:
© Jerry Schatzberg: "The Day the Whores Came Out to Play Tennis"
© The Estate of Diane Arbus: Mae West
William Claxton/Courtesy Demont Photo Management, LLc.: Barbra Streisand
Richard Avedon © 2008 The Richard Avedon Foundation: Jean Shrimpton, *Harper's Bazaar* cover, April 1965
WWD Archive, Condé Nast Publications Inc.: In my 77th Street apartment
Jean Vreeland: Diana Vreeland
© Richard Young: With Diana Cooper; with Collins and Warhol; Bailey, Lichfield, and author
Tim Jenkins/WWD Archive, Condé Nast Publications Inc.: Vreeland, Tree, Nicholson, and Eberstadt; Palmer and Hogg; Tracy Ward; Everett undressed; Bryan Ferry
Simon Upton/The Interior Archive: Hunting Lodge

All other illustrations are from the collection of the author.

A NOTE ABOUT THE AUTHOR

Nicholas Haslam was born in England at Great Hundridge Manor, Buckinghamshire, third son of diplomat William Heywood Haslam and Diana Ponsonby, granddaughter of 7th Earl of Bessborough. A frequent columnist for the London *Evening Standard* and *Sunday Telegraph* magazines, he is the author of *Sheer Opulence*.

A NOTE ON THE TYPE

The text of this book was set in Sabon, a typeface designed by Jan Tschichold (1902–1974), the well-known German typographer. Designed in 1966 and based on the original designs by Claude Garamond (ca. 1480–1561), Sabon was named for the punch cutter Jacques Sabon, who brought Garamond's matrices to Frankfurt.

Composed by Creative Graphics, Allentown, Pennsylvania

Printed and bound by Berryville Graphics, Berryville, Virginia

Designed by M. Kristen Bearse